ON LAND AND SEA

On Land and Sea

Native American Uses of Biological
Resources in the West Indies

LEE A. NEWSOM and ELIZABETH S. WING

THE UNIVERSITY OF ALABAMA PRESS
Tuscaloosa and London

Copyright © 2004
The University of Alabama Press
Tuscaloosa, Alabama 35487-0380
All rights reserved
Manufactured in the United States of America

Typeface: Janson Text

∞
The paper on which this book is printed meets the minimum requirements of American
National Standard for Information Science–Permanence of Paper for Printed Library
Materials, ANSI Z39.48-1984.

Library of Congress Cataloging-in-Publication Data

Newsom, Lee A.
    On land and sea : native American uses of biological resources in the West Indies / by
Lee A. Newsom and Elizabeth S. Wing.
        p. cm.
Includes bibliographical references (p.) and index.
    ISBN 0-8173-1314-1 (cloth : alk. paper) —
    ISBN 0-8173-1315-X (pbk. : alk. paper)
    1. Indians of the West Indies—Ethnobotany. 2. Indians of the West Indies—
Ethnozoology. 3. Indigenous peoples—Ecology—West Indies. 4. Human-plant
relationships—West Indies. 5. Human-animal relationships—West Indies. 6. Plant
remains (Archaeology)—West Indies. 7. Animal remains (Archaeology)—West Indies.
8. West Indies—Antiquities. I. Wing, Elizabeth S. II. Title.

F1619.3.E85 N48 2004
578.6′3′089970729—dc22

                                                                                    2003016298

We dedicate this book to the people of the West Indies, those who left their refuse for us to study and those who helped us to carry out this research in so many ways.

Contents

Figures

Tables

Preface

Our aim in writing this book is to present data derived from studies of plant and animal remains from archaeological sites in the West Indies and to use these data to better understand life on these islands in the past. The data that form the basis of this study come from an array of archaeological sites that span the times of occupation from the Archaic to the arrival of Europeans in the Caribbean. The biological remains come from sites excavated from islands off the coast of Venezuela, the Lesser and Greater Antilles, the Virgin Islands, the Bahamas, and the Turks and Caicos. These biological remains include very fragile carbonized seeds and tubers as well as robust shells of conchs. Thus preservation is uneven and the database does not include a complete inventory of the plants and animals used by past colonists of the islands. To compensate for the flawed and incomplete data we studied biological samples from as many sites as possible and concentrated on samples from sites where recovery strategies were optimal. We include data presented by other colleagues to increase the number of samples from critical periods and places. Despite the limitations of archaeological preservation, we do see patterns of past exploitation of resources.

The replication of patterns gives us the confidence that we can see a glimpse of the activities that sustained the lives of the early settlers in the West Indies. These patterns show clear differences between the resources used by people living on different island groups. For example, people living on small coral islands had access to quite different resources than did those people living inland on the larger islands. Similarly, groups of people with Archaic-period technology had a different impact on the environment than did subsequent people who built terraces and intensified agricultural production. We apply the concept of shifting baselines in charting the changes that are evidenced in the data from the islands (Jackson 1997; Jackson et al. 1996; Pauly 1995).

Without a paleontological, archaeological, or historical perspective it is hard to imagine what environmental conditions were like in the past. The archaeological data reveal changes wrought directly and indirectly by humans and the more widespread environmental fluctuations. Without this time perspective we may view a forested area as pristine when in fact it had been selectively forested, cleared, farmed, and reforested with second-growth trees that may support a different complex of plant and animal species. Shifting baselines in the West Indian Islands indicate initial forested islands, clearing, incipient agriculture and arboriculture, and ultimately agricultural intensification. At the same time fishing and gathering of land crabs and marine molluscs were the focus of the subsistence economy. Endemic rodents were hunted, managed, and introduced from island to island. When land crabs and reef fishes were overexploited there was a shift to more intensive gathering of molluscs and fishing pelagic species. In some places agricultural systems were intensified, perhaps in part to compensate for declines in protein sources. Trade networks were wide and some animal parts and domestic animals, dogs and guinea pigs, were dispersed. The most major shift in the baseline came with the European takeover, during which Old World domestic animals and plantation crops were introduced.

We hope that this review of the biological remains from the islands will be both interesting and conducive to further study. Our survey of the biological remains from archaeological sites has large gaps with no data from whole islands. We leave the reader with the challenge of many unanswered questions.

Acknowledgments

This research could not have been possible without the help of many people and support from a number of organizations. The work was initiated with the support of the National Science Foundation BNS 8903377. The NSF grant grew out of a paper written with the intention of summarizing the status of zooarchaeological work in the Caribbean by 1989 [Wing 1989]. This paper was published in the *Biogeography of the West Indies: Past, Present, and Future*, edited by Charles A. Woods. Zooarchaeological research and recovery methods have advanced greatly during the past two decades. Many new faunal and botanical samples were recovered using improved recovery techniques and form the basis of this research. This new work could not have been done without funding from the Virgin Islands Division of Archaeology and Historic Preservation; L'Association Archéologique Saint Martin; the Centro de Investigaciones Arqueologicas, Bieque, San Juan, Puerto Rico; PanAmerican Consultants, Inc.; the Municipio de Carolina, Puerto Rico; the San Juan National Historic Site, Puerto Rico; LAW Environmental and Engineering-Caribe, Miami; and funds from Marisol Meléndez Maíz and Samuel Wilson, in addition to the original NSF grant. Additional support was provided by grants from the National Science Foundation (Ref. #0106520), the National Geographic Society (Grant # 6260–98), the H. John Heinz III Charitable Trust, and the Consejo para la Protección del Patrimonio Arqueológico Terrestre de Puerto Rico (Antonio Curet and Lee Newsom, Tibes Archaeological Project).

We are also grateful to the various archaeologists who entrusted faunal and botanical samples to us for study. This study would not have been possible without the careful recovery of these samples by archaeologists and their confidence in us for identification and analysis. We have benefited immensely from their expertise and keen insights.

This work also could not have been accomplished without help from a number of scholars at the Florida Museum of Natural History and the Smithsonian Institution, who helped with identifications, and from a number of colleagues who granted permission for the inclusion of their data. Those who worked on many samples are Susan deFrance, Laura Kozuch, Irv Quitmyer, Sylvia Scudder, and Nathalie Serrand. Colleagues who granted permission to use their data are Lizabeth Carlson, Sandrine Grouard, Heleen van der Klift, Yvonne Narganes, and Elizabeth Reitz. Irv Quitmyer prepared the faunal figures, Molly Wing-Berman prepared the pen-and-ink drawing of the pottery representation of the hutía (Figure 7.3), Robin C. Brown photographed the maize and manioc specimens from En Bas Saline, Haiti, and Florence E. Sergile drafted all of the maps. Discussions with all of these colleagues and particularly Antonio Curet, Jack Ewel, Bill Keegan, José Oliver, Elizabeth Reitz, Miguel Rodríguez, Stephen Wing, and Tom Zanoni helped focus ideas for the interpretation of these bioarchaeological remains. We gratefully acknowledge them all.

ON LAND AND SEA

1
An Introduction to Native American Uses of Biological Resources in the West Indies

Native Americans have a long history in the Caribbean Islands, one spanning more than six millennia. They eventually occupied nearly every island of the archipelago and developed very complex and varied cultures. They quickly adapted to living in the West Indies and became adept at exploiting the natural resources of the island environment. Subsistence, in its broadest sense, is defined as the means of providing the necessities of life, including food and other items needed for health and comfort. Biological resources were the foundation of subsistence; they were deeply integrated into civic, ceremonial, ritual, and daily and occasional activities, and they provided foods, medicines, fuel for cooking and craft production, raw materials for fiber and other industries, magical and mind-altering substances, and more.

Native Americans were embedded in the Caribbean ecosystem as a keystone species. By means of their daily subsistence activities and other cultural practices, they were a biotic factor in the region. In this respect they were no different from people elsewhere. However, fragile biotic communities on small tropical islands are easily disrupted and quickly changed by human activity. Positioned in effect as a keystone species, colonists in the West Indies were responsible for biodiversity and landscape changes. Redmond (1999) has emphasized the importance of understanding the depth and diversity of human environmental impacts, both sustainable and destructive, to appreciate human-environmental interactions. This is essential to understanding long-term socioeconomic trends and intrinsic underpinnings of political economies, both historic and prehistoric. In the Caribbean, anthropogenic changes were largely the result of wood collection and land clearing for habitation sites and agricultural plots, but marine resources were also affected. The extent and scale of these activities on any given island at particular points in time ranged from limited to highly intensive extraction of biotic resources from marine and terrestrial environments. Useful plants and animals were maintained in the immediate vicinity of the human settlements, and staple crops were produced in cultivated fields known as *conucos* (Sauer 1966:51–53). On some islands the preparation of terraced slopes and ditch irrigation systems for intensive agriculture occurred.

Forest clearing for construction timber, fuelwood, and cultivation exposes soil to erosion and other changes and promotes ecosystem succession and disturbance (Ewel 1986; Ewel et al. 1981; Frelich and Puettmann 1999). The increased runoff associated with extensive clearing can affect adjacent freshwater aquatic and marine ecosystems by changing water quality and the character of nearshore habitats. Conversely, accumulations of refuse such as shell, bone, and charcoal may positively change the soil constituents and nutrient status, thereby attracting small animals such as land snails and providing suitable conditions for the growth of plants useful to humans (e.g., cycads and bottle gourds). Human exploitation of plant and animal resources thus has both direct and indirect consequences for the species that share the island ecosystem, and these consequences may necessitate or lead to new adaptations on the part of humans.

Overexploitation of animals results in both a decline in abundance and a reduction in the average individual size of the targeted species. Prolonged and intense fishing pressure can result in species growth problems: "growth overfishing," when reproduction is depressed because species fail to reach the size at which they become fully mature; and "recruitment overfishing," when the species population size is reduced to the point that no breeding takes place (Russ 1991). The decline of some species in the reef community through overfishing, such as carnivores, can result in a greater dependence by humans on reef herbivores until they too are overfished. Likewise, decreased availability of preferred plant species—for example, dense fuelwoods or a particular type of edible fruit—can lead to greater use of secondary species, including those from disturbed forest associations. This situation conforms to the summary rule in terms of the diet breadth (resource selection) model. Following the decline of a top-ranked resource in the optimal set and the resultant diminished foraging efficiency, the selection will progressively expand stepwise to include items of lower rank (Winterhalder and Goland 1997). Introductions of both plants and animals indirectly affect native flora and fauna by competition and selective consumption. For example, domestic dogs (*Canis familiaris*) accompanied people in the domination of worldwide ecosystems including the West Indies, and had the potential to catch and reduce the populations of lizards, ground-dwelling and flightless birds, and endemic rodents. The cultivation of introduced plants, such as fruit trees, that are managed at the expense of native flora may alter the natural structure and composition of vegetation. Such a change may have the effect of reducing the food plants and habitats of endemic species.

MANY AND VARIED USES

Plants and animals were put to many uses in the Caribbean, and food was chief among them. A balanced diet requires carbohydrates supplied by plants and proteins and fats provided primarily by animal flesh. By the time of historic contact with Europeans, the starchy tubers of manioc, or cassava (*Manihot esculenta*), were predominant among plants that provided a carbohydrate staple in the Caribbean Islands. Early Native American colonists carried manioc into the West Indies from the adjacent mainland. Manioc continues to be widely used as an important staple crop throughout tropical America (Norman et al. 1995). Little direct evidence of manioc or other edible tubers has been excavated or identified from archaeological sites in the Caribbean, but the microlithic chips from grater boards or coral tools used to shred and pulp the tubers, and the ceramic griddles on which cassava bread is typically cooked, are common constituents of archaeological deposits in the region. Manioc and other starchy root staples were supplemented in the Caribbean by seeds, fruits, and greens. Direct evidence for more than 100 plant species that could have contributed to the diet and overall subsistence economy among Caribbean Indians has been recovered from archaeological sites in the region (Newsom 1993a; Newsom and Pearsall 2003), as described in later chapters of this book. In addition to sustenance, some plants also probably had medicinal uses. The animal protein portion of the diet of the Native Americans living in the West Indies comes from both terrestrial and marine animals. The people choosing home sites located close to the shore relied heavily on marine organisms for food, whereas those living farther inland depended more on land animals. Animals that formed the basis of the diet were endemic mammals such as the rice rats (Oryzomyini) of the Lesser Antilles, introduced mammals and birds, oceanic birds, pigeons (Columbidae), land crabs (Gecarcinidae), molluscs—both snails and bivalves—and a great variety of fishes.

Some food items required special preparation because of the presence of poisonous constituents. For example, all cultivars of manioc contain varying concentrations of cyanogenic glucosides throughout their tissues, and these are hydrolyzed to hydrogen cyanide (HCN) when the plants are damaged from insect attack or other mechanical breakage of leaves, stem, bark, root, and tubers (Wilson and Dufour 2002). Manioc cultivars that contain higher concentrations of this toxic compound in their tissues must be put through an elaborate process to extract or neutralize the HCN before the tubers can be safely eaten. In the Caribbean, the shredded, mashed pulp of tubers was detoxified by washing, drying, and exposure to air, after which it was made into cassava bread or cooked with meat and fish in a stew known as a pepper pot. Some fish are or can be poisonous. Some species of puffer fishes (Tetraodontidae) have viscera containing tetraodotoxin, a poison that can be fatal if ingested. Other fishes, particularly large carnivorous fishes such as the great barracuda (*Sphyraena barracuda*), can acquire a poisonous component in their flesh that causes ciguatera poisoning if consumed.

Food is a necessity of life, as are medicines. Most medicines and mind-altering substances are derived from plants. Definitive evidence of these special-purpose plants and their particular uses is very difficult to recover archaeologically because the plant materials tend to have been completely processed and consumed. For example, leaves and bark that are dried, crushed, and steeped in medicinal teas or poultices leave little or no traces of their use. Among the special-purpose plants known to have been important in the Caribbean Islands are tobacco and a native tree legume that was the source of a snuff (Nieves-Rivera et al. 1995; Rouse 1992:14). Both plants had special significance among the historically known Taino of the region. For example, concerning tobacco: "The Indians of this island had a bad vice among others, which is taking a smoke they called tobacco, to leave the senses. This herb was most precious by the Indians, and it was planted in their orchards and farm lands for what I said; they insinuate if you take the weed and to smoke it was not only a sane stuff, but very sacred" (Fernández de Oviedo 1556, quoted in Nieves-Rivera et al. 1995). A narcotic snuff was made from the pulverized and powdered seeds of the tree called cojóbana or cojobilla (*Anadenanthera peregrina* [Liogier and Martorell 2000:69]) combined with crushed shell or lime. This mixture was inhaled directly into the nostrils through tubes made of pottery or wood as part of the important *cojoba* ritual that served primarily to communicate with the Taino deities and the spirit world (Alegría 1997a, 1997b; Nieves-Rivera et al. 1995). Cojóbana seeds contain an adrenergic agent known as bufotenine (the same as in certain poison toads, genus *Bufo*), a powerful hallucinogenic drug that strongly affects the cardiovascular and nervous systems and that can or should be used only in low doses (Dobkin de Rios 1984:120). This is another example of cultural materials associated with a particular plant, in this case combined for ritual and ceremonial purposes. Moreover, ritual purification involved vomiting induced mechanically by thrusting a shell or wood spatula down the throat (Alegría 1997a; Kaye 2001; Olazagasti 1997). Induced vomiting was also part of rituals focused on the treatment of disease. The shaman would ritually purify him or herself before entering into a trance state to confer with the spirit world regarding the cause and cure for the illness. Potential examples of this practice from ethnohistoric documents describe both the cojóbana tree and an herb called gioia used variously for this purpose (Rouse

1992:14). Nieves-Rivera et al. (1995) raise the question of whether hallucinogenic fungi may also have been used prehistorically in the Caribbean, based on their interpretations of wood and ceramic figurines that suggest mushroom forms. Thus even though evidence of particular plants used for such specialized purposes is often difficult to recover, the presence of these plants may reasonably be inferred from the presence of tightly associated ritual paraphernalia.

Other major uses of plant and animal resources were as raw materials. Probably most important among these were woods used as fuel and for building and construction. In the Caribbean archaeologists are beginning to reveal house constructions by the patterns of postholes and soil stains. Among the first examples are several structures, including a very large one about 19 meters in diameter, the remains of which were found at the Golden Rock site on St. Eustatius (Versteeg and Schinkel 1992). Patterns of postholes and associated house floors or activity surfaces are being located at other Caribbean sites, for example, at Luján I on Vieques, Maisabel in northern Puerto Rico, and Los Buchillones in Cuba (Jardines Macías and Calvera Roses 1999). The woods that were used for posts and rafters for these buildings or that served as fuel are being identified. Wood was also used to make canoes, containers, and furniture such as the stools known as *duhos*, as well as various tools and implements (Olazagasti 1997). Calabash tree fruits (*Crescentia cujete*) and conch shells (*Busycon* spp.) are almost ready-made bowls and containers. Cordage and plant fibers were used for items including fabrics, baskets, netting, fish traps, hammocks, slings, ropes, and fishing lines. Other tools and ornaments were made with shell, bone, teeth, and stone; plant and animal products such as fish poisons, tannins, gums, resins, hides, and other materials were undoubtedly also important to Native American lifeways in the Caribbean. Together, the manufacture of utilitarian and ornamental objects contributed to a rich material culture throughout the era of human occupation in the archipelago.

Among the most important and consistent uses of plant resources, aside from food, was as a source of fuel. Fuelwoods and tinder were burned not only to provide heat for cooking food but also for firing pottery and to extract valuable resins and other compounds from wood and other plant items (e.g., boiling palm nuts for their oils). Craft production such as ceramics manufacture requires the use of particular woods most suitable for adequate firing of clays; wood collection for this purpose tends to be very selective. Collecting fuelwood is one of the quickest ways humans can deforest an island or region. People who practice shifting cultivation use fire to clear land for cultivation. We presume that this form of land clearing was also practiced on the islands, as indicated in the early chronicles regarding cultivation in the Greater Antilles: "The Indians first cut down the cane and trees where they wish to plant it [maize]. . . . After the trees and cane have been felled and the field grubbed, the land is burned over and the ashes are left as dressing for the soil, and this is much better than if the land were fertilized" (Fernández de Oviedo 1959:13–14). Sustainable land-use practices were as important in former periods as they are today. Central to much archaeological research on long-term human socio-political and economic systems has been defining the threshold of resource sustainability in various environments. This is particularly important to understanding human existence in the circumscribed environments of island ecosystems.

An aesthetic or companionable use of plants and animals should not be ignored even when it is difficult to demonstrate. Body painting, tattooing, and scarification are practiced throughout the world. Body painting on ceremonial occasions was done in the Caribbean using jagua (*Genipa americana*), a tree in the madder (Rubiaceae) family, the seeds of which produce a black dye. Red paint, probably derived from the small tree known as achiote or annatto (*Bixa orellana*), was also used, especially preceding confrontations. Both of these trees may have been introduced from northern South America, and it is likely that they and other plants were tended in house gardens for their aesthetic appeal as well as their economic value. A number of animals were kept for purposes other than the meat they could provide. Among these were fully domesticated dogs and possibly also guinea pigs (*Cavia porcellus*) and parrots (the macaw, *Ara autochthones* [Wing 2001b:495]). Dogs are generally found in burials, indicating some degree of ritual associated with their death and therefore an attachment or intimate association with humans. The spotty distribution of guinea pigs suggests that they were either used as trade items or raised only at particular sites or locations or during particular periods. In addition to dogs and guinea pigs, several other captive mammals were introduced—for example, the agouti (*Dasyprocta leporina*) into the Lesser Antilles from the South American mainland, and the hutía (*Isolobodon portoricensis*), originally from Hispaniola, into Puerto Rico and the Virgin Islands (cf. Flemming and MacPhee 1999). The primary purpose for keeping these mammals may not have been consumption. Neither species persisted in captivity; agouti continue to live as wild animals on some of the Lesser Antillean islands, and the hutía (*Isolobodon*) is now apparently extinct (Woods et al. 2001). Macaws and other parrots may have been reared for their colorful feathers and as pets.

THE NATURE AND DIVERSITY OF EVIDENCE

The evidence for understanding ancient paleoethnobiologies comes from many sources, both direct and indirect. Direct evidence includes archaeological specimens of bone, shell, exoskeletal, macrobotanical, and microbotanical remains. Isolated finds outside an archaeological context are of little value because their association with cultural artifacts that can provide an approximate date or define an activity area are missing and cannot be re-created. Likewise, association with other plants and animals is vital for understanding the place of each organism in an economic system. Remains of plants and animals recovered from carefully excavated contexts using fine-gauge recovery procedures are the data that best provide a glimpse into past lifeways. Biological materials are fragile. Carbonized plant remains, in particular, must be recovered and handled with great care. Further, the larger the sample that can be recovered in such a way and identified, the more adequate the data sets and the more complete the resultant understanding of the past. For example, a zooarchaeological sample from two sites on Saba has a faunal list of 36 vertebrate taxa, of which 5 are birds. When the bird remains were identified from all of the recovered remains (of which the zooarchaeological sample was only a part), an additional 20 species were added to the faunal list (Steadman 1999; Wing 1996). These additional species include the common birds identified in the original sample plus 10 rare species. Together, these species provide a much broader view of the past association of people and animals, as well as a more complete picture of the native fauna of the islands before European colonization.

Plants and animals are represented in archaeological deposits in widely varied quantities and conditions. As might be expected, macrobotanical remains such as carbonized wood, nut shells, small seeds, and, especially, tubers and other soft plant tissues are the most rare and fragile. This is true despite the fact that fragmented charcoal is a commmon characteristic of anthropogenic soils in tropical regions and elsewhere (Teixeira et al. 2002). However, wood charcoal and other preserved plant specimens must be large or complete enough to include all of the morphological and anatomical features that permit identification. Sometimes trace elemental analysis can be very helpful in identifying or clarifying the presence of particular plants—for example, tobacco residues in pipe bowls—or of very small or highly fragmentary plant and animal remains. On the other end of the abundance spectrum are shellfish: snails and bivalves. Particularly at coastal sites these are so abundant that the task and cost of collecting, identifying, and quantifying them is overwhelming. Consequently, archaeologists sometimes discard these remains even though they provide evidence of past foraging activities. This is occasionally done despite the fact that information about the season and location of the foraging and the relative importance of foraging to fishing can be gleaned from such remains. Most Caribbean archaeologists now routinely collect a representative sample of invertebrate remains. Bone is usually intermediate in durability though sometimes very fragile. The more fragmentary a skeletal element, the more difficult it is to identify.

Microbotanical remains and bone chemistry also provide insights into past human conditions. Microbotanical remains are generally whole minute structures. These include pollen, spores, and cellular inclusions, such as starch grains and phytoliths (secreted crystalline structures). We refer to the work of other scholars who have studied these remains from the Caribbean. Anne Stokes (1998) did a pioneering study of stable isotopes of carbon and nitrogen incorporated into human skeletal tissue from various sites. We refer to some of her insights and compare them with evidence from macrobotanical and animal remains for a comprehensive picture of past diets.

Indirect evidence for human subsistence activities and economic behavior must also be considered in interpreting biological remains to reconstruct past ways of life. Such evidence is derived from material culture items like those mentioned earlier: cutting, grinding, and grating tools, fishing implements, and sometimes the landscape itself (e.g., terraced landforms and concentrations of fine particulate charcoal in sediments that reflect fire history and forest clearance). The sizes and abundance of sites, houses, and refuse deposits also provide indirect information about population density and potential means to sustain life at a given level of social organization and cultural complexity. The nutritional status and health of both the people and their captive animals can provide insight into the conditions of life. Because archaeological deposits tend to be fragile and incomplete, all clues from direct and indirect evidence must be taken into account to begin to understand the place of people in an island ecosystem.

By marshaling all of these data and comparing the results from a range of island conditions, we are able to provide some insights into Native American colonization of the West Indian Island archipelago. The focus of this work is threefold. First, we document the range of plant and animal taxa important to human subsistence in the region, and thus the intrinsic underpinnings of various economic and ethnobiological patterns. Second, we explore the sustainability of human economic systems in the islands, emphasizing the impact of people on the Caribbean landscape and on other species with which they shared the island ecosystem. In this milieu we investigate the limitations of island resources amidst growing human populations. This factor clearly has implications for human adaptations to resource depletion and for some of the dynamics behind increasing cultural complexity in the region along the settlement/time continuum. At least three responses are possible. One response is a shift to exploitation of new resources. This broadens the range of species included in the optimal set (Winterhalder and Goland 1997). Intensification of agriculture and animal husbandry—and all that these entail in terms of resource logistics, the mobilization of labor, and social complexity—

might be another compensation for failing wild or cultivated resources. Ultimately, abandonment of islands that can no longer sustain human populations may occur (Keegan and Diamond 1987). Third, we consider the processes of plant and animal domestication seen in the West Indies, and the role of captive animals and tended plants, in view of the longevity of socioeconomic systems in the islands of the archipelago.

2

Environmental Setting

The West Indian archipelago forms a sweeping arc from the coast of Venezuela counterclockwise across the Caribbean basin. The region is part of the Neotropics, though considerable portions of the archipelago are classified climatically as subtropical (Murphy and Lugo 1995; Nieuwolt 1977). The various islands of the Caribbean lie in a closely spaced chain surrounded by warm ocean waters. They can be divided into separate subregions based on their size, geological history, proximity to the mainland, and other features. The four primary physiographic subregions of the Caribbean that are distinct in a number of ways include the Greater Antilles, the Lesser Antilles, the Bahamas, and the southern Caribbean Islands. These island groups with their inherent geophysical and biogeographic characteristics consequently are vegetated and inhabited by different arrays of plants and animals. Thus the local floras and faunas and the relative availability of biotic and abiotic resources associated with individual island groups present various combinations of useful species, to which prehistoric human groups living on particular islands would have adapted in different ways.

The Greater Antilles, composed of Cuba, Jamaica, Hispaniola (including the Dominican Republic and Haiti), and Puerto Rico, are geologically the oldest and geographically the largest of the Caribbean Islands. The geological history of these islands is complex, and details of their formation are controversial (Hedges 2001). The proto-Antilles formed during the Cretaceous in the gap created by the divergence between the North and South American tectonic plates (Hedges 2001; Morgan and Woods 1986; Williams 1989). Early in the formation of the proto-Antillean island arc (65 mya), a tremendous asteroid or comet hit the earth in the Caribbean region (Hedges 2001; Kruge et al. 1994). This event had worldwide consequences, including the extinction of the dinosaurs and other major taxonomic groups, and doubtless destroyed most life that existed on the proto-Antilles. The Greater Antilles lie along the northern edge of the Caribbean plate that moved eastward and eventually collided with the Bahamas platform. During the eastward migration of the proto-Antilles, islands were periodically submerged and then reemerged, and parts of islands fused. The islands, as we know them today, formed by the mid-Cenozoic. Contacts formed and later broken between islands or continental landmasses have considerable implications for the biogeography of the Greater Antilles.

Study of the remains of plants and animals embedded in ancient amber (Poinar and Poinar 1999) reveals a glimpse of what a part of the proto-Antilles was like. These fossils indicate that a diverse tropical moist forest grew in Hispaniola 15 to 45 million years ago. This unique forest no longer exists in the Greater Antilles. The forest tree that produced the resin preserved as amber is an extinct species of the leguminous tree known as algarrobo (*Hymenaea protera*). Remnants of other forest canopy trees, understory shrubs, vines, and epiphytes are also preserved in the fossil resin produced by the ancient tree legume. Molluscs, crustaceans, spiders, scorpions, amphibians, reptiles, bird feathers, and mammal hair identified from the amber indicate a diverse fauna. Taken together, the remains of plants and animals preserved in the sticky resin reveal a surprisingly complete forest ecosystem.

This unique forest ecosystem became established on the newly formed land of the proto-Antilles while it was still close to North and South America. The land supporting the forest rested on the Caribbean plate as it moved to the east. At least some of the biodiversity of this moist tropical forest ecosystem is believed to be the result of vicariance (Iturralde-Vinent and MacPhee 1999). According to the vicariance model, some of the oldest plants and animals may have inhabited an island landmass while it was part of a mainland or larger island and drifted with it during the movement of the geological plate by tectonics. Most of the plants and associated animals of the moist tropical forest have their closest relatives in Central and South America. Some of the forest plants and associated animals still have generic representatives on Hispaniola, restricted to remnants of moist tropical forest. However, all of these ancient species, many of the genera, and at least one subfamily are extinct and many lineages no longer exist on Hispaniola or elsewhere in the Caribbean. Tectonic movement and environmental change associated with cooling and greater aridity during the Pliocene-Pleistocene (Higuera-Gundy et al. 1999) probably affected a turnover pulse relationship that resulted in the extinction and extirpation of the former tropical forest ecosystem and nearly synchronous turnover across diverse groups of organisms comprising that system (Behrensmeyer et al. 1992). The majority of the species that currently make up the West Indian biota dispersed to the islands on the wind or over water primarily from South America (Hedges 2001; Howard 1973; Judd 2001; Murphy and Lugo 1995).

The present island arc of the Lesser Antilles formed during the Eocene to Miocene epochs along the edge of the Caribbean plate. This island chain is actually composed of two arcs: an older one of coral limestone islands, which developed on ancient volcanic bases, and a younger arc of active volcanic islands (Watts 1987). The southern part of the island system—the Leeward Islands—never formed a connection with northern South America. However, rising and falling sea levels during the Pleistocene changed the conformation of individual islands, especially those on shallow banks, sometimes linking adjacent islands. A major fault trough, the Anegada trench, separates the northern Lesser Antilles, or Windward Islands, from the Virgin Islands and the Greater Antilles. Another deep-water trench separates the Yucatán peninsula from western Cuba, and a shallower one separates Grenada from Trinidad. The islands on either side of these troughs are wider apart. Otherwise the islands in the archipelago are quite close together and in many cases directly visible from one another.

The third group of islands, the Bahamas, is geologically the most recent. The many small low limestone islands in this group emerge from the very stable slowly rising block of crystalline limestone known as the Bahamian Foreland (Watts 1987). The Pleistocene sea-level fluctuation had a major effect on the size of the Bahamian landmass. During the Wisconsin glaciation a large land area was exposed. Conversely, the higher sea stands during the warmer interglacial periods were favorable for coral reef formation.

Finally, we recognize a fourth unique subgroup of islands in the Caribbean, sometimes called the southern Caribbean Islands. These small islands lie at the southern edge of the Caribbean basin and consist of the Netherlands Antilles—specifically Aruba, Bonaire, and Curaçao—plus the Venezuelan islands of Margarita and the small group known as Los Roques. The southern Caribbean Islands are generally located less than 50 km north of Venezuela.

CLIMATE

Climatic changes in the Caribbean have played a part in the distributions of plants and animals and thereby influenced human cultures when they came to occupy the region (see Chapter 3). Data on the regional climate history come from cores into lake sediments and the analysis of trace metals, stable oxygen isotopes ($\delta^{18}O$), and pollen sequences (Curtis et al. 2001; Higuera-Gundy et al. 1999). These data indicate fluctuating periods of dry and moist conditions. Relatively cool, dry conditions prevailed during the late Pleistocene to earliest

Holocene. Increased moisture during the early Holocene promoted expansion of mesophytic vegetation (~10500 to ~8500 ^{14}C years before present [B.P.]). This arid-to-mesic climate shift, in conjunction with sea-level rise, resulted in range reductions and extinctions in the West Indian vertebrate fauna from habitat alteration or elimination (Pregill and Olson 1981). Maximum moisture and the greatest extension of the forest habitats occurred in the early to middle Holocene during the interval between about 8500 and 3000 ^{14}C years B.P. This wetter period was followed by the return of drier conditions in the late Holocene (after ~3000–2500 ^{14}C years B.P.). Detailed paleolimnological research on lacustrine deposits in the Yucatán peninsula (Curtis et al. 2001; Hodell et al. 2001) demonstrates that superimposed on these broader patterns of temperature and moisture change is evidence for a series of firmly dated drought episodes. These have occurred on an approximately 200-year cycle during at least the past 2,600 years, coinciding with regular oscillations in solar activity. In addition, pronounced drought episodes are documented for the years around 585, 862, 986, and 1051 calendar years A.D., with a particularly severe, century-long drought during the interval A.D. 700 to 850. The extinction of many mammal species coincides with this late Holocene period, which entailed generally dry conditions and loss or decline of mesophytic forests. Much of this activity probably predated the impact of people on the biota of the West Indies (Curtis et al. 2001).

Today the climate of these warm, humid islands is dominated by easterly trade winds. The northeast trade winds blow moist air from the Atlantic. As the winds hit obstructions formed by the islands, the moisture in the winds forms clouds and precipitation. As a result, mean annual precipitation is generally greatest on the northern and eastern sides of the islands and on the highest mountains (Table 2.1). The highest peaks are usually shrouded in clouds and covered in cloud forest; elevations reach 3,177 m, 2,256 m, 2,006 m, and 1,338 m on Hispaniola, Jamaica, Cuba, and Puerto Rico, respectively (Murphy and Lugo 1995). The western and southern sides of the islands and the leeward sides of mountains are in the rain shadow and therefore are drier. The lowest rainfall is on small, low-relief islands such as those in the southern Bahamas, specifically the Turks and Caicos Islands, and in the Netherlands Antilles off the coast of Venezuela. Their average annual precipitation is generally between 200 and 750 mm. In much of the rest of the West Indies, the average level of rainfall is higher, between about 1,000 and 2,000 mm, but it may be as high as 4,000 mm to more than 7,000 mm in some upland areas, for example, over the Blue Mountains in Jamaica (Gumbs 1981) and on the windward slopes of mountains. Although the temperature varies little throughout the year, there are distinct dry and wet seasons on most of the islands. Peak periods of rainfall are strongly correlated with the annual movement of the Inter-Tropical Con-

Table 2.1. Summary of island characteristics

Island	Size (km^2)	Elevation (m)	Major Rock Types	Mean Air Temperature (C)	Rainfall (mm)
San Salvador	155	<30	L	24–25	1000–1250
Samana Cay	39	<30	L	24–25	750–1000
Middle Caicos	288	<30	L	24–25	350–750
Grand Turk	26	<30	L	24–25	350–750
Jamaica	11424	2256	L/S/M	25–28	760–7600
Hispaniola	76484	3177	L/S/M	25–28	1000–5000
Puerto Rico	8897	1338	L/S/M	25–28	1000–4500
Vieques	135	357	L/S	25–28	1000–2000
St. John	49	389	S/M/V	25–28	1000–2000
St. Thomas	70	209	S/M/V	25–28	1000–2000
St. Martin	34	485	L	25–28	800–2000
Saba	13	870	V	25	1200–2000
St. Eustatius	21	600	V	27	1000–2000
Nevis	130	985	V	25–28	1000–2000
Antigua	280	402	L/V	25–28	1000–1300
Guadeloupe	1702	1467	L/V	25	1240–1840
Barbados	440	400	L/S	23–29	1130–1250
Grenada	345	840	V	25–28	1000–2000
Venezuelan Federal Dependency	175	920	L/M	26–28	500–1000
Aruba	190	188	L/S/V	26–28	150–800
Bonaire	288	240	L/V	26–28	250–1000
Curaçao	443	372	L/V	26–28	250–1000

Source: Beard 1949; Stoffers 1956; Watts 1987:4

Note: The abbreviations for rock types are "L" for limestone; "M" for metamorphic; "S" for sedimentary; and "V" for volcanic.

vergence Zone (ITCZ); thus much of the region has a typically bimodal rainfall pattern (Nieuwolt 1977). The wet season is during the Northern Hemisphere's summer and fall (generally, a rainfall maximum occurs between June and November), but there is a short dry period of about 1 to 2 months' duration during the summer, and a longer dry season of 2 to 6 months during the winter and spring. The actual timing and extent of either wet or dry periods vary among the islands, from those that are generally wetter and have longer rainy seasons to drier islands that have longer dry periods or are too low in relief to stimulate orographic rainfall (Nieuwolt 1977).

Hurricanes are an obvious and important climatic influence in the region; the average number is about eight per year (Nieuwolt 1977). Hurricane frequency and extent in any given year in different parts of the Caribbean can have a considerable effect on the total annual rainfall and the local moisture budget. These storms also strongly influence vegetation dynamics as a fairly regular disturbance pulse (Lugo et al. 1981). Although they can be quite devastating and destructive, hurricanes and strong tropical storms can have net positive effects by creating openings in the canopy, stimulating forest succession, and, in many respects, fostering and maintaining high biodiversity (Reice 2001; Vandermeer et al. 2000). Earthquakes, volcanic eruptions, and tsunamis are additional hazards that occur in the region on a fairly regular basis (e.g., a volcano on Montserrat erupted most recently in 2001 and 2002) (Kruge et al. 1994; Tomblin 1981).

The surface current that sweeps through the Caribbean basin derives much of its power from the northern and southern equatorial currents that join forces along the northern coast of South America. The combined currents flow into the basin and circulate in a clockwise direction between the Antilles and Central America (Roberts 1997). A portion of the current flows into the Gulf of Mexico, and the rest flows between Cuba and Florida where it joins the Gulf Stream. There are countercurrents close to the Central American coast and other landmasses. A zone of upwelling occurs along the northern coast of Venezuela, affecting the Netherlands Antilles of Curaçao, Bonaire, and Aruba, as well as the Venezuelan islands of Los Roques.

As in the Pacific and other oceanic settings, the sea currents and prevailing winds affect the dispersal of animals and plants in the Caribbean. Most of the organisms that inhabited the islands when Native Americans first migrated into the West Indies are believed to have blown or floated to the islands (Howard 1973; Judd 2001; Morgan and Woods 1986; Williams 1989). One argument for waif dispersal of most of the land vertebrates is that the endemic fauna of the Greater Antilles is depauperate at higher taxonomic levels and unbalanced, lacking such mammal groups as marsupials, rabbits, and carnivores, nor is there fossil evidence of their past presence. New fossils continue to be found, adding to our fuller understanding of the faunal history of the islands. One example is the recent identification of a primitive rhinocerotoid ungulate from the Eocene of Jamaica (Domning et al. 1997). The currents favor rafting from South and Central America. Phylogenetic research and the Neotropical character of the flora and fauna of the West Indies supports this as the major source of founder populations (Baker and Genoways 1978; Hedges 2001; Howard 1973; Judd 2001; Morgan and Woods 1986; Simpson 1956).

Seeds are the mobile life stage of a plant. Lightweight seeds, such as those of orchids, may be blown from place to place. Buoyant fruit with tough exteriors and large stores of energy can withstand the rigors of long rafting journeys on ocean currents. Two such supertramps (Diamond 1975) are palm nuts (*Cocos* spp.) and bottle gourds (*Lagenaria* spp.). Mangrove trees that inhabit brackish shoreline environments in the tropics have fruits that are well adapted for waterborne dispersal. Another way in which plants disperse is as floating mats of vegetation or uprooted trees that provide rafts for both plants and animals (Gunn and Dennis 1976), and seeds are carried long distances by birds and other animal vectors of dispersal.

Currents also play a major role in the dispersal of marine organisms. Many fishes and invertebrates have pelagic eggs and larvae. Their dispersal is to some extent at the mercy of the currents, and their recruitment as adults into appropriate habitats depends on a source of larvae upstream (Roberts 1997). Land crabs (Gecarcinidae) produce planktonic larvae that may not replenish an island population annually or even as frequently as every six years, illustrating the role of currents and sources of larvae in maintaining island populations (Wolcott 1988).

With an improved understanding of plate tectonics, vicariance as a means of distribution of plants and animals is recognized as an alternative to crossing an aquatic barrier (Berlocher 1998). The distribution of terrestrial organisms by vicariance may be viewed broadly as encompassing organisms that occurred on a land fragment before it separated as an island from the mainland or from a larger island landmass. Vicariance also applies to biota on island fragments that merged to form a larger island such as the northern and southern parts of Hispaniola. Plants and animals might also have become distributed across land bridges when the sea level was low and islands on a shallow bank emerged to form a large landmass, such as the Bahamas during the Pleistocene (Hedges 2001).

The importance of vicariance in the distribution of West Indian vertebrates is still debated (Williams 1989; Woods 2001). The proto-Antilles separated from the continents during the Cretaceous, before many of the more advanced mammals had evolved. An exception is the insectivores that had evolved in North America by the Pliocene. The origin of the West Indian insectivores, *Solenodon* and *Nesophontes*, of the Greater Antilles may have been due to vicariance on the proto-Antillean archipelago (MacFadden 1980; Morgan and Woods 1986; cf. Ottenwalder 2001 and Whidden and Asher 2001). By the time most of the other advanced mammals had evolved, the connection between the proto-Antilles and the region between North and South America had broken.

The complex and diverse histories of the islands called the West Indies provided different opportunities for colonization by plants and animals. Overriding these geological differences are theories of island biogeography and the balance between the island area and distance from a source of propagules, as well as the numbers of successful colonists (MacArthur and Wilson 1967). Although nearshore habitats are not often considered in theories of island bio-geography, the size and configuration of these habitats do determine the abundance of marine fauna (in fact, even isolated terrestrial habitats or "resource islands" may be analyzed according to island biogeographic theory [Shafer 1990]). The Greater Antilles, whose large rivers drain an expansive land surface, have extensive estuaries and lagoons suitable for growth of mangrove forests and use by marine animals as nursery areas. Similarly, the diverse topography and substrates of these islands provide for a much richer flora with greater botanical species diversity than on small islands of the region.

COLONIZATION OF ISLANDS

Study of the colonization of islands not only provides a better understanding of island biota but also can be applied to research on biological colonization and diversity of habitat islands on mainland areas. This has important implications now for conservation biology and construction of wildlife preserves. The classic book *The Theory of Island Biogeography* by Robert MacArthur and Edward O. Wilson (1967) stimulated much of this work. Their theory on the dispersal and colonization of organisms describes the influence of geography on species diversity where the number of species demonstrates a positive, somewhat linear relationship with island size and proximity to sources of new colonists. It is based on an examination of the relation between area and species diversity, equilibrium between immigration and extinction rates of populations, and the evolutionary strategies adopted by successful colonizers. Further analysis of the distribution of species on islands has identified taxon cycles (Keegan and Diamond 1987; Levin 2000; Pianka 2000; Ricklefs and Cox 1972; cf. Gaston and Chown 1999). Taxon cycles have been described for plants, birds, ants, and other insects on various island archipelagoes. Four stages in dispersal, colonization, and evolution are described. In stage 1 a species inhabits an archipelago, is widespread, occurs on many islands, and may be in the process of invading new islands (expands its range); individual populations are similar or only slightly differentiated into distinct populations on the various islands. In this early stage the taxon is adapted to marginal, relatively unstable habitats, acting effectively as a pioneer or colonizer. In stage 2 of the taxon cycle, the distribution is still widespread and some differentiation to the level of subspecies exists between island populations. They begin to penetrate more mature, stable habitats. In stage 3 some of the differentiated taxa become extinct and the former range is fragmented because of extinctions; and by stage 4 a taxon is endemic to one island as a monotypic species. Eventually it may also go extinct.

Recent research combining new phylogenetic, ecological, behavioral, and morphological data from particular island faunas, for example, Galápagos finches, demonstrates that the allopatric model of differentiation and speciation (geographic separation promoting adaptive radiations) is inadequate to fully explain speciation without consideration of the role of changing environments, including number of islands, climate, and vegetation (Behrensmeyer et al. 1992; Grant and Grant 2002a, 2002b). Environmental archaeology, including zooarchaeology and archaeobotany, can contribute to this inquiry by providing details of past organisms, climates, and environments, and by clarifying the role of pre-industrial people in the distribution of island plant and animal populations. Moreover, natural ecosystems are "complex adaptive systems" (Costanza et al. 1997; Prugh et al. 1999): dynamic, inherently evolutionary, and with a limited degree of predictably. Thus, we argue and seek to demonstrate in later chapters that environmental archaeologists and others with an interest in human settlement must delve as much as possible beyond simple descriptions of hunting, fishing, and other cultural practices to appreciate as much as possible the problems and constraints underlying ecosystem dynamics. Such explorations are critical to our understanding of the role and impact of humans in natural ecosystems. This includes consideration of the basic distributions, replacement efficiency, and species relationships of taxa on individual islands, all of which have a direct bearing on the character, carrying capacity, and sustainability of human subsistence adaptations.

VEGETATION AND FLORISTIC PATTERNS

As predicted by the theory of island biogeography, both plant and animal species demonstrate greater species richness and endemism on the larger, older islands of the Greater Antilles than on smaller islands of the region. The larger landmass, dissected terrain, and range of elevations offer more habitats for this greater diversity. Moreover, these factors provide more niches for animal species. The islands of the younger, smaller Lesser Antilles have correspondingly fewer endemic plant species. Most of the islands have a mixture of plants originating from Central and South America (Beard 1944, 1949, 1955; Howard 1973; Watts 1987).

The pollen record from Lake Miragoane provides information about changes in the vegetation of Haiti during the last 10,000 years (Curtis et al. 2001; Higuera-Gundy 1989, 1991; Higuera-Gundy et al. 1999). Changing relative abundances of dry and moist forest pollen types chart environmental changes, including after human colonization of Hispaniola. The major arboreal taxa from the core samples include several trees typical of dry forest vegetation such as gumbo limbo (*Bursera*), cockspur (*Celtis*), bastard cedar (*Guazuma*), and pine (*Pinus*); in some pollen zones moist forest trees including trumpet tree (*Cecropia*), trema (*Trema*), and others are conspicuously present. The pollen from herbaceous weedy taxa, such as the grasses and copperleaf (*Acalypha*), increase in abundance relative to the pollen from trees around 600 to 700 years ago. The relative decrease in tree pollen coincides with an increase in the number of carbon particles and geochemical changes in the core. These changes possibly reflect human land clearing and agricultural activities, but they may be more strongly correlated with the late Holocene drying trend and decline in mesic forests after 3000 ^{14}C years B.P. A similar pattern of fluctuation in the quantity of charcoal particulate matter in a sediment core from Laguna Tortuguero in Puerto Rico is thought to be due to anthropogenic disturbances on that island (Burney and Burney 1994). A subsequent forest recovery event is documented for the Haitian flora by a sudden but short-lived increase in tree pollen that corresponds to the period A.D. 1852–1944. This regeneration episode was followed by a modern period of deforestation and soil erosion.

Plant communities in the Caribbean Islands, as elsewhere, depend to a great extent on the annual distribution of precipitation, evaporation, and temperature (Holdridge 1947, 1967; Holdridge et al. 1971). These factors also have considerable bearing on the potential for agriculture throughout the region and the particular types of crops that may be grown. According to Gumbs (1981), most agricultural areas in the region receive sufficient rainfall to support crop production; however, the strongly uneven distribution of that precipitation and the locations of water supplies (few rivers or no surface water on some islands) place constraints on agriculture and related activities. At higher elevations we could expect both cooler temperatures than are found closer to sea level and more moisture as the mountain peaks intercept the trade winds and the moisture carried in them. The mountain ridges of the Caribbean Islands support some of the richest, most lush vegetation formations, and they have at times supported agriculture. The characteristics of local soils can make a profound difference in the amounts of moisture they retain and make available to plants. Generally the more porous sandy or calcareous soils with low organic matter retain less water and therefore typically support only xerophytic thorn and cactus vegetation; these soils are unsuitable for plant cultivation.

The plant communities of the West Indies were first classified by Beard (1949, 1955) and a few other early naturalists, as reviewed by Woods (2001); they have since been further described by other botanists, ecologists, and foresters working regionally, subregionally, and on individual islands. The physiognomy of vegetation is strongly influenced by and varies primarily according to the amount and seasonal distribution of rainfall. Forest ecologists working in the Caribbean have applied Holdridge's (1947, 1967) bioclimatic classification system, comparing latitude, mean annual biotemperatures, and the aver-

Table 2.2. Summary of the major life zones and associated environmental parameters for the Caribbean Islands according to the Holdridge (1967) Life Zone classification system.

Holdridge System	Bioclimatic Parameters			
Life Zones	Total Annual Precipitation (mm)	Mean Annual Biotemperature (C)	Humidity Province	Potential Evapo-transpiration Ratio
Tropical Desert Scrub	125–250	>24	PerArid	8.00–16.00
Tropical Thorn Woodland	250–500	>24	Arid	4.00–8.00
Subtropical Thorn Woodland	250–500	<24	Semiarid	2.00–4.00
Tropical Very Dry Forest	500–1000	>24	Semiarid	2.00–4.00
Subtropical Dry Forest	500–1000	<24	Subhumid	1.00–2.00
Tropical Dry Forest	1000–2000	>24	Subhumid	1.00–2.00
Subtropical Moist Forest	1000–2000	<24	Humid	0.50–1.00
Tropical Moist Forest	2000–4000	>24	Humid	0.50–1.00
Subtropical Wet Forest	2000–4000	<24	Perhumid	0.25–0.50
Lower Montane Wet Forest	2000–4000	<24	Perhumid	0.25–0.50
Montane Rain Forest	2000–4000	<24	Superhumid	0.125–0.25
Lower Montane Rain Forest	4000–8000	<24	Superhumid	0.125–0.25
Subtropical Rain Forest	4000–8000	<24	Superhumid	0.125–0.25

Note: Dashed line denotes equal evapotranspiration ratio of 1.00; zones above that line have an overall moisture deficit, those below have a general moisture surplus.

age total annual precipitation, among other factors. The results indicate that the Caribbean Islands encompass as many as 13 major "life zones" (Ewel and Whitmore 1973; Lugo et al. 1981; Murphy and Lugo 1995); we judge these to include the life zones summarized in Table 2.2. Characteristic primary vegetation associations typify each life zone. However, in the case of the Holdridge system the term "association" refers not simply to a plant community per se but rather to a unique ecosystem: "a distinctive habitat or physical environment complete with an evolved naturally adapted community of plants and animals . . . defined by a range of environmental conditions within a Life Zone, together with its living organisms, within which the total complex of physiognomy of plants and activities of the animals are unique" (Holdridge et al. 1971:15). Therefore, individual life zones share common conditions for plant and animal growth.

It is important to understand that most of the Caribbean is classified as "subtropical" according to the Holdridge system because the mean sea-level biotemperatures tend to be below the 24°C limit that forms the boundary of the Tropical Latitudinal Region. This is despite the geographic position of the islands in latitudes generally characterized as "tropical" (Nieuwolt 1977). Truly tropical climates and life zones occur in the region at latitudes below about 12–15 degrees north (Ewel and Whitmore 1973:8); thus, about two-thirds of the way along the Lesser Antillean island arc in the approximate vicinity of St. Lucia. At the wetter extremes, the Caribbean life zones comprise various tropical and subtropical rain forest, wet forest, and moist forest associations. Dry and very dry forests, thorn woodlands, and desert scrub life zones occur in areas where a moisture deficit is the norm, that is, where mean annual precipitation is less than mean annual evapotranspiration, such as in the southern Caribbean Islands, the Turks and Caicos, and southwestern Puerto Rico. These associations as a whole span the superhumid through perarid humidity provinces (Holdridge 1947, 1967). Montane and lower montane forest associations, including cloud forests and palm breaks, also occur in the Caribbean at the highest elevations, as well as a number of notable edaphic associations (those in which the soils result in deviations from the climatic associations, e.g., because of unique mineral composition or poor or, conversely, excessive drainage) such as coastal mangrove forests or forests that grow on serpentine soils (Ewel and Whitmore 1973).

Approximately half of the vegetation in the Caribbean is actually classified within the dry forest life zones (Howard 1979; Murphy and Lugo 1995), areas that regularly experience a moisture deficit ranging from mild to relatively severe (evapotranspiration ratio >1.00 [Table 2.2]). The vegetation in these environments exhibits a number of specific xeromorphic adaptations such as having thorns and small or succulent leaves to cope with low available moisture. In general the dry forests are smaller in stature, simpler in structure and composition, and less species rich than wetter forest formations (Barnes et al. 1998; Bullock et al. 1995; Gentry 1995). Nevertheless, there are considerable differences among these forests according to geographic variation, mainly the effects of climate, soil, biogeographic considerations, and the history of disturbance (e.g., hurricanes and disruptive human activities) (Ewel and Whitmore 1973; Murphy and Lugo 1995). Interestingly, bird species richness and densities in the Caribbean tend to be higher in dry forests versus wetter forest types (Ewel and Whitmore 1973; Murphy and Lugo 1995).

A simple classification of the principal vegetation formations of the region, including zonal and nonzonal or edaphic associations, drawing in part from Beard (1949, 1955) and following Barnes et al. (1998) and Daubenmire (1978), is provided in Table 2.3. We emphasize that these are very simplistic categories and that we include them merely to provide a baseline to illustrate the general aspect and range of vegetation present in various Caribbean Island habitats. The aquatic ecosystems include freshwater and marine types. Mangrove and brackish swamp forests fringe protected bays and coastlines. Tough herba-

Table 2.3. Major types of vegetation and representative species

Vegetation Type	Dominant/Common Species
Saltwater shorelines: shallow marine; mangrove forest; brackish swamps; coastal strand, manchineel groves (nonzonal vegetation)	*Thalassia* sp., epiphytic algae; *Avicennia germinans, Conocarpus erectus, Laguncularia racemosa, Rhizophora mangle; Pterocarpus officinalis; Coccoloba uvifera, Chrysobalanus icaco, Erithalis fruticosa, Suriana maritima; Hippomane mancinella*
Freshwater ecosystems: ponds and streams; riparian woodland, freshwater swamp (nonzonal vegetation)	*Cabomba* spp., *Ceratophyllum* sp.; *Annona glabra, Ceiba pentandra*
Rainforest, wet-moist forests; various montane forest associations, cloud forest (mesophytic forest)	*Dacryoides excelsa, Diospyros* spp., *Hieronima* sp., Lauraceae, *Manilkara* spp., *Micona* sp., *Pouteria* spp., *Psychotria* sp., *Sloanea* spp., *Ternstroemia* sp.; *Cyathea* spp., *Cyrilla* sp., *Euterpe globosa*
Evergreen, semi-evergreen, mixed evergreen-deciduous, deciduous forest (xerophytic [seasonal] forest)	*Bourreria succulenta, Bursera simaruba, Ceiba pentandra, Cresentia* sp., *Hura crepitans, Hymenaea courbaril, Inga* spp., *Pisonia* spp., *Sideroxylon* sp., *Spondias* sp., *Swietenia* sp., *Tabebuia* spp.
Dry evergreen forest, bushland, cactus and thorn forest (microphyllous woodland)	*Acacia* spp., *Bucida buceras, Byrsonima* sp., *Caesalpinia* sp., *Calophyllum* sp., *Eugenia* spp., *Guaiacum* sp., *Inga* sp., *Manilkara bidentata, Pimenta racemosa, Zanthoxylum* spp.; *Cactaceae*
Grassland, savanna	*Byrsonima lucida, Croton* spp., Poaceae, *Heliotropium* sp.
Disturbed, secondary forest	*Cecropia peltata, Micona* spp., *Pisonia* sp., *Solanum* sp.

ceous and woody vegetation tolerant of winds and salt spray occur on more active coasts on sandy and coralline soils. This strand vegetation typically includes sea grape (*Coccoloba uvifera*) trees and associated woody and herbaceous plants such as railroad vine (*Ipomoea pes-caprae*). The various units of mesophytic forest, including true rain forests, are generally wet and humid, with rainfall distributed fairly evenly throughout the year. Xerophytic or seasonal forests are characterized by a seasonal rhythm in phenology (flowering, fruiting, leaf fall) attuned to alternating wet and dry seasons. These forests range from those that are fully deciduous during the dry season, to those that are semideciduous in areas with a shorter rainless period, to others that are primarily evergreen in locations where the annual moisture deficit is minor. The species diversity of evergreen seasonal forests is nearly as high as in mesophytic forests (Daubenmire 1978:243). Microphyllous woodlands and savanna vegetation occur in the driest locations throughout the Caribbean Islands.

Sparse tree cover characterizes the former, with generally widely spaced, very small-leaved (microphyll) or thorn-bearing shrubs and trees of low stature that are mostly deciduous. These "thorn woodlands" or "bushlands" are common on islands too low in relief to force orographic rainfall from the incoming trade winds, such as in the Turks and Caicos Islands and southern Bahamas, or in the driest rain shadows of mountains, such as in southwestern Puerto Rico. Grasslands or savanna vegetation in the Caribbean may be more edaphic (growth on infertile, shallow, or waterlogged soils) or derived (the result of regular fires or overgrazing) than a true climatic or zonal association. Various forms of disturbed and secondary forests are found throughout the region, having become increasingly prevalent since the presence of Europeans. For example, extensive deforestation of the Lesser Antilles for sugarcane production in the historic era has resulted in many areas in deflected successions and highly degraded woodlands, some of which may never recover their original or optimal forms.

As the dominant floristic elements of the Caribbean, the dry forests and related habitats have a long and varied history of human use. The microphyllous woodlands and savannas are used for grazing or browsing animals. Products long harvested from the microphyllous and xerophytic forests include dye (*Haematoxylon campechianum*), tannins (*Caesalpinia* sp.), essential oils (*Amyris* sp.), and firewood, and these environments have figured prominently in the production of sisal (*Agave* sp.), sugarcane, and pineapples (Daubenmire 1978). The hard dense wood of lignum-vitae (*Guaiacum* spp.) has long been sought to make sheaves, bowling balls, and other wood objects that require strength and resiliency. The Spanish began to harvest lignum-vitae ("wood of life") as early as 1508 for the valuable wood as well as for its (incorrectly) perceived value as a medicinal treatment for venereal disease (Fernández Mendez 1995; Record and Hess 1943:556). Other important timber species from the seasonal forests include mahogany (*Swietenia* sp.) and cedar or roble (*Tabebuia* spp.), among others. Finally, native mangrove forests are a common source of high-quality fuelwood in the Neotropics, and the wood may be used to produce charcoal (Little 1983; National Academy of Sciences 1980); the bark of these genera tends to contain high levels of tannin (Record and Hess 1943:129, 445, 566), a substance potentially useful for a variety of purposes.

Vertebrate Fauna

The vertebrates include animals with different modes of locomotion, which therefore colonized the islands from different sources (Table 2.4). Flying animals include both bats and birds for which the sea is less of a barrier to dispersal. Most species are derived from Central American taxa (Bond 1985; Koopman 1989). South America is the source of some Lesser Antillean bats. Some

Table 2.4. Habitats and characteristic vertebrate species of the West Indies

Habitats	Characteristic Animals
Forest and second growth	Oryzomyini, Capromyidae, Columbidae, Psittacidae
Freshwater swamps, marshes, and ponds	Ardeidae, Rallidae
Shoreline (nesting)	*Monachus tropicalis,** *Puffinus lherminieri*, Sulidae, Cheloniidae
Shallow inshore waters	*Trichechus manatus*, Cheloniidae, *Albula vulpes*, Belonidae, *Mugil* spp.
Pelagic	Clupeidae, Exocoetidae, Scombridae
Reef	Serranidae, Lutjanidae, Haemulidae, Labridae, Scaridae, Acanthuridae

* extinct

Table 2.5. Habitats and characteristic invertebrates of the West Indies

Habitat	Characteristic Animals
Land along the shoreline	Gecarcinidae, *Coenobatis clypiatus*
Intertidal sandy beach	*Donax* sp.
Rocky intertidal and shallow water	Echinoidea, Chitonidae, Fissurelidae, Littorinidae, Neritidae, *Arca zebra*
Mangroves	*Littorina* spp., *Murex* spp., *Crassostrea rhizophora*, *Isognomon alatus*
Shallow water and turtle grass beds	Portunidae, Lucinidae, Chamidae, Ostreidae, Strombidae, Fasciolariidae
Reefs	Palinuridae, Conidae

birds are oceanic, coming to land only to nest. Land mammals and reptiles generally have their closest relatives in South America (Morgan and Woods 1986). Marine mammals and reptiles, such as sea turtles, are widespread in tropical waters. The West Indian monk seal has closely related species in the waters of the Hawaiian Islands and the Mediterranean. Freshwater fishes are not abundant and played little role in human exploitation (Burgess and Franz 1989). Marine fishes, vital to the animal-protein portion of the economy, are primarily circumtropical. These include fishes that live near shore, those that are obligate reef dwellers, and species that are pelagic and oceanic (Nelson 1984).

Invertebrate Animals

The invertebrates that are most frequently used by people are echinoderms, primarily sea urchins, crustaceans—particularly crabs and lobsters—and molluscs, both bivalves and gastropods (Table 2.5). Other than the land crabs and land hermit crabs, these all live their entire lives in the sea. The land crabs are tied to the sea for the development of their larvae in the plankton stream.

In combination the environmental characteristics and biota of the Caribbean differ from those of any other area of the world in terms of origins, evolution, and intrinsic ecosystem dynamics. This being the case, researchers hoping to examine, for example, human colonization, subsistence adaptations, and various social developments in the region must be fully cognizant of the true nature of individual island environments, including the potentials, constraints, and limitations of the biotic resources, to adequately address anthropological problems.

3
Human Colonization of the West Indies

BIOGEOGRAPHIC THEORY

It is important to ask whether biogeographic principles as originally described by MacArthur and Wilson (1967) apply to human colonization of islands (Fitzhugh and Hunt 1997). They apply in two very important ways: (1) humans, like other organisms, have basic biological needs, and (2) islands have limited resources and clear constraints with which human cultures must cope. For colonization to be successful, an island must be large enough and have adequate resources to sustain a viable human population at the given scale and level of technology. Under almost any circumstance new colonists will affect the equilibrium of the existing fauna and flora of an island, which in turn affects the development of subsistence and economic patterns, among other things (Burney 1997; Keegan and Diamond 1987; Terrell 1997). At a very basic level, human colonists are similar to other organisms establishing viable populations on islands, but culture dictates the nature of human adaptation and the long-term outcome of colonization and settlement. Human colonists of the Caribbean originally represented a number of distinct mainland cultural traditions, each of which was ultimately transformed through unique adaptations, technological innovations, and intrinsic social dynamics in the various islands and subregions of the archipelago.

People must satisfy their subsistence requirements on a regular and frequent basis. In the island setting food resources are gleaned from the land as well as from the inshore waters. Possibly beginning with the earliest preceramic human groups of the region (Keegan 1994), and during the later Ceramic age, sources of wild food were augmented by food production that expanded the carrying capacity of the land. Such a broad diet required tools such as fishing equipment, containers for gathering, agricultural implements, and utensils for food preparation. The "tool maker" must also have materials for construction of shelter, clothing, ornaments, medicines, and more. The size and longevity of a human population on any given island depends to a large extent on the quality and quantity of resources and the resiliency and regeneration efficiency of those resources under human extraction pressure (Costanza et al. 1997; Prugh et al. 1999).

The colonization of islands by people as well as the plants and animals they brought with them set into motion a new equilibrium among the species in the island faunas and floras. Through the study of plant and animal remains from archaeological sites it is possible to document both the introduction of new species brought to the islands by people and the extirpation or extinction of endemic species (Pregill et al. 1994; Wing 1989). Not all species extirpations were necessarily the direct result of hunting or gathering pressures, but they may have been indirectly caused by competition exerted by people or their introduced animals, newly introduced diseases, or habitat disruption and change (Amorosi et al. 1997; Burney 1997; Keegan and Diamond 1987). Whatever the most immediate cause, a decline or loss of species coincided with the establishment of human colonies.

Of course human colonization differs in some important respects from that of plants and other animals. Discovery of an island may precede its colonization by people (Cherry 1984). Evidence from the Mediterranean Islands indicates that many of the islands were well known long before founding populations established settlements on them (Patton 1996). Probably the West Indian islands were known before colonists departed from the mainland. Many islands are close enough to be seen from neighboring islands. A further guide to navigation from one island to another is the visible cloud cover hovering over the islands. Clearly, large islands and those with high peaks and permanent cloud cover would be the easiest to see and are likely to have been discovered first (Keegan and Diamond 1987). The pattern of settlement along the coastline of Caribbean Islands indicates that the seas were less of a barrier to settlement than the interiors of islands (Rouse 1992). Mariners' skills, exploratory forays, and clouds over islands would have provided direction to explorers and potential colonists.

Maritime knowledge and navigational skills allowed people to control the direction of their exploration. They were not completely at the mercy of the currents and the prevailing winds for their destination. Maritime knowledge would also have permitted trade and communications between settlements on other islands and between islands and the mainland. This had the potential of renewing supplies, sources of rare materials, information, and gene flow.

The size of the human populations in the Caribbean Islands either as founding populations or as recently as A.D. 1492 has been debated for years with no clear consensus (Curet 1998). Site densities, sizes, and the level of cultural development at the time of contact suggest robust population levels. The rapid depopulation of Native Americans subsequent to European contact seems inconceivable if populations were indeed large, though there is considerable evidence to suggest widespread and substantial population losses (Wilson 2001). These conflicting impressions may be modified by subsistence data that indicate what population levels might be sustained before the Contact Era.

Research on the Marshall Islands in the Pacific examined the size of founder populations and the island characteristics that affect viability (Williamson and Sabath 1982, 1984). Characteristics that determine the success of a colony are the size of the island, its rainfall regime and availability of freshwater sources, reliance of the people on agricultural production, and the proximity of populations on neighboring islands. Horticulturists established viable populations on islands with adequate rainfall, particularly if they had opportunities to maintain contact with other island populations. Such founding populations had to be between 40 and 78 individuals. Other scholars working on colonization of islands in the Pacific suggest that a founder population of 20 to 25 individuals is large enough to establish an enduring colony (Irwin 1992). However, Diamond (1995, 1997) and others have shown that sustaining human populations of any size on small isolated islands can be extremely difficult and depends greatly on the ability of island dwellers to secure alternative resources when they encounter limitations.

These are figures for the Marshall Islands, which differ in many respects from the West Indies. Maintaining contact between populations on neighboring islands or with mainland areas may have been easier in the stepping-stone configuration of the Caribbean archipelago. The staple crops in the Pacific are taro, coconut, breadfruit, and sweet potatoes. According to ethnohistoric sources, the staple crops of the West Indies were manioc and several other tropical root crops, supplemented by various fruits. These records (Sauer 1966: 53–54) imply that bitter manioc cultivars were emphasized in the islands, based on the information that the first crop of tubers was available one to one and a half years after planting (which is typical of bitter cultivars) and that the tubers were prepared by grating, juicing, and baking the pulp (to eliminate toxins). The tubers of "sweet" or less bitter forms of manioc can be harvested for consumption within approximately six months of planting; despite the lack of clear mention, these are thought by Sauer to also have been produced by the Taíno. In general, bitter manioc cultivars produce higher yields than sweet forms (Wilson and Dufour 2002). Animal protein sources came primarily from the sea. Protein from fishes and molluscs was augmented by meat from introduced domestic pigs and chickens in the Pacific, but by wild or managed endemic rodents and birds in the Caribbean.

Systems analysts have quantified the sources of energy and costs of obtaining them for the subsistence horticulturists from Lamotrek Atoll in the Pacific (Odum 1971:105). By their calculations staple crops from the land support one person per acre. Protein sources come from a much larger area, including the lagoon and coral reef. Human density on the atoll and its surrounding waters is one person per 50 acres (or about 13 per square mile).

The productivity of manioc as a staple was quantified for people living in the South American lowlands. The average number of people who can be sustained by manioc is 37 per acre (15 per hectare) (Levin 1983). Manioc is low in protein and must be supplemented by animal protein to sustain health. Levin (1983:336) and others have concluded that calories from manioc were more than enough "to support aboriginal populations larger than those reported or inferred." It would appear that manioc is a more productive staple than the Pacific root crops. Nevertheless, the availability of protein, primarily fishes, to subsistence fishermen was probably a limiting factor setting an upper limit on population sizes (Beckerman 1994; Dufour 1994). In both the Pacific and the Caribbean, marine resources are gleaned from a very large area. These are sea turtles that migrate to the island shores to feed and breed as well as territorial subtidal molluscs and inshore fishes. Technological innovations are required to expand the range of fishing beyond the island shelf to the deep-sea waters and access to oceanic fishes such as tuna. One of these innovations is the more frequent use of watercraft, a change that accepts the greater dangers involved in fishing far from shore.

HUMAN COLONIZATION OF THE WEST INDIES

Establishing a chronology for the peopling of the Caribbean has been the research focus of many archaeologists since the 1940s. Chief among these scholars is Irving Rouse, whose 1992 book summarizes 50 years of research throughout the West Indies and northern South America. Others, such as Ricardo Alegría (1981, 1997a), William Keegan (1994, 2000), Jose Oliver (1999), Samuel Wilson (1997b), and Marcio Veloz Maggiolo (1993), continue to refine Rouse's work. We use their outline for the movement of people, their mainland roots, and the dates associated with those colonizing efforts.

Among the first migrants to enter the Caribbean in western Cuba and Hispaniola were people from Central America. These original inhabitants of the islands had a lithic technology emphasizing large chipped stone tools, and they did not manufacture pottery (Dacal Moure and Rivero de la Calle 1996; Wilson 2001). Evidence for their occupation—labeled Casimiran Casimiroid for the material culture subseries/series by Rouse (1992)—occurs in deposits across the islands of Cuba and Hispaniola and dates from about 3000–4000 to about 2000 B.C. (Dacal Moure and Rivero de la Calle 1996; Keegan 1994). A likely origin of these early migrants into the Caribbean Islands is the Yucatán peninsula (Veloz Maggiolo 1993; Wilson et al. 1998). This assumption is based on geographic proximity and on similarities in the stone artifacts. These early sites can inform us about the conditions in the Greater Antilles when people initially entered the island ecosystem. Unfortunately, few of these sites exist and those that have been found are not clearly habitation sites. Presumably the earliest of these colonists entered and became established in the islands as small bands of mobile hunter-gatherer-fishers who moved regularly between small base camps accumulating and leaving behind sparse refuse and other cultural debris. Consequently no data on the faunal or botanical remains from the earliest deposits are available.

Changes in the artifact inventories of the Preceramic sites in Cuba and Hispaniola occurred by at least 2000–1000 B.C. (Redondan and Courian Casimiroid subseries [Keegan 1994; Rouse 1992]). In addition to the flaked-stone industry involving blades and microliths, ground stone and shell tools, bowls, and ornaments or art objects appear in the archaeological record (Dacal Moure and Rivero de la Calle 1996; Keegan 1994; Veloz Maggiolo 1993). A number of sites are attributable to this period (Dacal Moure and Rivero de la Calle 1996; Veloz Maggiolo 1993), including several with relatively substantial midden and other domestic deposits. Such deposits indicate increasing human populations with larger, more permanent settlements and perhaps in a few areas the first signs of a sedentary or semisedentary lifestyle.

As early as 5500 B.C. another migration began of people who also produced no pottery, based primarily on evidence from the Banwari Trace site on Trinidad. Sometime between then and 2000 B.C. the migration(s) resumed or continued up the Lesser Antillean archipelago from Trinidad, the South American mainland, or both (Keegan 1994:266). Interaction between these Ortoiroid (Rouse 1992) Archaic-age people who migrated from northern South America and those who descended from earlier established colonists in the western Antilles may have occurred in Puerto Rico and the Virgin Islands (Keegan 1994; Lundberg 1991; Rouse 1992; Wilson 2001). A brief Archaic-age occupation also occurred between 1370 B.C. and A.D. 470 on the Netherlands Antilles off the coast of Venezuela (Haviser 1991a, 1991b). These people appear to have migrated directly from the South American mainland to the offshore islands.

In general, the early Caribbean peoples who are categorized as having Lithic- and/or Archaic-age cultures pursued a hunter-gatherer lifestyle (Keegan 1994; Rouse 1992). Their settlement patterns seem to have been characterized by varying degrees of residential or logistic mobility, evidently including short-term or seasonally revisited base camps located primarily along the coasts (Dacal Moure and Rivero de la Calle 1996; Rodríguez López 1997a). Evidence of any dwellings or other more permanent structures constructed during either the Lithic or Archaic age is basically lacking, though in some cases postholes in apparent alignments have been located and some midden deposits are extensive. Primary burials have been discovered in or near domestic contexts, including 11 inhumations at the Maruca site in southern Puerto Rico (Rodríguez López 1997a), and separate burial areas, some that perhaps functioned as formal cemeteries, are known from Cuba (Dacal Moure and Rivero de la Calle 1996) and are assigned at least to the latter part of this period. Food consumption practices resulted in the deposition of materials composed in large part of molluscan shell; it is clear that the molluscs were used for food and their shells for tools. The remains of vertebrates and plants are also found in some of these deposits; there is evidence to suggest that some Archaic groups were relatively more complex and may have been part-time or low-level food producers (Keeley 1995; Kelly 1995; Newsom 1993a; Smith 2001). This evidence is detailed in Chapters 6 and 7. As a whole, the Archaic-age sites are the earliest for which we have evidence for the exploitation of the island biological resources.

The various Archaic-age groups were followed into the West Indies by a mid–first millennium B.C. migration or, much more likely, a series of migrations of people from northern South America. These people came from the lowland tropical forest region of the Orinoco and other river basins of interior and coastal Venezuela and Guiana (Allaire 1997a; Keegan 1994, 2000; Oliver 1999; Wilson 2001). Unlike that of the earlier Archaic-age groups, the customary lifestyle of these first Ceramic-age migrants appears to have been fully sedentary, and they established permanent settlements in the islands. They produced pottery, and their subsistence practices included or perhaps emphasized staple tropical root-crop production. Settlement pattern studies based on individual islands, island clusters, and subregions (Haviser 1997; Siegel 1991; Wilson 1993) demonstrate the success of Ceramic-age colonization, though much more research needs to be conducted. The populations grew, becoming quite dense on individual islands (Haviser 1997; Wilson 1993). Ultimately these Ceramic-age groups spread nearly throughout the Lesser Antilles and into much of the Greater Antilles, resulting in the widespread presence of large archaeological deposits with abundant plant and animal remains. These materials are the primary focus of this book.

The first Ceramic-age colonists migrated up the Lesser Antillean island chain from northeastern Amazonia or, in some cases, may have taken a direct route by water from Trinidad/Venezuela north to the northern Leeward/Virgin Islands/Puerto Rico area, beginning about 500 B.C. (Keegan 1994, 2000; Oliver 1999). For the most part, these earliest or original Ceramic-age settlers are collectively attributed and assigned to an archaeological culture construct termed Saladoid (ca. 500 B.C.–A.D. 500/600 [Rouse 1992]), which is recognized as a distinct cultural complex until about A.D. 600 (Keegan 2000). Another early Ceramic-age cultural manifestation recognized by archaeologists working in the region as either distinct or perhaps in some way related to Saladoid groups is known as Huecoid or La Hueca (Oliver 1999; Rodríguez López 1997b), based on distinctive modes of ceramic manufacture and decoration. The exact nature of and relationship between the people represented by the numerous Saladoid sites and those who presumably were responsible for Huecoid sites, deposits, or strata are unclear, if they are separate at all. This question will only be resolved through more excavation and the collection of data. However vague at the moment, we allude to the presence of these apparently separate ceramic traditions because of the suggestion that they may represent distinct peoples and therefore indicate a greater degree of diversity of human groups—perhaps as separate ethnic groups or people with separate backgrounds and history—living in the region early in the Ceramic age aside from various mobile or semisedentary Archaic hunter-gatherers and village-dwelling Saladoid horticulturists, respectively.

Notwithstanding the foregoing discussion, there is considerable evidence that socially the Saladoid groups were relatively egalitarian. It has been suggested that they were organized into segmentary "Big Man" or "local-group" polities (Keegan et al. 1998), with individual communities integrated into larger multicommunity groups through kinship ties. They occupied permanent sites for long periods throughout the Lesser Antilles, Virgin Islands, Puerto Rico, and the eastern tip of Hispaniola (Haviser 1997; Keegan 2000; Rouse 1992; Siegel 1989). Individual communities on islands situated near particular habitats (e.g., coral reefs, mangrove forests, or arable soils) are likely to have cooperated and perhaps coordinated different aspects of food production, maximizing the use of patchy environmental zones and more productive areas through sharing, particularly during times of local shortfalls. A number of the habitation sites are located in the interiors of islands, but many of these show evidence for the use of marine shells and land crabs. Close study of these deposits reveals abundant vertebrate remains. Griddle sherds and related food-processing equipment commonly found in Saladoid sites indicate preparation of root crops, almost certainly manioc, as a staple crop. The actual plant remains, as we describe in subsequent chapters, indicate cultivation of a complex of plants and use of varied wild plant resources. Based on examination of postholes, houses are believed to have resembled the malocas still seen in northern South America (Versteeg and Schinkel 1992). These were substantial structures made of pole construction with thatch roofing, and some were large enough to house several families.

The next 500 years, from about A.D. 500–600 to 1000, saw many cultural and population changes in the West Indies. Sites became generally larger and more numerous as a response to population growth during this post-Saladoid period (Wilson 1989, 1993). This cultural period is known as the Ostionoid in the Greater Antilles and the Virgin Islands and the Troumassoid in the Lesser Antilles (Keegan 2000). The cultures of the West Indian people continued to diverge and diversify. Expansion and migration occurred to include new areas. A mosaic of different complex cultures arose.

In the entire region, particularly the Greater Antilles, social and political complexity continued to develop and evolve in unique ways. Eventually the first signs of simple chiefdoms and of social stratification began to emerge (Curet 1996; Curet and Oliver 1998; Keegan et al. 1998). As a part of this development, plant food production became more intensive. Landscape changes that left their mark included agricultural terraces and elaborately prepared ball courts and large plazas. Settlements extended farther inland, penetrating well into interior mountainous regions and away from the coastal settings inhabited by earlier populations. Eventually some people from the Greater Antilles moved into the Bahamas, establishing permanent settlements on those islands (Keegan 1992, 2000).

The Lesser Antillean populations also grew, as evidenced by an increased number of sites (Haviser 1997; Wilson 1993). Although the people living in those islands may have engaged in ball games such as in the Greater Antilles (Wilson 2001), they did not construct permanent ball courts. It seems that very little exchange or trade was carried on between the people living on either side of the Anegada Passage, the deep-water trough between the northern Lesser Antilles and the Virgin Islands. This is another question in Caribbean archaeology that remains to be clarified and resolved.

During the same period, the Netherlands Antilles of the southern Caribbean were settled by Ceramic-age people with a culture known as Dabajuroid. Contacts were maintained between people living on Los Roques, the Aruba-Bonaire-Curaçao island group, and those living on the mainland of Venezuela (Antczak 1995; Haviser 1987, 1991a, 1991b).

In the few centuries before the arrival of Europeans, there was a flowering of the Taino cultures in the Greater Antilles, northern Lesser Antilles, and Bahamas. On Hispaniola and Puerto Rico, at least, these chiefdoms with roots in the Archaic and Saladoid became very complex. They developed a strongly stratified society with caciques governing large villages and controlling many aspects of village life. There were complex, multifaceted interrelations and interactions between individual elites, separate segments of the society (e.g., elites or *nitainos*, commoners, and servants or *naborías* [Keegan 1997a; Keegan et al. 1998]), and with similar political entities (Keegan 1997b; Wilson 1990a,

1990b). Within the elite group were specialists known as *behiques*, shamans who were responsible for a range of demonstrative and transformative religious practices including divination and curing rituals (Schwimmer 1980). These individuals were believed imbued with the power to mediate between the everyday and spirit worlds; they performed curing and magicoreligious ceremonies that included the use of tobacco and hallucinogenic substances. For example, reiterating from Rouse (1992:14), a typical curing ceremony began with the shaman swallowing the herb gioia to induce vomiting (ritual purification), after which the shaman lighted a torch and sang while shaking a rattle, then approached the patient and pretended to suck an object from the latter's body. The object was considered to be the cause of the illness; thus through this ritual the stricken person was believed cured. The *behiques* also had a central role as interpreters of the Taino cosmology and the functioning of their religion, known as *cemíism* (Oliver 1997a, 1997c).

People in the Lesser Antilles also developed considerable diversity and cultural complexity. They continued to have contacts between islands, though it seems clear that the Leeward Islands and the Virgin Islands evolved and developed along a cultural trajectory more allied with the Greater Antilles groups, separate and largely distinct from developments in the Windward Islands to the south (Allaire 1997a). There is strong evidence also that contact with groups living on the mainland continued. In particular, trade and other social relationships were apparently maintained between residents of the Windward Islands and the mainland (Allaire 1997a, 1997b; Watters 1997). Populations in the Lesser Antilles continued to grow until about A.D. 1200, at which time population sizes declined and some islands may have been abandoned (Allaire 1997a; Wilson 1993). Sometime after this period a migration of Cariban-speaking people from northern South America occurred, resulting in the people known as Island Caribs (Allaire 1997a, 1997b).

Throughout the human occupation of the West Indies, cultures developed and human populations rose and fell. Human adaptations to these islands changed according to the conditions of the islands and the organizational capabilities of individual groups (Keegan et al. 1998), all part of an extended dynamic between the landscape and culture. Our examination of the plant and animal data associated with a range of archaeological sites aims to better understand these human adaptations and the complex interactions between human groups and the plants and animals with which people shared the islands.

4
Sources of Plant and Animal Samples and Methods Used to Study Them

SOURCES OF DATA

Our objective in undertaking this study is to base it on a good representation of samples that were carefully excavated from sites throughout the Caribbean. We use the word *sample* to mean an assemblage of plant or animal remains excavated from an archaeological site and associated with a specific context at that site. When sites are small or biological materials are poorly preserved, a sample may encompass the entire group of organisms recovered from the site. Large samples allow examination of variation in the representation of plants and animals related to different activity zones and changes through time. Our purpose is to examine variation in the uses of resources on various types of islands—small and large ones and those close or far from the surrounding mainland. Through this approach we are able to examine issues of human adaptation, island biogeography, and environmental change brought about by Native American colonists.

Faunal studies are more commonly undertaken than botanical ones and have a longer tradition in the region than does archaeobotanical research. Therefore, it is possible to cite zooarchaeological research conducted by several colleagues, including Lisabeth Carlson, Susan deFrance, Laura Kozuch, Yvonne Narganes, and Elizabeth Reitz. Their work integrates information from several animal classes, including vertebrates and invertebrates. DeFrance and Kozuch undertook the identification of animal remains in many of the faunal samples that form the core of this book. Important studies of biogeography that are in part based on archaeological remains of single vertebrate classes continue to be done by David Steadman and Storrs Olson on birds and by Gregory Pregill on reptiles. Macrobotanical research is relatively recent in Caribbean archaeological sites. The archaeobotanical work of Deborah Pearsall can be cited for studies in Puerto Rico, the Virgin Islands, and the Bahamas. We reference these studies, as well as some research of plant micro-remains and others undertaken on the island of Cuba, but our main focus is on our primary research and that of our students. This assures consistency in research methods.

The island groups for which we have data represent the major regions in the Caribbean as well as the southern Netherlands Antilles, sometimes called the "ABC" islands (Aruba, Bonaire, and Curaçao), and other small islands that lie off the coast of Venezuela (Figure 4.1). The southern Caribbean Islands are usually not included in archaeological and historical research describing the West Indies, but because they are biogeographically part of the Caribbean region and they provide information about plant and animal introductions onto islands close to the mainland, we include them. The other island groups recognized as subregions of the West Indies are the Lesser Antilles, Virgin Islands, Greater Antilles, and Bahamas, including the southern group of the Turks and Caicos Islands. Unfortunately, we have no samples of plant or animal remains from Cuba to incorporate here: the new research on these samples from Cuban sites is in various stages of analysis. This is particularly unfortunate because the island is the largest in the region, has the most diverse habitats, supports an important island fauna and flora, and has evidence of an early Preceramic human colonization from Middle America, as described in Chapter 3. We are glad that paleoethnobotanical and zooarchaeological research is now under way on Cuban sites and that this gap in our knowledge will soon be filled.

We concentrate on sites occupied by people who produced pottery and cultivated crops. A few of the sites and assemblages were deposited even earlier by Archaic-age groups. The results of research on these earlier deposits are discussed and contrasted with deposits of Ceramic-age people. Altogether there are plant or animal assemblages for nine Archaic-age deposits located on seven islands (Table 4.1). The Ceramic-age samples encompass all the geographic subregions of the Caribbean. These assemblages include four sets of material from the southern Caribbean Islands; samples from 13 sites (six islands) in the Lesser Antilles, including both early and later Ceramic-age components; 7 sites in the Virgin Islands and from Vieques, some again represented by earlier and later materials; 15 sites in the Greater Antilles, specifically Puerto Rico, Haiti, and Jamaica, some with early or late Ceramic-age materials; and finally, 14 sites in the Bahamas and Turks and Caicos, deriving from six of those islands (Table 4.1).

ARCHAEOLOGICAL RECOVERY STRATEGIES

Animal remains are often small and fragile and plant remains are even more so, requiring great care in their recovery and subsequent handling. Two basic

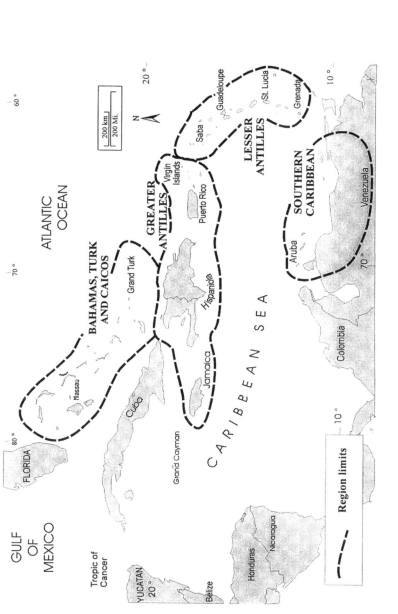

Figure 4.1. The West Indies. (By Florence E. Sergile)

Table 4.1. Sources of archaeobotanical and zooarchaeological assemblages

Period/Island	Site	Series	Excavator	Archaeobiological Reference
ARCHAIC				
Barbados	Heywoods	Ortoiroid	Drewett	Wing data
Antigua	Jolly Beach	Ortoiroid	Nodine	Newsom 1993a; Wing et al. 1968 and data
	Twenty Hill	Ortoiroid	Nodine	Newsom 1993a; Wing data
Nevis	Hichmans' Shell Heap GE-6	Ortoiroid	Wilson	Kozuch and Wing 2004; Newsom 2004
St. John, VI	Beach Access	Ortoiroid	Wild	Newsom 2001
St. Thomas, VI	Krum Bay	Ortoiroid	Lundberg	Pearsall 1989; Reitz 1989
Vieques	Puerto Ferro	Ortoiroid	Chanlatte, Narganes	Narganes 1991
Puerto Rico	Maruca	Ortoiroid	Rodríguez López	Narganes 1997a, 1997b; Newsom 1999b
	María de la Cruz	Ortoiroid	Rouse, Alegría	Newsom 1993a
CERAMIC				
Southern Caribbean				
Aruba	Tanki Flip	Dabajuroid	Versteeg	Newsom 1997; Grouard 1997
Bonaire	Wanápa	Dabajuroid	Haviser	Newsom 1991; Wing data
Curaçao	Santa Barbara	Dabajuroid	Haviser	Newsom data; Wing data
Los Roques	various		Antczak	Antczak 1999b
Lesser Antilles				
Antigua	Indian Creek	Saladoid	Rouse, Faber Morse	Jones 1985; Wing 1999
Barbados	Chancery Lane	Saladoid/post-Saladoid	Drewett	Wing 1991a
	Heywoods	post-Saladoid	Drewett	Drewett et al. 1993, Drewett, Rogers, and Newsom 2000; Wing 2000

Island	Site	Period	Investigator	References
	Hillcrest	Saladoid/post-Saladoid	Drewett	Wing 1991a
	Little Welches	Saladoid	Drewett	Wing data
	Silver Sands	post-Saladoid	Drewett	Wing 1991a
	Spring Head Cave	post-Saladoid	Drewett	Wing 1997
Grenada	Pearls	Saladoid	Keegan	Newsom 1993a; Fandrich 1990
Montserrat	Trants	Saladoid	Watters	Newsom data; Reitz 1994
	Windward Bluff	Saladoid	Watters	Newsom data
Nevis	Hichmans GE-5	Saladoid	Wilson	Kozuch and Wing 2004; Newsom 2004
	Indian Castle	post-Saladoid	Wilson	Kozuch and Wing 2004; Newsom 2004
	Sulphur Ghaut	post-Saladoid	Wilson	Kozuch and Wing 2004; Newsom 2004
Saba	Kelbey's Ridge	Saladoid/post-Saladoid	Hoogland	Wing 1996
St. Eustatius	Golden Rock	post-Saladoid	Versteeg	Newsom 1992; Klift 1992
St. Kitts	Sugar Factory	Saladoid	Goodwin	Wing and Scudder 1980
St. Martin	Hope Estate	Saladoid	Haviser, Hofman, Hoogland	Newsom and Molengraaff 1999; Wing data
Virgin Islands				
Jost van Dyke	Cape Wright	Ostionoid	Bates	Wing data
Tortola	Paraquita Bay	Ostionoid	Drewett	Wing data
St. Croix	Aklis	Saladoid/Ostionoid	Hayward	Newsom 1995b
St. John	Cinnamon Bay	Ostionoid	Wild	Quitmyer 2003
	Trunk Bay	Ostionoid	Wild	Newsom 2001; Wing data
St. Thomas	Tutu	Saladoid/Ostionoid	Righter	Pearsall 2002; Wing et al. 2002
Vieques	Luján I	Ostionoid	Rivera Calderón	Newsom 1999a; Quitmyer and Wing 2001
	Sorcé	Saladoid	Chanlatte, Narganes	Narganes 1982; Wing 1991b

Table 4.1. *Continued*

Period/Island	Site	Series	Excavator	Archaeobiological Reference
Greater Antilles				
Puerto Rico	Barrazas	Saladoid/Ostionoid	Meléndez Maíz	Newsom 1995a
	El Bronce	Ostionoid	Sickler Robinson et al.	Pearsall 1985; Reitz 1985
	El Fresal	Ostionoid	Meléndez Maíz	Newsom 1988, 1993a
	Maisabel	Saladoid/Ostionoid	Siegel	Newsom 1993a; deFrance 1990
	NCS-1	Ostionoid	Solis	Quitmyer and Kozuch 1996
	NCS-4	Ostionoid	Solis	Quitmyer and Brown 2001
	PO-38	Saladoid/Ostionoid	Garrow, Weaver	Newsom 1993a, 1999b
	Tibes	Saladoid/Ostionoid	Curet, Newsom	Newsom and Curet 2000; deFrance 1997
Hispaniola	EBS	Ostionoid/Taino	Deagan	Newsom 1993a, 1998a; Wing data
Jamaica	Bellevue	Ostionoid	Lee	Wing 1977
	Bengal	Ostionoid	Osborne	Wing 1972
	Cinnamon Hill	Ostionoid	Lee	Johnson 1976
	Rio Nuevo	Ostionoid	Vanderwal	Wing 1972
	Rodney House	Ostionoid	Lee	Scudder 1991
	White Marl	Ostionoid	Vanderwal	Wing 1972
Bahamas, Turks, and Caicos				
Crooked Island	CR-8		Keegan	deFrance 1991
	CR-14		Keegan	deFrance 1991
Grand Bahama	Deadman's Reef	Ostionoid	Berman	Berman and Pearsall 2000
Grand Turk	Coralie GT-3	A.D. 710–1170	Keegan	Carlson 1999; Newsom data
Middle Caicos	MC-6	A.D. 1437	Sullivan	Wing and Scudder 1983
	MC-12	A.D. 1040–1282	Sullivan	Wing and Scudder 1983
	MC-32	A.D. 1284	Keegan	Carlson 1994

Samana Cay	SM-2	950–1500	Hoffman	Kozuch data
	SM-7	950–1500	Hoffman	Wing data
San Salvador	SS-2, Palmetto	A.D. 1410–1654	Hoffman	Wing 1969
	SS-3, Minnis	A.D. 1050–1287	Winter	Winter and Wing 1995
	SS-9, Long Bay	A.D. 1460	Hoffman	Kozuch data
	SS-21, Three Dog	A.D. 750	Berman	Berman and Pearsall 2000; Newsom and Wing data
	SS-60, Major's Cave	A.D. 1500	Winter	Winter et al. 1997

texts, Pearsall (2000) for plants and Reitz and Wing (1999) for animals, discuss many aspects of recovery and analysis of biological remains. Archaeological recovery strategies have traditionally used 6-mm (1/4-inch) -gauge screens for sieving midden materials. These screens were adequate for recovery of most pottery, shell, and stone tools, which form the basis of the culture chronology for the West Indies. Therefore this traditional recovery strategy was adequate for the task. After the historical and chronological outline was established, Caribbeanists had other questions about human life in the islands. These questions concern human use of biological resources for what they reveal about subsistence, agriculture, animal management, and environmental change. Answers to these questions are based on study of the plant and animal remains, and they ultimately lead to insights about social dynamics and decision-making processes, human behavioral ecology, and more. A change in recovery strategy was required by this more focused direction in research.

Many of the animals whose remains are at the archaeological sites are small or have small fragmentary skeletal parts. To recover these, the site matrix must be sieved using fine-gauge screen, preferably 1.5 mm (1/16 inch) but at least 3 mm (1/8 inch). For best results the material should be sieved through stacked screens with the coarsest 1/4-inch mesh sorting the largest remains so that they do not break the smaller fragments as they are being sifted. To recover as complete a faunal assemblage as possible, exactly the same volume of midden material should be sieved through all sized screens and saved together as individual subfractions of the original sample. In this way it is possible to recover a sample of all or virtually all fragments of the animal remains from a given site location. Sieving is hard, time-consuming work, particularly when it has to be done carefully, but without this effort data are lost and the conclusions are biased as a result. Because archaeological sites are nonrenewable resources, it is our obligation to recover biological and cultural remains as carefully and thoroughly as possible and to preserve them for study.

Recovery of plant remains requires even more care. Broad interest in the development of agriculture in temperate regions spurred the development of flotation devices to recover fine plant remains (Wagner 1988; Watson 1997). These systems work on the principle that plant material is lighter in weight than other archaeological remains and will float to the surface when a sample is immersed in liquid. Reality is not so simple, however, as is so often the case with many new ideas and innovations. In practice, plant remains are often retained in the post-flotation heavy fractions because of differences in cell wall chemistry, amount of lignified tissues, relative density, and preservation factors. Moreover, when flotation devices are used in the Caribbean they are generally effective for small seed recovery but have a strong tendency to fragment larger plant specimens, particularly charcoal of the dense tropical hardwoods.

This fragmentation is largely due to the sudden moisture stress introduced into the cell structure of the generally friable plant tissues, causing them to break apart and separate along inherent planes of weakness (e.g., between growth increments or at the boundary between contiguous fiber and parenchyma zones in wood specimens).

Two examples serve to clarify this problem and demonstrate a typical pattern when water-recovery procedures are used to isolate plant remains from Caribbean sites. Midden samples for archaeobotanical analysis from the Luján I site on Vieques were collected as whole samples and then either dry-sieved or processed using water flotation (for comparison of the recovery procedures). The flotation samples yielded 0.6 g of wood charcoal per sample (n = 33 samples) and a single identifiable wood specimen. In contrast, the dry-sieved samples produced 12.26 g of charcoal per sample (n = 19 samples) and an average of 5.37 identified specimens per sample (range of 20). Even when these data are corrected for feature fill, the dry-sieve samples still produced 12 g of wood per sample compared with the flotation samples and an average of 6.5 specimens were identified. Similarly, flotation and dry-sieve samples from the Trunk Bay site produced 7.3 versus 32.7 g of wood charcoal per sample, respectively, and 22 compared with 69 total identified wood specimens. In both of these experiments the wood charcoal was considerably broken and reduced in flotation versus dry-sieved samples. The evidence for this is apparent not only in the diminished wood weights associated with the flotation sample groups but also in terms of the comparatively low number of wood specimens large enough for identification. Dense seed coats and like materials appear to suffer similar fates during flotation.

Repeated informal experiments conducted in the Environmental Archaeology Laboratory at the Florida Museum of Natural History demonstrated that wetting and drying carbonized plant remains caused this fragmentation (see, e.g., Newsom 1993a, 1998b). As a result, we urge that archaeobotanical samples from Caribbean sites—whether from buried floors and surfaces, features, middens, and other proveniences—be sieved dry and that water be avoided or used only when necessary for other reasons.

Dry-sieving is conducted by gently brushing the sediments and sample constituents through nested geological sieves with gauge sizes that include at least 4 mm, 2 mm, 1 mm, and 0.42 mm meshes (U.S. Standard Sieve numbers 5, 10, 18, and 40) to recover the plant remains. The individual sample fractions are then sorted directly into constituent plant remains. Sites with a large sand component can be sieved with a screen size that is slightly larger than the 0.42 mm mesh. The unsieved subsample (i.e., the material that passes through the finest sieve) should be retained to analyze for very small seeds such as tobacco (ca. 1 mm length by 0.5 mm width) and other fine materials, including shark dermal denticles. A further benefit of this sieve system is that it is equally suitable for the recovery of plant remains from wet sites. Waterlogged specimens do not float in solution but can be recovered by washing the sample through the series of sieves with a *gentle* stream of water (Greig 1989; Newsom 1987, 1993a). If flotation is to be implemented at a Caribbean site, then each sample first should be spread on a large tray and all larger charcoal (ca. 1/2 to 1 cm surface area), nutshell, and large seeds or seed coats carefully handpicked from the sample before flotation. Ceramic sherds and other visible artifacts can be removed at the same time, after which the sample residual may be floated and then carefully dried. In all cases, the sample volume must be recorded prior to sieving or flotation.

Care in recovery of the plant and animal remains and the size of the biological samples are fundamental to any good research on human use of environmental resources. When samples are too small or out of archaeological context, little can be said about the role of natural resources in the society. Samples must be large enough to encompass at least the dominant species that were used. Every site is different in respect to the density of biological remains, and within a site different activity zones vary in the composition, density, and fragmentation of these remains. Therefore no single rule can guide the archaeologist in decisions about the size of the excavation required for adequate biological samples. Generally an excavation that is 50 cm by 50 cm wide will provide an adequate faunal sample of the most common species in midden deposits. Such an excavation unit would be subdivided into strata or features and within the strata by arbitrary levels. The remains from each level should be identified separately, and during analysis the data from the levels within each stratum can be combined. Similarly, a 5- to 10-liter sediment sample usually provides an adequate botanical sample. Adequacy depends on the nature and amount of dispersion of materials in the provenience and the size of the feature being tested. Larger samples or multiple samples from a given feature, depending on its size, usually provide representative specimens. Samples of different volumes can be standardized in the laboratory for analytical purposes. To provide information about change through time or differences between activity areas, adequate samples must be taken from each stratum or each feature representing discrete activities.

One method of determining adequacy of sample size is based on the species-area or rarefaction curve (May and Stumph 2000; Reitz and Wing 1999). This curve is based on the principle that a given area can support a finite number of species. Similarly, humans tend to use a limited number of species gleaned from an area around the habitation site—the site catchment area—plus those that are traded or imported for special use. A sample of what was used should be large enough to reflect the universe from which it was taken and also contain common species, perhaps representing the staples, and other rarer species representing the special find or elite item. The rarefaction curve can be constructed by plotting the numbers of taxa and minimum numbers of individuals in samples from different sites or subsamples of a single site. As individuals are added the curve rises steeply, and as fewer and fewer new species are encountered an asymptote is reached. A sample could be viewed as adequate if a plot of the number of taxa and the minimum number of individuals falls on the curve beyond the asymptote. This guide for adequacy would not work for sites where people relied on very few species, such as historic sites in the Caribbean where European domestic animals formed the basis of the economy (May and Stumph 2000). Subsistence economies vary in the diversity of the species that were used and incorporated into the archaeological remains. However, within a site or between comparable sites and cultural components the rarefaction curve should serve as a guide to sampling adequacy of both plant and animal remains.

A standard for adequacy is the replication of faunal assemblages from a series of samples with few new taxa being added in additional samples. This does not mean that all the species in the site are recovered and identified. For example, five bird taxa and subsequently an additional one were identified from 37 subsamples of two neighboring sites on Saba. These include the few most common species in the site (Wing 1996). However, when all of the bird remains from all 191 excavated units were studied, a total of 22 taxa were identified (Steadman 1999). Steadman's larger study of the bird remains resulted in identification of the same common species encountered in the earlier study, but an additional 16 species not previously identified were recognized. Among these are rare and extinct species. A specialist such as Steadman also has the skill and knowledge to recognize the specific identity of highly fragmented remains. Thus a much fuller account is possible of the bird fauna on the island and of human association with birds. The additional subsamples examined may represent different activity areas associated with other uses of resources or simply a larger sample. If an additional study of the mammal remains were undertaken (as was done for birds from these two sites on Saba), the count of species would probably not change very much because so very few endemic mammals occurred on that island. Likely additions to that fauna would be marine mammals or introduced species that would be very interesting. The other information gained by a larger study would be a more complete sample of the rice rats, allowing better understanding of the age distribution of the animals that were caught. Study of all of the associated fishes would be a formidable task because they constitute the bulk of the remains from this small island.

Some sites where preservation is poor or the occupation was brief do not yield adequate samples by the measure of the rarefaction curve. Plotting the number of taxa and the minimum numbers of individuals on an island, rarefaction curve allows evaluation of how reliably those small samples represent the deposit and organisms that were used. The curves are useful to compare and access faunal data; they are equally informative and should be used to access samples of plant remains, particularly fuelwood residues (Newsom 1993a).

IDENTIFICATION AND LABORATORY PROCEDURES

Identification of both plants and animals is greatly facilitated by guides to identification and comparison with modern comparative specimens (Greig 1989; Reitz and Wing 1999). In all organisms details of anatomy and morphology must be considered before specific identifications can be made.

The aim of paleobotanists and paleoethnobotanists is to identify as much as possible an *affinity* with a given modern section, family, genus, or perhaps even species, taking into account inherent ecological and functional structural variation that may influence the identification process. Moreover, to specify or connect an ancient specimen with a particular extant species assumes a great deal about the nature of that particular species and may belie the inherent tendencies of plant genetics, plant biology, and the ephemeral nature of species as an entity through time (see, e.g., Hather 1994:2–4; Newsom 2002). Therefore, it is important to use a comparative collection intelligently and recognize that it has limitations, unless it may be demonstrated conclusively that the comparative collection encompasses the entire possible range of ecological and functional variability associated with given plant taxa, and also that it takes into account floristic dynamics induced by climate change and other factors. Particularly with wood identification, it is important to work first with regional anatomical keys and published descriptions of wood types, turning secondarily to collected comparative material and herbarium specimens to double-check results and compare further. This procedure avoids observer bias and eliminates any tendency to "shoehorn" identifications, as well as taking into consideration the problem of possible range extensions or local extinctions in past floras (taxa that may not be included in a modern comparative or herbarium collection and so could be overlooked). The same caveats apply to pollen and other microbotanical analyses.

Whether one is working with plants or animals, a detailed knowledge of the organism's anatomy, growth form, systematics, and ecology is essential. Identification of animal remains is usually based on details of the hard tissue anatomy, either bones or shells. Identification of plants often requires study of the size and shape of specimens (e.g., seeds) along with examination of the morphological and anatomical details of the surfaces (e.g., seed coats). Compound microscopy and electron microscope (SEM or TEM) analysis of surface details and the vascular tissues may be necessary to identify fragments of tubers. Identification of wood—whether waterlogged, fossilized, or carbonized—requires preparation of sections exposed along specific planes of reference to analyze three dimensionally the internal wood anatomy under high magnification.

Knowledge of the organisms of the Caribbean region and Neotropics and access to an appropriate comparative collection are required for research in archaeobotany and zooarchaeology. The comparative collection as a research tool is difficult and time consuming to build; therefore access to good zoological collections, herbaria, and xyleria is essential. Attention must be paid to both the letter and the spirit of the laws governing the collection of plants and animals when building a collection. These control when and if various species can be collected and whether they may be imported to other countries. Threatened and endangered species should never be taken. Proper documentation and permits should be secured before any collecting is done. Working within these regulatory bounds, when specimens are collected every effort must be made to also gather all pertinent information about the specimen. Such information includes where and when the specimen was collected, whether it was in flower or fruit, adult, pregnant, or juvenile. Data on the weight and appropriate measurements should be gathered.

The procedures for the preparation of comparative specimens depend on whether they are plants or animals. Voucher plant specimens are usually pressed, as is typical for herbarium specimens. Seeds and nuts are dried, and some may also be charred so that the shrinkage and deformation resulting from burning can be more easily compared with carbonized archaeological specimens. Comparative wood specimens are prepared by thin sectioning according to the three anatomical planes of analysis. Then the sections are mounted on glass slides to be compared with regional anatomical keys and ultimately also the archaeological wood samples. Specimens of animals need to have the soft tissues removed after all information on the specimens is recorded. Nothing further needs to be done except washing molluscan shells. In preparing vertebrates the first step is to remove the skin, viscera, and muscle masses. Final cleaning of the fleshed carcasses of vertebrates can be achieved in several ways depending on the facilities that are available. Fleshed carcasses can be boiled, followed by the time-consuming task of removing the flesh; however, care must be exercised because prolonged cooking will soften bones. They can be macerated, a process by which the specimen is immersed in water where bacterial action breaks down any remaining soft tissue. This procedure usually causes odors, but they are reduced when specimens are frequently rinsed. A colony of dermestid beetles can be used to clean dried carcasses. All stages of this insect will eat dried tissue. For successful use of this technique, infestations of spiders that feed on the insects must be controlled and beetles must not be permitted to escape, because they also consume books and other organic materials. Specimen preparation should be done in a clean, dry area that is devoted to this function. Access to water is also important.

Comparative specimens should be catalogued so that all pertinent data can be recorded and kept in one place. Each specimen should also have a tag including basic information such as the catalogue number, specific name, locality in which the specimen was collected, the date, and the name of the collector. The catalogue number allows the specimen to be associated with additional information, including the information on the tag. All skeletal elements of animal specimens should be identified by catalogue number. This number should be written with black indelible ink on each bone of a vertebrate except those that are too small. Those smallest elements, as with small seeds, should be put in a glass vial or a curation-quality plastic self-sealing bag and the catalogue number written on an identification tag inserted with the small specimens. By these precautions specimens can be used for identification without danger of losing or mixing elements of different specimens.

QUANTIFICATION AND ANALYSIS

Plants and animals are used in different but overlapping ways that in part account for the differences in their remains. Both are basic to subsistence. However, most animals that are eaten leave behind inedible bones or shells, whereas plants are usually entirely consumed. Exceptions to this are inedible shells of nuts, large stony pits of fruits, maize cobs, and wads of chewed fibers. Most remains of edible plants in archaeological sites are accidentally burned seeds, nuts, or fragments thereof that otherwise could have been eaten, leaving no trace.

These differences in the past uses and preservation of plants and animals make integrating data derived from studies of their remains difficult. Reconstruction of former economies requires different approaches to quantification of the remains. The most basic recording of identification data is similar, and basic quantification common to both plant and animal studies is the count and weight of identified remains. However, interpretation of these remains may be different. For example, a comparison between the numbers of purslane (*Portulaca* sp.) seeds and herring (Clupeidae) bones in the same sample probably does not reflect their relative importance to the former subsistence. A site with bone, shell, and carbonized wood may indicate the animal contribution to the diet and burned fuel or construction wood. Contribution of plants to the diet may rely at least in part on indirect evidence from artifacts, that is, tools and other items such as griddle sherds (the broken remains of ceramic griddles traditionally used to cook manioc) that are associated with plant food processing and cooking techniques.

Measurements are also made and tabulated for both plant and animal remains. Measurements of whole seeds, bones, or individual cell types in wood aid in specific identification of those specimens. Measurements of seeds, skeletal parts, or shell parts can be used as a proxy for the size of the whole animal or fruit. Growth-ring widths are important measurements in wood specimens, bivalves, and some skeletal structures as indicators of past growth and environmental conditions. The sizes of animals and seeds of plants can be altered by cultural selection such as domestication, by technology and choice used for catching or gathering, and by natural selection. The interpretation of size profiles is discussed further under the heading of analysis.

Methods of evaluating the relative importance of particular organisms at a site are different when applied to plants and animals. Ubiquity and density data (quantity taxon/unit volume) of each plant species identified in samples throughout the archaeological site is a means of estimating importance or rarity of a taxon (Popper 1988). Ubiquity, usually applied to plant remains, is the frequency of a taxon among the total set of *proveniences* examined and is expressed as a percentage. For example, if a particular taxon occurs in 5 of a total of 10 proveniences, its ubiquity score would be 50%, reflecting its presence among half of the contexts analyzed. (Note that total number of *samples* may differ from the number of *proveniences sampled;* thus ubiquity is based on occurrence among proveniences only [except in cases where the ratio of samples to proveniences excavated is the same, equal], to provide an estimate of how common is a particular taxon at the site in general; proveniences may undergo multiple sampling, therefore using sample total may inflate the figures and skew interpretations of relative importance.) In cases where samples and specimens are relatively few, individual taxa may be simply reported by presence (X). Density is the weight or count of plant fragments, usually wood charcoal, in a given volume of soil; seed count per volume of sample is often used. The total number identified (NI) is typically reported for wood specimens. An estimate of minimum number of individuals (MNI) is a means of estimating the relative importance of different animal taxa. The value of MNI is that it takes into account the great differences that exist between the numbers of identifiable elements found among animals. For example, fishes have several hundred bones, whereas clams have two valves, and a snail has a single shell and, sometimes, a calcareous operculum. MNI is a way to give individuals equal weight in terms of relative abundance. MNI is normalized and presented in terms of relative abundance. When MNI is calculated, the unidentified bone and shell is not included. Similarly, when applied to plant remains, MNI is tabulated from seed scars (i.e., the seed hylum, which is one per seed), excluding other seed coat fragments that lack the diagnostic scars. The amount of unidentified bone, shell, and seed coats varies from site to site and probably has more to do with fragmentation that results from destructive processes such as trampling, particularly in high-use areas of a site where more foot traffic would have occurred.

Plant and animal remains are sometimes quantified as a ratio between different sample constituents, such as seeds to nuts, or the relationship between two animal species or groups of species (Johannessen 1988; Miller 1988). Such quantification may reveal changes through time in important economic elements.

ANALYTICAL METHODS USED TO EXAMINE RESEARCH OBJECTIVES

Our main objective is to provide data for a better understanding of human adaptation to the West Indian Island setting. A major aspect of human settlement in the Caribbean islands is the use of the islands' biological resources. People rarely use biological resources in their natural abundance. Instead, people select or target species because they are choice food items, are easily caught with the techniques available, or provide some particular benefit such as wood that burns long and hot or fruits that are sweet and provide energy. In addition to targeted species, side-catch is used but perhaps not preferred (Meehan 1982). To compare samples of different sizes, the data are normalized and presented as percentages. Those species that are most abundant are presumed to be the targets of exploitation.

Human adaptation in this environment includes evaluating issues of island biogeography in terms of the differences and limitations of the resources in each of the regions. Changes in the plants and animals used reveal the ways in which people exploited and changed the island landscape. Focused gathering, hunting, and fishing can result in overexploitation of the plant and animal populations limited by the island landmass and surrounding marine environments. Overexploitation and introductions affect the island biogeography and ultimately the island landscape.

The analytical methods described below are intended to reveal some of these aspects of human adaptation to the West Indian ecosystems. Other methods are used in zooarchaeological and archaeobotanical research, but we confine our discussion to methods used in this volume. We also present data as fully as possible so that they can be used for other research.

Subsistence and Resource Exploitation

Samples from the West Indies tend to be diverse, well over 100 taxa of animals alone. To better understand the relative importance of different habitats or functions of resources, species lists may be grouped according to the classes of organisms, the habitats in which species are typically found, or the ways in which resources were presumably used. By such groupings, contrasts can be made between woods and seeds, terrestrial and marine animals, or wild and managed species. These groupings can be expressed in percentages, permitting comparisons of activity areas within sites, between deposits associated with different periods, and among sites from different islands.

Information on the management of animals and cultivation of plants usually relies on the presence of animals and plants that were not endemic to an island, for example, guinea pigs, maize, and manioc in the Caribbean, all of which derive from mainland source areas. The absence of species from paleontological or early archaeological sites followed by their relatively sudden appearance in later deposits gives evidence for introductions and hence control and management.

Ancillary Information

Ancillary information can be used to suggest specific activities. Common tools excavated from archaeological sites are adzes made from either stone or shell. These were probably used to cut and shape wood. Based on the sizes of some of the post molds and the arc or curvature of growth rings observed in wood specimens from the posts (e.g., as large as 20–80 cm in diameter at the Golden Rock site), some very large trees were felled and used in the construction of houses, some of which were quite substantial (floor area up to 214 m^2 [Newsom 1992; Schinkel 1992:table 23]). Canoe building also required woodworking tools. Fishhooks are very rare in West Indian sites but were probably used to catch larger carnivorous species such as tuna, grouper, and jacks. Explanations for the rarity of fishhooks and lures in West Indian sites are that they may have been made of some material such as wood or thorns that does not preserve well.

Supplementary insight into the past economy and subsistence practices can come from documents based on eyewitness accounts of Native American ways of life from the first European explorers. Often these accounts do not address critical issues in sufficient detail to permit a full understanding of all facets of the economy, and they may sometimes misrepresent the true nature of activities. Some of the early accounts do, however, describe the structure of the houses, the size of the canoes, and some other details of the life of Native Americans as first seen by Europeans (Fernández de Oviedo 1959). Clearly some watercraft must have been used to explore and colonize the island archipelago. The descriptions add details about size and form but not necessarily on the wood that they were built of or the tools used to build them. A paddle has been found in waterlogged conditions on Grand Turk, and the shape corresponds to paddles used presently in South America (Keegan 1997b:57). The wood appears to be a native type (*Zanthoxylum* sp., wild lime) in the citrus family.

Dietary Compositions and Health

Our understanding of the dietary composition of people living in the past rests on the plants and animals identified and assumed to be food resources and their relative abundance. Because all organisms do not contribute the same amounts of food, an estimate must be made of the average live weight or potential amount of meat each species could have contributed. Such estimates are based on several assumptions. The basic assumption is that the people who deposited the remains consumed the estimated weight of meat contributed by each species. The other assumption is that what is recovered even with the most careful recovery strategy is not necessarily the remains of everything that was eaten. Some animals are very large, for example, manatee (*Trichechus manatus*). These were probably butchered at the shore and only meat was carried back to the home site, so little evidence of this activity turns up in the midden deposit. The meat of large animals was also probably distributed throughout the community. Filleted or split fishes may have been preserved for trade after removing the heads and viscera, leaving only skull bones at the site, and at the other end of the trade network there is little or no evidence for fish consumption. The greatest disparity between midden remains and past dietary items lies in the contribution of plants and animals. Ethnographic studies indicate that the diets of most people are composed of far more plant foods than animal protein. Estimating yields of ancient crop species is fraught with difficulties, though it may provide important baselines to consider.

Documenting size change is important in analysis of both plants and animals. Burning and charring introduces size changes in the specimens. A burned bone or seed may be 10% smaller than it was before it was burned. Even greater shrinkage is seen in other burned plant parts (e.g., maize cobs [King 1994]). Such changes must be kept in mind when a measurement is used to estimate the size of the whole animal or the plant specimen. Estimates of body size of animals are based on allometric correlation between measurements of skeletal elements and body weight or standard length. The allometric formulas are based on modern comparative specimens of species encountered in the archaeological sites of a region. The constants used here are presented in Table 4.2. The coefficient of variation (100 x standard deviation/mean) is frequently used with seed assemblages (Cowan 1997; Decker and Newsom 1988; Newsom 1993a) to evaluate morphological variability within the assemblage, hence the possible presence of separate cultivars or landraces maintained through selective planting and breeding.

Size profiles may change as a result of the methods of fishing or gathering

Table 4.2. Allometric constants used to estimate body weight or standard lengths

Measurement	N	Slope b	Y intercept a	r^2	Reference
(1) X = width of teleost atlas; Y = total weight	43	2.53	0.872	0.87	Wing 2001a
(2) X = aperture height of marine snails; Y = total weight	59	1.93	-1.64	0.96	Reitz and Wing 1999
(3) X = merus height of terrestrial crabs; Y = total weight	25	1.842	0.508	0.90	deFrance 1990

Note: These use the formula $\log Y = \log a + b (\log X)$, where X is the measurement of a skeletal, shell, or exoskeletal element taken in mm and Y is the estimate of body weight in g.

plants or shellfish. A large hook, if successful, will catch a proportionally large fish, and coarse-gauge netting will allow small fishes to escape through the mesh. Human selection may play a part in determining the size profile of the shellfish at a site if the humans gather only the largest snails on the rocks. Of course, recovery methods that do not use fine-gauge sieves bias the size profile of the sample. Size change may also come about through selection. Some of the most stringent selection results from domestication. Progression toward domestication is management of a captive or cultivated segment of a population that interbreeds and may diverge in size from ancestral populations in the wild.

Further insight into broad dietary constituents may be gained through analysis of stable isotopes of carbon and nitrogen in bones of humans. Stokes (1998), and before her Keegan and DeNiro (1988), van Klinken (1991), and Ambrose and Norr (1993), experimented with the isotopes of carbon and nitrogen incorporated in bone collagen and carbonate by the plants and animals that are known or expected to have contributed to the Native American diet in the West Indies. By setting parameters for the isotopic signature for different food combinations, it was possible to get insight into the prehistoric diet. Stokes (1998) took samples of human bone from many of the same sites where both plant and animal remains were identified, making it possible to indicate what species were contributing to isotopic values reflecting the whole diet and the animal protein portion of the diet.

Another line of evidence of general diet and health is obtained from biological anthropology. Studies of human remains can indicate malnutrition and disease resulting from some dietary inadequacy or imbalance. Human remains may also indicate other features of the past way of life such as warfare, accidents, physical stress, and infant mortality (Larsen 1997; Larsen et al. 1996; Sandford 2002). Population dynamics such as population growth can be seen indirectly in the number and sizes of the archaeological sites on an island, rather than in the physical remains (Wilson 1997b). Evidence for stress in human populations can also be detected in the biological remains as overexploitation of resources.

Evidence for Overexploitation

Overexploitation can manifest itself in many ways and cause population changes. Chief among these in terms of faunal resources is size change. In plants, the growth increments may demonstrate predictable trends under the stress of human extraction pressure. Ultimately a change in forest structure and composition may occur as individual species are continuously harvested while in the vigorous growth stages or are altogether locally eliminated. Measurements must be relied on to document size change and must be applied to material from successive strata. Overexploitation by artisanal or subsistence fishermen and gatherers can result in a decline in the body size of territorial organisms. Such size and age reduction, called growth overfishing, occurs when fishing intensity is great enough that the larger and older individuals are selectively removed from the local population, leaving only the smaller individuals. With increased fishing intensity the size and age of the individuals of a species are reduced, resulting in a population with primarily immature individuals that are too young to reproduce and maintain the population.

Species that have large population reservoirs in the oceans (fish) or ocean-dispersed propagules (e.g., mangrove trees and land crabs) may not be affected by focused exploitation. An exception is relentless capture of animals that use particular breeding grounds, such as sea turtles or monk seals. Heavy hunting pressure on those individuals programmed to return to the beach where they were born can exterminate a local segment of the population.

Size differences could also be interpreted as exploitation of different age classes. For example, the juveniles of many species of fish grow and mature in nursery grounds and then as adults move into other habitats. Fisheries biologists studying modern fish populations have information about what age and size and during which season juveniles are restricted to nursery grounds. Allometric correlations between skeletal measurements and standard length can identify individuals that are juvenile or adult (Table 4.2). Fishing technology may focus on the juvenile fishes in the nursery grounds or the technology may resort to catching juvenile individuals when the adult fishes become scarce.

Population changes may accompany size declines through time. Top predators in an ecosystem such as a coral reef, or the dominant trees in a mature forest, are most vulnerable to extraction by people. Predatory fishes are usually aggressive and eager to take a baited hook or enter a baited trap. These fishing techniques selectively target species that are high in the food web. As a consequence their abundance declines relative to that of herbivorous fishes (Russ 1991; Wing and Wing 2001). Similarly, large mature trees have some of the best, straight-grained wood for lumber and dugout canoes, and some of the dense tropical hardwoods make the best house posts because of their well-developed heartwood and resistance to decay and insect attack. Many of these trees are very slow growing and thus not easily replaced under sustained extraction by humans. Two examples of such loss and the consequences are the local elimination of preferred large yo ni (*Cedrela odorata*) trees after decades of their use for canoe manufacture by the Maijuna of the Peruvian Amazon (Gilmore et al. 2002), forcing the use of alternative species, and the complete elimination of trees adequate for canoes in some of the Pacific Islands, effectively stranding their occupants (Diamond 1995, 1997; Redmond 1999). A forest ecosystem may be inadvertently maintained in a secondary state of succession by such actions, or even in a fully deflected state from which the original forest may never recover.

Extreme overexploitation of both plants and animals results in extinction of vulnerable species. The most vulnerable species are those that evolved on an island in the absence of people and other predators. Some species isolated on islands lose the ability to escape new predators by hiding or flying (Quammen 1996). David Steadman (1995) has documented the extirpation and extinction of many endemic island bird species shortly after colonization by people and their domestic animals in the Pacific.

As was mentioned, woods used for construction or fuel have qualities that make some tree species more suitable than others. For most purposes, fuelwood should burn long and hot. A decline in the quality of fuelwoods may indicate overexploitation. Likewise, use of second-growth wood species for fuel and construction suggests that mature trees were no longer available (Newsom 1993b).

Island Biogeography and Human Behavioral Ecology

An island's size and distance from the mainland or a large island has an effect on the species diversity of the island (MacArthur and Wilson 1967; May and Stumpf 2000; Quammen 1996). Species-area relations may be modeled and expressed by a power function: $S = cA^z$, where S is the number of species of a given taxon on an island, A is the area, and c and z are fitted constants related on the one hand to the inherent biotic richness of the particular biogeographic region, and to the difficulty of reaching a given island on the other (Shafer 1990:26–27; Whittaker 1998:115). These anticipated differences between islands can be tested by measures of species diversity or by richness (Ludwig and Reynolds 1988; Ricklefs and Schluter 1993). Richness is a count of the number of different identified taxa in a sample of a given size. A very common test for diversity known as the Shannon-Weaver function, also referred to as the Shannon-Wiener function, is described in Reitz and Wing (1999).

Both the Shannon-Weaver diversity index (H′), which incorporates even-ness (Pileu's index [J′], basically the distribution of abundance among species in a community), and richness provide an indication and measure of diversity. Both are sensitive to sample size. It must also be remembered that animals that were used in the past and recovered at an archaeological site are not the same, per se, as the current fauna of the island. Many plants and animals were not used by previous cultures or were not preserved and recovered by archaeologists. However, a large island would be expected to have a more diverse fauna; if animals were caught opportunistically, we would expect greater diversity on large islands and on those close to the mainland.

People have contributed to extinction of species and have introduced new species onto islands worldwide (Burney 1997). Both possibilities also must be viewed from the perspective of the island biota before and after Native American colonization in the Caribbean. The presence of species in paleontological or early archaeological deposits and their absence in later and modern faunas and vegetation are potential evidence of extinction. Similarly, the absence of a species in paleontological or paleobotanical collections and its sudden presence at a later archaeological site suggests an introduction by people. This introduction may have been intentional, such as the agouti (*Dasyprocta leporina*), or possibly such an uninvited fellow traveler as the tree frog in the Lesser Antilles.

Landscape and Environmental Change

One of the basic contributions of biological remains from archaeological sites is the information and details they convey to describe the natural environment and landscape dynamics. Plant and animal data sets may provide information on different natural communities or aspects of the same communities, and they may be mutually complementary. For example, identification of two genera of oysters from the Lujan I site on Vieques (described in Chapter 7) indicates that mangrove forests grew near the site, even though mangrove plant remains were not identified among site deposits. Together, the archaeobotanical and zooarchaeological data from Lujan I provide a more complete picture of the environment at the time of human occupation of the site. The changes brought about by exploitation and extraction practices affect the plant and animal populations on islands. Further landscape changes are the result of intensive horticulture, irrigation, and terracing of the slopes for agriculture. The extent of these landscape changes distinguishes between the post-Saladoid in the Lesser Antilles and the Ostionoid of the Greater Antilles. Extensive land-scape modification occurred on the larger islands (Oliver et al. 1999). Some forest clearing can provide large ecotonal zones that may promote popula-tion growth of weed species and some rodents. The increase in weed species, second-growth wood, and rodents may be the signature for land clearing and agricultural activities spurred by human population growth. Along with the plant and animal macroremains, pollen, diatoms, phytoliths, foraminifera, and other microremains are useful indicators of landscape modification and change (Burney 1997).

5
Southern Caribbean Region

INTRODUCTION

The southern region encompasses the islands that lie off the coast of Venezuela. These include the Netherlands Antilles of Aruba, Bonaire, and Curaçao ("ABC" islands), Margarita Island to the east, and the small islands in between. We have not analyzed nor do we have references to comparable studies of faunal or botanical remains excavated from Margarita Island. Therefore, this chapter is concerned with studies of biological resource use as seen at sites on the "ABC" islands and the smaller offshore islands from Los Aves to La Blanquilla (Figure 5.1). The information on animal use on the offshore islands is based on the research of Andrzej Antczak (1999a, 1999b). Faunal studies of samples from the "ABC" islands are based on analyses made by several people, whereas all the botanical research was done by Lee Newsom.

We allude to work on Trinidad, but we do not emphasize that island because it is essentially a continental island that has separated from the mainland in relatively recent times. Trinidad is large and has a diverse vegetation and land fauna. Detailed zooarchaeological research that considers both vertebrates and invertebrates has not been carried out on Trinidad, nor have archaeobotanical investigations been undertaken. Consequently, the work done on Trinidad is not comparable to that done on the other islands. Faunal studies from sites on Trinidad are, however, interesting from the standpoint of documenting the changes that took place after the island separated from the mainland, while remaining in proximity to the continent.

Nutrient-rich waters with abundant and diverse marine resources surround the "ABC" and related offshore islands, but land resources are minimal to absent. Annual rainfall is very low and the terrestrial environments are very arid with sparse vegetation, as we describe below. Conversely, and compared with

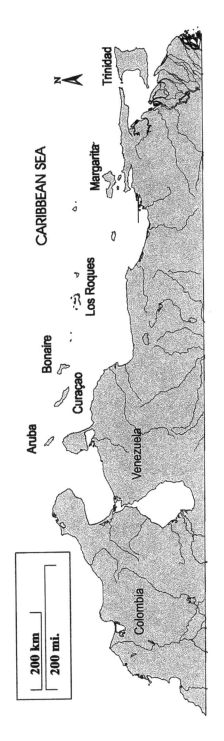

Figure 5.1. Southern Caribbean region. (By Florence E. Sergile)

the other West Indian islands, however, these are relatively close to the rich resources of the mainland. The focus of this chapter is the resources that attracted people to these islands despite the dangers inherent in the voyage from the mainland. That fact alone potentially can raise or enhance the functional carrying capacity of these southern Caribbean Islands. Fairly extensive and long-term settlements have been located archaeologically on the three "ABC" islands, even though freshwater and terrestrial vegetation are limited. To what extent was contact with mainland culture maintained and were mainland resources used to satisfy physical and social needs of islanders? We might expect that people living on the smaller offshore islands depended more heavily on continental resources than did people living on the larger "ABC" islands. It has been suggested that these islands and settlements may have functioned together in a settlement/resource interaction sphere that included the mainland (Haviser 1987). Information from this southern Caribbean region provides insight into the strength of inter-island ties and those between island and mainland people, as well as control of resources by the occupants of these islands.

ENVIRONMENTAL CHARACTERISTICS

The islands from Aruba to Margarita lie parallel to the Venezuelan coast and are all relatively small and dry. The islands from Curaçao to La Blanquilla are oceanic and separated from the mainland by the Bonaire Trench, which is more than 1,000 m deep. Aruba and Margarita Islands, at the ends of the offshore chain, are on the continental shelf. Cold, nutrient-rich water wells up from the deep trench around these islands and nourishes abundant marine life. The islands themselves have low precipitation (e.g., 270–844 mm annually on Curaçao; as low as 150–200 mm on Aruba [Stoffers 1956]) and high evaporation accelerated by the trade winds. Thus, these semidesert islands support a xeric, thorn scrub and very dry forest vegetation. Many of the islands are fringed by mangrove forest. Although this climate does not promote dense vegetation, it does produce conditions for evaporation of seawater; the result is extensive salt deposits.

The fauna is derived from northern South America either by natural dispersal or naturalized species brought to the islands by people (Eisenberg 1989; Husson 1960). As would be expected, the number of mammals on these islands corresponds roughly with the size of the island. The mammal fauna is most diverse (31 species) on Margarita, the largest (1,150 km^2) island (Eisenberg 1989). The next largest island, Curaçao (443 km^2), has 14 mammal species, excluding those introduced by Europeans. The smaller of these Venezuelan islands have no native mammals but do support lizards, including iguana (*Iguana iguana*), and land crabs (Gecarcinidae).

In contrast to the land, the surrounding sea supports a rich biota. Oceanic birds, the West Indian monk seal (*Monachus tropicalis*), and sea turtles (Cheloniidae) use the beaches as rookeries. The shallow-water lagoons are home to conchs (*Strombus* spp.) and other molluscs and are nursery grounds for some fishes. A diverse fish fauna inhabits the coral reefs skirting the islands and shallow inshore waters.

CULTURE HISTORY AND MATERIAL CULTURE

The cultural history of these islands extends back to migrations that predate ceramic-producing groups that arrived later. As elsewhere in the Caribbean, Archaic deposits are scarce. They do occur on Aruba, Curaçao, and La Blanquilla, dating between 2000 and 1600 B.C. The deposit on Aruba is a shell midden evidently associated with a large cemetery known as Malmok (Versteeg et al. 1990). Between 60 and 70 skeletons were excavated from the Malmok cemetery. Similar burials are present at a site that dates to about 3800 B.P. at St. Michielsberg in Curaçao (Haviser 1985, 1989; Versteeg et al. 1990:36–37). In both cases molluscan shells are associated with the burials. The carapaces of sea turtles (*Chelonia mydas*) are either above or below about 10% of the burials at Malmok and are also present among the St. Michielsberg burials (Haviser 1985; Versteeg et al. 1990). The Malmok burials suggest some degree of social stratification with some apparently high-status males (Versteeg et al. 1990). An Archaic site dating to about 3300 B.P. was found on Bonaire (Haviser 1991a). A signature or characteristic tool type at the Archaic sites, aside from the later deposit on Bonaire, is a type of gouge made from conch shell (*Strombus* sp.) (Haviser 1989, 1991a, 1991b; Versteeg et al. 1990). The remains of sea turtles and conchs (Figures 5.2, 5.3) are also present in the Archaic deposit on the island of La Blanquilla (Antczak and Antczak 1992).

Ceramic-age deposits in the southern Caribbean Islands are larger and more abundant and reflect more complex social structure and activities. The pottery styles found at sites on the "ABC" islands are derived from the Falcón region, geographically close on the Venezuelan mainland (Oliver 1997b). These styles are known as Dabajouroid and were produced from about A.D. 800 to time of contact. The Las Aves archipelago, made up of small islands immediately east of Bonaire, was occupied around A.D. 1200 by people who also produced Dabajouroid pottery styles (Antczak and Antczak 1992). Caribbeanists believe these colonists maintained contact with each other and with the mainland. The islands of Los Roques and La Orchila east of Las Aves were occupied between A.D. 1100 and 1300. Their pottery styles are associated with the Valencioid tradition, corresponding to the more eastern mainland of Venezuela. One of the sites in the Los Roques archipelago had a brief Ocumaroid

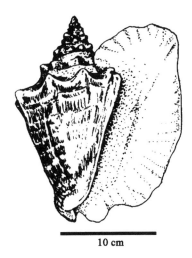

10 cm

Figure 5.2. Queen conch, *Strombus gigas* Linnaeus, 1758, is particularly common at sites in the southern Caribbean region and on the Bahamas Turks and Caicos. (From Fischer 1978, vol. 6 STROM Strom 2)

occupation. Sites on the easternmost island, La Blanquilla, have both Valencioid and Saladoid styles of pottery suggesting influences from central and eastern Venezuela. Native populations were decimated shortly after European contact (Versteeg 1991). These offshore islands had a complex history of settlement, resource extraction, ritual activity, and interaction between island and mainland people of different cultural affiliations.

ISLAND RESOURCES

Almost without question, human groups were originally attracted to the southern Caribbean Islands because of their wealth of marine resources, prominent among which are sea turtles, conchs, fishes, and possibly salt (Antczak and Antczak 1992). The data on plant and animal resources used by people on these islands are uneven for a number of reasons. Chief among these are the differences between archaeological sites and methods of faunal analysis. The botanical remains from the major Ceramic-age sites—including Tanki Flip (Aruba), Wanápa (Bonaire), and Santa Barbara (Curaçao)—were all studied by Newsom (1991, 1997, laboratory data) with comparable results, though the overall number of samples analyzed from these sites individually and together is comparatively few. For this reason the plant identifications for Aruba and Curaçao are indicated simply by presence (X); the Wanápa site on Bonaire was sampled somewhat more extensively, and therefore site ubiquity values are in-

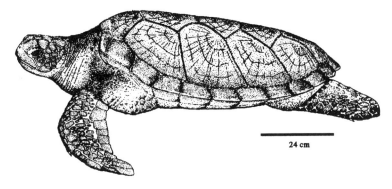

24 cm

Figure 5.3. Green sea turtle, *Chelonia mydas* (Linnaeus, 1758), is represented at many sites throughout the Caribbean. (From Fischer 1978, vol 6 CHEL Chel 1)

cluded in the sections and tables that follow. Despite the limitations, the archaeobotanical and zooarchaeological data that have been generated from sites in this island group nevertheless are the first to describe the nature of the prehistoric biota, and they provide preliminary insights into human adaptations and the overall patterns of resource use in this small subregion of the Caribbean. Interesting patterns of resource use emerge (Tables 5.1, A-1, A-2).

Evidence for Use of Forest Products

Some of the southern Caribbean Islands may have been more extensively forested during the period of prehistoric human occupation than they are today, though it is difficult to say for certain based on the present information. Unfortunately, no seeds or other remains of edible plants have been identified thus far from archaeological sites in these southern Caribbean Islands, though some fragmentary specimens have been recovered. However, well-preserved carbonized wood specimens have been recovered from various deposits at three sites, and from these it has been possible to identify a number of woods that were used by prehistoric people living in the area. We can at least infer indirectly some of the plant foods potentially available to the inhabitants of these islands, based on the presence of species recognized among the wood remains that are known also to produce edible fruit.

The wood types most frequently associated with the archaeobotanical samples from Aruba, Bonaire, and Curaçao are lignum-vitae (*Guaiacum* sp.) (Figure 5.4), buttonwood (*Conocarpus erectus*), caper tree (*Capparis* sp.), and strong bark (*Bourreria* sp.), probably *B. succulenta* or "watakeli" (Table 5.1). These trees are all very drought tolerant or able to withstand high soil salinity, and they are major constituents of the xerophytic forest habitats as well as mangrove forest

Table 5.1. Plant resources used by Ceramic-age people living in the Netherlands Antilles

Taxa			Islands/Sites		
Family # Samples/Wood NI	Scientific Name	Common Name	Aruba* Tanki Flip 07/83	Bonaire Wanápa 45/312	Curaçao* Santa Barbara 10/67
Bignoniaceae	*Tabebuia* sp. and/ or *Cresentia* sp.	cedar, kibra-hacha or cala-bash, kalebas		51	X
Capparidaceae	*Capparis* sp.	caper tree, oliba	X	42	
Combretaceae	*Conocarpus erectus*	buttonwood, grijze mangel	X	39	X
Boraginaceae	*Bourreria (succulenta)*	strong bark, watakeli		24	X
Euphorbiaceae	cf. *Hippomane mancinella*	cf. manchineel, manzaliña	X		
Fabaceae	*Caesalpinia (coriaria)*	divi-divi, waaiboom	X		
Fabaceae		legume family, tree legume			X
Flacourtiaceae	*Casearea (tremula)*	geelhout, palu di Bonaire		15	
Flacourtiaceae	cf. *Xylosma (arnoldii)*	roseta		15	
Sapotaceae	cf. *Bumelia (obovata)*	boxwood, palu di lechi		6	
Zygophyliaceae	*Guaiacum* sp.	lignum-vitae, pokhout	X	84	X

Note: *Abundance is measured by ubiquity across the site for larger sets of samples, as described in the text, or simply by presence (X) for a few samples and specimens identified.

and fringing salt flats, in the case of buttonwood (Broeders 1967; de Boer 1996). In addition to these, a Bignoniaceous wood is conspicuously present (51% ubiquity) among the proveniences analyzed from Wanápa, Bonaire, and the same is among the samples from Santa Barbara. This particular wood is provisionally assigned to either calabash tree (*Cresentia* sp.) or cedar (*Tabebuia* sp.), or perhaps both, depending on inherent anatomical variation among individual wood specimens. Like the other taxa mentioned, both of these trees are native to the local xerophytic woodlands.

Buttonwood was identified among approximately 40% of the proveniences analyzed from Wanápa, Bonaire, and it is the most abundant taxon from Santa

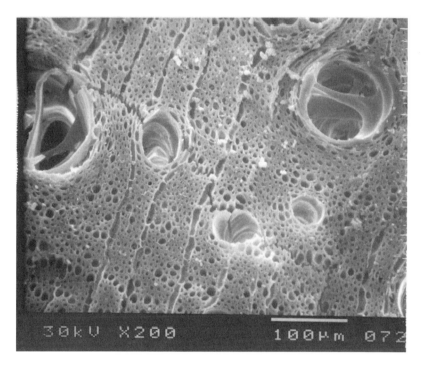

Figure 5.4. Lignum-vitae (*Guaiacum* sp.) wood, cross-section anatomical perspective. Santa Barbara site, Curaçao (provenience C-036, 77-103 cmbs) (1350x magnification).

Barbara, Curaçao, at approximately 70% ubiquity and comprising 67% of the specimens identified (Newsom 1991; laboratory data). Lignum-vitae proved to be very conspicuously present among the Wanápa proveniences (84% ubiquity) and was identified in half of the proveniences analyzed from Santa Barbara (Newsom 1991; laboratory data). Caper tree was identified among 42% of the proveniences from Wanápa. The common presence among the sites and the high relative ubiquities of these xerophytic forest tree taxa may be an indication that these forests were once more widespread or better developed than at present because these woods are very slow growing. For example, *Guaiacum* trees growing in Mexico (from Sonora to Oaxaca) produce wood at the very slow rate of approximately 10 cm per decade (Record and Hess 1943:556). Thus in the similarly very arid conditions of the "ABC" islands these trees would grow slowly and be very slow to replace themselves in the local forests. This has clear implications for the level at which woods in these islands can be sustainably harvested.

Other woods identified from the archaeological contexts at the Wanápa site include a type assigned to the sapote family (Sapotaceae, cf. *Bumelia obovata*, "palu di leche") and two woods in the Flacourtiaceae: *Casearia* sp., cf. *C. tremula* or "geelhout," and a wood closely matching the genus *Xylosma* or "roseta" (Table 5.1). A wood identified to the genus (*Caesalpinia* sp.) was identified among the samples from Tanki Flip, Aruba. It very likely represents the interesting local species known as divi-divi (*C. coriaria*), which often exhibits a very contorted, wind-blown form ("windboom") on these islands (Broeders 1967:95–97). All of these trees are associated with tropical very dry forests or thorn woodlands (see Tables 2.2 and 2.3). One additional wood taxon from Tanki Flip belongs to the spurge family, Euphorbiaceae, and is closely matched with *Hippomane mancinella*, the manchioneel. This coastal tree species has highly toxic exudates in the bark, leaves, and fruit; however, the timber is not toxic and may be used for construction and other purposes (Record and Hess 1943:159–160).

The Tanki Flip site on Aruba has evidence of wood used in food preparation or other activities that would involve burning wood, based on the associations of wood with particular hearth features. A wood closely matched to the genus *Capparis* sp. (oliba, raba) was recovered from three hearth features, in one case, along with the divi-divi-type wood; another wood type provisionally assigned to the spurge family (Euphorbiaceae) was identified from an additional hearth or possible kiln (Newsom 1997). By their associations with separate posthole features, buttonwood and lignum-vitae seem to have been used to build structures that burned, or the material represents charcoal displaced from hearths or firepits. Based on their having been burned and in some cases also the association with hearthlike proveniences, it is apparent that most or all of the woods identified from these archaeological sites in the southern Caribbean Islands were collected for use as fuels at one time or another. They are all well suited to this purpose, being hard, dense woods; several are common fuel-wood crops (Little 1983).

Concerning other potential economic uses of the islands' vegetation and based on the identifications mentioned above, we note several possibilities to illustrate the considerable economic potential of the local flora, though it is merely conjecture with regard to the prehistoric inhabitants of the islands. The calabash tree produces large, hard container fruits that are potentially useful for a range of purposes, for example, as bowls, water jugs, scoops, containers, and fishnet floats; the pulp and seeds are edible and have value as medicinal treatments for colds and respiratory ailments (Ayensu 1981:53; de Boer 1996:33). The bright orange berries of strong bark or watakeli attract birds and are also edible by humans (de Boer 1996:37; Morton 1990:28); the leaves, twigs, and bark of this small tree have also been used medicinally (Ayensu 1981:58). *Caesalpinia* sp., the likely divi-divi, is a tree legume. The pods have high tannin content (30–50% tannin and tannic acid), making them very astringent; they have been used to make a gargle for sore throat and for other health care purposes (Ayensu 1981:66). According to de Boer (1996:95), the pods were harvested and shipped to Europe to produce tannin, used in leather tanning in the nineteenth century. Broeders (1967:164) indicates that divi-divi fruit are edible. The leaves of some species of *Bumelia* are boiled with those of other dry forest trees for a postpartum tea (Ayensu 1981:168). Lignum-vitae is a true multipurpose tree. The resin, wood, bark, flowers, and leaves have been employed in a wide range of medicinal treatments: for cuts and bruises, sore throat, rheumatism, fever, arthritis, and other body pains; as a laxative, an arbortifacent, and more (Ayensu 1981:196). According to Record and Hess (1943:558), the resin, sometimes used in modern pharmaceuticals, is known as *guaiac* or *guaiaci* resin. It is collected by cutting the bark, after which it seeps out in droplets or "tears" from the live tree; it can also be extracted by heating sticks of the wood, causing the resin to ooze out, or boiling chips and sawdust in water. Finally, the caustic latex from manchineel is reported to have been used as a poison to tip darts and arrows (Ayensu 1981:89), and so may have been useful for hunting birds or other fauna. These or similar plant products and uses were probably very important to everyday life and existence on these small islands. Undoubtedly they were not the enticement to settle the islands, as we indicated above, even though the islands, particularly the larger ones, may once have had more plant resources.

Use of Marine Resources

Marine resources, on the other hand, may have been the chief attraction of the islands to human colonists. The only endemic land animal abundantly represented in the archaeological deposits is iguana (*Iguana iguana*). Otherwise the

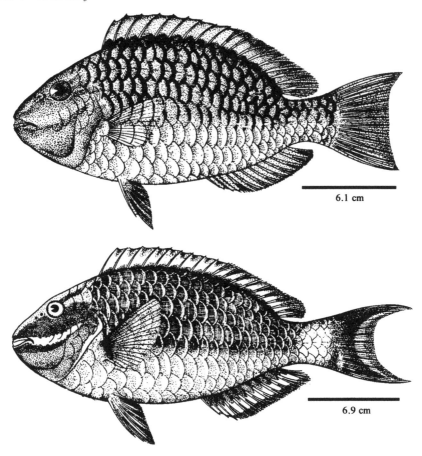

6.1 cm

6.9 cm

Figure 5.5. Stoplight parrotfish, *Sparisoma viride* (Bonnaterre, 1788), is the most frequently identified parrotfish at sites in the West Indies. The top fish has the brown and red color pattern of the female, and the bottom fish has the green and yellow orange markings of the male. (From Fischer 1978, vol. 4 SCAR Spari 4)

faunal data show quite consistent focus on certain marine animal resources throughout these islands (Table 5.2). The most important among these are sea turtles (Cheloniidae), groupers (Serranidae), jacks (Carangidae), snappers (Lutjanidae), grunts (Haemulidae), parrotfishes (Scaridae), and queen conch (*Strombus gigas*) (Figures 5.2, 5.3, 5.5, 5.6, and 5.7; Table A-1). These same animals still sustain the modern fishery (Antczak 1991).

The estimated sizes of the fishes have some implications for the methods that might have been used to procure them. Estimates of the sizes of animals whose remains consist only of the surviving hard tissues, bone or shell, may be

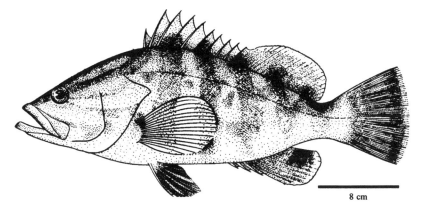

Figure 5.6. Nassau grouper, *Epinephelus striatus* (Bloch, 1792), and other serranid species are frequently identified from West Indian sites. (From Fischer 1978, vol. 4 SERRAN Epin 22)

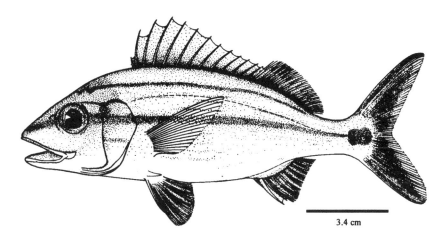

Figure 5.7. Tomtate grunt, *Haemulon aurolineatum* Cuvier, 1829, along with other species of the genus are frequently identified from West Indian sites. (From Fischer 1978, vol. 4 POMAD Haem 2)

made by comparison with specimens for which both the skeletal or shell size and the total live weights are known (Reitz and Wing 1999; Table 4.2, this volume). Because growth is allometric, the best way to estimate size is by application of an allometric formula based on an array of specimens with known weights and dimensions. A dimension that correlates well with body weight in fishes is the width of the vertebral centrum. Measurements of unidentified fish

Table 5.2. Summary of vertebrate and crab remains

| Habitats | Islands/Sites | | | |
| | Curaçao; Santa Barbara | | Bonaire; Wanápa | |
	MNI	%	MNI	%
Vertebrates				
Terrestrial	21	11.5	16	38
Freshwater and shore	24	13.2	0	0
Shallow inshore waters	37	20.3	10	23.8
Coral reefs	98	53.9	13	30.9
Pelagic	2	1.1	3	7.1
Sample size	182	77.8	42	82.4
Crabs				
Terrestrial	49	94.2	8	88.9
Shallow inshore waters	3	5.8	1	11.1
Sample size	52	22.2	9	17.7
Total	234		51	

Note: Remains arranged according to the habitats in which they are usually found and divided between vertebrates and crabs. This table is based on the detailed faunal list in Table A.1. Quantification is by minimum number of individuals (MNI) and expressed as a percentage.

vertebrae are expected to give the average fish size as well as the range of sizes in fishes from a particular deposit. These measurements taken for unidentified fishes from the Santa Barbara site on Curaçao and the Wanápa site on Bonaire give different results, though they are consistent within each site (Table 5.3). Measurements from Santa Barbara are on average larger and the range in sizes is greater than those from Wanápa. Estimates of the weight of fishes in the Santa Barbara deposit range from 141 to 13,849 g with a mean weight between 753 and 951 g. The estimated weights of the fishes from Wanápa range from 43 to 7,648 g with a mean between 265 and 374 g.

Size differences in animal remains can come about in several ways. The lower end of the size range of fishes, for example, can be lost through a recovery strategy that does not incorporate fine-gauge screen (at least 2 mm). A coarse-screen sieving strategy normally will not affect the upper end of the size range unless some selection occurs in the specimens that were saved. Other factors that affect sizes of fishes represented in a deposit are the methods used to catch the animals. For example, the size range of fishes caught with hook and line relates to the size of the hook and the strength of the line; this applies only to those species that will take a baited hook. Similarly, the size

Table 5.3. Size and range of unidentified fishes from Santa Barbara, Curaçao, and Wanápa, Bonaire, based on the width of vertebral centra (mm)

Provenience	Number	Mean (mm)	Standard Deviation	Range (mm)	Mean Estimated Weight (gm)
Santa Barbara, Curaçao					
118/117 lv. 7–8	79	6.8	3.7	3.2–19.6	951
118/117 lv. 9–10	36	6.2	2.3	3.5–15.8	753
Wanápa, Bonaire					
88/124 lv. 2	50	4.1	1.7	2–10.9	265
88/124 lv. 3	59	4.7	1.8	2.1–12	374
88/124 lv. 4	78	4.1	1.8	2.5–15.5	265

Note: Estimates of total body weight (gm) are made using the allometric formula $\log Y = 2.53 (\log X) + 0.872$, where Y is body weight and X is the vertebral width.

range of fishes caught in traps is limited by the size of the trap entrance and the sizes of the openings in the fabric of the trap. Large size ranges suggest that several different fishing techniques were used.

The differences in the types of fishes in the assemblages from Santa Barbara and Wanápa may account for some of the differences in the size ranges of fishes seen at the two sites. Grouper, with an average estimated weight of 4,712 g, are relatively abundant in the deposits from Santa Barbara and absent at Wanápa. Despite the relatively small sample from Wanápa, several species are present, such as herrings (Clupeidae), squirrelfishes (Holocentridae), and surgeonfishes (Acanthuridae), fishes that tend to be small. These are absent from the much larger sample from Santa Barbara. These differences may affect the size range seen at the two sites but probably do not account for all of the difference.

How accurately midden deposits reflect the use of large animals is always open to debate. Large marine animals such as marine mammals and sea turtles may be shared among members of the community, and the skeletal remains of a single individual may be deposited in a number of different middens. Alternatively, they, as well as queen conchs, may be butchered on the shore and the largest shells or bulk of the skeleton never brought to the site. These animals may be underrepresented in any single midden sample. This may be true for the shells of queen conch at the Tanki Flip site, where the majority of whole shells were juvenile individuals based on the low average shell weight (45 g) of complete individuals in the archaeological deposit (Reinink 1997:149). Nevertheless, some large specimens were used for the manufacture of shell tools, made with the large lip found only in more mature individuals (Serrand 1997: 195). The thick lips and columella of large individuals were also used for the manufacture of tools on some sites on Bonaire (Haviser 1991a:162–163). The abundance of shell fragments at sites on Aruba and Bonaire suggests that conch shell tools were made on the site, but this does not preclude that shells were also deposited at the resource extraction site. Conch shells were found at both an extraction site close to the shore and around the hearth of an occupation site on a smaller offshore island (Antczak 1999a, 1999b).

The extinct monk seal (*Monachus tropicalis*) is probably underrepresented at sites because it was a large animal that may have been butchered on the shore, its meat then distributed. Two foot bones (cuboid and distal epiphysis of a metatarsus) of a monk seal were found at the Santa Barbara site (77/103 level 7–8). These represent examples of specimens documenting the southern end of the former range of this extinct animal and are therefore of both zoogeographic and zooarchaeological significance.

Introduced Animals and Animal Parts

A distinctive characteristic of the faunal remains of these offshore islands is the presence of exotic animals, those that do not naturally occur on the islands. Many of these exotic animals are represented by worked bone artifacts, but others are unmodified (Antczak 1995). Bone artifacts from sites on Dos Mosquises and Cayo Sal in the Los Roques archipelago include bone flutes made of the radius of two species of deer (*Mazama* sp. and *Odocoileus virginianus*) and pendants made of perforated teeth of crab-eating fox (*Cerdocyon thous*), peccary (*Tayassu tajacu*), and tapir (*Tapirus terrestris*). Young ocelots (*Felis pardalis*) and margay (*F. weidii*) are represented in the sites on Dos Mosquises by the front parts of the skulls: maxilla and mandible. These elements may represent the skeletal parts kept with skins of the brightly marked cats. Worked bone or tooth artifacts may have been brought to the islands as tools and ornaments rather than as live animals. However, some of the exotic species may represent animals brought to the islands alive rather than as prepared treasures.

Exotic animals found at sites of other islands are also represented by a combination of worked and unmodified bone. Two exotic species were found at the Wanápa site on Bonaire. One is an ocelot represented by an ulna that was polished to a point at the distal end; the other is a juvenile capuchin monkey (*Cebus* sp.) represented by 10 unmodified bones. The artifact made of ocelot bone was probably brought to Bonaire as a fully formed tool. The capuchin monkey was doubtless a pet that died in captivity.

Two animals that are closely associated with people are agouti (*Dasyprocta* sp.) and guinea pigs (*Cavia porcellus*). Agouti remains are reported from the Santa Cruz site on Aruba (Hooijer 1960) and Sint Jan II on Curaçao (Hooijer 1963), and guinea pig from the Santa Barbara site. Wherever humans and agoutis occur together, people, now as in the past, use and sometimes tame them. They adapted to captivity and introduction into the Lesser Antillean islands as well as into Aruba and Curaçao. Guinea pigs are fully domesticated, though wild populations still occur along a broad arc over South America (Eisenberg 1989). The guinea pig remains from the Santa Barbara site are probably all from the same young individual. The humerus and femur are unfused, and the height of the mandibular symphasis is 10 mm, which is small but within the range of the domestic species. Guinea pigs were domesticated in the Andes of Peru and are endowed with important cultural roles in divination, healing, and sacrifice (Morales 1995). Whether these attributes were associated with the guinea pigs found at Santa Barbara is not possible to determine, but their presence, as elsewhere in the West Indies, indicates wide distribution of this domestic animal.

CONCLUSIONS

The southern Caribbean Islands fall into two groups according to their size as well as their diversity and abundance of natural resources. The "ABC" islands in the west are large and supported permanent settlements from the Archaic period to the present time. The offshore Venezuelan islands to the east are all small, but the lagoons surrounded by the islands of the archipelagoes have rich and abundant marine resources. Settlements on these islands were semipermanent or temporary camps.

The Ceramic-age cultures in these two island groups also differ. The people living on the "ABC" islands had Dabajouroid culture and established themselves on the islands around A.D. 800. Los Aves also was occupied by people with Dabajouroid culture but was established later—around A.D. 1200—than the neighboring islands to the west. The Dabajouroid culture was derived from the adjacent mainland Falcón region. Human residents of the other offshore islands had primarily Valencioid culture derived from central Venezuela. They ventured to these islands about A.D. 1100.

A dynamic tension may have existed among people living on these islands (Antczak and Antczak 1991). People extracting resources from the offshore islands and their immediate marine environments may have discouraged any encroachment by people with Dabajouroid cultures from the west. At the same time, people living on all the islands maintained ties with the mainland (Oliver 1997b).

The driving force for the occupation of these islands was the presence of marine resources, especially the conchs, sea turtles, fishes, and salt deposits. Being much larger than the other islands and able to support forest resources—fuelwood, wood products and construction materials, edible tree fruits, and terrestrial animal populations—the "ABC" islands were also capable of sustaining permanent human communities with some degree of social stratification. The small offshore islands were settled later in time and only on a semi-permanent basis. Although comparison of the abundance of exotic animal remains is difficult because there is no control for the size of the excavated volume, it appears that relatively more exotic material was present on Los Roques than at the sites on the "ABC" islands. Some of these exotic materials may be related to ritual: to ensure safe passage to these islands and luck in the pursuit of marine resources (Antczak 1995). The exotic fauna at sites on the "ABC" islands include the guinea pig, capuchin monkey, agouti, and paca, which could potentially be maintained alive on islands with more natural resources.

The plant remains recovered from the "ABC" islands sites represent primarily fuelwood. Some samples may have included construction materials. Definitive food remains were not recovered among the various botanical samples analyzed, but at least some of the soils have the potential to have supported root crops as long as adequate moisture was maintained (Haviser 1987, 1991a, 1991b; Norman et al. 1995:271–278).

6
Lesser Antilles

The Lesser Antilles is an arc of more than 20 small islands forming stepping stones between northeastern South America and the Greater Antilles and Virgin Islands (Figure 6.1). The islands of the Lesser Antilles are relatively close together. Most are close enough for the cloud cover over neighboring islands to be visible. The distances between islands, approximately 50 km, made exploration of the island chain relatively easy. The first step from Tobago on the South American continental shelf to Grenada, the southernmost of the Antillean island chain, is the longest distance, 105 km. Barbados is the most isolated island in the archipelago, lying 161 km east of the main axis of the island chain. Favorable ocean currents also facilitated exploration of the Antilles with paddled canoes. The South Equatorial Current that flows across the Atlantic is deflected northward from the Guyanas and meets the water flowing from the mouth of the Orinoco River. When the river is in full flood stage during the summer, it diverts part of the Equatorial Current northward to the Windward Islands. The relatively short distances between the individual islands, along with the favorable ocean current, promoted colonization of the Antilles by people from northeastern South America. After colonization began it seems to have proceeded rapidly (Rouse 1992).

Islands provided different conditions for life and resources than did the mainland. Characteristics of human adaptation (Kirch 1980) to these differences are one of the issues explored in this chapter. We discuss the extent to which people brought resources with them to duplicate or at least partially simulate mainland life, and the new resources that were used. How was traditional knowledge gained in a mainland setting applied to island life? As Terrell (1997) has pointed out, a small colonizing group may simply or will almost certainly be unable to reproduce in full the culture from which it derived;

Figure 6.1. Lesser Antilles. (By Florence E. Sergile)

therefore founder effects, transformations of traditional knowledge and practices among migrating societies are almost ensured from the beginning. We
seek to clarify something of the nature and development of these cultural
changes in the Caribbean Islands from a socioeconomic perspective. What
changes in the economies of the island people were made as a result of their
move to a new environment or overexploitation of the more limited island

plant and animal populations? Or is it incorrect or inappropriate to assume that occupants of the islands followed negative economic ecology trends (i.e., an overall trajectory of overexploitation under the assumption of endless supply [Costanza et al. 1997])? Data from the plant and animal remains excavated from a series of Lesser Antillean islands are presented and discussed in the light of these issues.

ENVIRONMENTAL CHARACTERISTICS

The islands can be grouped in two different ways: they may be divided into the Windward Islands south of Dominica and the Leeward Islands north of Guadeloupe, or as the inner arc of volcanic islands and the discontinuous outer arc of limestone islands. The division of Windward and Leeward has a historical origin referring to the course set by Columbus during his second voyage and followed by many subsequent voyages. Sailors took advantage of the northeastern trade winds to sail from the Canary Islands across the Atlantic and through the Dominica Passage between the islands of Guadeloupe and Dominica and then northward along the leeward coast of the more northern Lesser Antilles (Sauer 1966:192). These two groups of islands took their names from the course set by early navigators. Many of the individual islands observed or visited during Columbus's second voyage were also named. The division between volcanic and limestone islands relates to their geology and environmental history, which determines their physiography, elevations, and climate. The volcanic islands include Grenada, the Grenadines, St. Vincent, St. Lucia, Martinique, Dominica, the western portion of Guadeloupe, Montserrat, Redonda, Nevis, St. Kitts, St. Eustatius, and Saba. Many of the volcanoes that formed the islands are still active or have been in the recent past (an eruption on Montserrat occurred as recently as the past two years). The limestone islands include Barbados, Marie Galante, the eastern portion of Guadeloupe, La Désirade, Antigua (which also has a volcanic district), Barbuda, St. Barthelemy, St. Martin, Anguilla, and Sombrero.

The islands of the Lesser Antilles are relatively small but are surrounded by the Caribbean Sea on the west and the Atlantic Ocean on the east. The islands range in size from only about 13 km^2 for Saba to 1,700 km^2 for Guadeloupe, with an average size of about 400 km^2. Island size is related to the diversity of species that can be supported (MacArthur and Wilson 1967). The surrounding sea also provides essential food resources in the island setting. The size of the island shelf may be added to the dry land above high tide as habitat for biotic organisms and a resource base for human colonists. This island shelf varies according to the geological makeup of the island. The limestone islands tend to have wider shelves than the volcanic ones.

Another important condition for life on an island is rainfall and the plant life it promotes. When moist air carried by the trade winds is intercepted by land, precipitation is initiated. Many of the volcanic islands with high mountains receive more rain, between 1,500 and 2,500 mm per year, than islands with low relief (Watts 1987). This amount of rainfall can sustain seasonal, and in some cases, moist to wet tropical forest associations. Dry cactus and thorn scrub vegetation grows on parts of islands in the rain shadow or on islands with very low relief or excessively well-drained soils. Mangrove forests fringe many of these islands. In addition to promoting growth of vegetation, rainfall supplies water held in catchment basins, ponds, and marshes. Rainfall and reliable sources of fresh water are critical for plant and animal life and to establish conditions suitable for colonization by humans, especially those reliant on plant cultivation.

CULTURE HISTORY

The earliest deposits associated with human activity in the Lesser Antilles are those related to Archaic people and date around 5000 B.C. (Keegan 1994:266). Archaic groups manufactured stone and shell tools, but they did not produce pottery. Their settlements in this part of the Caribbean generally appear to have been impermanent or ephemeral. Archaic-age sites are relatively small and, compared with later sites, somewhat rare. Most of the sites in the Lesser Antilles are located in the Leeward Islands, fueling speculation that these first colonists came from the Greater Antilles instead of from South America by way of Trinidad (Allaire 1997a). However, evidence from sites occupied between 5000 B.C. and 2000 B.C. in the southern Lesser Antilles supports the hypothesis of a primary route of migration from Trinidad and northern South America (Davis 1988a, 1993; Keegan 1994:266). Much of the information about the source and culture of these people comes from the tools they left behind. Interestingly, the traits associated with tool manufacture at the Jolly Beach site in Antigua appear to represent a blend of two Preceramic traditions (Rouse 1992:67ff.). The tool assemblage has characteristics of the Archaic cultures of the Greater Antilles (originally derived from Middle America and termed "Casimiroid") and those of the Archaic cultures of Trinidad and others of the southerly islands (collectively called "Ortoiroid" [Rouse 1992:67; cf. Keegan 1994]; Chapter 3, this volume). Caribbean Archaic groups were primarily generalist fisher-foragers, with an emphasis on marine foods. The presence of ground stone tools at their sites is almost certainly related to plant food preparation (e.g., grinding small grains such as the panicoid grasses), but this inference has not been tested.

The subsequent major phase of migration of Ceramic-age people began around 400–500 B.C. and clearly arose in the Orinoco basin of northeastern South America (Allaire 1997a; Keegan 2000; Rouse 1992). The cultural tradition of the earliest of these migrants is known as Saladoid. Regional developments and associated demographic increases and population movements on the mainland may have been the primary impetus for migration, which resulted in the relatively rapid migration of ceramic-bearing people throughout the Lesser Antilles (Allaire 1997a; Keegan 2000). These people established permanent settlements, produced fine pottery, planted crops, and managed animals. Their staple is presumed to have been manioc and similar root crops, largely based on the widespread presence of cooking and processing equipment at Saladoid sites, as described in Chapter 3. These tools could be used to process starchy root pulps into bread roasted on thick and durable ceramic griddles, just as had occurred for centuries in the mainland, greater Amazonia/ Orinoco source region (Oliver 2001). Manioc is relatively tolerant of soil and moisture conditions, but for high yields it requires open space with no shade and as much sunlight as possible (Rehm and Espig 1991:43). The shifting cultivation that must have been practiced by these first horticulturists to create agricultural plots for manioc and any other crops would have resulted in the first major anthropogenic disturbance and disruption of the natural forests and vegetation of the islands. Although the Saladoid and other/related early Ceramic age (e.g., Huecoid [Chapter 3]) groups appear to have been essentially egalitarian, there is evidence for more elaborate social structure and differentiation, including a complex belief system with ceremonial activity (Curet 1996; Keegan 2000).

Major cultural changes occurred between A.D. 500 and 1000 throughout the Caribbean, and in the Lesser Antilles relevant groups are sometimes termed "post-Saladoid." Substantial population growth is indicated by the increase in the number of sites and their sizes (Keegan 2000; Wilson 1989, 2001). This was a time when the cultures within the Lesser Antilles diversified and diverged from those in the Virgin Islands and the Greater Antilles. Trade and interaction was conducted with other island and mainland people. Some population loss and site abandonment occurred after about A.D. 1200 (Wilson 2001). The events unleashed by Columbus's voyage of discovery in 1492 changed the Native American cultures and the flora and fauna of the islands forever.

PATTERNS OF BIOTIC RESOURCE USE IN THE LESSER ANTILLES

Evidence for the prehistoric uses of plants and animals in this part of the Caribbean comes from sites located on a number of islands (Table 4.1). Just as archaeological deposits are not all the same, so too the remnants of plants and animals differ from site to site. Differences in the plant and animal assemblages may be the result of access to different arrays of resources, choices or technology in the exploitation of resources, conditions for preservation of organic remains, excavation of different activity areas and temporal units, and archaeological recovery strategies. The chronological position of the sample, the associated material culture, and the ecological setting of the site are important considerations in any evaluation of the plant and animal data (Table 4.1). Although we are primarily concerned with resource use during the Ceramic age, use of biotic resources by people during the preceding Archaic age provides information about the initial stage of adaptation to the island ecosystem. Therefore, we precede the presentation of data from Ceramic-age sites with a summary of the information from Archaic-age sites. Presentation of the data from Ceramic-age sites is by island, and the information is in chronological order when more than one site from an island was studied.

Archaic Age

Only a few Archaic-age sites have plant and animal remains that have been studied. They include a component of the Heywoods site in Barbados (Wing 2000), Twenty Hill and Jolly Beach in Antigua, and Hichmans' Shell Heap (GE-6) on Nevis (Table 4.1). Only samples of vertebrate remains were studied from the Heywoods and Jolly Beach sites concerning the faunal aspect of subsistence, and only botanical information is available for the Twenty Hill site. Hichmans' Shell Heap includes invertebrate remains as well as vertebrates (Kozuch and Wing 2004; Wing 2001b). Plant remains from both Hichmans' Shell Heap and Jolly Beach were also analyzed.

The faunal remains from the Archaic-age samples resemble later assemblages in many but not all respects. Fishes, particularly those living in reef areas, make up the majority of the vertebrates. The most abundantly represented family of fishes is the parrotfishes (Scaridae) (Table 6.1). Remains of the endemic rice rats are also abundant. Absent from all three deposits are managed or domestic animals such as the agouti (*Dasyprocta leporina*) and the domestic dog (*Canis familiaris*).

The molluscs from Hichmans' Shell Heap make up the bulk of the faunal remains from that site, with a minimum of 615 individuals and a focus on two species. These are the West Indian topsnail (*Cittarium pica*) with 51% (Figure 6.2), and turkey wings (*Arca zebra*) with 37% of the molluscan MNI. The other mollusc species as well as these two abundant ones are all found in rocky, inshore waters. Crab remains are not common in these faunal samples.

Plant remains excavated from Archaic deposits in the Lesser Antilles thus far derive from very few samples (Table 6.2) and are generally few in number

Table 6.1. Vertebrate remains identified from Archaic-age sites

| Taxa | | Islands/Sites | | | | | |
| Scientific Name | Common Name | Barbados Heywoods | | Nevis Hichmans' Shell Heap | | Antigua Jolly Beach | |
		MNI	%	MNI	%	MNI	%
Terrestrial							
Brachyphyla sp.	bat	0		0		1	0.8
Oryzomyini	rice rat	3	11.5	7	4.7	13	10.3
Columbidae	pigeon	2	7.7	0		0	
Passerine	perching bird	1	3.8	0		0	
Iguanidae	iguana	0		0		3	2.4
Indeterminate lizard	lizard	0		0		2	1.6
Alsophis antillensis	racer	0		0		4	3.2
Subtotal		6	23.1	7	4.7	23	18.3
Freshwater or Shore							
Sula sula	red-footed booby	0		2	1.4	0	
Rallidae	rail	1	3.8	0		0	
Subtotal		1	3.8	2	1.4	0	
Shallow Inshore Waters							
Monachus tropicalis	monk seal	0		2	1.4	0	
Cetacean	whale or porpoise	0		0		1	0.8
Chelonia mydas	green sea turtle	1	3.8	0		0	
Cheloniidae	sea turtle	1	3.8	5	3.4	4	3.2

Continued on the next page

Table 6.1. *Continued*

Taxa		Islands/Sites					
		Barbados Heywoods		Nevis Hichmans' Shell Heap		Antigua Jolly Beach	
Scientific Name	Common Name	MNI	%	MNI	%	MNI	%
Indeterminate shark	shark	0		0		1	0.8
Indeterminate ray	ray	0		0		3	2.4
Elops saurus	ladyfish	1	3.8	0		0	
Malacanthus plumieri	sand tilefish	0		2	1.4	0	
Caranx sp.	jack	0		3	2.0	6	4.8
Carangidae	jacks	1	3.8	1	0.7	4	3.2
Sparidae	porgies	0		4	2.7	5	4.0
Sphyraena sp.	barracuda	1	3.8	12	8.1	1	0.8
Subtotal		5	19.2	29	19.6	25	19.8
Coral Reefs							
Muraenidae	moray eels	0		2	1.4	0	
Holocentrus sp.	squirrelfish	0		1	0.7	1	0.8
Epinephelus sp.	grouper	1	3.8	3	2.0	8	6.3
Mycteroperca sp.	grouper	2	7.7	2	1.4	1	0.8
Serranidae	groupers	0		11	7.4	2	1.6
Lutjanidae	snappers	0		3	2.0	4	3.2
Haemulon sp.	grunt	1	3.8	7	4.7	3	2.4
Halichoeres sp.	wrasse	0		2	1.4	3	2.4
Labridae	wrasses	1	3.8	3	2.0	0	

		MNI	%	MNI	%	MNI	%
Scarus sp.	parrotfish	2	7.7	5	3.4	5	4.0
Sparisoma viride	stoplight parrotfish	2	7.7	0		0	
Sparisoma sp.	parrotfish	0		30	20.3	36	28.6
Scaridae	parrotfishes	0		0		0	
Acanthurus sp.	surgeonfish	1	3.8	16	10.8	0	
Balistidae	triggerfishes	1	3.8	4	2.7	7	5.6
Diodon sp.	porcupinefish	1	3.8	1	0.7	2	1.6
Subtotal		12	46.2	90	60.8	72	57.1
Pelagic							
Physeter catodon *	sperm whale	1	3.8	0		0	
Belonidae	needlefishes	1	3.8	18	12.2	2	1.6
Scombridae	tuna	0		1	0.7	0	
Indeterminate fish	fish	0		1	0.7	4	3.2
Subtotal		2	7.7	20	13.5	6	4.8
Total		26		148		126	

* from spoil bank and not necessarily the marsh clay

Note: Abundance is based on minimum number of individuals (MNI) and expressed as a percentage. Families are arranged according to the habitats in which the taxa are usually found.

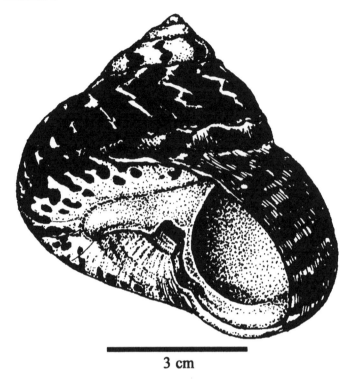

3 cm

Figure 6.2. West Indian topsnail, *Cittarium pica* (Linnaeus, 1758), is common at sites in the Lesser Antilles, Virgin Islands, and Bahamas. (From Fischer 1978, vol. 6 TROCH Citt 1)

of specimens, analogous to the case of two of the sites from the "ABC" islands (Chapter 4). Thus with the exception of Twenty Hill, identifications from these sites are provided on the basis of simple presence (X). The archaeobotanical identifications include at least five taxa represented by seeds, as well as an additional unidentified seed type, and one of these plant families is also represented by wood (Table 6.2). Fruit trees in the sapodilla family (Sapotaceae) are represented by seeds and wood fragments from Twenty Hill on Antigua, and by seed remains from Hichmans' Shell Heap, Nevis. The seed specimens consist of individual carbonized fragments of seed coat that conform very closely to those that characterize two genera in the family, *Manilkara* sp. and *Sideroxylon* sp. (bulletwood and mastic bully, respectively). Therefore individual specimens could derive from either or both genera, both of which produce edible fruit. Similarly, the Sapotaceae wood belongs to a particular anatomical group in the family that encompasses several genera, including mastic bully as well as star apple (*Chrysophyllum* sp.) and others (Record and Hess

Table 6.2. Plant remains identified from Archaic-age sites in the Lesser Antilles

	Taxa			Islands/Sites	
Form/Family	Scientific Name	Common Name	Antigua Twenty Hill 13/2	Antigua Jolly Beach 3/0	Nevis Hich. Shell 9/0
# Samples/Wood NI					
Tree Seed/Nuts					
Rutaceae	*Zanthoxylum* sp.	wild lime	15		
Sapotaceae	*Manilkara/Sideroxylon* sp.	sapote, mastic bully	46		X
Ulmaceae	*Celtis* sp.	cockspur	77		
Herbs/Grains					
Acanthaceae	cf. *Siphonoglossa* sp.	cossie balsam			X
Papaveraceae	*Argemone mexicana*	Mexican poppy		X	
Seed, Other					
seed unidentified					X
Nonwood, Other					
parenchyma tissue					X
Wood					
Sapotaceae	*Chrysophyllum/Sideroxylon* wood anatomical group	star apple, mastic bully, etc.	8		
Twenty Hill type 1			8		

Note: Abundance is based on site ubiquity, expressed as a percentage of all proveniences analyzed; some plant identifications are reported by simple presence (X). Plant taxa are arranged by specimen category (seeds, tree/herb, parenchyma tissue, wood).

1943–1948); any of these could be the ultimate source of the archaeological wood (and could possibly represent additional sources of edible fruit). *Celtis* sp., cockspur, and *Zanthoxylum* sp., wild lime, are also native dry forest trees; they are relatively common in the woodlands where the sites are located. Cockspur has edible fruit and the presence of the fruits or seeds of wild lime might represent use of its various parts for medicinal purposes (Ayensu 1981:167). We note that the occurrence of either of these two taxa among the deposits at Twenty Hill could be incidental (i.e., naturally deposited). However, we think this is not the case because the seeds derive from culturally produced midden deposits, the quantities of cockspur seeds increase with depth, and the wild lime seeds are primarily concentrated in one excavation level at the site (Newsom 1993a). These spatial distributions are possible indications that the taxa were gathered for consumption by the site's inhabitants, rather than having randomly become incorporated into the deposits by natural fruit fall from nearby trees. Moreover, as will be seen below and in succeeding chapters, these two seed types occur with regularity among archaeological deposits in the region and so by default, if anything, seem to have paleoethnobotanical significance.

Other seeds from Archaic-age sites derive from herbaceous or slightly woody plants. Seeds that are provisionally assigned to the genus *Siphonoglossa* sp. (Acanthaceae; Table 6.2), cossie balsam, were recovered from Hichmans' Shell Heap on Nevis. This plant is documented among the floras of the northern Lesser Antilles, though it does not seem to have been recorded as part of the modern vegetation of Nevis (Howard 1989:372–373), a very interesting fact. The archaeological presence on that island, assuming the identification is correct, could indicate a broader natural range in prehistory. Alternatively, it may indicate that this plant was utilized by the prehistoric people of Nevis, resulting in its occurrence on the island. Cossie balsam is potentially another species that had medicinal value (at least it has been used as tea to treat colds [Acevedo-Rodríguez 1996:50]). One additional seed type has been identified from among this particular set of sites and samples: Mexican poppy (*Argemone mexicana*), from Jolly Beach on Antigua (Table 6.2). This is yet another plant with potential medicinal significance (Ayensu 1981:140), but a cautionary note is again warranted. The poppy is a cosmopolitan weed of disturbed environments throughout the Neotropics, including Antigua (Howard 1988:274–275), so there is a strong possibility of natural deposition. Unlike cockspur and wild lime, this particular taxon has not demonstrated a strong association with archaeological sites in the region, nor is there anything unusual about its occurrence as regards cossie balsam. The single poppy seed was recovered from a midden at the site, but otherwise it has no clear association with the prehistoric occupation and so may be incidental to any prehistoric cultural activities at Jolly Beach.

Small bits of carbonized unidentified parenchymatous tissue such as make up the starchy interiors of soft plant organs like roots and tubers were also recovered in the samples from the Hichmans' Shell Heap on Nevis. It is possible that these specimens are the remnants of edible tubers, though in their fragmentary, pulverized state they lack diagnostic anatomical structure or any outward morphological characteristics for definitive taxonomic placement.

Ceramic Age

Grenada

The major site on Grenada is Pearls, located on the northeastern coast of the island within view of the sea. This large, ca. 60.7-hectare site was excavated first by the Bullens (1964) and subsequently by Keegan and Cody (1990) in 1988 and 1989. The claim by the earlier excavator that "not many food bones were uncovered at the Pearls site" was clearly a function of inadequate recovery (Bullen 1964:22). The much-disturbed surface of the site is strewn with bone and shell to date, and the excavations by Keegan and Cody recovered large samples of vertebrate and invertebrate remains as well as plant seeds and small bits of unidentified wood. Mammals (Lippold 1991), vertebrates (Fradkin ms), and vertebrates and invertebrates (Fandrich 1990) excavated by Cody were studied by others.

We reanalyzed a small sample (GREN P3) that we use to exemplify the fauna from the Pearls site (Table B-1). As at other sites in the West Indies, fishes dominate the vertebrate fauna (Table 6.3a). Both reef fishes and offshore fishes like tuna (Scombridae) and horse-eye jack (*Caranx latus*) are important (Figures 6.3 and 6.4). The component that is missing is the invertebrates. However, Fandrich found that the virgin nerite (*Neritina virginea*) was overwhelmingly abundant, making up from 58 to 60% of the invertebrates in the samples she studied (GREN A1). Associated species typical of the rocky intertidal zone such as chitins, other nerites, and West Indian topsnails are also present in GREN A1.

A characteristic of faunal assemblages that sets Grenada apart from the other Lesser Antilles is the number of mammals from the mainland. These include the agouti (Figure 6.5), which is found in most other Ceramic-age sites in the Lesser Antilles. Opossum (*Didelphis* sp.) is also present in the deposits at Pearls, as well as at the site of Grand Anse in St. Lucia (Wing and Reitz 1982). Domestic dog remains are also reported from Pearls (Lippold 1991).

The seeds that came from the 1989 excavations at Pearls all represent edible tree fruits (Table 6.4). Conspicuously present among the samples from this site are palm nut fragments, perhaps from the spiny palm (*Acrocomia aculeata*), and well-preserved seeds and seed coat fragments of mastic bully (*Sideroxylon* [formerly known as *Masticodendron*] sp.) (Figure 6.6). These taxa demon-

Table 6.3. Summary of the exploitation of key habitats based on the relative abundance of vertebrates usually associated with these habitats

Islands/Sites

Archaic-Age Deposits	Barbados	Nevis	Antigua
	Heywoods	Hichmans'	Jolly Beach
Terrestrial	23.1	4.7	18.3
Freshwater or shore	3.8	1.4	0
Shallow inshore	19.2	19.6	19.8
Coral reefs	46.2	60.8	57.1
Pelagic	7.7	13.5	4.8
Sample size (MNI)	26	148	126

Saladoid Sites	Grenada	Barbados			Montserrat	Nevis	St. Martin	
	Pearls	Hillcrest	Chancery	Welches	Trants	Hichmans	Hope Estate Early	Late
Terrestrial	22	3.8	0	9.5	45.4	50	42.9	52.8
Freshwater or shore	4.9	0	0	0	1	1.6	4.3	1.1
Shallow inshore	24.4	30.8	20	28.6	13.4	6.3	15.7	18
Coral reefs	31.7	46.2	66.7	47.6	39.2	32.8	32.9	23.6
Pelagic	17.1	19.2	13.3	14.3	1	9.4	4.3	4.5
Sample size (MNI)	41	26	15	21	97	64	70	89

| Post-Saladoid | Barbados | | | | Nevis | | St. Eustatius |
Sites	Hillcrest	Silver Sands	Chancery	Heywoods	Sulphur Ghaut	Indian Castle	Golden Rock
Terrestrial	20	8.8	9	6	9.3	16.8	19.2
Freshwater or shore	5	1.8	1.5	0	0	0	0.4
Shallow inshore	15	9.5	7.5	16	17.4	8	8.6
Coral reefs	40	72	68.7	18	63.4	67.2	30.9
Pelagic	20	7.9	13.4	60	9.9	8	41
Sample size (MNI)	20	454	67	50	172	125	525

Note: Detailed information about the faunal samples is presented in Appendix B. The sites are grouped according to the time period of occupation.

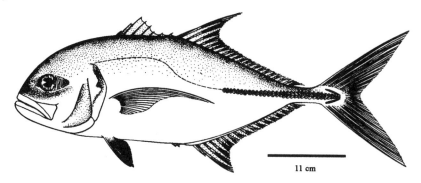

Figure 6.3. Horse-eye jack, *Caranx latus* Agassiz, 1831, is frequently identified from Lesser Antillean sites. (From Fischer 1978, vol. 1 CARAN Caranx 8)

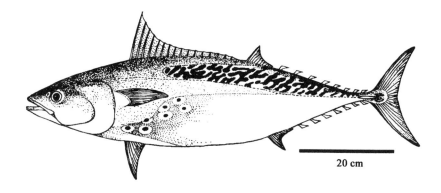

Figure 6.4. Little tunny, *Euthynnus alletteratus* (Rafinesque, 1810), is the most common scombrid at Lesser Antillean sites. (From Fischer 1978, vol. 4 SCOMBR Euth 1)

strated 83% and 100% ubiquities among the proveniences analyzed (Table 6.4). Cockspur seeds were also identified among the samples from Pearls (33% ubiquity).

Barbados

Barbados is more isolated in the Atlantic than the other islands of the Lesser Antilles (Drewett 1991, Drewett et al. 2000). This more remote position as well as the locations of the sites around the island influence the resources that were used. The site of Hillcrest is on the eastern coast and has Saladoid and evidence of post-Saladoid occupations. Chancery Lane, on the southern coast, also has evidence of Saladoid (A.D. 180–380) and post-Saladoid occupations. The Saladoid site of Little Welches and the post-Saladoid site Silver Sands are also located on the southern coast. Heywoods, located on the western coast,

Figure 6.5. Agouti, *Dasyprocta* sp., is a rodent that is associated with people wherever they coexist. It was introduced into the Lesser Antilles during the Ceramic period. (From National Academy of Sciences 1991:198).

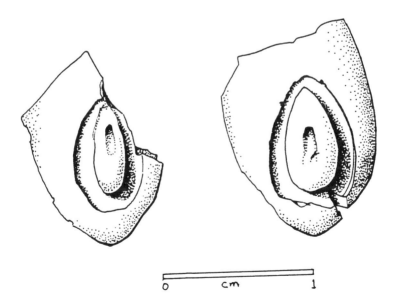

Figure 6.6. Sapotaceae (mastic bully [*Sideroxylon* sp.]) seed fragments showing intact hila. Pearls, Grenada, Unit 196, sample no. 9.

Table 6.4. Seeds and other nonwood remains identified from Ceramic-age sites

Taxa			
Family/Form	Scientific Name	Common Name	Grenada Pearls
Tree Seed/Nuts			
Anacardiaceae	cf. *Comocladia* sp.	poison ash	
Anacardiaceae	*Spondias* sp.	mombin	
Annonaceae	*Annona sp.*	sour sop	
Aracaceae	*Acrocomia aculeata*	spiny palm	
Aracaceae		palm family	83
Fabaceae	*Hymenaea courbaril*	stinking-toe, locust	
Rutaceae	*Zanthoxylum* sp.	wild lime	
Sapotaceae	*Sideroxylon* sp.	mastic bully	100
Ulmaceae	*Celtis* sp.	cockspur	33
Herbs/Grains			
Aizoaceae	*Trianthema portulacastrum*	trianthema	
Fabaceae	cf. *Crotalaria* sp.	rattlebox	
Malvaceae	*Malva/Sida* sp.	broomsedge	
Poaceae	Paniceae, panicoid group	panicoid grass	
Portulacaceae	*Portulaca* sp.	purslane	
Verbenaceae	cf. *Verbena* sp.	verbena	
Nonwood, Other			
Bignoniaceae	*Cresentia (cujete)* [rind]	calabash tree	
cf. Euphorbiaceae	cf. *Manihot* sp. [tuber]	manioc	
Parenchyma-dense		?endosperm ('nutmeats')	
Parenchyma-loose		?tuber remains	
Bark/rind fragment		bark and/ or rind	

has a small Archaic deposit and a larger post-Saladoid deposit (A.D. 830–1040) from which both plant and animal remains were recovered (Tables B-2 and B-3).

The Saladoid samples from Hillcrest, Chancery Lane, and Little Welches are small but have many vertebrate characteristics in common (Table 6.3). Jacks, particularly the bigeye scad (*Selar crumenophthalmus*), are abundant in each of these samples. The jacks identified only to family at Chancery Lane are small and probably referable to bigeye scad or one of the other related small in the Lesser Antilles

	Islands/Sites				
Barbados Heywoods	Nevis Hichmans	Nevis Indian Castle	St. Eustatius Golden Rock	St. Martin Hope Estate	Montserrat Trants
				4	
X					
X					
X					
X					
				8	
				4	
		X	67	16	
					X
				4	
				4	
				16	X
				4	
				29	
X					
	X				
		X			
	X	X		4	
	X				

species. Parrotfishes (Scaridae) are abundant in all the Ceramic-age sites. In other respects the faunal assemblages of the Saladoid and post-Saladoid samples from the same locations differ. Rice rats are abundant at Hillcrest and Silver Sands (Table 6.3 and B-3). Dog burials are a feature of the Silver Sands site. All four post-Saladoid deposits—Hillcrest, Silver Sands, Chancery Lane, and Heywoods—have a greater abundance of flyingfishes (Exocoetidae) than in the earlier deposits. In addition to abundant flyingfish, the post-Saladoid sample from Heywoods has abundant tuna (Scombridae). The jack that is abundant at Hillcrest, Chancery Lane, and Silver Sands is the horse-eye jack (*Caranx latus*) instead of the bigeye scad common to Saladoid deposits.

The Archaic faunal assemblage from Heywood contrasts markedly from the post-Saladoid (Tables 6.1 and 6.3). In the Archaic sample rice rats are common (12%), as are pigeons (8%), and parrotfishes make up 15% of the assemblage. No flyingfishes, scads, or tuna were identified from the Archaic deposit, though these fishes are common in the post-Saladoid deposit at the same site. This indicates quite a change in the use of vertebrates.

The evidence from the seed and wood remains recovered from the Ceramic-age deposit at Heywoods (Tables 6.4 and 6.5) indicates a fairly diverse array of items used in subsistence practices. A number of these items came from water-logged deposits with superb organic preservation and associated with prehistoric structures at the site (Drewett, Rogers, and Newsom 2000). The remains of edible fruits include hog plum (*Spondias* sp.), soursop (*Annona* sp.), and spiny palm (Table 6.4). Also identified among the nonwood plant remains were pod fragments from the tree legume known as "stinking toe," or West Indian locust (*Hymenaea courbaril*). The pods may have served a number of purposes: their resin can be used as a varnish to waterproof boats and containers, as incense, and for a variety of medicinal purposes (Ayensu 1981:70; Drewett, Rogers, and Newsom 2000). Rind fragments from calabash (*Cresentia cujete*), the native tree gourd, were also identified. Ten wood taxa were identified from Heywoods (Table 6.5), primarily dense tropical hardwoods that would be excellent for fuel or durable construction. Here again we have evidence for the presence of a Sapotaceae wood, in this case strongly matched to the genus *Sideroxylon* sp. (synonym *Mastichodendron*), mastic bully, because of the exceptional anatomical preservation. This wood served as post supports for at least two wooden structures (Drewett, Rogers, and Newsom 2000). That this was an excellent choice for this purpose can be observed in the following excerpt from Record and Hess (1943:507): "the timber is used in heavy construction of all kinds, vehicles, ox-yokes, fence posts, railway crossties, and to a small extent in furniture . . . [The wood is] very hard, heavy, tough, and strong . . . not easy to work, but finishes smoothly." As indicated above, this particular tree, mastic bully, also has edible fruit and so represents an additional resource that is likely to have been consumed by the site's inhabitants. Silk-cotton (cf. *Ceiba* sp.) wood is very light and buoyant and is known to have been used widely to make dugout canoes; the seedpod produces fiber that may be used in ways similar to cotton.

Montserrat

Large samples of plant and animal remains were recovered from the Trant's site on Montserrat. Steadman et al. (1984) present a detailed discussion of the vertebrate fauna from the Trant's site. A study by Reis and Steadman (1997) describes the birds from this site including a new species to Montserrat. Reitz (1994) identified and analyzed the vertebrate remains, integrating the data from the different vertebrate classes. Her faunal list is presented here (Table B-4). It accompanies data on the seeds and charcoal identified from the same excavations (Tables 6.4 and 6.5).

The Trant's site is important for our understanding of prehistoric uses of plant and animal resources in several respects. This site is relatively early, having been occupied during the Saladoid period from about 480 B.C. to A.D. 200 (Reitz 1994). The site is located on the eastern shore of the island in a similar position to Hillcrest on Barbados, Pearls on Grenada, and Hichmans' Shell Heap on Nevis. The composition of the remains is of particular interest. This site is the only one known with two rice rat species designated A and B (Oryzomyini A, B [Table B-4]) until taxonomic revision of the West Indian rice rats is completed. Both species are now extinct. The remains of two dogs were also identified in the Saladoid deposit, and agouti were encountered in the more superficial stratum with historic remains. Three bird species identified from the Trant's site material no longer occur on Montserrat. These are shearwaters (*Puffinus lherminieri*), purple gallinule (*Porphyrio martinicus*), and a parrot (*Amazona* sp.) with affinities to the Greater Antillean parrots (Reis and Steadman 1999).

Reef carnivores such as the grouper (Serranidae), snapper (Lutjanidae), and grunt (Haemulidae) dominate the fishes in the faunal sample (Reitz 1994). The most abundant fish is the grouper (*Mycteroperca* sp.), all represented by small individuals with an average atlas width measurement of 2.26 mm (range 1.7 mm–3.2 mm). A fish with an atlas of that size would be estimated to weigh 59 g. Grouper of the genus *Epinephelus* are on average twice as large, with an average atlas width of 5.07 mm (range 2.35 mm–7.39 mm). Parrotfishes (Scaridae), the reef omnivores that are usually very common, are only represented by a single individual.

A rich diversity of plant remains is represented, both at Trants and at the contemporaneous Windward Bluff site, also on Montserrat (Table 4.1). Plants represented by seeds and probably used for food are trianthema (*Trianthema portulacastrum*) and purslane (*Portulaca* sp.) (Table 6.4). All parts of these herbaceous plants are edible, and trianthema seeds are relatively high in protein content (32.9% [Carr et al. 1985:510]). Tentative identification of guava (*Psidium guajava* [Table 6.5]) wood charcoal suggests the presence of an edible fruit. The most commonly identified wood types and often most abundant charcoal remains at Trants and the several other Lesser Antillian sites analyzed are lignum-vitae (*Guaiacum* sp.) and strong bark (*Bourreria* sp.), the former with site ubiquities as high as 80 to 95% (Table 6.5). These woods are exceptional for their hardness and durability. Lignum-vitae wood is particularly

Table 6.5. Wood taxa identified from Ceramic-age sites in the Lesser Antilles

Taxa			Barbados Heywoods	Nevis Hichmans
Family	Genus/Species	Common Name		
# Samples/Wood NI			24/28	36/752
Mangrove and Strand				
Euphorbiaceae	*Hippomane mancinella*	manchineel	X	
Fabaceae-Caesalpoid	cf. *Caesalpinia* sp.	gray nickers		
Malvaceae	cf. *Hibiscus* sp.	mahoe		
Polygonaceae	*Coccoloba uvifera*	sea grape		26
Simaroubiaceae	cf. *Suriana maritima*	bay cedar		
Theophrastaceae	*Jacquinia* sp.	joe wood		5
Interior				
cf. Annonaceae		custard apple family		
Aracaceae		palm family	X	
cf. Bignoniaceae		bignonia family	X	
Bombacaceae	cf. *Ceiba* sp.	silk cotton tree	X	
Boraginaceae	*Bourreria* sp.	strong bark, strong back		84
Boraginaceae	*Cordia* sp.	geiger tree, anaconda		
Celastraceae	*Maytenus (elliptica)*	mayten		84
Celastraceae	*Maytenus (phyllanthoides)*	mayten		
Celastraceae	cf. *Maytenus* sp.	mayten, rockwood		
Erythroxylaceae	cf. *Erythroxylum* sp.	redwood		
Euphorbiaceae	*Croton* sp.	pepper bush		
Euphorbiaceae	*Drypetes* sp.	whitewood	X	
Euphorbiaceae	cf. *Hura* sp.	sandbox tree		
Fababeae-Mimosoid	cf. *Pithecellobium* sp.	blackbeard, cat's claw		
Fabaceae-Papilionoid	cf. *Dalbergia* sp.	rosewood	X	
Fabaceae-Papilionoid	*Piscida (carthagenensis)*	fish poison, bois á enivrer		5
Fabaceae	Caesalpinoideae/Mimosoideae	tree legumes		
Meliaceae	cf. *Swietenia* sp.	mahogany	X	
Myrtaceae	cf. *Eugenia* sp.	stopper, black wattle	X	79
Myrtaceae	cf. *Pimenta* sp.	bay rum tree		
Myrtaceae	cf. *Psidium guajava*	guava		
Nyctaginaceae	*Pisonia* sp.	pull-back, hold-back		

Islands/Sites					
Nevis Indian Castle	Nevis Sulphur Ghaut	St. Eustatius Golden Rock	St. Martin Hope Estate	Montserrat Trants	Montserrat Win. Bluff
17/54	06/45	50/280	68/628	99/526	02/21
			2		
				3	
	X			1	
		5			
			16		
			2	1	
X	X		2	48	
			4	[1]	
	X		27	4	X
				1	
		5			
				4	
[X]		[10]		[1]	
	X				
					X
X		10	2	10	
				6	
X					
				1	
				[10]	
				1	

Continued on the next page

Table 6.5. *Continued*

Taxa				
Family	Genus/Species	Common Name	Barbados Heywoods	Nevis Hichmans
# Samples/Wood NI			24/28	36/752
Rubiaceae	cf. *Erithalis fruiticosa*	black torch		
Rubiaceae	*Guettarda (elliptica)*	silver wood		
Rubiaceae	cf. *Psychotria* sp.	wild coffee		10
Rubiaceae		madder family		
Rutaceae	*Amyris elemifera*	torchwood		58
Rutaceae	*Zanthoxylum* spp.	wild lime, satinwood		[5]
Sapotaceae	*Chrysophyllum/Sideroxylon* wood anatomical group	star apple, mastic bully	X	[5]
Sapotaceae		sapodilla family		
Ulmaceae	cf. *Celtis* sp.	cockspur		
Zygophyllaceae	*Guaiacum* sp.	lignum-vitae	[X]	95

*Brackets indicate provisional assignment

dense and very difficult to work but would be a very high-quality source of fuel. Strong bark wood is described as fine textured, with a fairly straight grain and easily worked (Record and Hess 1943:100). We can add, as described in Chapter 5, that the fruits from this small tree are edible, and lignum-vitae has considerable potential for a variety of ethnobotanical purposes.

Nevis

Archaeological sites on Nevis yielded abundant plant and animal remains associated with the long occupation of the island. The Archaic site of Hichmans' Shell Heap (GE-6) (790–520 B.C.) is very close to the subsequent occupations by Saladoid people at Hichmans site (GE-5) (100 B.C.–A.D. 600) and by post-Saladoid people at Indian Castle (GE-1) (A.D. 650–880). Sulphur Ghaut (JO-2) (A.D. 900–1200) is located on the opposite (west) coast. These provide the opportunity to trace changes in resource uses through time. Although the coastal locations of the Saladoid and post-Saladoid sites are nearly the same, the landscape and the plant and animal populations undoubtedly changed as a result of human exploitation pressures. The two post-Saladoid sites provide a larger sample for the later period.

The relative abundances of the most common organisms in the three Ceramic-age sites are presented in Table 6.6. It seems evident that neither location nor

Islands/Sites					
Nevis Indian Castle	Nevis Sulphur Ghaut	St. Eustatius Golden Rock	St. Martin Hope Estate	Montserrat Trants	Montserrat Win. Bluff
17/54	06/45	50/280	68/628	99/526	02/21
		21		1	
				1	
		10			
X	X			[4]	
[X]	[X]	21	2	[1]	
		10		1	
			4	[3]	
	X				
X	X	37	80	34	

period of occupation clearly determines similarity in the relative abundances of these organisms; however, some interesting differences are apparent. Among the prominent woods, sandbox tree (cf. *Hura* sp.) predominated at Sulphur Ghaut, followed by torchwood (*Amyris elemifera*) and strong bark, while lignum-vitae is definitively most abundant among the samples from Hichmans site and Indian Castle. Strong bark is also highly conspicuous among the Hichmans proveniences analyzed. Lignum-vitae, strong bark, torchwood, and most others of the wood taxa identified are all commonly associated with tropical-subtropical dry forests (xerophytic seasonal and microphyllous forest formations [Table 2.3]). The conspicuous presence of these woods throughout the spatial and temporal series from Nevis demonstrates the long and widespread presence of this forest and its lengthy history of human use on the island, particularly the sustained extraction of the woods for fuel. However, some subtle changes may be indicated. Newsom (2004) has suggested that the apparent decline in emphasis and use of lignum-vitae (Table 6.6) and conversely the increased or first-recorded presence of species like sandbox tree, fish poison (*Piscida* sp.), pepper bush (*Croton* sp.), and cockspur (*Celtis* sp. [Table 6.5]), which are generally all components of dry scrub vegetation, by the post-Saladoid period may signal important landscape dynamics. This may have involved the progressive local elimination of the slow-growing dominants of the

Table 6.6. Most abundant plant and animal remains represented at three Ceramic-age sites on Nevis

Most Common Plants and Animals	Saladoid	Post-Saladoid	
	Hichmans (355+)	Indian Castle (1024)	Sulphur Ghaut (3988)
Lignum-vitae	95% ubiquity	25% wood ID	4% wood ID
Strongbark	84% ubiquity	8% wood ID	12% wood ID
Mayten	84% ubiquity	0	4% wood ID
Stopper	79% ubiquity	4% wood ID	0
Torchwood	58% ubiquity	4% wood ID	32% wood ID
Rice rats	30% vert. MNI	7% vert. MNI	5% vert. MNI
Grouper	13% vert. MNI	15% vert. MNI	12% vert. MNI
Grunt	5% vert. MNI	5% vert. MNI	36% vert. MNI
Parrotfish	3% vert. MNI	10% vert. MNI	3% vert. MNI
Surgeonfish	2% vert. MNI	23% vert. MNI	4% vert. MNI
Land crabs	38% invert. MNI	5% invert. MNI	1% invert. MNI
Donax	0	14% invert. MNI	78% invert. MNI
Topsnail	7% invert. MNI	12% invert. MNI	1% invert. MNI
Nerites	12% invert. MNI	22% invert. MNI	3% invert. MNI
Tree snails	32% invert. MNI	21% invert. MNI	3% invert. MNI

Note: Total size of the sample of animals expressed as MNI is in parentheses next to the name of the site. Quantification differs according to the organism identified. Plant ubiquity is expressed as the percentage of the samples from the site in which the taxon occurred among the samples studied. Plant percentage ID is the frequency of a particular taxon among all identified wood specimens.

dry forests, especially lignum-vitae (Beard 1949:82–83), concurrent with the expansion of secondary forests and possible deflection of forest successions to dry scrub, depending on the intensity of these changes. Such a situation is predictable in view of a continual need for wood resources coupled with increasing land clearance to produce root crops. The material culture remains from these sites, that is, the tuber-processing equipment such as graters and griddles, and the presence of provisionally identified manioc tuber remains and similar parenchymatous fragments (likely also from tubers [Table 6.4]), are evidence of horticultural practices. Increasingly arid conditions, as described in Chapter 2, may have been an additional factor influencing changes in native forest habitats.

Concerning the fauna, terrestrial organisms such as rice rats, land crabs, and tree snails predominate in the Saladoid sample (Tables 6.3, 6.6; Table B-5). Grouper are approximately equally abundant in all three sites. The two obligate reef fishes, parrotfishes and surgeonfishes, are more abundant at Indian

Castle than at either of the other sites (Table 6.6; Table B-6). Juvenile grunts and donax dominate the faunal collection from Sulphur Ghaut (Kozuch and Wing 2004).

In addition to changes in species composition, the size ranges of the individuals represented at the sites have implications for reconstruction of the fishing technology and the condition of animal populations. Measurements that correlate well with live body weight are the width of the vertebrae in fishes and the height of the mandible in land crabs (Reitz and Wing 1999). Fish vertebrae are not easy to identify to species; therefore measurements were taken of all the specimens that could be identified to family (Table 6.7). The exception is the measurements of the specimens identified to bigeye scad that are sufficiently distinctive to identify to species. The other specimens identified only to jacks undoubtedly include several species, some of which get as large as the horse-eye jack. Vertebral sizes and crab mandible width are smaller in the post-Saladoid than in the Saladoid sample. A change in the composition of the species within each family or a decline in the size of territorial species may account for this.

St. Eustatius

The Golden Rock site is a late to post-Saladoid (Keegan 2000; Versteeg and Schinkel 1992) occupation located on the low land below the Quill, the volcanic cone, and equally distant from the Atlantic and Caribbean shores. This was the first site to reveal some of the details of the internal dynamics, configuration, and layout of a Saladoid settlement. Altogether six circular structures were identified that were variously built, rebuilt, and abandoned, with new ones erected in their place; most or all of these appear to have been houses, living space devoted to domestic and related activities. A similar ebb and flow of midden accumulations occurred in conjunction with the series of settlement phases at the site, all of which took place over the course of a lengthy history of occupation during the seventh to ninth centuries A.D. (Schinkel 1992). Van der Klift (1992) identified the vertebrate remains (Table B-7). Taverne (Taverne and Versteeg 1992) identified the molluscs but did not quantify them in a fashion comparable to the vertebrate component of the fauna. According to Taverne, "The midden consisted mainly of *Cittarium pica*, the West Indian topsnail. This species outnumbered by far all the other species. *Nerita tessalata, Nerita versicolor, Purpura patula* [now called *Plicopurpura patula*], *Strombus gigas, Tectarius muricatus*, and chitons are relatively abundant" (Taverne and Versteeg 1992:84). Vertebrates that are particularly abundant at Golden Rock are rice rats, grouper, and scads. These appear to be identifiable to either the genus *Trachurus* or *Decapterus* (van der Klift 1992). Although the precise identification of the scad is inconclusive, both genera are ecologi-

Table 6.7. Comparison of the sizes of selected animals from sites on Nevis

Taxa	Saladoid Hichmans				Post-Saladoid Indian Castle				Post-Saladoid Sulphur Ghaut			
	#	x	Range	Weight	#	x	Range	Weight	#	x	Range	Weight
Indeterminate fish	75	7.2	3.4–14.4	1099.1	135	3.7	1.6–9.5	203.96	765	3.3	1.4–13	152.7
Grouper	13	7.7	3.6–9.9	1302.6	8	4.3	2.9–7.5	298.3	12	5.2	2.8–7.5	482.5
Grunt					2	4.1		264.5	4	3.7	3.4–4	203.96
Jacks	1	6.5		848.5	19	4.8	3.3–11	394.0	116	4.1	1.8–12.5	264.5
Bigeye scad									30	3.4	2.5–4.1	164.7
Parrotfishes	1	9.9		2460.1	6	4.4	2.3–6.6	316.2	4	4.2	2.6–7.4	281.1
Surgeonfishes					15	2.4	1.8–3.4	68.2				
Tuna	60	10.3	3.4–14.4	2719.4	7	8.6	5.9–9.4	1722.98	187	9.6	4.6–13.9	2275.9
Land crabs	14	8.6	7.5–10.7	169.57	3	6.2	4.2–8.5	92.8	46	7.4	4–11.2	128.6

Source: Kozuch and Wing 2004

Note: All fish measurements are the width of the vertebral centrum and the land crab measurements are the height of the mandible. These measurements are in mm. Symbols: # is the number of specimens measured, x is the mean measurement, range is the smallest and the largest, and weight is the estimated weight (gm) of an animal with the mean measurement using the allometric constants presented in Chapter 4 (Table 4.2).

cally similar, living in pelagic waters and occupying a niche that is low in the food web.

Golden Rock archaeobotanical remains are limited to cockspur seeds (67% ubiquity; Table 6.4) from the midden deposits, and nine wood taxa from midden and posthole samples (Newsom 1992, 1993a; Table 6.5). The cockspur seeds (Table 6.4) and scale insect tests (*Margarodes* sp.) from the midden have interesting distributions. Their abundance changes dramatically through the excavated column. Cockspur is most common in the lower levels and absent in the uppermost, whereas scale insect tests, also called ground pearls, are absent in the lower levels but abundant in the upper ones. Scale insects typically attach themselves to grass roots. The presence of cockspur and possibly the star apple and/or false mastic (*Chrysophyllum/Sideroxylon* wood group) suggests use of the fruits of these trees for food. Most abundant are wood specimens of lignum-vitae (37% ubiquity), followed by wild lime/satinwood (*Zanthoxylum* spp.) and black torch (cf. *Erithalis fruiticosa*) (Table 6.5). Trees of all three types provided the posts to construct the houses and other structures at Golden Rock (described above). Post diameters were estimated from the curvature of the growth rings exhibited in individual wood specimens and found to range from 10 to 18 cm (Newsom 1992).

St. Martin

Hope Estate is a large Saladoid site located approximately 2 km inland at the northern end of the island. The vertebrate remains can be separated into early and late Saladoid components (Table 6.8; Table B-8). This allows for a comparison of vertebrate use during the early Ceramic age rather than only between the Saladoid and post-Saladoid, which is also marked by major cultural changes. The invertebrates are associated only with the early deposit. The plant remains including both seeds and wood can also be divided into these early and later cultural components, including those excavated from deposits ascribed to an early Huecan Saladoid occupation (ca. 300–400 cal B.C. to about 50 cal B.C.) and others recovered from deposits identified with an evidently subsequent Cedrosan Saladoid (ca. cal A.D. 255 to 650) presence at the site (Hoogland 1999; Newsom and Molengraaff 1999; and see Chapter 4).

More seeds were recovered from this site than from any other in the Lesser Antilles; however, most of these represent weedy incidentals (Table 6.4). Among the economic taxa are the tree fruits mastic bully and cockspur, as at several of the other sites in the Lesser Antilles. There may also be two forbs that provided sustenance to various inhabitants of the site, one with edible grains (panicoid grass) and another (purslane [*Portulaca* sp.]) with edible seeds and vegetative parts, thus a potential potherb. Rattlebox (cf. *Crotalaria* sp.) and wild lime potentially represent medicinal plants (Ayensu 1981).

Nine woods were identified from carbonized remains at Hope Estate (Table

Table 6.8. Comparison of the sizes of selected animals from early and late Saladoid deposits at Hope Estate

Taxa	Early Saladoid				Late Saladoid			
	#	x	Range	Weight	#	x	Range	Weight
Needlefishes	17	7.5	3.2–8.9	1218.7	25	5.0	4–6.5	436.9
Grouper	5	6.2	4.8–9.4	752.9	2	5.8		636.0
Jacks	30	5.9	3.1–8.9	664.1	20	4.5	3.6–5.8	334.7
Wrasses	2	6.1		722.6	1	6		692.98
Parrotfishes	1	7.3		1138.2	3	5.6	4.9–6	581.99
Tuna					27	10.6	7.3–14.6	2924.3
Indeterminate fish	40	5.2	3.3–8.6	482.5	37	5.7	3.7–8.5	608.6

Source: Wing 2001a, 2001b

Note: All fish measurements are the width of the vertebral centrum (mm). Symbols: # is the number of specimens measured, x is the mean measurement, range is the smallest and the largest, weight is the estimated weight (gm) of an animal with the mean measurement using the allometric constants presented in Chapter 4 (Table 4.2).

6.5). Once again, lignum-vitae and strong bark were identified. Lignum-vitae is highly prominent throughout the site deposits, with 80% overall site ubiquity. Mayten (*Maytenus* sp., probably the species *M. elliptica*) is also relatively abundant (27% overall ubiquity; Table 6.5). Lignum-vitae wood was clearly important to the Huecan occupation; it demonstrates an 81% ubiquity for that period alone. The wood of this tree continued to be sought for fuel and perhaps as well for other purposes during the later Cedrosan period (60% ubiquity); however, a much more diverse array of woods was used during that period (a total of 7 taxa during the Huecoid occupation [n = 33 proveniences] versus 16 associated with the Cedrosan component [n = 27 proveniences]). The expanded breadth of woods procured and used in the later period may be an indication of less specific cultural preferences or could be a sign that preferred but slow-growing lignum-vitae had by then become scarce. Several of the taxa associated with the Cedrosan component are commonly found in subtropical dry forest environments, but they also occur in secondary forests; thus their presence may indicate landscape changes and the resulting differences in the relative availability of trees that provided wood for fuel, construction, and other purposes.

The vertebrate remains from both the early and the later Saladoid deposits at Hope Estate have a greater relative abundance of terrestrial species than do the other sites studied in the Lesser Antilles (Table 6.3). In the earlier deposit pigeons (Columbidae) predominate. In the later deposit pigeons are still abundant but rice rats are more so, making up 50% of the vertebrate individuals

Table 6.9. Summary of the exploitation of key habitats based on the relative abundance of invertebrates usually associated with these habitats

Habitat	Time Period/Islands/Site				
	Saladoid			Post-Saladoid	
	Nevis Hichmans	St. Martin Hope Estate		Nevis	
				Sulphur Ghaut	Indian Castle
		Early	Late		
Terrestrial crabs	38.5	20.8	4	4.8	7.3
Terrestrial snails	32	50.8	93	3.4	21.1
Rocky or sandy intertidal	25.4	9.4	2	86.6	60.7
Shallow inshore	1.7	4.2	1	4.9	9.5
Coral reefs	2.4	14.8	0	0.3	1.4
Sample size (MNI)	355	715	1066	3787	422

Note: Detailed information about the faunal samples is presented in Appendix B. The sites are grouped according to the time period of occupation.

(Wing 1995). Fishes are primarily those that inhabit reefs. A shift can be seen in the reef fishes from a predominance of reef carnivores, such as groupers (Serranidae) and snappers (Lutjanidae), to an equal abundance of reef carnivores and reef herbivores and omnivores, such as parrotfishes (Scaridae) and wrasses (Labridae) (Table 6.8). Some size changes in fishes based on the width of their vertebral centra can be seen (Table 6.8).

Invertebrate data comparable to vertebrate data are available only for excavation Unit 16, Zone 18 (Table 6.9; Table B-8). In many respects the invertebrate assemblage is similar to the vertebrate one in the relatively greater numbers of terrestrial species represented. Both land hermit crabs (*Coenobita clypeatus*) and land crabs (Gecarcinidae) (Figure 6.7) are abundant, making up 21% of the MNI of the invertebrate fauna. Tree snails (Bulimulidae) and seagrape snails (Xanthonychidae) together make up 36% of the invertebrate fauna. Both reinforce the terrestrial character of the fauna. The most abundant marine mollusc is the jewelbox (Chamidae). This was a shell used to make beads, and its abundance may be due to this industry.

DISCUSSION

Plant and animal remains from Lesser Antillean sites document traditions in the use of diverse marine and terrestrial resources. Repeated representation of certain key species suggests a focus on particular plants and animals useful for food, fuel, and utilitarian purposes. Traditional foods that were used and well

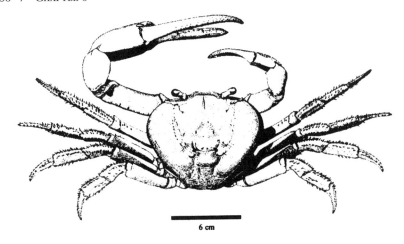

6 cm

Figure 6.7. Blue land crab, *Cardisoma guanhumi* Latreille, 1852, as well as other members of the family Gecarcinidae, is particularly common at early Saladoid sites. (From Fischer 1978, vol. 6 GECAR Cardis 1)

established in a cuisine may or may not have originated in the mainland homes of the people who migrated to the West Indian islands, because it appears that native Caribbean resources (e.g., reef fishes and native tree fruits) were readily adopted as foods by Caribbean migrants. Similarly, select woods like lignum-vitae and strong bark were commonly used for fuel to provide the best heat; efficaceous medicinal plants, and plant and animal products that have utilitarian properties, were also part of the cultural heritage of the island colonists. Under any circumstance the transplantation of well-honed traditions from a mainland setting to oceanic islands requires some modifications. Terrestrial resources of the islands are less diverse than those of the mainland, yet they have unique characteristics and possibilities that appear to have been quickly recognized by the early settlers in the region. The surrounding marine environment supports a rich and varied fauna and promotes important strand and mangrove vegetation. An important change from an economy based on mainland resources to one on an island is the prominence of maritime resources.

The data derived from studies presented here provide insight into the extent to which mainland traditions were transplanted to the islands and the modifications made to establish island economies derived in part from the mainland. Samples of plants and animals taken from strata progressively through time provide opportunities to trace changes in the use of resources. Samples from different island settings also indicate the adjustments made to sustain the island life.

Archaic deposits are rare, but those samples that exist provide the first evidence for human adaptation to the island environment. In general, an oppor-tunistic collection strategy seems to have characterized Archaic-age human adaptations in the Lesser Antilles. The seeds associated with the one site on Nevis, Hichmans' Shell Heap, and one on Antigua, Twenty Hill, indicate use at least of native trees: sapodilla (mastic bully and/or bulletwood) and cockspur fruits, as well as wild lime in some capacity. However meager, the archaeobotanical evidence for the Lesser Antillean Archaic is seemingly in-dicative of materials retrieved entirely from the natural vegetation and pro-vides no clear indication of the presence of plant staples or gardening practices. The one possible exception is cossie blossom, given its apparently more re-stricted modern range. However, the data currently are too limited to discern with certainty any evidence of plant cultivation during the Archaic period. Similarly, though the faunal samples from these Archaic sites are likewise rela-tively small, two introduced animals typically associated with later deposits in the Lesser Antilles are absent. Their absence may simply be the result of small sample sizes, or management of captive or domestic animals may not have been part of Archaic-age economic patterns.

One of these captive animals is the agouti, a large rodent (Figure 6.5). Agoutis are associated with people throughout the New World tropics and were introduced into the Lesser Antilles during the Ceramic age. Their re-mains are relatively more common at sites in the southern part of the Lesser Antilles and are never an important component of the vertebrate fauna or pre-sumably of the diet. This distribution obeys biogeographic principles and indicates that agoutis were difficult to maintain in captivity. The other intro-duced animal is the domestic dog. Dog remains are found more often in buri-als and are relatively rare among midden remains, which suggests an intimate association with human groups and a cultural significance over and above a food resource. Dog remains tend to be slightly more common in later Ceramic-age sites than in earlier occupations.

Another domestic animal found only in late Ceramic-age sites is the guinea pig (Figure 7.2). Guinea pig remains were identified at sites from Curaçao, Puerto Rico, and the Virgin Islands. In the Lesser Antilles they are identified only from sites on Antigua (Wing 1999; Wing 2004). The presence of guinea pigs is apparently exclusive to Antigua in this subregion of the Caribbean, and it would appear to set that island apart as the source of some trade item that could have been exchanged for these animals or the presence of some control-ling human influence allowing for their acquisition. The presence and distri-bution of these domestic animals remains unexplained until more of them are found and their specific contexts are better understood.

The importance of terrestrial animals in the vertebrate faunal samples and presumably to the economies is greater at sites closest to the mainland and those located farther inland on islands. For example, at Pearls on Grenada, land animals make up 22% of the vertebrate sample. At Hope Estate on St. Martin, land animals make up between 43% and 53% of the vertebrate fauna. Pearls is on the coast, and Hope Estate is 2 km inland. This greater use of terrestrial resources may be more a function of island biogeography and local catchment areas than attempts to necessarily mimic the mainland economy, as has been intimated or hypothesized in earlier studies (Goodwin 1980; Jones 1985; Roe 1989; Rouse 1989). The vertebrate fauna from Pearls includes more agouti than from any other site studied. Another introduced animal, an opossum, is also part of the fauna. Opossum were also identified from the Grand Anse site on St. Lucia but are not found beyond these southernmost sites (Wing and Reitz 1982). This distribution conforms to the expectations of island biogeographic principles (MacArthur and Wilson 1967). The abundance of land animals at the Hope Estate site may reflect accessibility of inland resources in preference to the more distant marine habitats. Such a choice would have an energetic basis usually referred to in catchment analysis and optimal foraging models (Kelly 1995), in which the energetic cost of procuring resources far from the home site must be taken into account in balancing the food value obtained.

A tradition for gardening and cultivating useful plants was derived from the mainland and undoubtedly modified for each island's ecosystem. A South American staple, manioc, was evidently introduced into the islands along with the technology (grating equipment, pottery griddles) used to process and cook the bread made from this tuber. Ceramic griddle sherds are a common cultural artifact, and the isolated finds of possible tuber fragments and bits of parenchymatous plant tissues at various sites in the region may be remnants of actual manioc tubers (Table 6.4). Plants that initially invaded cleared areas and that may have been tolerated and even become garden crops may have included trianthema, purslane, and panicoid grass (e.g., *Setaria* spp., foxtail millets). Fruit trees were probably cultivated or their growth promoted. Frequent identification of the seeds and woods of fruit trees such as cockspur and sapodillas (mastic bully and relatives) from most sites, possible guava from Trants, Montserrat, sea grape from Sulphur Ghaut, Nevis, and hog-plum and soursop from Barbados attest to their importance. A number of plants were used for utilitarian purposes beyond wood, such as the gourds produced by the calabash tree and perhaps the resin from stinking toe pods, lignum-vitae wood and bark, and the fiber from the silk-cotton tree. Medicinal uses of plants would likely require a period of experimentation. Much of the original knowledge about the properties of the same, related, or similar plants may have been gained on the mainland. Plants with known medicinal properties include silk cotton, calabash, croton, sandbox, fish poison, lignum-vitae, and purslane, to name a few, all of which occur at a number of sites (Ayensu 1981; Honychurch 1986; Williams and Williams 1961).

Evidence for change in subsistence patterns can be seen in both plant and animal remains. Changes in species composition through time can be the result of changing technology and more intensive exploitation of certain resources. The intensity of exploitation can itself affect plant and animal populations. Signs of overexploitation in these collections are decline in size of species, replacement of primary forest plants by second-growth species, decrease in the relative abundance of carnivorous reef fishes, and ultimately absence in the record, whether through extinction or population decline below economically viable levels.

Many of the woods found in Lesser Antillean sites represent dominant components of local dry forests. Lignum-vitae, strong bark, and wild lime are examples. Clearly the inhabitants of the various sites focused on readily available species from local forests, particularly lignum-vitae and strong bark. From an economic standpoint the dry forest woods collectively are superior fuelwoods by virtue of their generally high resin content, their coppicing ability, and their dense anatomical structure, all of which are beneficial in terms of supply and burning characteristics (Ewel and Whitmore 1973:10–20; National Academy of Sciences 1983:6; Record and Hess 1943; Wartluft and White 1984). That many of the dry forest trees are able to sustain coppicing was a potentially important factor not only to forest longevity but also to the long-term existence of human settlements. Coppice growth is an aggressive response to the stress of regular cycles of cutting and harvest, after which the tree responds by producing strong, prolific shoot growth. Regeneration is relatively rapid, and the trees continue to respond in this manner as long as harvesting is not too frequent or severe. Thus the dry forests of the islands theoretically have a natural capacity to sustain relatively great wood extraction pressures. This natural resiliency of the forests may have indirectly benefited the human populations living on the islands, translating in cultural terms to a fairly stable local wood supply and considering in particular that there are no alternative sources of fuel (e.g., peat, dung) in this environment. However, there is some tentative indication among the later deposits on these islands for the prevalence of second-growth trees or weed species that grow in disturbed conditions, at least based on the data from sites on Nevis and from Hope Estate, St. Martin.

Subtle, progressive alteration of local forests is a predictable consequence of a sustained, even low-intensity, human presence in most any insular environment. There is a continuous need for wood extraction, including selective cutting of woods preferred for cooking, construction materials, dugout canoes, and wooden implements. Shifting horticulture would contribute to this thinning through regular episodes of burning and land clearance, potentially altering the inherent forest dynamics. It may be that lignum-vitae—a wood commonly associated with early Ceramic-age sites—was locally eliminated on individual islands such as Nevis and St. Martin by the time of the later Saladoid, post-Saladoid, and Ostionoid settlements. Other species such as fish poison would have become relatively more abundant in the secondary forest, which may explain their presence among the later sites or deposits at Hope Estate, Golden Rock, and Sulphur Ghaut. Certainly differences in use of taxa by the occupants of individual sites and during different periods were dictated by cultural preferences; however, alternatives may have been sought as traditionally used or preferred woods were in short supply or eliminated. Moreover, as forested area becomes diminished, the replacement capacity of the woody vegetation on islands may be severely impeded or entirely lost. Drawing from island biogeographic theory, distance and area effects would have been highly important factors as progressively greater distances from seed sources to replenish vegetation potentially ensued (Harris 1984). The cumulative negative effects of cropping and rotation on the soils and vegetation in a circumscribed area (Ewel 1986) also would have influenced the nature of human settlement in these islands. Herbaceous plants that typically grow in disturbed conditions are purslane, panicoid grass, trianthema, and croton, among others. The presence of these suggests landscape changes that were probably brought about by human pressure on mature forests—opening the canopy in more densely forested tracts and, in general, promoting disturbed vegetation by burning and land clearing for gardens and fruit tree cultivation, among other activities. Such a change in vegetation and microhabitats could perhaps also account for the increased presence of rice rat remains at sites such as Hope Estate, given that small rodents tend to frequent ecotones and patchy environments.

One of the most noticeable changes in these biotic assemblages is the decline in land crabs that appears to coincide with the end of the Saladoid (Rainey 1940). Land crab exoskeletons are strikingly abundant and clearly visible in lower archaeological strata. Strata with fewer crab remains often have more molluscan shells and are deposited above the crab-rich lower strata. A decline in size through time can be documented when measurements are taken of the sizes of the crabs, as is seen in the neighboring sites, Hichmans and Indian Castle, on Nevis. Rainey (1940) first described this faunal change and attributed it to the apparent cultural change that it seemed to accompany (ceramics styles appear to change coincidentally). However, decrease in land crab abundance does not always coincide with the end of the Saladoid period. Typical characteristics of overexploitation are decreased abundance as well as decline in size of the individuals in the population. This change in the land crabs usually comes toward the end of the Saladoid, the first intensive occupation of the islands, but decreases in crab remains can come after initial occupation whether during the Saladoid or post-Saladoid periods.

Similar changes in abundance and size are observed in fish remains (Wing and Wing 2001; Wing 2001a). Comparison in relative abundance and size of reef fishes in the early and late deposits at many sites show changes similar to those of the land crabs and topsnails. The most apparent change is a decrease in reef fishes among all fishes. Accompanying this decrease is a decline in the average size of the individuals in each family, and a relative decrease in more aggressive carnivorous species with a corresponding increase in herbivorous and omnivorous species. These changes can be seen in Tables 6.7 and 6.8 by comparing the sizes of grouper and parrotfishes in the early and late deposits of the sites of Hichmans and Indian Castle on Nevis and Hope Estate on St. Martin. The change in relative abundance in reef carnivores and reef herbivores at the early deposits at Hichmans compared with the later deposits at Indian Castle can be seen in Table 6.9. Carnivorous reef fishes are twice as abundant as herbivores in the early deposits whereas in the later deposit they are 10% less abundant. A similar change in relative abundances of reef carnivores and herbivores can be seen in grouper, parrotfishes, and surgeonfishes in the neighboring sites on Nevis (Tables B-5 and B-6). Even though the relative abundance of groupers is the same at Hichmans and Indian Castle, parrotfishes and surgeonfishes are much more abundant in the later deposit. The sites where these changes have been studied are Hope Estate, Kelbey's Ridge on Saba, Hichmans and Indian Castle, and sites in Puerto Rico and the Virgin Islands that will be discussed in the next chapters.

The decline in size of the reef fishes through time has the characteristics of the phenomenon known as growth overfishing seen in modern fisheries. Growth overfishing is "when fishing intensity reaches a point where fish are caught before they have time to grow" (Russ 1991:605). Another characteristic of overfishing on reefs is that the more aggressive, most easily caught, and often primary fish used for food are reef carnivores. Therefore, they are disproportionately removed from the population by fishing early in the occupational sequence.

At the same time that changes in reef fishes appear, an increase can be seen in offshore fishes such as tuna, large jacks—particularly horse-eye jack—and flyingfishes. Even if these pelagic fishes come close to shore, some sort of watercraft is needed to successfully fish for them. Those fishing farther from shore would have to accept the increased risk of such an enterprise. The increased demands of a growing human population, declining terrestrial animals such as land crabs, and declining reef fish catches might leave little choice except taking on the riskier offshore fishing. We have no evidence for more production of captive animals such as agouti to supplement the meat protein in the

Table 6.10. Distribution of vertebrate taxa according to the niches in which they typically belong and the estimated biomass of reef fishes compared with inshore and pelagic taxa

General Niche	*St. Martin* Hope Estate							
	Early Deposit				Late Deposit			
	MNI	%	Estimated Biomass	%	MNI	%	Estimated Biomass	%
Terrestrial	30	43			47	53		
Freshwater/shore	3	4			1	1		
Reef carnivores	15	21			14	16		
Reef herbivores	8	11			7	8		
Total reef	23	33	17502	70	21	24	15939	65
Inshore/pelagic	14	20	7449	30	20	22	8590	35
Total	70		24951		89		24529	
	Kelbey's Ridge							
Terrestrial	21	11			56	27		
Freshwater/shore	6	3			3	1		
Reef carnivores	76	39			43	21		
Reef herbivores	83	42			85	41		
Total reef	159	81	129592	92	128	62	58985	73
Inshore/pelagic	11	6	10627	8	20	10	21372	27
Total	197		140219		207		80357	
Nevis	Hichmans				Indian Castle			
Terrestrial	32	50			21	17		
Freshwater/shore	1	2			0			
Reef carnivores	14	22			35	28		
Reef herbivores	7	11			49	39		
Total reef	21	33	24230	70	84	67	24956	74
Inshore/pelagic	10	16	10301	30	20	16	8662	26
Total	64		34531		125		33618	

Source: Wing 2001a, 2001b

Note: Data are from early and late deposits at Hope Estate (St. Martin), Kelbey's Ridge (Saba), and Hichmans and Indian Castle (Nevis).

diet of growing human populations, though rice rats might have served to partially alleviate this problem at Hope Estate. More intensive horticulture may have accompanied offshore fishing—perhaps the change in the fuelwood assemblages on Nevis and St. Martin that suggest wood extraction from secondary forests is an indirect indication of this, though expanded horticultural activity is more clearly seen in the Greater Antilles. This possibility will be discussed in the next chapter. Another solution to the problem of feeding growing populations on small islands is emigration. Some Lesser Antillean islands may have been abandoned when Europeans arrived (Wilson 2001).

7
Greater Antilles and the Virgin Islands

INTRODUCTION

The four islands of the Greater Antilles—Cuba, Jamaica, Hispaniola, and Puerto Rico—represent 88% of the landmass of the West Indies (Watts 1987: 4). Associated with the Greater Antilles and to their east are the islands of Vieques, nearby Culebra, and the group of islands known collectively as the Virgin Islands (Figure 7.1). The Virgin Islands and Vieques are situated on the relatively shallow island shelf contiguous with Puerto Rico. These islands are small, with a total landmass of 418 km^2. The Virgin Islands are separated geologically and culturally from the Lesser Antilles by the Anegada Trough, which is deep, 4,500 m below sea level, and wide—approximately 90 km between the nearest of the Virgin Islands and Lesser Antilles. The physiographic features of the Greater Antilles and the associated Virgin Islands promote a more diverse flora and fauna than are seen in the Lesser Antilles. This greater diversity in turn theoretically provided greater opportunities for resource exploitation for human colonizers and subsequent cultural developments. These are some of the ways in which the Greater Antilles and Virgin Islands are distinct from the Lesser Antilles to the south.

The broader resource base, the inherent "natural capital" (Costanza et al. 1997; Prugh et al. 1999) of the Greater Antillean islands sustained large human populations before A.D. 1492. These populations derived or arose from at least two different directions and mainland traditions. At the earliest, separate groups of people with stone-tool industries migrated from Middle America into the western Greater Antilles, and from South America up the Lesser Antilles into eastern Puerto Rico (Keegan 1994). Later, ceramic-producing groups migrated up the Lesser Antillean island chain and into the Virgin Islands and Greater Antilles. Very distinctive cultural developments, particu-

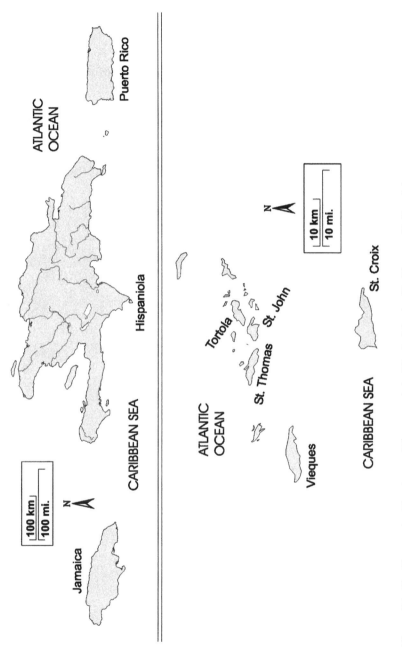

Figure 7.1. *Top*: Greater Antilles; *bottom*: Vieques and the Virgin Islands. (By Florence E. Sergile)

larly the transition from essentially egalitarian to stratified societies (Curet 1996), with roots in these separate traditions, occurred in the Greater Antilles and spread from there. A part of that cultural development entailed intensification of agriculture, major landscape changes intentionally planned and carried out by people, and chiefdom-level social organization presumably controlling the production and distribution of some resources. The diverse environment and the complex cultural history are accompanied by flexibility and innovation in the exploitation of plant and animal resources.

ENVIRONMENTAL CHARACTERISTICS

The geological history of the Greater Antilles involved spread of the ocean floor between North and South America along with Caribbean tectonic plate movement, resulting in fusion and splitting of ancient islands to achieve the conformation of the present islands. This geological history influenced the landforms as we know them. Each of the Greater Antillean islands has elevations of more than 1,000 m, and Hispaniola has peaks as high as 3,175 m. The Virgin Islands' maximum elevation is around 500 m. On small islands this elevation produces a very rugged landscape with steep hillsides presenting challenges to a horticulturist. The geological history of the Greater Antilles also controlled the manner in which plants and animals colonized the land.

Complete agreement does not exist among scholars concerning this colonization. Two primary modes of colonization—vicariance and dispersal—are at the center of the debate, as described in Chapter 2. Human dispersal into the islands took place by watercraft of some sort, dugout canoes, or composite vessels like catamarans. Here the debate concerns the routes that were taken. Did people go from one island to the next nearest island, or were intervening islands skipped? Clearly, people promoted the dispersal of plants and animals from one island to another, either intentionally or incidentally along with other transported materials. Some of these organisms became naturalized, whereas others required care; their remains are associated only with archaeological deposits.

The uplifted and dissected terrain of the Greater Antilles provides the conditions for many different plant communities. High elevations intercept moisture brought by the trade winds, thereby creating the conditions for perpetually wet (rain) forests (Watts 1987). High-elevation forest associations, known as upper montane, cloud, or mist forest, grow on the higher peaks between about 900 and 1,500 m in Puerto Rico, Hispaniola, and Jamaica. Moist to wet evergreen forests are adjacent to mountains, on their windward sides, at elevations between 200 and 900 m, and in riparian settings. Seasonal forests are found at elevations below 200 m on the leeward sides of islands adjacent to mountains. Seasonal forest formations generally occur where annual precipitation ranges between 750 and 2,000 mm, but where the uneven distribution of rainfall during the year influences plant life cycles, that is, the timing of vegetative, flower, and fruit production. These seasonal forests are believed to have been the dominant vegetation before it was cleared by people (Watts 1987; and see Chapter 2 concerning tropical and subtropical dry forest associations). The driest zones such as in southwestern Puerto Rico, with less than 750 mm of annual precipitation, support cactus, thorn, or scrub vegetation. Mangrove and strand forest vegetation grows along the coasts.

The aquatic habitats found in the Lesser Antilles also occur in the Greater Antilles and Virgin Islands. However, because of the larger land area and the greater size of the rivers that drain it, the estuaries are bigger in the Greater Antilles. These provide the habitat for fishes and molluscs that prefer less saline conditions of the surrounding Caribbean Sea and Atlantic Ocean. Some fishes, such as mullets (Mugilidae) and drums (Sciaenidae), require estuarine waters for parts of their life history. The coasts are indented with bays bracketed by rocky headlands. Sea grass meadows grow in inshore waters, and coral reefs form patch and barrier reefs. These all support rich vertebrate and invertebrate faunas.

CULTURE HISTORY

The cultural history of the Greater Antilles is the most complex among the four major subregions of the Caribbean. The first evidence for human presence is based on culturally modified shell and lithic materials deposited about 6,000 years ago. One early stone-tool tradition and its variants, termed by Rouse (1992:54) Casimiroid series or Casimiran subseries, appear to derive from Middle America, probably Yucatán. In the Caribbean the Casimiroid series is known only from Cuba and Hispaniola. These people evidently produced no pottery, at least not originally, but had a well-developed chipped stone tool industry. The earliest evidence of this migration is from sites dated to around 4000 B.C. (approximately 4000 to 400 B.C. [Keegan 1994:264–265]).

Other deposits with ground stone and/or shell tools but still lacking pottery and dated to around 5000 to 200 B.C. are collectively ascribed to the Caribbean Archaic age and an Ortoiroid tradition(s), with the earliest dates coming from sites in the southern Lesser Antilles (Keegan 1994:265–270). The Archaic-age deposits and tool assemblages of the Greater Antilles and Virgin Islands appear to have characteristics derived from both the early Middle American colonists and the Archaic people who migrated up the Lesser Antillean chain from northern South America. Eventually the culture of the early people who migrated from Middle America developed in situ from elements associated with the Casimiroid archaeological series, resulting in two named subseries (Redondan in Cuba and Courian in Hispaniola). Similarly,

Archaic sites in Puerto Rico and the Virgin Islands, associated with the Ortoiroid series of Rouse (1992), have been classified according to three primary complexes defined largely on the basis of differences in the tool types (Keegan 1994:268). In general the Archaic-age peoples of the Virgin Islands and Greater Antilles seem to have settled and lived along the coasts, where evidence of their former existence consists primarily of marine shell scatters. Thus Archaic-age groups had a maritime-based existence and are characterized by archaeologists as basically generalist hunter-gatherer, fisher-foragers. The degree to which these populations were logistically mobile or partially sedentary is still debated, and there are probably not enough data at this point to specify much definitive about Archaic settlement patterns in the region, aside from what was described earlier in Chapter 3.

The various flaked and ground stone tools of the early Caribbean human groups are believed to have been primarily associated with processing edible plants, though this remains to be tested by experimental archaeology and analysis of starch grains and trace organic residues on tool surfaces. In particular, it has been suggested that wild grains and the subterranean stems of marunguey or guáyiga (*Zamia* sp.; Cycadaceae) were important plant food items (Newsom 1993a; Veloz Maggiolo 1996:101–114, 1997). These inferences are largely based on discovery of desiccated remains of *Zamia* leaves found in prehistoric domestic deposits in a cave in the Dominican Republic (Veloz Maggiolo and Vega 1982) and on the presence of small grains at Archaic sites. Almost certainly a wide variety of wild plants and animals were used by Archaic people, and they probably also produced tools and other objects out of perishable materials like plant fibers and wood.

Most Caribbean archaeologists agree that some groups of foragers persisted in portions of Cuba, Jamaica, and western Hispaniola well into the time when Ceramic-age populations migrated into the eastern Greater Antilles and Virgin Islands (Dacal Moure and Rivero de la Calle 1996; Rouse 1992:52). There is mounting evidence that in many areas Archaic groups were not necessarily displaced but coexisted or were assimilated by Ceramic-age settlers in various locations of the Lesser and Greater Antilles (Keegan 1994:270–272).

The first Ceramic-age populations migrated from northeastern South America up the island chain into the Virgin Islands and eastern Greater Antilles, Puerto Rico, and the eastern tip of Hispaniola. The initial Ceramic-age migration and settlement is known broadly as "Saladoid" but may have consisted of separately organized and autonomous local groups with distinctive cultural traits (Keegan 2000:139–140). The Saladoid period is judged to have lasted from about 500 B.C. to A.D. 600 (Keegan 2000). Many of these sites—for example, Maisabel, in northern Puerto Rico—are also coastal, a location that provided easy access to coastal and marine resources (Siegel 1991). Saladoid sites are larger and more abundant than the preceding Archaic ones. Maisabel and

Tibes (Table 4.1) represent relatively large long-term settlements, including habitation and burial areas, or formal cemeteries (Maisabel). The two sites are particularly significant because they demonstrate apparently continuous histories of occupation spanning the early Saladoid ("Hacienda Grande") into the Ostionoid ("Santa Elena" and "Esperanza" material culture complexes) eras, or from about 200 B.C. to around A.D. 1200. This span of occupation brackets the period when simple chiefdoms first arose in the region; Tibes in particular may represent an early form of chiefdom social organization. The indications of cultural complexity and presumed presence of social ranking during the later occupation at Tibes include changes in mortuary patterns and the construction of ball courts and large plazas, among other things (Curet et al. 1998). In general, Saladoid archaeological deposits from this region indicate that people used a wide range of wild plants and animals, cultivated plants and raised domestic dogs, produced finely crafted pottery, and worked shell to form tools and ornaments such as beads. They also engaged in ritual activity including burial of domestic dogs.

Population growth and cultural development accelerated at the end of the Saladoid period after A.D. 500. This post-Saladoid period, also called the Ostionoid, is characterized by political and social complexity evolving in some cases into various levels of chiefdom or chiefdom-like organization (Keegan et al. 1998). Presumed manifestations of this development were control of symbolism, resource production, and distribution; complex trade relationships; major landscape changes in some areas such as construction of ball courts and large plazas, as well as agricultural terraces and ditch irrigation systems for intensive agriculture; cultivation of domestic crops; and maintenance of domestic and managed animals (Alegría 1983; Curet 1996; Krieger 1930:488; Oliver 1997c; Oliver et al. 1999; Ortíz Aguilu et al. 1991). The Taino who greeted Columbus arose from this cultural development. The site of En Bas Saline on Haiti was a large chiefly center that flourished from about A.D. 1200 until the occupation was truncated by European contact shortly after 1492 (ca. A.D. 1250 to 1510, cal. C14 [Deagan 1987]). In part, as indicated above, the people with Archaic cultures may have invigorated this cultural development (see Keegan 2000:149–150), whereas those in the western portion of the Greater Antilles may have persisted as an ethnic minority into the post-Columbian era.

BIOTIC RESOURCES IN THE GREATER ANTILLES AND VIRGIN ISLANDS

The landmasses of the collective Greater Antilles, on the one hand, and the Virgin Islands, on the other, are very different (Figure 7.1). This has an effect on species richness and the overall diversity of plants and animals endemic to the two groups of islands. The range in sizes of the individual Virgin Islands is similar to that of the Lesser Antilles. The difference between the two groups of smaller islands is that the Virgin Islands are closely situated and genetically related to Puerto Rico, and are all close together (except St. Croix, which is separated and on a shallow water platform), whereas the Lesser Antilles are located on the far side of the deep Anegada Trough and are generally relatively dispersed. As we will see, these natural features make a big difference in the plants and animals used during the prehistoric Ceramic age.

Archaic Age

The four samples of plants and fauna from Archaic-age deposits expand our appreciation of the knowledge and control of natural resources during this period (Krum Bay, St. Thomas; Beach Access, St. John; María de la Cruz, Puerto Rico; Maruca, Puerto Rico). A large sample of plants and vertebrates was recovered from Krum Bay on St. Thomas, Virgin Islands (Pearsall 1989; Reitz 1989). The Krum Bay site consists primarily of a shell midden located on the southern coast of St. Thomas. Two dates indicate that it was occupied around 1530 and again around 1680 B.C. (Reitz 1989). Small but important samples of plant material were also identified from midden deposits at the Beach Access site on St. John, as well as the María de la Cruz rockshelter and the Maruca site, located in eastern and western Puerto Rico, respectively. A large sample of vertebrate and invertebrate faunal material was analyzed from Maruca (Narganes 1997a, 1997b). Most of the plant remains from the rockshelter were recovered before systematic archaeobotanical research began in the region (Newsom 1993a; Rouse and Alegría 1990); however, new excavations at the site in the late 1990s by Miguel Rodríguez resulted in additional archaeobotanical specimens for analysis. The Beach Access materials derive from limited probing associated with a cultural resources survey of St. John. Even though the samples of plant remains from these two sites are small, they nevertheless contribute to the overall understanding of Caribbean Archaic-age plant use.

As a group, plant remains from these four sites are diverse, and certain taxa have very interesting social implications related to their ultimate origins. The remains include seeds of tree fruits, small edible seeds from herbs, and wood charcoal, among other classes of botanical materials (Table 7.1). Collectively, at least 10 edible seed/fruit types and 15 different wood species were identified. The edible tree fruits mastic-bully (*Sideroxylon* sp.; possibly also *Manilkara* cf. *M. bidentata*, bulletwood) and sapodilla (*Manilkara* cf. *M. zapota*, níspero) were very conspicuous among Krum Bay proveniences (Pearsall 1989; and see Newsom and Pearsall 2003). Also present variously at the sites were palm nutshells (cf. *Acrocomia media*, corozo), wild avocado (*Persea americana*), West Indian cherry (*Malphigia* sp.), wild fig (cf. *Ficus* sp.), and yellow sapote

(*Pouteria campechiana*). The presence of a sapodilla-type fruit (i.e., based on seeds that conform very strongly with the species *M. zapota*) at Krum Bay is important not only as evidence of early subsistence practices but also because some species, including *M. zapota*, now widely distributed in the Greater Antilles, are considered native to Mexico and Central America (Liogier and Martorell 2000:154). Likewise, the cultivation of fruit trees is suggested by the presence of the yellow sapote and wild avocado among the Archaic deposits at the María de la Cruz shelter. Both of these are exotics, again from Mexico and Central America (Liogier and Martorell 2000:62, 154; Newsom 1993a; Newsom and Pearsall 2003). Each of these trees has a long history of association with Neotropical home gardens on the mainland. Thus some of the plant remains may represent evidence for the presence of Archaic-age arboricultural practices in the Caribbean, as well as the importation of plants during this early period. It would seem that subsistence practices incorporated planted and perhaps fully managed trees. Valued trees may have been transported with these hunter-gatherer migrants when they established themselves in the islands or they continued to maintain contact with the mainland after they settled in the region, or both. Moreover, it is possible that the introduced trees were maintained along with native mastic bully and other useful fruit-bearing trees. Under any circumstance the evidence suggests that the subsistence adaptations of Archaic-age groups in the region did not simply center necessarily on collected plant resources.

Herbaceous plants with edible seeds or greens include trianthema (*Trianthema portulacastrum*), panicoid grass (Poaceae/Paniceae), and portulaca (*Portulaca* sp.) (Table 7.1). If not maintained in a small garden setting, assuming a somewhat more settled existence for Archaic-age human groups, these taxa should have been readily available from nearby disturbed habitats, including shell middens and repeatedly trafficked areas or revisited camps.

Wood charcoal from the Archaic sites includes plants found in a variety of different habitats from coastal vegetation such as mangrove forests (white mangrove [*Laguncularia racemosa*] and buttonwood [*Conocarpus erectus*]), as well as trees found in inland dry forests typically found at various elevations. Wood from two mangrove taxa was particularly conspicuous among Krum Bay deposits, along with an acacia-like tree legume (Fabaceae, cf. *Acacia* sp.) (site ubiquity values for these three taxa range from 39% to 97% [Table 7.1; Pearsall 1989]). The palm wood specimens identified from Maruca (Table 7.1) could represent either construction materials, wood implements, or wood burned as fuel.

The remains of animals from the Greater Antilles Archaic-age sites reflect a diverse use of resources typically found in a relatively restricted number of habitats (Tables 7.2a and 7.2b). Land vertebrates are rare and introduced mammals are absent. The predominant molluscs are pearl oyster (*Pinctata imbricata*)

Table 7.1. Plant remains from Archaic-age sites in the Virgin Islands and Greater Antilles

| | Taxa | | Islands/Sites | | | |
| | | | St. Thomas | St. John | Puerto Rico | |
Family/Form	Scientific Name	Common Name	Krum Bay	Beach Access	María de la Cruz	Maruca
# Samples/Wood NI			54/1018	02/27		10/5
Tree Seed/Nuts						
Aracaceae	cf. *Acrocomia* sp.	spiny palm, corozo				X
Combretaceae	*Conocarpus erectus*	buttonwood, mangle botón				X
Lauraceae	*Persea americana*	avocado, wild variety			X	
Malpighiaceae	*Malpighia* sp.	West Indian cherry	3			
Moraceae	cf. *Ficus* sp.	wild fig, jaguay	10			
Sapotaceae	*Manilkara* sp.	sapodilla, níspero	52			
Sapotaceae	*Sideroxylon* sp.	mastic bully	45		X	X
Sapotaceae	*Pouteria campechiana*	yellow sapote			X	
Herbs/Grains						
Aizoaceae	*Trianthema portulacastrum*	trianthema, verdolaga	23			
Cactaceae		cactus family	3			
Convolvulaceae		morning glory family	3			
Euphorbiaceae		spurge family	6			
cf. Fabaceae		bean family, wild variety	3			
Malvaceae		mallow family	19			
Poaceae	Paniceae, panicoid group	grass family, panicoid group	6			X
Portulacaceae	*Portulaca* sp.	purslane, verdolaga	16			

			Nonwood, Other		Wood
			Possible fruit rind	Parenchyma tissue	
Mangrove and Strand					
Combretaceae	*Conocarpus erectus*	buttonwood, mangle botón	X		39
Combretaceae	*Laguncularia racemosa*	white mangrove, mangle blanco			45
Simaroubiaceae	cf. *Suriana maritima*	bay cedar		X	45
Interior					
Aracaceae		palm family		X	
Bignoniaceae	*Tabebuia* sp.	cedar, roble			39
Capparidaceae	*Capparis* sp.	caper tree			16
cf. Celastraceae		staff tree family			61
Euphorbiaceae	*Croton* sp.	soldier whip, lechecillo			3
Fabaceae-Mimosoid	cf. *Acacia* sp.	acacia			97
Fabaceae-Mimosoid	*Leucaena leucocephala*	campeche			16
Guttiferae	*Clusia rosea*	cupey			26
Moraceae	*Ficus* sp.	wild fig, jagüey			6
Piperaceae	*Piper* sp.	higuillo			23
Rutaceae	*Zanthoxylum* sp.	wild lime, espino rubial, espino			X

Note: Abundance is based on site ubiquity, expressed as a percentage of all proveniences analyzed; some plant identifications are reported by simple presence (X).

Table 7.2a. Vertebrate remains identified from Archaic-age sites of Krum Bay, St. Thomas, Puerto Ferro, Vieques Island, and Maruca, Puerto Rico

| Taxa | | Islands/Sites | | | | | |
| | | St. Thomas Krum Bay | | Vieques Island Puerto Ferro | | Puerto Rico Maruca | |
Scientific names	Common names	MNI	%	MNI	%	MNI	%
Terrestrial							
Mammal	mammals	2	1.5	2	5.9	1	3.8
Hesperopsomys insulans	spiny rat	0		0		1	3.8
Bird	bird	1	0.8	0		0	
Falconidae	hawks	0		0		2	7.7
Columba sp.	pigeon	0		1	2.9	5	19.2
Zenaida sp.	dove	0		0		1	3.8
Indeterminate snake	snakes	1	0.8	8	23.5	0	
Subtotal		4	3.1	11	32.4	10	38.5
Freshwater or Shore							
Ardeidae	herons	0		1	2.9	0	
Casmerodius albus	great egret	0		0		2	7.7
Anatidae	ducks	0		0		2	7.7
Subtotal		0		1	2.9	4	15.4
Shallow Inshore Waters							
Cheloniidae	sea turtles	4	3.1	6	17.6	2	7.7
Carcharhinus sp.	requiem shark	1	0.8	1	2.9	0	

Centropomus sp.	snook	1	0.8	0		1	3.8
Caranx hippos	crevalle jack	0		4	11.8	1	3.8
Carangidae	jacks	4	3.1	1	2.9	0	
Sparidae	porgies	7	5.3	0		0	
Sphyraena sp.	barracuda	1	0.8	0		1	3.8
Gobiomorus dormitor	bigmouth sleeper	0		0		3	11.5
Subtotal		18	13.7	12	35.3	8	30.8
Coral Reefs							
Epinephelus sp.	grouper	15	11.5	0		2	7.7
Mycteroperca sp.	grouper	1	0.8	0		0	
Lutjanidae	snappers	16	12.2	1	2.9	1	3.8
Anisotremus surinamensis	black margate	0		0		1	3.8
Haemulon sp.	grunt	2	1.5	0		0	
Halichoeres sp.	wrasse	2	1.5	0		0	
Lachnolaimus maximus	hogfish	1	0.8	0		0	
Labridae	wrasses	2	1.5	0		0	
Scarus sp.	parrotfish	6	4.6	0		0	
Sparisoma sp.	parrotfish	60	45.8	4	11.8	0	
Balistidae	triggerfishes	2	1.5	0		0	
Diodontidae	porcupinefishes	2	1.5	5	14.7	0	
Subtotal		109	83.2	10	29.4	4	15.4
Total		131		34		26	

Source: St. Thomas (Reitz 1989), Vieques Island (Narganes 1991), and Puerto Rico (Narganes 1997a, 1997b).
Note: Abundance is based on minimum number of individuals (MNI) and expressed as a percentage. Families are arranged according to the habitats in which they are usually found.

Table 7.2b. Most common crustaceans and molluscs identified from Archaic-age sites

	Taxa			Islands/Sites	
Family	Scientific Name	Common Name	St. Thomas Krum Bay NISP	Vieques Island Puerto Ferro NISP	Puerto Rico Maruca NISP
Terrestrial–Crabs					
Coenobitidae	*Coenobita clypeattus*	land hermit crab		27	4
Gecarcinidae	*Cardisoma* sp.	land crab		89	6998
Subtotal				116	7002
Terrestrial–Gastropods					
Land snails		land snails		123	12
Subtotal				123	12
Freshwater					
Pseudothelphusidae	*Epilobocera* sp.	crab		0	2515
Subtotal					2515
Rocky Intertidal					
Trochidae	*Cittarium pica*	W. I. topsnail		2422	7
Neritidae	*Neritina* sp.	nerite		181	363
Muricidae	*Chicoreus* sp.	murex		834	131
Subtotal				3437	501

Shallow Inshore (rocky, sandy, or attached to roots)

Archidae	*Arca zebra*	turkey wing	X	146	1326
Pteriidae	*Pinctata* spp.	pearl oyster	X	110	3
Ostreidae	*Crassostrea rhizophorae*	Caribbean oyster		3509	1709
Lucinidae	*Lucina pectinata*	thick lucine		7201	284
Veneridae	*Chione cancellata*	cross-barred venus		193	1050
Strombidae	*Strombus* sp.	conch		396	161
Subtotal				11555	4533
Other Invertebrates				1492	2264
Total Invertebrate NISP				16723	16827
Total Vertebrate NISP			3459	199	150

Note: Data are from the same sources as Table 7.2a. Abundance is based on count of identified specimens (NISP). Unquantified abundance is indicated by x. Families are arranged according to the habitats in which they are usually found.

and turkey wing arc (*Arca zebra*). Both of these molluscs are abundant in the wild today, where they are found attached to rocks in shallow water. The vertebrate remains indicate focused exploitation on reef fishes, in particular parrotfishes (*Sparisoma* spp.). Typical reef carnivores such as grouper (Serranidae), snapper (Lutjanidae), and grunt (Haemulidae) are also abundant but only about half as abundant as the parrotfishes. The recovery strategy used by the archaeologist (Lundberg 1989) did not include sieving with fine-gauge screen; consequently, remains of smaller fishes may have been lost.

Archaic-age uses of plants and animals in the Virgin Islands and Puerto Rico, as reflected primarily at Krum Bay and Maruca, suggest two approaches to the procurement of resources. In terms of the terrestrial environment, plants were collected from the natural vegetation—fuelwood, herbs, fresh fruit—and there is the intriguing possibility that others were introduced into the islands and cultivated in small-scale gardens, perhaps along with some native taxa. The human settlements were established in open or perhaps intentionally cleared locations, and we might infer that the continuous or regular human presence produced or enhanced the habitat and growth conditions for weedy plants typical of disturbed environments. Thus, rather synergistically, many plants potentially useful to human subsistence in the Caribbean may have occurred in greater frequencies in the vicinity of human settlements, where they entered into an ecological and potentially coevolutionary dynamic with humans, much as has been modeled for the Archaic period of eastern North America (Rindos 1984; Smith 1995). All of the small seed taxa (herbs/grains, Table 7.1) represent ruderal species with various food or medicinal potential. Wood resources also were undoubtedly used for multiple purposes.

In contrast to the use and possible management of plants, we have no evidence that any animal was introduced into the Caribbean Islands or managed there during the Archaic age (Narganes 1997a, 1997b; Reitz 1989). The only possible overlap is the focus on mangrove and coastal strand habitats in the exploitation of plants and animals. Mangrove and strand habitats can supply fuelwood, and the adjacent shallow water is a source of shellfish attached to mangrove roots and rocks and fishes that feed in inshore nursery grounds. Fishing was focused on the reef. Reef fishes were probably caught in traps made of plant fibers.

Ceramic Age

During the Ceramic age, sites become increasingly abundant in both the Virgin Islands and the Greater Antilles (Wilson 1997b). They demonstrate a range of adaptations to different environmental conditions by changes in types and locations of sites through time as well as some adverse effects of human exploitation on animal populations. The position of the Virgin Islands between the Greater Antilles to the west and the Lesser Antilles to the southeast allows examination of the sources of influences on the economies of these island people. We will present the data from these two groups of islands separately and then discuss the results for the region.

Virgin Islands and Vieques

Faunal and botanical data from the small islands east of the Greater Antilles come from Vieques Island, politically now a part of the Commonwealth of Puerto Rico, and from St. Thomas, St. John, Tortola, Jost van Dyke, and St. Croix, all islands in the Virgin Islands group. Seed remains were recovered from the Tutu site on St. Thomas, from Trunk Bay, St. John, and from the Luján I site, Vieques; wood charcoal was identified from all three of these sites as well as from Aklis, St. Croix (Tables 7.3 and 7.4). Both vertebrate and invertebrate remains are analyzed from Luján, Tutu (early and late deposits), Trunk Bay, and Cinnamon Bay (Table 7.5; Tables C-1 and C-2). Vertebrate remains only are analyzed from Paraquita Bay on Tortola and Cape Wright on Jost van Dyke (Table 7.5; Table C-1). In combination, these data document the uses of biotic resources, both terrestrial and aquatic, by people living on these small islands during Saladoid and post-Saladoid times.

The plant assemblages from these primarily later Ceramic-age Ostionoid settlements provide evidence for the use of a more diverse array of economic taxa compared with the Archaic-age sites discussed above (Table 7.1). Among these are a definitive domesticate—maize (*Zea mays*)—and one or perhaps two additional garden taxa, guava (*Psidium guajava*) and cotton (cf. *Gossypium* sp.) (Table 7.4). The possible cotton seeds could derive from cultivars or native wild species; however, maize could not be a native wild species in the West Indies. In addition, Piperno (2002) identified plant opal phytoliths belonging to the family Cucurbitaceae, the pumpkin-gourd-squash family, in samples from Tutu. These have the potential to represent domesticated species of gourd, squash, or pumpkin, though they could also derive from any of several native wild taxa (Liogier and Martorell 2000:202–204). The maize kernel specimens from Tutu come exclusively from Chican Ostionoid deposits (A.D. 1140–1350) at the site, thus the later period of occupation (Newsom and Pearsall 2003; Pearsall 2002). Provisionally identified also are a few edible-fruit-bearing tree taxa that likewise could represent wild or maintained individuals (Table 7.3). As in the Lesser Antilles (Chapter 6) and Archaic-age deposits from this area, Sapotaceae (cf. *Sideroxylon* sp., mastic bully) seed remains are present at each of these sites. The weedy herbaceous taxa recorded for Tutu may be incidentally present or, perhaps with passion flower, also called parcha (*Passiflora* sp.) and panicoid grass, could represent food remains. Nonwood plant remains are lacking from the Aklis site.

Table 7.3. Seeds and other nonwood remains from Ceramic-age sites in the Virgin Islands and Vieques

Taxa			Islands/Sites			
Family/Form	Scientific Name	Common Name	St. Croix Aklis	St. John Trunk	St. Thomas Tutu	Vieques Luján
Garden/Conuco						
Malvaceae	cf. *Gossypium* sp.	cotton			X	
Myrtaceae	*Psidium guajava*	guava, guayaba		X	X	[X]
Poaceae	*Zea mays*	maize			X	
Tree Seed/Nuts						
Bombacaceae	cf. *Ceiba* sp.	silk cotton, ceiba		X		
Goodeniaceae	*Scaevola plumieri*	ink berry, bosborin		X		
Malpighiaceae	cf. *Byrsonima* sp.	paralejo			X	
Moraceae	cf. *Ficus* sp.	wild fig, jaguay			X	
cf. Rutaceae	cf. *Zanthoxylum* sp.	wild lime, espino rubial				X
Sapotaceae	cf. *Sideroxylon* sp.	mastic bully		X	X	X
Sapotaceae		sapodilla family				
Ulmaceae	*Celtis* sp.	cockspur		X		

Herbs/Grains

Family	Taxon	Common name				
Cheno-Amaranth	*Chenopodium/Amaranthus*	apazote	X			
Fabaceae		bean family	X			
Malvaceae	*Malvastrum* sp.	false mallow	X			
Passifloraceae	*Passiflora* sp.	passion flower, parcha	X			
Poaceae	*Paniceae, panicoid group*	panicoid grass	X			
Poaceae		grass family	X			X
Portulacaceae	*Portulaca* sp.	purslane	X			
Portulacaceae	*Talinum* sp.	verdolaguilla	X			
Solanaceae	*Solanum* sp.	nightshade	X			

Nonwood, Other

Family	Taxon	Common name				
Aracaceae		palm family (leaf, fiber)		X		
Bark/rind				X	X	
Parenchyma tissue		?: root/tuber		X	X	

Note: Values are site ubiquity or presence/absence.

Table 7.4. Wood identifications from Ceramic-age sites in the Virgin Islands and Vieques

Taxa			Islands/Sites			
Family	Scientific Name	Common Name	St. Croix Aklis 32/11	St. John Trunk 28/92	St. Thomas Tutu 100/409	Vieques Luján 144/684
# Samples/Wood NI						
Mangrove and Strand						
Chrysobalanaceae	cf. *Chrysobalanus* sp.	coco-plum			4	
Combretaceae	*Conocarpus erectus*	buttonbush, mangle botón		[X]		
Interior						
Anacardiaceae	cf. *Comocladia* sp.	poison ash, carrasco		X		
Bignoniaceae		bignonia family		[X]		
Bixaceae/Ebenaceae	cf. *Bixa orellana*, *Diospyros* sp.	achiote or guayabota				7
Boraginaceae	*Bourreria* sp.	strong bark, palo de vaca	[X]	X	6	6
Boraginaceae	*Cordia* sp., *C. laevigata*	capá colorado	X			2
Burseraceae	*Bursera simaruba*	gumbo-limbo, almácigo				
Capparaceae	*Capparis* sp.	caper tree, burro				2
Celastraceae	*Elaeodendron xylocarpum*	marble tree, aceituno			8	
Celastraceae	*Maytenus* sp.	mayten, cuero sapo, boje				13
Combretaceae	*Bucida* (*buceras*)	oxhorn bucida, ucar, bucaro				33
Euphorbiaceae	*Croton* sp.	pepper bush, adormidera	[X]	[X]	21	4
Euphorbiaceae	cf. *Savia* sp.	garrote			23	
Euphorbiaceae	cf. *Phyllanthus* sp.	sword-bush, bayoneta			2	
Fabaceae-Mimosoid	cf. *Acacia* or *Leucaena* sp.	acacia			73	
Fabaceae-Mimosoid	cf. *Inga* or *Pithecellobium*	guaba or cat's claw		[X]		
Fabaceae-Papilio	*Andira* (*inermis*)	bastard mahogany, moca				4

Family	Taxon	Common name				
Fabaceae-Papilio	*Piscida (cartbagenesis)*	fish poison, ventura	X		4	8
Hernandiaceae	cf. *Hernandia (sonora)*	mago, toporite	X			1
Lauraceae	cf. *Nectandra (coriacea)*	laurel avispillo				2
Myrtaceae	*Eugenia (confusa)*	stopper, grajo				13
Myrtaceae	*Psidium (guajava)*	guava, guayaba	X			
cf. Myrtaceae	*Psidium* sp. or *Eugenia* sp.	guava or stopper myrtle family	X		8	
Oleaceae	cf. *Forestiera* sp.	ink bush, hueso blanco				1
Rhamnaceae	*Krugiodendron (ferreum)*	black ironwood, baraico				2
Rubiaceae	*Exostema (caribaeum)*	quinine bark, albarillo				1
Rubiaceae	cf. *Randia (aculeata)*	nacte, tintillo				
Rutaceae	*Amyris (elemifera)*	torchwood, tea		[X]	2	1
Rutaceae	*Zanthoxylum* sp.	wild lime, espino rubial	X	[X]		1
Sapotaceae	*Chrysophyllum/Sideroxylon* wood anatomical group	caimito, mastic bully, tabloncillo	X			17
Sapotaceae	*Manilkara* sp. group	bulletwood, ausubo			[11]	24
Simaroubaceae	*Picramnia (pentandra)*	bitter bush, guarema				7
Sterculiaceae	*Sterculia (S. apetala)*	Panama tree, anacagüita				7
Zygophyllaceae	*Guaiacum* sp.	lignum-vitae, guayácan			19	

Note: Values are site ubiquity or presence/absence.

Table 7.5. Summary of the distribution of vertebrates and invertebrates in the primary habitats in which they are found in the Virgin Islands

Habitats	Islands/Sites						
	Vieques	St. Thomas		St. John		Tortola	Jost van Dyke
	Lujan	Tutu Early	Tutu Late	Trunk Bay	Cinnamon Bay	Paraquita Bay	Cape Wright
Vertebrates							
Land	15.6	5.8	10.6	3.4	4.8	16.1	5.1
Freshwater and shore	4	0.8	1.3	3.4	1.4	3.3	1
Shallow inshore	19.1	24	41.1	12.4	12.9	13.3	21.2
Reef	58.3	57.9	37.7	75.3	73.5	63.3	55.6
Pelagic	3	11.6	9.3	5.6	7.5	3.3	17.2
Sample size	199	121	151	178	147	30	99
Invertebrates							
Land–crabs	0.4	18.9	23.1	4.2	4.1		
Land–snails	6.4	72.7	16.3	0	0		
Rocky intertidal	26.9	7.3	43	74.4	72.7		
Shallow inshore	66.3	1.1	17.6	21.4	23.2		
Sample size	7301	465	221	379	267		

Note: Values are in minimum number of individuals (MNI) and expressed as percentages.

The wood types that are conspicuously present at sites from the Virgin Islands and Vieques are strong bark (*Bourreria* sp.), pepperbush (*Croton* sp.), and tree legumes (Fabaceae), including fish poison (Table 7.4). Species richness is relatively high for the Luján I assemblage, with 20 individual wood taxa identified. These are generally representative of dry coastal forest and mangrove habitats; however, Panama tree (*Sterculia* sp., cf. *S. apetala*) is an exotic. *Bucida* sp., ucar, a live oak–like tropical hardwood, was prominent among habitation areas at Luján. Rivera Calderón was able to identify a number of house structures at this site, and ucar seems to have been preferred for making the primary posts and structural supports for the buildings. This was an excellent choice, ucar being one of the heaviest, strongest, and densest of native woods. Moreover, ucar is durable in contact with the ground and resistant to attack by dry-wood termites (Little and Wadsworth 1964:388). Wood use at the Tutu site appears to have placed heavy emphasis on an acacia-like tree legume (73% ubiquity) (Table 7.4). Lignum-vitae, so conspicuous among the wood taxa recorded from the Lesser Antilles sites and the southern Caribbean Islands, was only identified from Tutu (19% ubiquity) in the Virgin Islands/Vieques archaeobotanical assemblages.

Vertebrate remains from the Virgin Islands and Vieques can be grouped according to the habitat in which they are usually found. These categories are terrestrial, freshwater, and shore, shallow inshore waters, coral reefs, and pelagic (Table 7.5). The terrestrial animals include native birds like pigeons (Columbidae) and introduced mammals that were either domesticated (dogs [*Canis familiaris*] and guinea pig [*Cavia porcellus*]) or almost certainly tame and managed (hutía [*Isolobodon portoricensis*]) (Figures 7.2 and 7.3). The freshwater and shore animals include birds that live and nest along the shore, and freshwater turtles (*Trachemys* sp.). The shallow inshore waters group includes most of the same fishes found in this habitat in the Lesser Antilles. The primary difference is that more estuarine species were used, such as tarpon (Elopidae) and mullet (*Mugil* sp.). The coral reefs and pelagic species encountered at sites in the Virgin Islands are virtually the same as those from the Lesser Antilles. As in the Lesser Antilles, animals typically found in coral reef habitats contribute the greatest numbers of individuals (MNI) to the samples. In collections from Vieques and the Virgin Islands, coral reef fishes contribute more than 58% of the vertebrate individuals. Pelagic species are those that swim in the surface water, often in schools; some may come close to the shore. Others typically stay offshore. Pelagic species encountered at these sites are herrings (Clupeidae), flyingfishes (Exocoetidae), needlefishes (Belonidae), and tuna (Scombridae), especially little tunny (*Euthynnus alletteratus*).

In many respects the vertebrate faunal assemblages from Vieques and the Virgin Islands are similar to those from the Lesser Antilles; however, they differ

Figure 7.2. Guinea pig, *Cavia porcellus* Erxlaben, 1777, was domesticated in the Peruvian Andes and introduced into the West Indies during the Ceramic age. Its distribution is spotty and includes sites in the southern Caribbean region, the Lesser and Greater Antilles, and the Virgin Islands. (From National Academy of Sciences 1991:240)

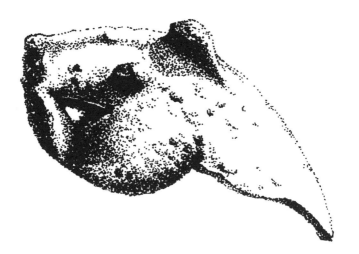

Figure 7.3. A sculptured clay head is almost certainly a hutía, *Isolobodon portoricensis*. The image was made available by Yvonne Narganes and has the provenience Sorcé, Vieques, Centro de Investigaciones Arqueológicas, Universidad de Puerto Rico. The head was part of a Saladoid vessel oriented so that when the vessel is right side up, the animal is on its back. (Figure based on a photograph by Molly Wing-Berman)

in some important ways. The most important introduced animal identified from Vieques and the Virgin Islands is the hutía. It is believed to be native to Hispaniola and introduced by people into Puerto Rico and islands immediately to the east (Wing 1993). It has never been found in Lesser Antillean sites. Similarly the agouti (*Dasyprocta leporina*), common in the Lesser Antilles, is not present in the Virgin Islands. An agouti was tentatively identified from the Sorcé site on Vieques Island, but the specimen has been lost and its identity cannot be verified. Other introduced animals found in the Virgin Islands and absent or rare in the Lesser Antilles are the shrew, *Nesophontes edithae*, and the pond turtle, *Trachemys* sp. Pond turtles occur abundantly in the early historic site of Puerto Real on Haiti and occasionally at other Greater Antillean and Virgin Islands sites. Although abundant remains of pond turtle were identified from Puerto Real, their remains are virtually absent from the late pre-Columbian site at En Bas Saline located nearby (Reitz and McEwan 1995). This would suggest some aversion to pond turtles by the Taino at En Bas Saline. A single pond turtle carapace specimen was found at the Spring Bay site on Saba (Wing 1996). The later occupation on Saba has other cultural ties to the Greater Antilles confirmed by the fragment of turtle shell. Otherwise this distribution of land and freshwater animals, aside from the fully domestic ones, has a clear boundary between the islands to the south and those to the west of the Anegada Passage.

No such geographic demarcation is seen in the distribution of domestic animals (Wing 1993). Dogs are the most abundant domestic animal in the Caribbean and are generally found in burial contexts, or their teeth are modified for ornaments often associated with human burials. Dog remains that do not come from burial contexts usually are not sufficiently complete to reveal characteristics of size, morphology, and abnormalities. A large sample of dogs came from the early Ceramic-age Sorcé site on Vieques Island (Wing 1991b). These dogs, as do many others in the West Indies, exhibit modification of the lower dentition. Thirty percent of the mandibles from Sorcé are missing the crown of the lower fourth premolar. In many cases the root of the premolar is still in the jaw and bone has grown over the alveolus, indicating that the tooth was not congenitally missing. The dogs of the West Indies exhibit a number of congenital abnormalities in the dentition, such as the absence of the first premolar and the last molar in the lower jaw. This is different from the fourth premolar that was clearly intentionally broken out. West Indian dogs are uniformly small. The similarities that can be seen in the dogs of the West Indies may be the result of a small founder population that subsequently interbred.

The other domestic animal is the guinea pig (*Cavia porcellus*). Its distribution does not follow any clear geographic pattern. These animals are typically associated with late prehistoric deposits. Guinea pig remains are found in

Puerto Rico, Vieques, and the Virgin Islands in addition to those reported from deposits on Antigua and Curaçao (Chapters 5 and 6). Introduction of both domestic animals was probably from northern South America.

Coral reefs were the source of the most vertebrates for the inhabitants of the small islands between Puerto Rico and the Lesser Antilles (Table 7.5). More than 50% of the individuals (MNI) in the Virgin Islands samples are species typically found in coral reef habitats, except in the late deposit from Tutu. The contribution of coral reef fishes is even higher, 83%, in the Archaic deposit from Krum Bay, St. Thomas (Table 7.2a). Most of the species associated with reefs tend to be territorial and include predatory fishes such as grouper (Serranidae), snapper (Lutjanidae), and grunts (Haemulidae) as well as fishes lower in the food chain such as parrotfishes (Scaridae) and surgeonfishes (Acanthuridae). The same significant trend is seen in the Virgin Islands as was found in the Lesser Antilles (Wing 2001a; Wing and Wing 2001). Successive deposits at the Tutu Archaeological Village are compared to examine changes in animal uses through time. These deposits are called early (context 2044N1837E), with a date of 1380 B.P., and late (context 2036N1842E), with a date of 560 B.P., in text and tables. The changes that were observed in these successive deposits include decreased size of reef fishes as indicated by measurements of the vertebral centra and a shift in reef species composition to relatively fewer predatory fishes in the later deposits (Tables 7.6a and 7.6b). This decline in reef fishes can be measured by the decrease in their estimated biomass, relative abundance of individuals (MNI), or mean trophic level. A comparison of the early and late deposits from Tutu also shows the decrease in relative abundance of reef fishes and a corresponding increase in species caught in shallow inshore waters, such as herrings (Clupeidae) (Table 7.5). As in the Lesser Antilles, these changes in the reef fauna through time are attributable to overfishing pressures (see Chapter 6 and Wing and Wing 2001). In the Lesser Antilles the decline in reef fishes is associated with a change in the fishing strategy toward more offshore fishing for tuna (Scombridae Thunnini) and large jacks (Carangidae, i.e., *Caranx latus*).

Aside from the changes, the complex of species obtained from the major habitats is very stable. For example, Trunk Bay and Cinnamon Bay are located side by side on the northern coast of St. John. They both have surprisingly similar distributions of both vertebrates and invertebrates grouped by habitats (Table 7.5). Luján (Vieques Island) and Paraquita Bay (Tortola), both located on south-facing bays, show reliance on very similar complexes of habitats based on the groupings of MNI of species by the habitat in which they are usually found. This would suggest similar exploitation strategies practiced on islands in the same general Virgin Islands ecosystem.

Table 7.6a. A comparison of the sizes of selected animals from the early (N2044 E1837, level I) and late (N2036 E1842, level B) deposits at Tutu

Site/Taxa	Saladoid				Post-Saladoid			
	#	x	Range	Weight	#	x	Range	Weight
Tutu								
Herring	59	1.8	1.1–2.4	33.0	38	1.6	1.3–3.2	24.5
Jack	254	4.97	2.6–10.3	430.3	25	5.4	1.8–12.4	530.8
Grouper	37	7.3	1.6–21.6	1138.2	16	3.2	2.0–8.2	141.3
Snapper	35	4.7	1.1–21.8	373.6	18	2.96	1.3–5.6	116.0
Parrotfish	21	5.3	2.3–8.9	506.3	53	2.5	1.3–4.9	75.7
Indeterminate fish	314	3.7	1.3–11.7	204.0	313	2.6	1.0–8.9	83.5
Crab	139	10.8	7.5–13.5	258.0	21	8.5	4.2–10.7	166.0
					Tutu			
Main St. Topsnail	44	80.6	30.3–96.5	109.5	7	45.8	30.5–61.7	36.8

Source: Wing, deFrance, and Kozuch 2002.

Note: All fish measurements are the widths of the vertebral centrum, land crab measurements are the height of the mandible, and topsnail measurements are the height of the aperture. These measurements are in mm. Symbols: # is number of specimens measured, x is the mean measurement, range is the smallest and the largest measurement, weight is the estimated weight (gms) of an animal with the mean measurement using the allometric constants presented in Chapter 4 (Table 4.2).

Table 7.6b. Distribution of vertebrate taxa grouped according to the niche in which they typically belong and the estimated biomass of reef fishes compared with inshore and pelagic taxa

Tutu	Early Deposit				Late Deposit			
General Niche	MNI	%	Estimated Biomass	%	MNI	%	Estimated Biomass	%
Terrestrial	7	5.8			16	10.6		
Freshwater/Shore	1	0.8			2	1.3		
Reef Carnivores	51	42.2			25	16.6		
Reef Herbivores	19	15.7			32	21.2		
Total Reef	70	57.9	65831	85	57	37.7	6274	31
Inshore/Pelagic	43	35.5	11645	15	76	50.3	14049	69
Total	121				151			

Source: Wing, deFrance, and Kozuch 2002
Note: The data are from the early and late deposits at Tutu presented in Table C.1.

Invertebrates are grouped as terrestrial crustaceans, terrestrial molluscs, rocky intertidal, and shallow inshore species that might be found on sandy or muddy bottoms, among sea grass, or attached to rocks or roots (Table 7.5). Terrestrial crustaceans are land crabs (Gecarcinidae) and land hermit crabs (Coenobitidae), and of these the land crabs are particularly abundant in Saladoid-period sites. The terrestrial molluscs include some species that could have been eaten, but most of the species in this category are very small commensal species. Commensal species are attracted to refuse discarded by people. Abundant small snails may indicate that the deposit accumulated slowly (Wing et al. 2002). Small land snails may also have been transported inadvertently from island to island with vegetation, thereby extending their distribution. Because these commensal animals are typically incidental to the sample and do not contribute to the diet, they are not quantified in the summary table even though they may have implications for site formation processes and biogeography.

The distribution of individual animals in the three other groups—terrestrial crustaceans, shallow inshore, and rocky intertidal—varies according to the cultural context and environmental conditions near the site (Table 7.5). The early deposits at Tutu demonstrate the intensive use of land crabs during the Saladoid occupation. The decline in abundance of land crabs and their decrease in size is probably the result of overexploitation. This decline is followed by an increase in snails gathered from the rocky intertidal zone. The West Indian topsnail (*Cittarium pica*) predominates among those intertidal animals. Although the West Indian topsnail increases in abundance, the individuals in the later deposit are on the average smaller than those in the early deposit. These population changes in crabs and topsnails are indications of the pressure on local resources.

All pairs of deposits do not show changes in the faunas attributable to over-exploitation as great as was documented at Tutu. Both the vertebrates and the distribution of invertebrates from Trunk Bay and Cinnamon Bay are virtually the same. This is true even though the Trunk Bay site was occupied earlier than the Cinnamon Bay site and Trunk Bay is considered an occupation site, a general settlement, whereas Cinnamon Bay is thought to be a civic-ceremonial center where important ritual and communal activities were performed and where some segments of the society (i.e., elites) may have lived (Wild 2001). The critical factor that is not known is the size of the human population at each site. Currently archaeobotanical samples from Cinnamon Bay are being analyzed (Newsom, laboratory data), and we will be interested to see how the resulting data compare with those from Trunk Bay and other sites.

The complex of invertebrates from Luján differs from that in the other small-island sites in the Virgin Islands (Table 7.5). In the deposits from Luján, the inshore habitats predominate based on the great abundance of tree oysters (*Isognomon alatus*) and Caribbean oysters (*Crassostrea rhizophora*) and secondly of lucine clams (Lucinidae). Both of the oysters can be found attached to the roots of mangroves that may have been in the area where shellfish gathering focused. In addition to lucine clams and oysters, one midden at Luján, midden B, has a very large number (326 MNI) of coquina (*Donax denticulatum*), whereas the other middens at the same site have few or none. The assumption is that the middens are contemporaneous; if that is so, some form of fishing rights may have regulated the gathering of coquina.

Procuring useful plants, wood, vertebrates, and invertebrates posed different challenges to Native Americans living in the smaller of the Caribbean islands. Local environmental conditions play a major role in determining the presence or absence of a particular complex of species. For example, in the Caribbean the coastal zone promotes the growth of mangroves (*Avicennia germinenans, Laguncularia racemosa, Rhizophora mangle*), sea grape (*Coccoloba uvifera*), and buttonwood (*Conocarpus erectus*), whereas the rocky intertidal zone is inhabited by topsnails (*Cittarium pica*), nerites (Neritidae), limpets (Fissurellidae and Acmaeidae), and chitons (Chitonidae). Plants and invertebrates are similar in having to be found, but once located they are usually readily taken. Capture of vertebrates poses a more complex problem because most have to be caught with some equipment, even if it is rudimentary. Some sort of fishing equipment must be used to catch fishes. Perhaps the simplest is adding fish poisons derived from the shredded bark of fish poison (*Piscida carthagenensis*) and a few other trees to shallow, enclosed water and gathering up the stupefied fish. The type of fishing equipment imposes a filter on the array of species caught, and then people choose what to consume among the species in the catch. These differences may account for the relative diversity of plants and invertebrates in the deposits and the greater uniformity among the vertebrates represented in the samples.

Rare species in the past environment may have been actively sought and appear to have been more common in the past than today. For example, parrots have had enduring appeal for their bright plumage and their social behavior. In the past they may have been selectively caught. This exploitation would have endangered the viability of their populations, resulting in extinction and extirpation of many taxa (Pregill et al. 1994). The presence of rare species is also a function of sample size; the larger the sample, the greater the chance of finding rare species.

Greater Antilles

Our main source of data on plants and animals excavated from archaeological sites in the Greater Antilles is Puerto Rico, with some information from Hispaniola and Jamaica (Table 4.1). Unfortunately, we have no comparable data from Cuba; however, we allude to relevant identifications and limited analyses from that island. Puerto Rico is the smallest (8,865 km^2) of the four Greater Antillean Islands and has the lowest elevation (1,338 m). As would be predicted, Puerto Rico has the fewest endemic land mammals; most of these are bats (Woods 1989:789). Cuba and Hispaniola have the largest landmasses, the most complex topography, and the greatest habitat diversity; consequently, they host the greatest number of taxa among many classes of animals such as mammals (Woods 1989:789) and freshwater fishes (Burgess and Franz 1989: 276). The larger islands also have bigger rivers and estuaries, providing habitats for more abundant estuarine fishes and molluscs. The diverse ecological zones reflecting varied soil fertility and rainfall promote the rich native vegetation of the Greater Antilles. Even though Puerto Rico is not the largest of the Greater Antilles, it is many magnitudes larger than any of the Lesser Antilles or Virgin Islands. This size difference permits examination of traditions of human exploitation honed on small islands and transferred to the larger island with its greater, more diverse resource potentials.

Macrobotanical evidence from Puerto Rico and Hispaniola derives for the most part from later Ostionoid deposits, though it includes some Saladoid materials (Table 4.1). The evidence demonstrates the use of many different wild plants and the cultivation of fruit trees and crops (Tables 7.7 and 7.8).

The list of trees possibly associated with home gardens is much richer and more definitive than was evident in the areas discussed previously. Among the trees that produce edible fruits and other useful products are soursop (*Annona* sp.), papaya (*Carica papaya*), guava (*Psidium guajava*), and several Sapotaceae as indicated by seed and wood remains (*Bumelia* sp., lechecillo; *Chrysophyllum/ Sideroxylon* group, star apple or caimito, mastic bully; *Manilkara* group, ausubo, níspero; *Pouteria* sp., jácana, almendrón). Genip or quenepa (cf. *Melicocca bijugata*) and sea grape (*Coccoloba uvifera*) also produce edible fruit. Panama tree (*Sterculia* [*apetala*]) is a member of the chocolate family, Sterculiaceae, which has seeds that are edible when ground; they can also be made into a beverage and when roasted are said to taste like peanuts (Little and Wadsworth 1964:340; Martin et al. 1987:122). Guaba (*Inga* sp.) has edible pods, and maví (cf. *Colubrina* sp.) and guácima (*Guazuma ulmifolia*) are used to make fermented beverages. Achiote (*Bixa orellana*) and jagua (cf. *Genipa americana*) are the sources of a red dye and a black dye, respectively, and calabash or higüera (*Cresentia cujete*) produces gourdlike container fruits. Palms are multipurpose plants providing in some cases edible fruit, but also wood, thatch, and fiber for cordage and other purposes. Finally, the seeds of cojóbana (cf. *Anadenanthera* sp.) are the source of a narcotic snuff.

This mention requires clarification: the genus *Anadenanthera* and the closely related *Piptadenia* have been at times or in various regions treated as the same (i.e., subsumed under the same name [e.g., *Piptadenia peregrina*]), creating some confusion in the literature. The two genera are not distinguishable based on wood anatomy; thus either genus, that is, the tree source of the narcotic snuff or its close relative, in theory may be the true identification for the archaeological wood remains. However, it is important to note that only *Anadenanthera peregrina* is recorded for the flora of Puerto Rico (see Liogier and Martorell 2000:69), whereas *Piptadenia* spp. are absent. This suggests that the true identity of the wood is in fact *Anadenanthera peregrina* or cojóbana, also known as cojobilla or cojoba.

Among those just indicated are several trees—including papaya, genip, achiote, Panama tree, and possibly also jagua—that definitively or very likely represent introductions from outside the region. Genip and achiote are native to lowland South America (Liogier and Martorell 2000:111, 127; Record and Hess 1943:89, 491). Jagua may likewise derive from that region: "the tree occurs sparingly in the virgin forest of eastern Brazil, rarely averaging more than one per acre, but is abundant in and about towns and villages, since it is planted as a shade tree or comes up spontaneously and is protected because of its fruit. The fruit, which is about 2 inches in diameter, has a leathery shell enclosing a dark pulp that is edible though not very palatable. The juice, transparent at

Table 7.7. Seeds and other nonwood remains from Ceramic-age sites in the Greater Antilles

Taxa			Islands/Sites								
Family/Form	Scientific Name	Common Name	Puerto Rico, North				Puerto Rico, South				Haiti
			Barrazas	Maisabel	NCS-1	NCS-4	Bronce	Fresal	PO-38	Tibes	EBS
Garden/Conuco											
Convolvulaceae	cf. *Ipomoea batatas*	sweet potato, batatas									X
Euphorbiaceae	*Manihot esculenta*	manioc, yuca									41
Onagraceae	*Oenothera* sp.	evening primrose			20	X		X	X	2	24
Poaceae	*Zea mays*	maize									34
Solanaceae	*Capsicum* (*annuum*)	pepper, pimiento, ají									7
Cultivated Trees											
Annonaceae	*Annona* sp.	soursop, guanábana	12		4					[1]	[3]
Bignoniaceae	*Cresentia cujete*	calabash, higüera	[4]		8						
Bixaceae	*Bixa orellana*	anatto, achiote			4						
Caricaceae	*Carica papaya*	papaya, lechosa							X		

Family	Taxon	Common name	[4]	[28]	[8]			[7]
Malpighiaceae	*Malpighia* sp.	W.I. cherry, acerola						[7]
Myrtaceae	*Psidium guajava*	guava, guayaba						[7]
Sapotaceae		sapodilla family			20	X		
Other Trees								
Araceaceae	cf. *Acrocomia media*	spiny palm, corozo			12	X	X	3
Fabaceae-Mimosoid		bean family, mimosoid group						17
Malpighiaceae	cf. *Byrsonima* sp.	candle berry, paralejo, nance					6	
cf. Myrtaceae		myrtle family						3
Herbs/Grains								
Aizoaceae	*Trianthema portulacastrum*	trianthema, verdolaga		5	8	X		27
Cactaceae	cf. *Opuntia* sp.	prickly pear, tuna						4
Capparaceae	cf. *Cleome* sp.	spider flower					X	
Chenopodiaceae		goosefoot family, apazote			4	X	X X	17

Continued on the next page

Table 7.7. Continued

	Taxa			Islands/Sites								
				Puerto Rico, North				Puerto Rico, South				Haiti
Family/Form	Scientific Name	Common Name	Barrazas	Maisabel	NCS-1	NCS-4	Bronce	Fresal	PO-38	Tibes	EBS
Convolvulaceae		morning glory family					X				
Euphorbiaceae		spurge family			4						
Fabaceae	cf. *Desmodium* sp.	bean family (wild)			8	X	X				
Fabaceae	cf. *Vigna* sp.	bean family (wild)			4						
Hypoxidaceae	*Hypoxis* sp.	star grass, coquí	54		4	X		X	X		3
cf. Labiatae	cf. *Ocimum* sp.	wild basil, albahaca			4						
Malvaceae	*Malvastrum* sp.	false mallow					X				
Malvaceae	*Malva/Sida* type	mallow family herbs	8								3
Passifloraceae	*Passiflora* sp.	passion flower, parcha			4			X			
Poaceae	*Paniceae*, panicoid group	grass family, panicoid group	[4]		8						10
Poaceae	(NCS-1 grass morph 2)	grass			4						

									[3]
Poaceae	(NCS-1 grass morph 3)	grass				4			
Poaceae		grass family						X	17
Portulacaceae	*Portulaca* sp.	purslane, verdolaga						X	
Rosaceae	*Rubus* sp.	wild raspberry, fresa de montaña					X		
Solanaceae	*Solanum* sp.	nightshade, yerba mora				12			3
Nonwood, Other									
Arecaceae		palm family (frond, fiber)	5	X		4			
Bark/rind				X	3	16			
Stem/vine			X			X	X		
Root/tuber/parenchyma				X	5	X			

Note: Values are site ubiquity or presence/absence.

Table 7.8. Wood identifications from Ceramic-age sites in the Greater Antilles

	Taxa	
Family	Scientific Name	Common Name

Samples/Wood NI

Mangrove and Strand

Combretaceae	*Conocarpus erectus*	buttonwood, botoncillo
Polygonaceae	*Coccoloba uvifera*	sea grape, uva de playa
Rhizophoraceae	*Rhizophora mangle*	red mangrove, mangle colorado
Simaroubiaceae	cf. *Suriana maritima*	bay cedar, guitarán
Verbenaceae	*Avicennia germinans*	black mangrove, mangle negro

Interior

Anacardiaceae	cf. *Comocladia* sp.	poison ash, carrasco
Anacard/ Lauraceae	*Metopium* sp. or *Ocotea* sp.	poisonwood or laurel
Annonaceae	*Annona* sp.	soursop, guanabana, relatives
Annonaceae	cf. *Oxandra* sp.	lancewood
cf. Apocynaceae		dogbane family
Aracaceae		palm family
Bignoniaceae	*Tecoma stans*	roble amarillo
Bignoniaceae	*Tabebuia* sp.	white cedar, roble
Bignoniaceae	*Cresentia* sp. or *Tabebuia* sp.	calabash tree or roble
Bignoniaceae		bignonia family
Boraginaceae	*Bourreria* sp.	strong bark, palo de vaca
Boraginaceae	*Cordia* sp., *C. alba*	capá, capá blanco
Boraginaceae		borage family
Burseraceae	*Bursera simaruba*	gumbo-limbo, almácigo
Capparaceae	*Capparis* sp.	caper tree, burro, sapo
Celastraceae	*Elaeodendron xylocarpum**	marble-tree, aceituno
Celastraceae	*Gyminda** or *Crossopetalum* sp.	mala mujer, maravédi
Celastraceae	*Maytenus* sp. or *Torralbasia* sp.	mayten or boje
Celastraceae	*Maytenus* sp.	mayten, cuero de sapo

Islands/Sites								
Puerto Rico, North				Puerto Rico, South				Haiti
Barrazas 89/308	Maisabel 45/290	NCS-1 40/53	NCS-4 30/99	Bronce 90/1340	Fresal 05/60	PO-38 35/67	Tibes 255/368	EBS 106/1296
				[70]				67
				32		[12]		
								57
							50	
								81
			12					
								5
				2				
			6					
14								
		4		2				33
				12				
		16						
			53	28				
	6							
			18				62	
							25	
				12				
14								
				32				
	6							
							12	
							25	
							[25]	

Continued on the next page

Table 7.8. *Continued*

Taxa		
Family	Scientific Name	Common Name

Samples/Wood NI

Combretaceae	*Bucida (buceras)*	oxhorn bucida, ucar, bucaro
Erythroxylaceae	*Erythroxylum* sp.	false cocaine, cocaína falsa
Euphorbiaceae	*Croton* sp.	pepper bush, adormidera
Euphorbiaceae	*Gymnanthes (lucida)*	oysterwood, yaití, tabaco
Euphorbiaceae	*Hura crepitans*	sandbox, javilla
Euphorbiaceae	*Jatrophia* sp.	tártago emético
Euphorbiaceae or Rubiaceae	cf. *Hyeronima* sp. or *Genipa americana*	cedro macho or jagua
Fabaceae-Mimosoid	cf. *Inga* or *Pithecellobium*	guaba or uña de gato
Fabaceae-Mimosoid	cf. *Anadenanthera* sp.*	cojobilla, cojoba
Fabaceae-Papilionoid	*Andira (inermis)*	bastard mahogany, moca
Fabaceae-Papilionoid	cf. *Andiria* sp. or *Lonchocarpus*	moca or palo hediondo
Fabaceae-Papilionoid	cf. *Lonchocarpus* sp.	palo hediondo, genogeno
cf. Fabaceae		bean family (tree legume)
Lauraceae	cf. *Aniba* sp., *Licaria* sp., *Ocotea* sp.	canelillo, canelón, aguacatillo
cf. Malpighiaceae	cf. *Byrsonima* sp.	candle berry, paralejo, nance
Malvaceae	cf. *Abutilon* sp. or *Hibiscus* sp.	mallow family
Malvaceae	*Thespesia [syn. Montezuma]* sp.	maga
cf. Melasto-mataceae	cf. *Mouriri* sp.	caimitillo
cf. Meliaceae	cf. *Trichilia* sp.	mariaco, guayabacón
Moraceae	*Ficus* sp.	wild fig, jagüey, jagüello
Myrsinaceae	*Ardisia* sp.	bádula, mameyuelo
Myrtaceae	cf. *Eugenia* sp.	stopper, grajo
Myrtaceae	*Psidium* sp. or *Eugenia* sp.	guava or stopper
Pinaceae	*Pinus* sp., *sect. Diploxylon*	pine, hard pine anatomical group

Islands/Sites								
Puerto Rico, North				Puerto Rico, South				Haiti
Barrazas 89/308	Maisabel 45/290	NCS-1 40/53	NCS-4 30/99	Bronce 90/1340	Fresal 05/60	PO-38 35/67	Tibes 255/368	EBS 106/1296
							37	
				2				
[7]				70				
[7]							12	
								14
							12	
7								
42	6	4				16	37	24
							62	
				[4]			37	
21								
7								
				9				
							62	5
							37	
7								
	25	24					25	
							12	
							25	
	[6]		6		[X]		12	
							12	9
	[6]							9
								19

Continued on the next page

Table 7.8. *Continued*

Taxa		
Family	Scientific Name	Common Name

Samples/Wood NI

Family	Scientific Name	Common Name
Rhamnaceae	cf. *Colubrina* sp.	snake-bark, mabí, maví
Rhizophoraceae	cf. *Cassipourea guianensis*	palo de toro
Rubiaceae	*Exostema (caribaeum)*	quinine bark, albarillo
Rubiaceae	cf. *Randia (aculeata)*	randia, nacte, tintillo, uvillo
Rubiaceae	cf. *Genipa americana*	jagua
cf. Rubiaceae		madder family
Rutaceae	*Amyris (elemifera)*	torchwood, tea
Rutaceae	*Zanthoxylum* sp., type 1	satinwood type, acetillo
Rutaceae	*Zanthoxylum* sp., type 2	wild lime type, espino rubial
Rutaceae		citrus family
Sapindaceae	cf. *Melicoccus bijugatus*	genip, quenepa
Sapotaceae	cf. *Bumelia* sp.	lechecillo
Sapotaceae	*Chrysophyllum/Sideroxylon* anatomical group, form 1	star apple, caimito, mastic bully, tabloncillo anatomical group
Sapotaceae	*Chrysophyllum/Sideroxylon* anatomical group, form 2	star apple, caimito, mastic bully, tabloncillo anatomical group
Sapotaceae	*Manilkara* sp. group	bulletwood, ausubo, níspero
Sapotaceae	*Pouteria* sp.	bully-tree, jácana, almendrón
Sapotaceae		sapodilla family
Sterculiaceae	*Guazuma ulmifolia*	guácima
Sterculiaceae	*Sterculia (S. apetala)*	Panama tree, anacagüita
Ulmaceae	cf. *Trema* sp.	guacimilla
cf. Vitaceae	cf. *Cissus* sp.	bejuco de gongolí
Zygophyllaceae	*Guaiacum* sp.	lignum-vitae, guayacán

*Elaeodendron xylocarpum synonym *Cassine xylocarpa*; *Gyminda* synonyms *Myginda*, *Rhacoma*;
Note: Values are site ubiquity or presence/absence.

Islands/Sites								
Puerto Rico, North				Puerto Rico, South				Haiti
Barrazas 89/308	Maisabel 45/290	NCS-1 40/53	NCS-4 30/99	Bronce 90/1340	Fresal 05/60	PO-38 35/67	Tibes 255/368	EBS 106/1296
								19
								5
				30				
							25	
								9
							12	
							[12]	
								[14]
							[25]	[5]
			12					
								9
								9
			29				75	24
							12	
24			6					9
	56				[X]			
					[X]	25		
[57]							25	[5]
	6							
	7							
							25	
				9			12	

Anadenanthera synonym *Piptadenia* [in some cases].

first, soon turns black and leaves an indelible stain on everything it touches" (Record and Hess 1943:464–465). Panama tree is also considered to be native to northern South America (Liogier and Martorell 2000:123; Little and Wadsworth 1964:340); the archaeological record is based on wood remains from a Saladoid context at Maisabel and also from the Luján I site on Vieques, mentioned above. The center of origin for the genus *Carica* (papaya) is generally thought to be Central America (Rehm and Espig 1991); however, Prance (1984:92) argues for an Andean origin. Wild species of *Carica* are not known from Puerto Rico, the island from which the archaeological material derives (El Parking site [Table 7.8]). However, one species is recorded for Jamaica, *C. jamaicensis* (Urb.) (Adams 1972), but it is important to note that this species may now be subsumed under species *C. papaya*, as is the original *C. portoricensis* (Liogier and Martorell 1982:115), that is, what were once thought to be native wild species of the genus *Carica* are now considered instead to represent feral *C. papaya*. Perhaps another species once occurred on Puerto Rico and is now extinct, but it is perhaps more likely that this identification represents a human introduction of non-native *Carica papaya* into the Caribbean. Moreover, papaya pollen was identified from the Sanate site in the Dominican Republic, possibly dating to about A.D. 1050 (Fortuna 1978; García Arévalo and Tavares 1978:32–35). These various tree taxa were evidently introduced during the Ceramic age and then maintained for the products they provide. The presence also among these sites of certain herbaceous plants such as pepper and evening primrose suggests that Caribbean home gardens were diverse with multiple strata incorporating herbs, vines, shrubs, and trees.

Food crops and staples were also introduced into the Greater Antilles or developed there. These include the important tropical food staples, manioc (*Manihot esculenta*) and maize (*Zea mays*), based on tuber specimens, cob fragments, and kernels from En Bas Saline, Haiti. Manioc pollen is reported from the Manoguayabo site near Santo Domingo in the Dominican Republic (Nadal et al. 1991), also associated with the relatively late Chicoid ceramics (ca. A.D. 1200–1500 [Rouse 1992:107]). In addition, another type of root crop, sweet potato (cf. *Ipomoea batatas*), may be among the preserved tuber remains from En Bas Saline (Table 7.7). Microbotanical data from a sediment core sample dating to after cal. A.D. 410 from a pond adjacent to the Maisabel site potentially represent additional evidence for the presence of sweet potato prehistorically in the Caribbean based on pollen grains that compare favorably with the genus (Newsom and Pearsall 2003). However, alternatively the pollen of native wild *Ipomoea* spp., of which there are several (Liogier and Martorell 2000:163–165), may account for the grains. Phytoliths from the sediment core likewise may suggest the presence of two additional gathered or perhaps cultivated root crops, given specimens classified to the family Marantaceae and to the genus

Canna sp. (Newsom and Pearsall 2003). Again, though possibly deriving from introduced cultivars, several native wild species, including endemic *Canna pertusa* and various members of the Marantaceae that occur in wet areas (Liogier and Martorell 2000:252), may have produced the plant crystals; some of these wild taxa, however, may include edible species. Under any circumstance, the broken sherds of ceramic griddles, used to prepare manioc bread, are common indicators throughout the West Indies of the cultivation and consumption at least of root crops, manioc in particular, in the absence of the plant remains themselves. The manioc tuber fragments (Figure 7.4) from the En Bas Saline site on the northern coast of Haiti (41% ubiquity [Table 7.7]) are the first to actually be recovered from Caribbean archaeological deposits. Plant macroremains of maize have only been identified at sites in the Greater Antilles and Virgin Islands, including the very fragmentary kernel specimens from the Tutu site on St. Thomas, mentioned above, and several kernels and a cob fragment from En Bas Saline (Newsom and Deagan 1994). The En Bas Saline kernels are intact and well preserved and clearly represent two races of maize: one is a popcorn and the other a flour-type maize (Figure 7.5). The former possibly represents the race "Chandelle" and the latter the maize known as Early Caribbean (Bretting et al. 1987; Brown 1953, 1960; Brown and Goodman 1977; Newsom 1993a; Newsom and Deagan 1994). Early Caribbean is thought to be a very old indigenous race, a "remnant of one of the earliest types introduced into Europe" (Brown 1953:161), and it is not closely related to any known maize in either Central or South America (Bretting et al. 1987). The overall ubiquity of maize is 34% at En Bas Saline. However, maize, along with seeds identified as pepper (*Capsicum* sp., e.g., chili, *Capsicum annuum*) and evening primrose (*Oenothera* sp.) (Figure 7.6), is primarily associated with high-status contexts at that site, specifically an elite structure (interpreted as the residence of the cacique) and two large pit features located in the center of the site, suggesting that these plants were valued apart from simply supplying food; that is, some special social significance may have been attached to them (special foods reserved for elites or that were integral to feasting and communal activities) (Newsom 1998a; Newsom and Deagan 1994).

According to Las Casas (Sauer 1966:57), three types of pepper were regularly used by the Taino Indians, two of which were domesticated; the third was evidently wild. One of the domesticates is described as having long, red, finger-shaped fruit (e.g., *C. annuum*) and the other had smaller round, cherry-like fruits and was more pungent (perhaps *C. chinensis*? [see Pickersgill 1984]). The wild pepper reportedly had small fruit but was not further described; it is possible that this was a related genus like *Physalis*, ground cherry, rather than *Capsicum*. The *Capsicum* seeds from En Bas Saline may represent any of these ethnohistorically mentioned types, but if either of the two former, then they

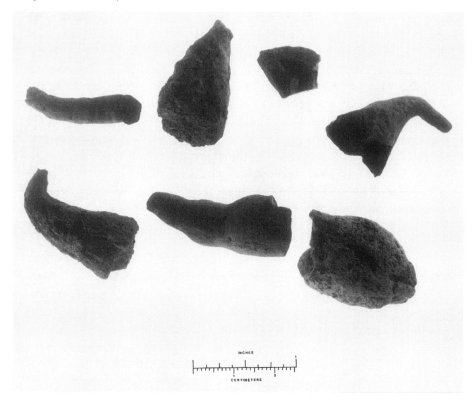

Figure 7.4. Carbonized remains of manioc (*Manihot esculenta* [Euphorbiaceae]) tubers from En Bas Saline, Haiti (lower right is from Field Sample 6317; otherwise specimens are from Field Sample 3746).

would also represent a plant introduction, the species deriving ultimately from Mexico and perhaps northern South America and cultivated widely in other mainland areas. The evening primrose may represent a plant used for ritual or medicinal purposes derived from the psychoactive properties of the seeds (Newsom 1993a, 1998a). It is intriguing that this taxon was identified from six of the nine Ceramic-age sites (Table 7.7), including Tibes and En Bas Saline, both of which were major civic-ceremonial centers. The seeds are ubiquitous (20% presence) at site NCS-1, another Ostionoid settlement in northern Puerto Rico, as at En Bas Saline. It is especially interesting to consider the presence of evening primrose, a mild narcotic, in conjunction with the possible cojóbana wood from Tibes (Table 7.8). Snuff made from ground cojóbana seeds was fundamental to Taíno cajoba ritualism (Alegría 1997a, 1997b). The

Figure 7.5. Carbonized maize (*Zea mays* [Poaceae]) kernels from En Bas Saline, Haiti, Field Sample 6316. Kernel morphology suggests two races of maize: popcorn (*left*), and a floury-endosperm type (*right*).

likely presence of the wood, particularly at a regional population center such as Tibes, may be an indication of trees grown at or near the site to facilitate the ritual activities that took place there. The Spanish chronicles mention a still unidentified herb that was also used for ritual purposes. Perhaps this was evening primrose. Particularly noteworthy is that the evening primrose genus, *Oenothera* sp., does not now occur in Puerto Rico or in Haiti. The modern distribution includes a limited area of the Dominican Republic and some isolated locations in Cuba (Henri Liogier, personal communication 1998; Liogier 1989:134–147; Sauget and Liogier 1957:62–70). This indicates either that the plant had a broader natural range in the past or that it was specifically maintained in Ceramic-age gardens outside that original range. This situation may be analogous to the introduction of hutías from Hispaniola to Puerto Rico during the Ceramic-age occupations of the region. The presence of evening primrose among the later Ceramic-age deposits is discussed in more detail below.

In addition to the important staple crops and other taxa mentioned above are several other plants that were probably food resources at the Ceramic-age settlements of the Greater Antilles. They include trianthema, goosefoot family (Chenopodiaceae), panicoid grass (Figures 7.7 and 7.8), and purslane. Only at

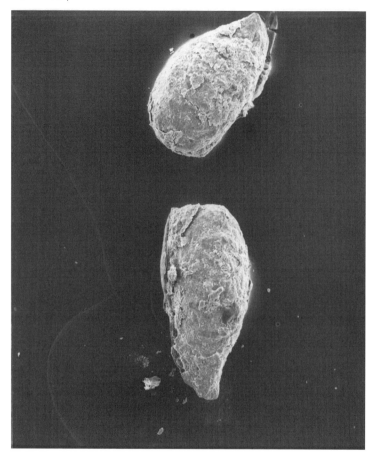

Figure 7.6. Evening primrose (*Oenothera* sp. [Onagraceae]) seeds from En Bas Saline, Haiti (Field Sample 7020) (65x).

En Bas Saline do any of these grains occur in frequencies and ubiquities that suggest more intensive use; however, this is difficult to judge considering the nature of use (ground seeds or entire plant consumed) and preservation factors. These finds are generally quite consistent with the plants recovered from sites in the Virgin Islands and Lesser Antilles discussed in previous sections. Star grass or coquí (*Hypoxis* sp.), however, is identified exclusively from the Greater Antilles sites and is prevalent among them (six sites and 54% ubiquity at Barrazas [Table 7.7]). Star grass may have been used for food or for its medicinal properties (Bailey and Bailey 1976:586; Moerman 1986:231). Some of these herbaceous plants may also represent taxa that were cultivated and fully integrated with the domiciles of the sites in a home garden setting that in-cluded herbs such as chilis and evening primrose, passion flower vines, and trees such as those indicated in preceding paragraphs; however, there are no indications from the seed morphologies of changes normally associated with domestication of small grains (i.e., the seed coat characteristics, sizes, and shapes are all consistent with those of wild species).

It is not a coincidence that many of the herbaceous taxa frequently encoun-tered among the sites are plants that typically grow in anthropogenic environ-ments. Successful gardening has to start with clearing before seeds can be sown and successfully grown or vegetative growth planted. Such gardening and other human activities expose the land for weedy species in a form of niche expansion; some species may eventually be used and further propagated, others collected casually or secondary to other activities. Vestiges of terraces can still be seen in some areas of Puerto Rico, suggesting intensification of plant pro-duction with a very organized system of agriculture (Oliver et al. 1999; Ortiz Aguilú et al. 1991; Petersen 1997). These terraces and other landscape changes created level land for planting. In general, the nonwood plant assemblages (Table 7.7) suggest a fairly focused reliance on plant foods from horticultural plots, gardens, and wild habitats, with perhaps greater emphasis on domesti-cated taxa later in the sequence, at least as represented by En Bas Saline, Haiti. The archaeological deposits at En Bas Saline date between about A.D. 1200 and the early contact period, thus reflecting the conditions prevalent at the time of European expansion. Unfortunately, not enough associated clear con-textual information or data were collected from the sites with both Saladoid and Ostionoid components (Table 4.1) to compare seed and other food remains between the earlier and later periods that might suggest any significant trends in plant use. At Tibes, however, both the evening primrose seeds and the cojóbana-type wood are associated with Ostionoid contexts, thus the period when the ball courts were in use and the site functioned as a chiefly center (Newsom and Curet 2000, 2003). Moreover, potentially very significant is that the area of the site where these plants have been recovered demonstrates the highest overall level of botanical species richness thus far documented for Tibes. This may signal the presence of high-status residence(s) or that unique activities occurred in the northern sector of the site, similar to the spatial dif-ferences in the presence of plant remains at En Bas Saline, Haiti. Additional excavation and research at Tibes may clarify whether this area was reserved for the cacique or other high-status individuals, or whether important ritual or communal activities took place at the site.

More than 60 types of wood have been identified from the Greater An-tilles sites (Table 7.8). Intensively used wood species at En Bas Saline, a coastal

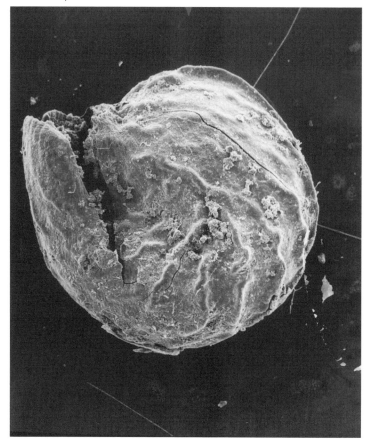

Figure 7.7. Trianthema (*Trianthema portulacastrum* [Aizoaceae]) seed from En Bas Saline, Haiti, Field Sample 7422 (39x).

site, are from the mangrove forest and include black mangrove (*Avicennia germinans*), red mangrove (*Rhizophora mangle*), and buttonwood (*Conocarpus erectus*), with ubiquity values ranging from 57 to 81% of the proveniences sampled. Newsom (1993b) has suggested that the natural resiliency of mangrove trees to withstand human extractive practices may have been an important factor in the longevity of the chiefdom centered at En Bas Saline. Another potentially very important benefit is that because mangrove trees grow at the water's edge in a habitat fully unsuitable for crop production, there would have existed no conflict between competing necessary resources, that is, between land required for crop production and the wood lots needed for a steady supply of fuelwood. Moreover, since the fruits of mangroves are water dispersed,

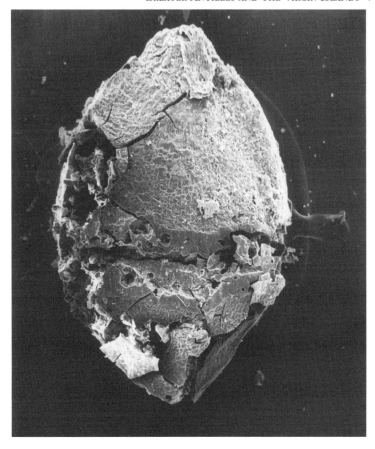

Figure 7.8. Panicoid grass (Poaceae, panicoid group) grain from En Bas Saline, Haiti (Field Sample 7197), showing partial preservation of glumes (*upper left corner*) (48x).

mangrove forests can quickly regenerate because of the regular influx of new propagules from nearby maritime shores, even if the forests undergo local elimination.

Tibes, on the southern coast of Puerto Rico, demonstrates a diverse array of wood taxa; 29 types have been recognized thus far. Conspicuous among those deposits are strong bark, the cojóbana-type tree legume, and a wood in the laurel family (Lauraceae), each present at 62% ubiquity. Lignum-vitae charcoal is prominently associated with a domestic activity area at Tibes, located through remote sensing and excavations (Curet et al. 2003). The charcoal was recovered from a hearthlike feature and adjacent midden deposit, both of which are associated with a living floor that includes a broken ceramic griddle (*buren*) in situ near the hearth (Newsom and Curet 2000, 2003). At the nearby El Bronce site a wood very much like buttonwood and adormidera (*Croton* sp.) seem to have been preferred fuels, both with ubiquity values of 70%. At the other sites woods in the legume (Fabaceae), bignonia (Bignoniaceae), and sapodilla (Sapotaceae) families seem to have been most important (Table 7.8). The Puerto Rican endemic maga, *Thespesia* (*T. grandiflora*, syn. *Montezuma grandiflora*), of the cotton family (Malvaceae), was identified from one-quarter of the proveniences tested (ubiquity values 24 to 25%) at Maisabel, NCS-1, and Tibes. Posthole and other features from Maisabel indicate that almendrón (*Pouteria* sp., e.g., *P. multiflora*) was preferentially used for building construction during all periods, but particularly the Saladoid; it is the sole wood taxon recovered from more than half (56%) of the proveniences analyzed at that site. *Pouteria* spp. wood, long recognized as suitable for durable construction, is a good choice for posts, particularly because the heartwood is highly resistant to decay (Record and Hess 1943:501).

Animal remains are from fewer sites but give an intriguing if incomplete picture of the full range of exploitation of resources in the Greater Antilles. Contributing to the diversity in the use of resources are the large landmasses of the Greater Antilles, the greater richness in the flora and fauna, and the growing social complexity that included controls of the access to some resources. The suggestion of controls was seen in the distribution of maize, pepper, and perhaps also evening primrose and cojóbana, among others. Access to coquina—a small water-edge-dwelling bivalve—at Luján, described above, may also have been controlled. Although coquina does not seem to be a high-status food, it makes up 15% of the invertebrate individuals in midden B and is present only in trace quantities in the other middens at Luján. The abundance of coquina could be incidental to access to the sandy beaches that may have been controlled. More typically prestige would be associated with imported domestic, tame, and managed animals or animals imbued with special cultural significance.

The most widespread managed animal in the Greater Antillean region is the hutía (*Isolobodon portoricensis*). It is believed to be native to Hispaniola and moved as a captive animal to Puerto Rico and the Virgin Islands. It has not yet been found in Archaic-age deposits and is less common in early Ceramic-age deposits than later ones (Wing 1993). Sites located inland, farther from the rich resources of the sea, have a greater relative abundance of the hutía (Table 7.9; Table C-3). For example, hutía are a major contributor (17.4%) to the vertebrate individuals at the site of El Bronce, located 7.3 km inland. At coastal sites such as Maisabel and En Bas Saline, marine vertebrates predominate.

Table 7.9. Summary of the distribution of vertebrates and invertebrates in the primary habitats in which they are found in the Greater Antilles

Habitats	Puerto Rico		Haiti	Jamaica					
	Bronce	Maisabel	EBS	Rodney	White Marl	Bellevue	Cinnamon	Bengal	Rio Nuevo
Vertebrates									
Land	31.3	17.5	15	29.1	61.9	88.8	11.1	22.7	20.9
Freshwater and shore	12.2	2.6	3	2.7	0	1.6	1.2	3	2.5
Shallow inshore	38.3	23.3	23.5	35.5	28.1	7.2	6.8	7.6	17.4
Reef	17.4	33.9	54	31.8	9.5	1.6	65.4	59.1	49.6
Pelagic	0.9	22.8	4.5	0.9	0.6	0.8	15.4	7.6	9.7
Sample size	115	189	200	110	713	125	162	132	599
Invertebrates									
Land–crabs	0.4		0						
Land–snails	89.3		0						
Rocky intertidal	9.2		0.7						
Shallow inshore	1.1		99.2						
Sample size	1776		11117						

Source: El Bronce (Reitz 1985), Maisabel (deFrance 1990), and Rodney House (Scudder 1991).
Note: Values are in minimum number of individuals (MNI) and expressed as percentages.

The large endemic Jamaican rodent known as cony (*Geocapromys brownii*) is equivalent in many respects to the hutía in Puerto Rico. They are rodents of about the same size. They increase in abundance at sites farther from the coast. For example, three sites that are located increasingly farther from Kingston Harbor and the coast are the Rodney House site with 19% cony among the vertebrate fauna, the White Marl site with 50%, and the Bellevue site with 82% (Scudder 1991; Wing 1993). The Bellevue site is located 6 km inland in the mountains above Kingston. The great abundance of cony at some sites may reflect either reliable access to wild populations or management. Cony evolved in the absence of large predators and are therefore particularly vulnerable to hunting with dogs. Where they can find deep rock crevices in which to escape, they continue to maintain viable population levels (Wilkins 2001).

The most widespread domestic species, dogs (*Canis familiaris*), are associated with sites throughout the Ceramic-age in the Greater Antilles. They are usually found in burials and may be associated with human burials. Teeth have been modified either with a drill hole through the root of the tooth, usually the canine, or with a bas-relief design carved into the root (Rímoli 1977). Most of these clearly come from ritual contexts.

The other domestic animal found more abundantly in Greater Antillean sites than elsewhere in the Caribbean is the guinea pig (*Cavia porcellus*). These animals are reported ethnographically from the Dominican Republic, where they were called cori. This name is a cognate of *cuy*, the name used for these animals in Peru, where they were originally domesticated. They were probably domesticated for 2,000 years before they were introduced into the West Indies, where they are consistently found in late prehistoric contexts. Our evidence to date indicates that they are most abundant at sites in Puerto Rico. They were also carried into the Virgin Islands, where they are reported from Luján (Vieques Island) and Cinnamon Bay (St. Johns). The only site where we have found them to be common is NCS-1 (5 km inland on the Rio Grande Arecibo in northwestern Puerto Rico). At this site guinea pigs represent 11% of the vertebrate fauna, making them slightly more abundant than the hutía (Quitmyer and Kozuch 1996). Guinea pigs clearly played an important role in the economy of the people living at NCS-1. They have also been identified at the elite ceremonial center at Tibes, suggesting their special role in Taino culture (deFrance 1997).

At all sites, even those located fairly far inland, resources from the sea are the focus of the acquisition of animals (Table 7.9; Tables C-3 and C-4). The two sites located farther from the coast, El Bronce and White Marl, have many similarities despite being on different islands (Reitz 1985). Tibes is located close to El Bronce, and both are Ceramic-age sites occupied for several centuries. El Bronce is located 7.3 km inland on the Rio Bucana near Ponce.

The Rio Bucana flows into Caleta de Cabullon, a small southward-facing bay fringed with mangroves. White Marl is located beside the Rio Cobre and 5.6 km inland from Kingston Harbor, also on the southern side of the island. The White Marl site was excavated in 1964, when coarse-gauge screen was used to recover the faunal remains. As a consequence the component of small fishes that were probably part of the assemblage are missing and the larger land animals may be relatively more abundant in the sample than in the deposit from which it was taken. The El Bronce site was excavated in 1981 and the faunal sample was recovered using 1/8-inch screen. Despite the differences in the recovery strategies and the location of the sites on different islands, the faunal assemblages are remarkably similar.

The vertebrate assemblages from both of these sites are similar in respect to the relative focus on the different habitats that were exploited (Table 7.9). The predominant land mammals are different genera, *Isolobodon* and *Geocapromys*, but these large rodents are similar in size and conformation. The hutía was probably managed in captivity. The cony may also have been managed or reliably accessible. Among the marine vertebrates, fishes from inshore estuarine habitats predominated. The species included in this group and abundant at these two sites are snook (Centropomidae), porgy (Sparidae), mullet (Mugilidae), and sleeper (Eleotridae). Reef fishes are only about half as abundant as species typically found in inshore estuarine habitats.

The faunal assemblages from two other Greater Antillean sites, Maisabel and En Bas Saline, are very similar to each other and differ markedly from White Marl and El Bronce (deFrance 1990). The Maisabel site is located west of San Juan, Puerto Rico, on the northern side of the island. It is situated close to the shore and was occupied during the Saladoid period from about A.D. 200 to 500. En Bas Saline in located on the northern coast of Haiti near Cap Haitien. It was occupied during the end of the pre-Columbian era. At both sites land vertebrates are varied including hutía, pigeons (Columbidae), iguanas (Iguanidae), and other lizards and make up between 15% and 17.5% of the vertebrate fauna. Shallow inshore species are equally abundant, constituting 23.5% of the fauna. The big contributors to the fauna are the reef fishes, at 34% and 54% of these two assemblages. The fauna from Maisabel differs from that at En Bas Saline in having more pelagic fishes, primarily herrings (Clupeidae) and needlefishes (Belonidae).

Changes can be seen in the reef and inshore fish components of successive deposits from Maisabel. Early and late deposits at Maisabel show a decline in the sizes of reef fishes and a shift of reef species to those that are lower in the trophic level through time (Wing and Wing 2001). Changes in fishing through time can be seen in the estimated biomasses of reef fishes compared with inshore/pelagic fishes in the early and later deposits at Maisabel. In the early deposit at Maisabel, which dates to 1850 B.P., the estimated biomass of reef fishes is 61% (8,333 g), and inshore/pelagic fishes make up 39% (5,297 g) of the total estimated biomass of aquatic vertebrates. In the later deposit at Maisabel, which dates to 1350 B.P., the estimated biomass of reef fishes is 14% (1,296 g) and that of inshore/pelagic fishes is 86% (7,953 g) of the total aquatic estimated biomass (Wing 2001). These changes were also seen at the Tutu site, St. Thomas, and sites in the Lesser Antilles. In the early deposit at Tutu, which dates to 1380 B.P., the estimated biomass of reef fishes is 85% (65,831 g) and that of inshore/pelagic fishes is 15% (11,645 g) of the total aquatic vertebrate biomass. In the late deposit at Tutu, which dates to 560 B.P., the estimated biomass of reef fishes is 31% (6,274 g) and that of inshore/pelagic fishes is 69% (14,049 g) of the total estimated aquatic vertebrate biomass (Table 7.6b). Similar changes can be observed in fisheries today and are evidence of overfishing. The size decline indicates that the fishing effort was intense enough that fishes did not have the time to grow to their full potentials, "growth overfishing" (Russ 1991). The relative decrease in predatory species is also symptomatic of overfishing because the fishes that aggressively take a hook or lure and therefore can be caught most easily are eliminated from the population. This reduces the abundance of predators relative to herbivores and is responsible for the species shift. Overfishing of the reef fishes may have been pressure put only on a local reef. To compensate for the decline of the reef fish populations, the inshore and pelagic fishes were more intensively sought. Particularly important among the inshore and pelagic species were the tuna (Scombridae: Thunnini) and the needlefishes (Belonidae). The shift to greater dependence on inshore and pelagic species would have required a change in fishing strategies, perhaps accepting the greater risk involved in fishing farther from shore.

The distribution of molluscs at Maisabel and En Bas Saline differ substantially even though their vertebrate assemblages were similar (Table C-4). The Maisabel sample is composed primarily of rocky intertidal species such as the nerites (Neritidae) and periwinkles (Littorinidae). In contrast, the En Bas Saline sample is composed of clams (Lucinidae, Donacidae, and Veneridae) and the coffee melampus (*Melampus coffeus*). The coffee melampus is a small snail found in the intertidal zone on mud in mangrove areas. It could probably be gathered in huge numbers and cumulatively provided a substantial protein source. The apex of these shells were removed, suggesting that they may have been modified for use as tinklers, strung and worn around the wrist or ankle (K. Deagan, personal communication, 25 November 2002).

The vertebrate pattern seen at El Bronce and White Marl compared with Maisabel and En Bas Saline does not mean that there are not many other variations. Availability in the local environment plays a major role in the focus of resource exploitation. Technology and choice moderate the use of resources that are available. The difference in the faunal assemblage between sites also indicates flexibility in the food quest resulting from a variety of methods to capture a range of species. In chiefdom levels of society, such as may be represented by some of the Ostionoid populations, there exists a measure of social control over access to resources. Such control typically results in unequal access to resources, as was seen in the presence of maize and perhaps also other plants in higher-status contexts at En Bas Saline.

DISCUSSION

The use of plants and animals was flexible to take advantage of locally occurring resources and knowledge gained through familiarity with the properties and behaviors of plants and animals so that they could be managed. The importation and management of plants follows a different trajectory than that of animals. Introduced plants but no introduced animals occur in Archaic-age sites. By the late Ceramic age, agriculture was not only practiced but evidently intensified, judging from the diversity of crop and garden species and the preparation of formal fields, at least in some areas. The fields, *conucos*, consisted of series of small circular earthen mounds about 1 foot high and 3 to 4 feet in diameter that served to provide growing platforms for crops (Las Casas 1971:110; Sauer 1966:51–54). At least in some regions this field preparation included extensive terraforming to construct irrigation ditches (Hispaniola [Krieger 1930:488; Sauer 1966:53, 64]) and linear growing platforms or terraces on mountain slopes (Puerto Rico [Oliver et al. 1999; Ortíz Aguilu et al. 1991]). Animals such as the dog and guinea pig were domesticated elsewhere and introduced widely into the West Indies. The hutía and Jamaican cony were intensively used at inland sites, but they did not greatly augment the diet when land crabs and reef fishes declined. We do not have evidence for the increase in availability of these rodents as a result of land clearing and cultivation of herbs and fruit-bearing trees.

It is clear that plants were vital to the capture of animals and the processing of meat for food. Travel between islands was by canoe made from the trunks of large trees. Fishes were caught with plant-fiber nets; produce from the garden and molluscs from the shore were carried in nets and bags made from cotton or other plant fibers. Reef fishes were caught and captive animals were held in traps probably made of reeds or wattle tied with plant fibers. So plants and animals were completely intertwined in these economies, even though collection and cultivation of plants was land based and the majority of animals were marine. The interface between land and sea, the mangrove forest, was exploited for wood, organisms clinging to their roots and juvenile fishes feeding below.

The uses of plants are diverse, and many of the species identified from seeds and carbonized wood differ from site to site in the Greater Antilles and associated smaller islands. This apparent diversity may be a function of preservation, appropriate recovery strategies, and sample size, but it is likely that cultural and social factors account for much of the observed variation. Collectively, herbaceous ruderal plants and fruit-bearing trees are two groups of plants that appear increasingly important or evident in this subregion. The weedy plant presence may have been positively correlated with land clearance, or some of the first invaders of disturbed ground. Some of the weedy species and fruit trees, some evidently established as early as the Archaic period, were probably actively encouraged or intentionally cultivated.

Newsom (1993a) and Newsom and Pearsall (2003) have interpreted the paleoethnobotany of the Caribbean as a synergistic system, a human plant-use dynamic that evolved along with human settlement and cultural developments in the islands, unique and apart from life in the original homelands. This is particularly clear with regard to the plant remains discussed in this chapter. From the outset of human occupation in this island group, the general subsistence pattern evidently included (1) home gardens; (2) selections of arboreal and perhaps also herbaceous plants from the natural vegetation; and (3) introduced plants primarily in the form of exotic fruit trees. We posit a continuation and expansion of these practices with the entry of the Saladoid-ceramic-bearing groups into the Greater Antilles. That is, the early Ceramic-age people of the Caribbean arrived in the Greater Antilles, as did their Preceramic or Archaic predecessors, with an established tradition of subsistence gardening focused on a select group of taxa, some of which they transported themselves. That the Archaic-age plant introductions derive from Central America and those of the Ceramic-age mainly from South America is undoubtedly a reflection of the original homelands and established traditions of the separate human groups. This may also signal the continuation of important traditions and social ties with these mainland areas. Plant food production by the Saladoid and later Ceramic-age groups centered on prepared plots emphasizing root crops and eventually included maize and other cultivars. For example, peanuts (*Arachas hypogaea*), another crop from the Amazon region, have been identified from Ceramic-age midden deposits excavated at the Birama site in central Cuba (Delgado Ceballos et al. 2000). This is particularly significant because it represents the first identification of this crop in the region, verifying ethnohistoric records that mention peanuts as a common crop among the Taino of the Greater Antilles. Likewise, pollen identified as tobacco, another introduced plant, from the Sanate site in the Dominican Republic (Fortuna 1978; García Arévalo and Tavares 1978) and possibly dating to about A.D. 1050, represents the first evidence also to verify ethnohistoric mention of this plant in the region. It is important that even though most of the crops, particularly manioc and other root crops, derived from mainland areas, ultimately implementation of the production system in the island environments was a uniquely Caribbean manifestation. As was shown of the Archaic-age settlements, it appears from their ubiquitous presence among the various sites' deposits that fruit-bearing trees like native mastic-bully (which has also been identified from an Archaic-age site in Cuba [Hernández Cano and Navarrete Pujol 1999]) and a few small wild grains (e.g., trianthema) were an important part of Ceramic-age subsistence in the Greater Antilles.

The woods used for fuel and for building are primarily from the coastal mangrove, subtropical dry forests, or lower montane forests. Characteristics that may have been sought were a high resin content and density, making woods resistant to decay and insect damage and therefore particularly useful for construction and efficient for fuel. To some extent our record may be biased because of the differential burning and heating characteristics of individual wood taxa, with hard, dense woods used as fuelwood surviving better compared with lighter, less dense types. Some trees, such as mangroves (e.g., *Avicennia germinans*) and various dry forest taxa, may have been coppiced (Ewel and Whitmore 1973:10–20; Newsom 1993b) (as opposed to simple collection of fallen deadwood). This coppice response, i.e., the inherent ability of particular tree species for rapid shoot growth after cutting, could have enhanced the wood supply and therefore raised the threshold of sustainability, since local forests would have been able to sustain greater and longer extraction pressures by humans. Such a situation hypothetically could have resulted in management practices that relied on this growth characteristic exhibited by trees that produce strong and prolific shoots in response to the stress of regular cycles of cutting and harvest.

Another form of management is cultivation of fruit trees. This may range from tending trees in the wild by clearing away competing vegetation to active arboriculture involving planting, pruning, and protecting the fruit tree and harvesting the fruit. This also generally denotes ownership of the trees and their products.

Agriculture as we tend to think of it involves soil preparation, planting, tending, and harvesting on a regular schedule. It involves knowledge of the requirements of the plants cultivated and of their uses. In addition to food, cultivated plants provide drugs, medicines, dyes, fibers, and fish poisons, which all potentially played a part in the developing Caribbean cultures.

Archaeobotanical data from Greater Antilles sites illuminate plant use and the dynamic relationships between people of the Caribbean and their local flora. The collective identifications form initial profiles of plant use that correspond with early, late, and final stages of migration, settlement, and social organization in particular island groups. Thus the Archaic-age deposits analyzed here provide glimpses of wood selection corresponding with these early occupations, and at least tentative evidence that some form of gardening was practiced before the migration of Saladoid horticulturists from northern South America (Newsom and Pearsall 2003). Fruit-bearing trees were an important part of Ceramic-age subsistence, judging by their ubiquitous presence among the sites and their deposits. The archaeobotanical evidence appears to demonstrate that throughout the Ceramic-age gardening and arboriculture became increasingly important. Finally, late Ceramic sites, including the Classic Taíno site of En Bas Saline on Hispaniola, provide some of the first definitive evidence verifying the presence of the root staples and other crops described in ethnohistoric documents.

Although plant cultivation and management practices were well advanced during the Ceramic age, management and domestication of animals does not seem to have been equally important in the economy. The hutía was a managed animal that was intensively used at inland sites such as El Bronce, but it was not used more intensively in later deposits at Tutu after reef fishes declined. Possibly the management of these animals posed technical difficulties, particularly in the Virgin Islands farther from the diverse resources of the larger islands. The relative rarity of guinea pig remains suggests that this truly domestic animal was not bred in great numbers in order to compensate in the diet for the decline of reef resources. With the decline in reef fishes, some people appear to have shifted their focus to offshore pelagic fishes, despite the inherent danger of fishing far from shore. This also suggests that other reefs along the coast may not have been accessible, either because they were too far or because they were controlled by other people.

The plant and animal remains from the Greater Antilles illustrate flexibility in the use of natural resources and at the same time a clear focus on the resources in particular habitats. Cultivation of plants appears to have been far more developed than domestication of native West Indian animals. Even fully domestic animals and managed species do not seem to have augmented the food supply when evidence for overexploitation of wild resources is evident. At inland sites, however, use of managed animals was greatly increased, and we have no evidence that those populations became overexploited. On the coast, overexploitation of land crabs and reef fishes and the decline of those resources was compensated for by expansion of the fishing effort to pelagic species including those typically found offshore. This indicates that it may have been easier to modify and expand the fishing enterprise than to further pursue animal husbandry of native species. At least in some areas, enhanced production of plant staples may have helped to fill this void—adding species as well as developing terraces and irrigation are forms of intensification—however, this must have concerned primarily tropical root crops because evidence of maize is minimal. We discuss this possibility in greater depth in Chapter 9.

8
Bahamas Archipelago

INTRODUCTION

The focus of much of the archaeological research on the Bahamas archipelago centers on the timing of the first human colonization of these islands, the source or sources of colonists, and the first sighting of these islands by Europeans. The Bahamas archipelago is composed of two modern nations, the Commonwealth of the Bahamas and the Turks and Caicos Islands (Figure 8.1). The Bahamian landscape and natural resources contrast markedly with those of the neighboring islands of the Greater Antilles. In most respects, the potential productivity of the land is poorer and the terrestrial resources more meager. This raises the question of why these islands were colonized and how the colonists sustained themselves. Although archaeological exploration of the Bahamas archipelago began as early as the 1880s and continued through the twentieth century, very few faunal studies accompany the archaeological investigations and even less paleoethnobotanical information is available. Even today at the beginning of the twenty-first century, when these studies are considered an integral part of archaeological research and the methods for optimal recovery of plant and animal remains are well known, our information about Native Americans' use of natural resources is meager. Despite the paucity of material, however, the diversity of taxa identified from Bahamian sites is relatively high and reveals unique patterns of resource use.

What we present here is a preliminary review of the plants and animals used by the colonists of these islands, hindered by small samples. The initial impetus for colonizing the Bahamas may have been the exploitation of special resources such as salt and shellfish, particularly conch (*Strombus gigas*) (Sears and Sullivan 1978:23). We concur with Keegan and others that it is highly likely that the Ostionoid people living on the islands of Hispaniola and Cuba

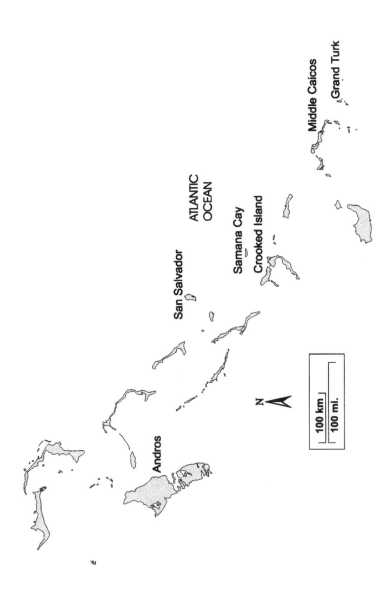

Figure 8.1. Bahamas, Turks and Caicos. (By Florence E. Sergile)

knew about the adjacent islands of the Bahamas archipelago and their resource potentials well before they actually settled in the Bahamas. Exploratory trips are hard to document in the archaeological record. However, colonists apparently bypassed islands closest to the Greater Antilles to occupy islands farther away. This may demonstrate informed choice. If the lure of the Bahamas was access to special resources, exploratory trips to the islands probably preceded colonization. Sedentary settlement was relatively later in the overall history of the West Indies, beginning around A.D. 700–750, if not somewhat earlier (W. F. Keegan, personal communication April 2001).

ENVIRONMENTAL CHARACTERISTICS

The Bahamas archipelago is composed of 35 low limestone islands and more than 600 cays that extend over 1,000 km and are oriented along a northwest-to-southeast axis (Correll and Correll 1982; Morgan 1989; Olson and Pregill 1982) (Figure 8.1). The islands emerge from banks on a large limestone platform. During the Pleistocene, sea-level fluctuations exposed the banks around present-day islands, thereby forming five large islands and a few smaller ones. Sea level may have been as much as 120 m lower during the peak of the Wisconsin glaciations, 17,000–18,000 years ago, than it is today. At this lower sea level stand, the dozen or so present-day islands and their surrounding banks were exposed forming the five large islands. With the rise in sea level after the Pleistocene, only the highest parts of these islands remain as dry land and the banks are under 3 to 30 m of water. These characteristics—the geologic history, small size, low elevation, low and very seasonal rainfall, and subtropical location—account for the relatively depauperate recent land fauna (Morgan 1989).

The islands of the archipelago can be grouped according to several different biogeographic criteria. The archipelago is divided into two zoogeographic regions separated by the Crooked Island Passage, between Long Island and Crooked Island. The islands to the north of this passage are larger and were very large during the periods of lowest sea levels in the Pleistocene. Those to the south of the passage are smaller today as they were during the Pleistocene.

Another way of subdividing the archipelago is by bioclimatic conditions, taking into account the geographic position of each island, mean annual biotemperatures, annual rainfall, and effective evapotranspiration, and thus the major life zones with their characteristic forms of vegetation (Holdridge 1947, 1967). These climatic parameters vary along the south-north gradient in the Bahamas. The archipelago trends 1,000 km longitudinally across about 6 degrees latitude. The northern islands (Grand Bahama, Great and Little Abaco, Bimini, Andros, the Berry Islands, and New Providence) experience somewhat seasonal, generally cooler conditions and normally receive the most rainfall, between 1,200 and 1,600 mm recorded annually (Keegan 1992; Sears and Sullivan 1978). The central Bahamas (Exuma, Long Island, Eleuthra, San Salvador, and Crooked Island) receive between 800 and 1,100 mm of rainfall annually. The southern Bahamas (Inagua and the Turks and Caicos Islands) receive the least rainfall, less than 800 mm (generally between about 330 and 750 mm). The northern Bahamas fall within the humid-subhumid provinces according to the Holdridge Life Zone system (1947, 1967), and the vegetation in this northern zone is characterized as tropical to subtropical dry forest. Dry secondary woodlands variously described as coastal coppice, whiteland and blackland communities, and localized stands of pine forests predominate today (Correll and Correll 1982). The central and southern Bahamas islands, with less moisture, are in the subhumid to semiarid humidity provinces. The projected natural vegetation is classified as very dry tropical forest. Currently these islands are dominated by secondary xerophytic broadleaf scrub or, in more exposed or degraded areas, by thorn woodland (Morgan 1989:687). Strand vegetation, coastal coppice, and mangrove forests, as well as tidal flats, salt marshes, and some freshwater plant formations, occur throughout the archipelago (Correll and Correll 1982).

These biogeographic factors have considerable implications for the colonization of the islands, affecting not only forest structure and composition but also the characteristic faunal biota. The availability of fresh water is a major consideration in the small dry islands, particularly the southern Bahamas region, where this may depend entirely on rainwater collection.

CULTURE HISTORY

Colonization of the Bahamas was late in the cultural history of the West Indies. Some of the earliest dates for permanent settlements are around A.D. 700–750. The islands were undoubtedly explored and the resources of the islands known before permanent settlements were established. Explorers and early settlers came from the Greater Antilles. Support for the origins of the first settlers in the Bahamas comes from pottery sherds with characteristic Greater Antillean cultural affinities. Sites such as the Coralie site, believed to be representative of the initial colonization on Grand Turk, have imported wares identified as Ostionan Ostionoid subseries, originating from Hispaniola (Keegan 1997b:21). This pottery was not simply made on Grand Turk in the style of the pottery from Hispaniola. The clay from which the pottery was made was tempered with mineral sand not found in the Bahamas. A distinctive pottery type, Arroyo del Palo, was found at the Three Dog site on San Salvador, which is also believed to signify an early occupation in the Bahamas (Berman and Gnivecki 1995). The Arroyo del Palo pottery has Cuban affinities. It is likely that the colonists of the Bahamas came from both Greater Antillean islands, and possibly even from the islands east of Hispaniola (e.g., Puerto Rico, Virgin Islands).

Once firmly established in the Bahamas, the settlers began making distinctive pottery attributed to the Palmettan Ostionoid subseries (formerly called Palmetto ware [Rouse 1992]). These ceramics are produced from local red clay and tempered with shell. Clay resources in the Bahamas are poor and are derived from windblown sediments traced to Africa (Carlson 1999:29; Keegan 1997b:38). Pottery styles within the Palmettan Ostionoid subseries differ somewhat from island to island, making it possible to distinguish pottery made on Crooked Island from that made on Abaco, among others (Keegan 1997b:39). A particularly interesting type of pottery is "Palmetto Mat Marked," which has impressions of woven fabric (Hutcheson 2001). This is interesting for what it reveals about the techniques of basketry and also the use of plant materials in fiber industries. The historic inhabitants of the Bahamas are known collectively as the Lucayan Taino (Rouse 1992), or simply Lucayans.

USERS OF PLANTS AND ANIMALS IN THE BAHAMAS

The uses of plant and animal resources throughout the Bahamas archipelago are not equally well known (Table 4.1). Archaeological exploration has centered on the southern islands, Grand Turk and Middle Caicos, and on the central island of San Salvador. Some additional archaeobotanical and zooarchaeological work has been conducted on materials excavated from Samana Cay and Crooked Island. Although faunal remains have been excavated from the northern islands, the results of those studies are not yet available. The same problems of unevenness in recovery strategies and inclusion of invertebrates with vertebrates apply to the sites in the Bahamas as to the other West Indian islands. These differences in the data must be kept in mind in evaluating the assemblages. Despite the spotty representation of faunal and botanical assemblages, or perhaps because of it, the Lucayan use of resources appears very diverse, suggesting flexibility in the food quest. We will first discuss plant and animal use on each island or group of islands and then compare the islands with each other.

Turks and Caicos (Southern Bahamas)

One of the earliest occupations in the Bahamas is the site of Coralie (GT-3) on Grand Turk (Carlson 1999). It was occupied from A.D. 705 to 1170 (B.P. 1280 ± 60 to 900 ± 50) (Carlson 1999:52). Excavations at this site were extensive and faunal samples are large, including both vertebrate and invertebrate remains

(Table 8.1 and Table D-1). Analyses of plant materials recovered from the site are currently in progress; the preliminary data are discussed here. The Coralie faunal assemblage is outstanding for the diversity of species including extirpated and extinct forms. One particularly interesting extinct animal is an undescribed large tortoise (*Geochelone* sp.) (Carlson 1999). Characteristics of this fauna are the absence of the Bahamas hutía (*Geocapromys ingrahami*), the presence of a diverse bird assemblage, abundant rock iguana (*Cyclura carinata*), reef fishes (particularly grunts [Haemulidae]), and conch (*Strombus gigas*) (Carlson 1999). This large sample of animal remains deposited at the inception of human settlement in the southern end of the archipelago allows comparison of this assemblage with later deposits.

Recovery strategy can have an impact on species composition and size distribution of the faunal remains. As we have seen in many deposits in the West Indies, the species represented do not grow to large sizes, and the range in sizes includes small individuals. To understand the contribution of plants and animals to the prehistoric economy, it is important to examine the full range of species and their sizes. The complex of reef fishes in many West Indian sites indicates overexploitation of the reefs, as indicated by the decline in the sizes of fishes and a shift to relatively more species low in the food web (Wing and Wing 2001). To make this case for overfishing, the full range of species and individuals must be present. The other aspect of the fishing enterprise that a full range in size reveals is the techniques used. The strength of the line, size of the hook, gauge of the trap mesh and size of the entrance, gauge of netting, and length of a seine all determine the kinds of fishes caught and their sizes. Therefore, the kinds and estimated sizes of fishes caught can be used to interpret the fishing technology that may have been employed.

The faunal remains from the Coralie site were recovered using 6 mm mesh screens. An experiment with finer-gauge recovery did not yield enough faunal specimens to make the extra effort fine-sieving would require worthwhile to the archaeologists (Carlson 1999). (Separate fine-sieved [0.42 to 4.0 mm] samples were recovered for archaeobotanical analysis.) Nevertheless the small end of the size range of recovered animals may be missing, with the mean of vertebral measurements skewed a little to the large end of the range. With this possibility in mind, the size range of the represented fish species is from 5.25 to 16.10 mm vertebral width, representing fishes estimated to weigh from 0.43 to 4.3 kg (Carlson 1999:75). Because Coralie is believed to be the first settlement on Grand Turk, the fish represented in the deposit are those that were selected from a pristine marine environment. Although a 4 kg fish is large, it is not like the enormous individuals one might expect from unfished waters.

The absence of fishes larger than 4 kg can be accounted for in two ways. Limitations of the fishing technology, including the use of watercraft to fish

Table 8.1. Summary of the faunal assemblages with organisms grouped according to the habitats in which they are typically found

Turks and Caicos

	GT-3 (Coralie) Carlson 1999 % MNI	MC-6 Wing and Scudder 1983 % MNI	MC-12 Wing and Scudder 1983 % MNI	MC-32 Carlson 1994 % MNI
Vertebrate				
Land	45	9	3	7
Freshwater and shore	3	3	1	2
Shallow inshore	13	48	13	31
Reef	38	37	84	60
Pelagic	0	2	0	0
Total	958	139	127	97
Invertebrate				
Land	7			
Rocky intertidal	24			
Shallow/inshore	65			
Reef	4			
Total	1289			

Crooked Island and Samana Cay

	CK-12 deFrance 1991 % MNI	SM-2 % MNI	SM-7 % MNI
Vertebrate			
Land	4	1	2
Freshwater or shore	0	0	0
Shallow and inshore	11	5	2
Reef	84	20	11
Pelagic	1	74	86
Total	185	196	186

Continued on next page

far from shore, would confine most fishing to shallow inshore waters. Very large animals such as monk seals, manatee, sea turtles, and large fishes may have been butchered on the shore and only occasional small fragments of their bones brought back to the site. Large animals may also have been subdivided among the members of the community, further reducing the numbers of skeletal remains deposited in the midden. Although remains of sea turtles are com-

Table 8.1. *Continued*

San Salvador

	SS-2 Palmetto Grove Wing 1969 % MNI	SS-3 Minnis Ward Winter and Wing 1995 % MNI	SS- 9 Long Bay % MNI	SS-21 Three Dog Berman 1994 % MNI
Vertebrate				
Land	1	0	2	2
Freshwater and shore	0	0	0	0
Shallow inshore	1	11	10	5
Reef	98	84	87	93
Pelagic	0	5	1	0
Total	991	38	143	57
Invertebrate				
Land				11
Rocky intertidal				11
Shallow/inshore				76
Reef				3
Total				112

Source: Coralie site (Carlson 1999); Middle Caicos sites (Wing and Scudder 1983; Carlson 1994); Crooked Island site (deFrance 1991); San Salvador sites (Wing 1969; Wing and Winter 1995; Berman 1994).

Note: Details of the faunal assemblages can be found in Tables D.1 and D.3, the Coralie site (GT-3); D.2, the Middle Caicos sites of MC-6, MC-12, and MC-32 sites; D.4, the Crooked Island site CK-14 and two sites from Samana Cay SM-2 and SM-7; D.5 and D.6, the San Salvador sites of Palmetto Grove, Long Bay, Three Dog, and Minnis Ward.

mon, those of large marine mammals are rare, and large fish bones are almost never found in Bahamian sites studied thus far.

The rock iguana had also not previously faced predation on the scale imposed by Native Americans. Remains of an individual iguana in the Coralie deposit suggest an animal estimated to have weighed 5 kg, exceeding the known size of iguanas living in the Bahamas today (Carlson 1999:73).

The 18 tortoises, one of which has a plastron length of 340 mm, persisted throughout the occupation at Coralie but are known from no other sites and are now extinct (Carlson 1999:138, 235). The coincidence of human colonization and the extinction of these tortoises suggest that people directly or indirectly caused their demise.

The relative abundance of land vertebrates such as the rock iguanas, tortoises, and birds at Coralie sets it apart from other sites in the Bahamas (Table 8.1). Several reasons can be proposed to explain this unusual abundance of land vertebrates at Coralie. The recovery procedures and reliance on large samples sieved with 6-mm-gauge screen may have played a role in the terrestrial characteristics of the faunal assemblage. The first occupants on Grand Turk had access to animal populations never before hunted by people, which may account for the greater abundance of land animals. However, the initial occupation on other islands such as San Salvador, which is six times larger than Grand Turk, did not result in the same terrestrial dominance of the vertebrate fauna. A dominance of terrestrial animals in other West Indian faunas is associated with sites that are located inland. Even a few kilometers' distance inland can make a big difference in the importance of land animals. The Coralie site, however, is located close to the coast and near the mouth of North Creek, a large inland lagoon. It is within .5 km of the seashore and access to the reef. In addition to land animals, the focus at Coralie was on reef fishes and shallow inshore molluscs, as is typical of most other sites in the Bahamas.

The archaeobotanical assemblage from the Coralie site is very well preserved and consists primarily of abundant large (commonly >4 mm cross-section surface area), carbonized wood specimens. We describe these materials below, along with other paleoethnobotanical data from the Bahamas island system.

Three archaeological sites on Middle Caicos illustrate how proximity to a particular habitat affects the compositions of faunal remains (Table 8.1 and Table D-2). Two sites, MC-12 and MC-32, are located along the northern coast of Middle Caicos Island overlooking barrier reefs, turtle grass meadows, and patch reefs. MC-32 is east of MC-12 and has closer access to a large brackish-water pond on the inland side of the site. The third site, MC-6, is located on the southern side of the island adjacent to an extensive mangrove swamp and a shallow lagoon bounded by East and West Caicos Islands and other small cays.

A marine focus is evident in all three archaeological sites on Middle Caicos (Tables 8.1 and Table D-2). Reef fishes predominate in the samples from the two sites on the northern side of the island facing the sea. MC-32 has more shallow inshore and many more pelagic vertebrates than MC-12. The pelagic species are very small silversides probably caught with nets along the shore. Their presence in MC-32 and not in MC-12 is probably the result of the different recovery strategies used at the two sites. One might think that silversides, being such small fishes, were of no consequence to the diet. Yet they were a source of protein and calcium and may have been added to a pepper pot to increase its nutrient value. Land vertebrates are not abundant though still interesting. A single dog is represented in MC-12 deposits, evidence that this animal was introduced into the Bahamas.

Although shallow inshore vertebrates are more common in the sample from MC-32 than the one from MC-12, they are very abundant in the sample from MC-6. Shallow inshore waters and tidal drainage was the primary source of vertebrates for the people living at MC-6. The most important species are bonefish (*Albula vulpes*) and small sea turtles (Cheloniidae). One Bahamas hutía (*Geocapromys ingrahami*) is represented at this site.

Invertebrates were studied at only one site in the Turks and Caicos group: Coralie (Carlson 1999). Conch (*Strombus gigas*) is the most abundantly represented of these taxa, constituting 30% of the invertebrate fauna (Table 8.1 and Table D-3). Nerites and topsnails (*Cittarium pica*) are second in abundance. The Governor's Beach site (GT-2) is a shell bead–manufacturing activity area on Grand Turk. A large number of beads and shell debitage, approximately 5,600 whole and broken disc beads, 3,400 polished shell or bead blanks, and 13,000 pieces of shell debitage were studied from this site (Carlson 1995:99). The primary raw material for making these beads was conch (*Strombus gigas*) shell and red jewelbox (*Chama sarda*) shell. The archaeological recovery techniques were not at the time of investigation designed to recover archaeobotanical samples; consequently very little food refuse was encountered.

Crooked Island and Samana Cay (Central Bahamas)

The faunal assemblages from Crooked Island and Samana Cay are examples of the versatility in the food quest by the Lucayan people. The Crooked Island site of CR-14 has an assemblage that is virtually identical to that of MC-12, described above. In both assemblages the reef component predominates. The faunas from Samana Cay also include an important reef component, but the most abundant fishes are very small juvenile fishes.

The faunal assemblages from the two sites on Samana Cay, SM-2 and SM-7, are similar to each other and different from other samples in the West Indies. The major contributors to the Samana Cay fauna are very small individuals of goatfish (Mullidae) and tuna (Scombridae) (Table 8.1 and Table D-4). In addition to the small goatfishes and tunas are flyingfish or halfbeaks (Exocoetidae/Hemiramphidae), squirrelfishes (Holocentridae), and jacks, including bar jacks (*Caranx ruber*) and bigeye scad (*Selar crumenophthalmus*). The vertebral widths of these small fishes average between 1 and 2 mm. These small juvenile fishes may be caught among floating mats of Sargassum weed. Small-gauge netting would be required to catch such small fishes.

Adjacent to these sites is a large conch shell deposit. It has been described as a "causeway"—thus a cultural feature on the landscape—and consists of a vast accumulation of conch shells (Judge 1986:586–587). The causeway is at right angles to the shore and stretches from one embayment to another on the island. Interestingly, the conchs that make up the causeway were opened in two different ways. Some had round holes in the shells to extract the meat, and others appeared to have holes cut with a tool like a machete (Hoffman, personal communication 1986). This suggests that the shells were accumulated both before and after colonization by Europeans. Unfortunately, sampling was not designed to determine the relative number of shells opened by the different tools and techniques or their depositional sequence, which might have clarified the proportion deposited before A.D. 1492. It is likely that conch was an important resource in the past as it is today.

San Salvador (Northern Bahamas)

Intense archaeological investigation has occurred on San Salvador. Interest in the archaeology of San Salvador was in part spurred by the possibility that this island was the first landfall of Columbus's first voyage. Native American colonization and cultural development in the Bahamas was also motivation to study the archaeology of this island. It lies in the relatively moist subtropical region of the archipelago. The island has one of the earliest sites in the Bahamas, the Three Dog site (SS-21). The occupation at the Three Dog site was A.D. 750 (1290 ± 90 to 490 ± 70 B.P.) (Berman 1994). San Salvador also has a possible Spanish contact site, Long Bay (SS-9), with a date of A.D. 1460 as well as European artifacts including glass beads. A small sample from the Major's Cave site (SS-60) appears to be associated with a burial that was accompanied by funerary offerings, including food items, dating to A.D. 1500 (450 ± 50 B.P.) (Winter et al. 1997). Two of these faunal samples, Three Dog and Majors Cave sites, are small with a total vertebrate MNI from 41 to 57, respectively (Tables 8.1 and Tables D-5 and D-6). However, in general the faunal samples from San Salvador are similar to each other and to MC-12 and CR-14 assemblages from the southern and central Bahamas, respectively. The defining characteristic is the predominance of reef fishes in each of these samples (Table 8.1). Reef fishes make up more than 75% of the vertebrate fauna, among which parrotfishes are the most important except at Major's Cave, where triggerfishes are most abundant. Invertebrate remains from the Three Dog site demonstrate an emphasis on shallow inshore molluscs, very similar to the pattern observed at the Coralie site (GT-3) in the Turks and Caicos region (Table 8.1).

PLANT USE IN THE BAHAMAS

Little direct evidence of plant use is available from sites in the Bahamas. This is more a matter of the paucity of systematic sampling for archaeobotanical remains than of poor preservation. However, the isolated specimens and assemblages that have been analyzed indicate intelligent and fairly consistent uses of botanical resources. Evidence for a uniquely Bahamian paleoethnobotany derives from hypotheses about potential key resources and factual information based on identifications of plant specimens excavated from archaeological deposits in this archipelago.

Fragmentary information from historic documents indicates that the Lucayans had both small and large canoes, were adept at making various forms of basketry, and lived in post-supported shelters (Keegan 1997b; Sears and Sullivan 1978). Early Spanish accounts tell us about watercraft described as small canoes for localized fishing and very large canoes big enough to carry 150 people (Keegan 1997b:58), perhaps for more ambitious inter-island or ocean-going expeditions. A small canoe recovered from a blue hole on Andros Island has projections at the bow and stern as described by Oviedo and is reported to be made of mahogany (Keegan 1997b:58). Two paddles have been found: one from a cave on More's Island and said to be made of cedar (Judge 1986:583), the other from peat deposits at North Creek near the Coralie site on Grand Turk and made of wild lime (*Zanthoxylum* sp. [Newsom, laboratory data]).

Lucayan skill in basketry is revealed by basket- or mat-impressed pottery (Hutcheson 2001). The range of basket or mat patterns exhibited in the impressions demonstrates some of the versatility in this craft. Plant fibers such as from retted palm or grass leaves were probably used. We can also assume skill in net making based on ethnographic reports of hammocks and the presence of small fishes that were probably caught with nets. Some of the pottery sherds either with or without mat impressions are of the form typically used to bake breadstuffs, as from root crops or maize tortillas. Lucayans reportedly processed various geophytic starchy organs—perhaps manioc tubers or the subterranean stems of zamia (*Zamia* sp.)—for their carbohydrate staple. Manioc was a widely used staple in the West Indies and may have been an important crop in the Bahamas as well. However, the native cycad *Zamia* sp. is as likely or more likely to have been the primary starch staple in this island group, whether cultivated or gathered from wild populations. Possible evidence for zamia use, or perhaps even the introduced yautía (*Xanthosoma* sp.), comes from potential starch grains isolated from a chert microlith from the Three Dog site on San Salvador (Berman and Pearsall 2000).

Specimens of carbonized and uncarbonized seeds and wood, including complete wood objects, have been identified from at least four sites in the Bahamas (Table 8.2). Hog plum (*Spondias* sp.), strong bark (*Bourreria* sp.), and cocoplum (*Chyrsobalanus icaco*) all produce edible tree fruits. They were recovered in the vicinity of the human burial in Major's Cave, suggesting the possibility that they represent ritual offerings in conjunction with the mortuary activity in the cave (Winter et al. 1997).

Wood items and fuelwood remains indicate a clear choice for species with exceptionally hard, dense wood, including buttonwood (*Conocarpus erectus*), sea grape (*Coccoloba uvifera*), red mangrove (*Rhizophora mangle*), black mangrove

Table 8.2. Plant Remains from Bahamas archipelago sites (reported by simple presence [X])

Family	Genus/Species	Common Name	Grand Turk Coralie	San Salvador Major's Cave	San Salvador Three Dog	Grand Bahama Deadman's Reef
Seeds/Nuts						
Anacardiaceae	Spondias sp.	hog-plum		X		
Boraginaceae	Bourreria sp.	strong bark		X		
Chrysobalanaceae	Chrysobalanus (icaco)	coco-plum		X		
Combretaceae	Conocarpus erectus	buttonwood		X		
Sapotaceae	Sideroxylon sp.	mastic bully			X	
Wood						
Mangrove/Strand						
Combretaceae	Conocarpus erectus	buttonwood	X		X	[X]
Polygonaceae	Coccoloba sp.	sea grape/pigeon plum				X
Rhizophoraceae	Rhizophora mangle	red mangrove				X
Verbenaceae	Avicennia germinans	black mangrove				X
Interior						
Aracaceae		palm family	X			
Boraginaceae	Bourreria sp.	strong bark	X			
Celastraceae	Gyminda* or Crossopetalum sp.	boxwood/cherry	X			
Cupressaceae	cf. Juniperus sp.	cf. red cedar				X
Erythroxylaceae	Erythroxylum sp.	false cocaine			X	
Euphorbiaceae	Croton sp.	pepper bush	[X]		X	
Fabaceae-Mimosoideae	cf. Acacia sp.	cf. acacia				X
Fabaceae-Papilionoideae	Piscida (carthagenesis)	fish poison				X

Family	Taxon	Common name				
Malvaceae	cf. *Hibiscus* sp.	cf. mahoe				X
Myrtaceae	*Eugenia* sp.	stopper				X
Myrtaceae	*Psidium* sp. or *Eugenia* sp.	guava/stopper			X	
Nyctaginaceae	*Pisonia* sp.	water mampoo				X
Rhamnaceae	*Krugiodendron (ferreum)*	black ironwood			X	
Rubiaceae	*Exostema (caribaeum)*	quinine bark		X		
Rutaceae	*Amyris* sp.	torchwood, white torch				X
Rutaceae	*Zanthoxylum* sp.	wild lime type			X	
Sapindaceae	*Thouinia* sp.	quicksilver				X
Sapotaceae	*Chrysophyllum/Sideroxylon** anatomical wood group	star apple, mastic bully wood group				X
Zygophyllaceae	*Guaiacum* sp.	lignum–vitae	X	X		

*Gyminda synonyms *Myginda, Rhacoma; Sideroxylon* synonym *Mastichodendron*

(*Avicennia germinans*), strong bark, black ironwood (*Krugiodendron* sp.), lignum-vitae (*Guaiacum* sp.), and more (Table 8.2). One such wood, false cocaine (*Erythroxylum* sp.), demonstrated a 75% presence among the proveniences analyzed from the Three Dog site on San Salvador (Berman and Pearsall 2000). Black ironwood is known as one of the most hard and dense in the world, with a specific gravity (an indirect measure of density and hardness) between 1.34 and 1.42 (Record and Hess 1943:441). By way of comparison, species of mahogany, a wood that is considered to be moderately dense and hard, have specific gravities between about 0.50 and 0.60, and lignum-vitae, another exceptionally dense wood, between about 1.10 and 1.32 (Record and Hess 1943:374, 554). Subtropical dry forests and mangrove/ strand associations are inherently quite rich in such taxa; thus the evident preference for these hard, dense woods may simply be a matter of local abundance and availability rather than deliberate choice. Moreover, it is difficult to imagine that such hard, dense woods could have been readily cut with shell tools; thus we surmise that most of the carbonized wood derives from deadwood collections gathered and used as fuel. Another consideration is preservation bias, these relatively dense woods having the greatest chance of surviving burning and long-term burial. Most of this wood charcoal was used as fuel, judging by associations with hearths or burned features. Some charcoal may be the remnants of burned house construction posts, though we have no direct evidence of that. A wooden bowl from Major's Cave and a mortar from Watling's Bluehole were preserved in undisturbed and anaerobic conditions offered by the bluehole and cave (Winter and Pearsall 1991; Winter et al. 1997). These objects were made of lignum-vitae and mahogany (*Swietenia mahogani*), respectively. Berman and Pearsall (2000:222) report wooden objects from the Deadman's Reef site, Grand Bahama, made from stopper (*Eugenia* sp.), red mangrove, buttonwood, and a tree leguminous wood.

In general, botanical remains from Bahamas sites tell us more about the technological aspects of subsistence—manufacture of objects from wood and fiber, wood for fuel—than about plant production for dietary purposes on these relatively arid islands.

We are hopeful that the current research with botanical samples from the Turks and Caicos and new excavations in the Bahamas islands will improve our understanding of dietary uses.

CONCLUSIONS

Sites in the Bahamas offer a unique view of resource use by the Lucayan Taino during the last thousand years of cultural development in the West Indies before the European social and ecological takeover. Although all of the Bahamas islands have not been explored archaeologically and relatively few sites have detailed investigations of plant and animal remains, those samples that are available reveal great flexibility in the use of resources. Only one site, Coralie (GT-3), has the time depth, good preservation, and large sample size to allow discussion of changes in the faunal assemblage through time (Carlson 1999). The relatively late occupations of short duration set studies of resource use in the Bahamas apart from the rest of the West Indies, where many locations were occupied for hundreds of years. This also raises the question of what features of the Bahamas archipelago attracted colonists from the larger islands.

The diversity of faunal assemblages in the Bahamas is startling even though reef fishes are at the core of this diversity. At only two sites (Samana Cay) is the vertebrate reef component less than 35%. The reef component in the faunal samples from sites on San Salvador constitutes 75% or more of the vertebrate individuals and is dominated by parrotfishes, particularly the stoplight parrot-fish (*Sparisoma viride*). The sites on Samana Cay have an important reef fish component, but numerically the very small Sargassum fish individuals pre-dominate although they were probably less important as biomass sources. The faunal samples from sites on Middle Caicos show exploitation that is finely at-tuned to extraction of resources in the closest habitats to the site. Thus we see predominant use of inshore waters by the people living along the southern shore adjacent to the shallow lagoon, whereas people living along the northern coast depended more heavily on the fishes from the nearby coral reefs. Conchs (*Strombus gigas*) were very abundant at Coralie, evidently as a food resource. They were a primary shell for the bead industry at GT-2 and were probably abundantly used on Samana Cay. In particular, the heap of shells at SS-2 indi-cates they were important at that site. However, conchs do not appear to have been important to the inhabitants of the Three Dog site, unless we are missing this element of subsistence because the shell was deposited elsewhere, perhaps at the shore.

Terrestrial faunal resources, primarily rock iguana (*Cyclura carinata*), are most important at the Coralie site. The extinct tortoise (*Geochelone* sp.), though not abundant numerically, would have provided a lot of meat to the prehistoric diet. The native capromyid rodent, *Geocapromys ingrahami*, is rare or absent from all faunal samples studied thus far. No introduced rodents from the Greater Antilles have been found in faunal assemblages from the Bahamas.

The effects of sustained human exploitation can be seen in changes in the faunal assemblages associated with a sequence of deposits such as is seen at Coralie (Carlson 1999:138). Trends of change appear in a comparison between the faunal composition of the early and late contexts at Coralie. The observed trends through time are declines in birds, especially boobies (*Sula* spp.), and in the primary reef carnivores (Serranidae, Lutjanidae, and Haemulidae). Documented also is a decline in number and sizes of green turtles (*Chelonia mydas*) and increases in reef omnivores (Labridae and Scaridae), rock iguana (*Cyclura carinata*), and conchs (*Strombus gigas*). Only one of these changes is statistically significant, and that is the increase through time in the abundance of conchs relative to the decrease in sea turtles, birds, reef carnivores, and cherry jewel-box (*Chama sarda*) (X^2 = 24.02). Carlson (1999:142) argues that the increase in conch relates to the increase in the number of hearths in later contexts rather than to a dietary change. However, the trend of relative decline in many of the other resources would have resulted in changed faunal assemblages and presumably diet. It is possible that the increase in conchs represents a prepared, stored, and commercial enterprise, drying or salting conch meat for future food, trade, tribute, or exchange. Had the Coralie settlement lasted longer it is possible that the trends would have become significant. These changes were probably wrought by hunting and fishing pressures.

9
Toward a Synthetic Caribbean Paleoethnobiology

The information presented in this volume represents basic data on plant and animal remains from an array of archaeological sites in the West Indies. This crucial biological information from archaeological sites and the ecology of the settled islands is fundamental to interpretations of human colonization and adaptations for life on tropical island archipelagoes. In this chapter we examine some of the constraints and opportunities involved in resource extraction and food production in island ecosystems. We explore issues of resource diversity between island groups, cultural differences between colonizing people, sustainability of subsistence practices involving plant and animal populations in view of human population growth, human manipulation of the environment and its resources, and some of the ways in which biotic organisms may have contributed to the ritual and symbolic aspects of culture in the Caribbean. Finally, we contrast the pre-Hispanic use of resources with the changes wrought by Spanish explorers and the ensuing European takeover (Crosby 1986).

Biological resources are deeply integrated into the overall fabric of human existence on several levels. The most fundamental is their role in everyday life through use for food and medicine, but they also play an important part in spiritual belief systems and are integral to nonfood subsistence concerns (e.g., fuelwood and construction materials and the whole array of objects from fish traps to baskets, to bowls and beads). The introduction of organisms into island ecosystems adds to the number and kinds of resources available for human use but also changes the endemic flora and fauna in subtle or sometimes overwhelming ways. Such introductions offer insight into the source of cultural influences and serve as a measure of those things that were viewed as important to the settlers, and how they managed risk in terms of food surpluses and shortages. We discuss not only how the environment sustained colonists but also the role of people as a force in environmental and landscape change.

ORIENTATION OF THE WEST INDIAN ARCHIPELAGO AND MAINLAND SOURCES OF COLONISTS

A defining feature of the island chain is its location in the New World tropics in a climate that promotes the growth of diverse tropical and subtropical vegetation, and surrounded by warm seas that allow for coral reef formation. However, the groups of islands within the archipelago provided different ease of access, resources, and potentials for exploitation. In this regard the geometrical properties of island biogeographic theory—distance, configuration, area, and isolation effects—come to the fore as important considerations, as in other island systems (Diamond 1997; Kirch 1984, 1986; Rainbird 1994). The islands of the southern Caribbean group are close enough to the South American mainland to permit continued interaction between people living on the mainland and the islands. These islands and settlements may have functioned together in a settlement–resource interaction sphere that included the mainland (Haviser 1987). The islands of the Lesser Antilles are all small with fewer ecological niches and evolved native organisms than the Greater Antilles. The islands of the Bahamas and Turks and Caicos have rich marine resources but poor soils, limited access to fresh water, and therefore limited potentials for plant cultivation. Some of the smaller and isolated islands in both the Bahamas and Lesser Antilles, which individually may not long sustain human populations, became functionally incorporated into local resource and interaction spheres, allowing for human survival by taking advantage of the differentially occurring assets between islands (Haviser 1991c). Trade and continuous interactions with the Greater Antilles or the South American mainland are also evident (Watters 1997). Human colonists of all these island groups came with traditions developed in different tropical areas that may have prepared them in different ways for life in the island ecosystem.

The colonization of the West Indies could have originated from three mainland regions each inhabited by people with different cultural backgrounds. The island archipelago is oriented within the Caribbean Sea close to mainland shores of South, Middle, and North America. At the southern extreme, the distance from Trinidad and Tobago to Grenada is 105 km (65 miles); that from the Yucatán peninsula to western Cuba is 200 km (124 miles); in the north, from the Florida Keys to Cuba is 161 km (100 miles), and to the Bahamas is 129 km (80 miles) (Rouse 1992:3). The northeastern coast of South America was the source of most pre-Hispanic colonists. The number and intensity of separate colonization ventures are still debated. Middle America, particularly the Yucatán peninsula, appears to have been the homeland of some of the earliest Caribbean colonists (Rouse 1992). Groups of people brought their stone tools, hunting, fishing, and perhaps plant-tending traditions to Cuba, Hispaniola, and Puerto Rico. In some cases their archaic successors or descendants apparently brought with them important home garden fruits, such as yellow sapote, wild avocado, and perhaps also sapodilla, which are native to Middle America and were probably early introductions into the islands. The southern coast of Florida is closer to Cuba and the Bahamas than the Yucatán is to Cuba. However, the ocean currents and trade winds do not favor travel from Florida to either the Bahamas or the Greater Antilles. No contact with Florida is firmly documented, and if contact occurred it was at best minimal until historic times.

Colonists, who came from different mainland regions, brought with them their ethnic identities and "social memory" (Levy and Holl 2002), including their varied cultural traditions, established cuisines, concepts concerning economic resources, and subsistence practices. They also moved through the islands at different rates, bringing with them various evolved cultures compared with Caribbean settlement and adaptations. Beyond the initial migrations they undoubtedly interacted as they encountered one another on different islands along the route (Levy and Holl 2002; Terrell 1997). People who took part in the major migration(s) from northeastern South America, and who left the deepest mark of all the early migrants, brought with them traditions originally developed and honed in the lowlands of the Orinoco Valley (Rouse 1992). As with all archaeologically defined cultures, they produced distinctive artifacts, and they cultivated crops, hunted game, fished along the rivers and coast, and reared domestic dogs. Their staple crop was manioc, and the root-crop production may have included additional geophytic starch sources such as arrowroot (*Xanthosoma* sp.). The practices developed to grow and prepare manioc tubers became part of Saladoid settlement and subsistence adaptations in the insular setting. Associated with all of these activities were funds of knowledge and dynamically evolved traditions. The choice to migrate to the islands required modifications of these traditions in the face of different island resources and environments.

RESOURCES OF ISLAND GROUPS AND DIVERSE
PATTERNS OF EXTRACTION

Native flora and fauna of the island chain resulted from colonization primarily by dispersal. Most plants and animals were dispersed by floating in the sea, rafting on plant mats or logs, being transported by birds, or being carried by the wind. Colonization by people was by watercraft that could be controlled to some extent. People were accompanied on these sea voyages by plants and animals that were intentionally and unintentionally brought along. These organisms and the people they came with had an impact on the endemic fauna and flora.

The islands with their depauperate terrestrial faunas would not have sustained a culture focused on hunting for very long. On the other hand, the abundant marine resources close to shore provided a rich alternative. This alternative source of protein, perhaps combined with relatively low human populations experiencing little or no population pressure, may explain why foragers of the earlier Preceramic periods and those who may have survived in the Greater Antilles up to historic contact (Chapter 3) seem to have practiced little or no plant cultivation. This would be analogous to the situation of relatively sedentary coastal foragers in Peru who had good access to marine and littoral resources, as well as access to knowledge about plant cultivation and crops, but who appear to have chosen not to add plant production and tending to their subsistence practices, or to have delayed that process (Hastorf 1999). Furthermore, in an effort to explain when and why hunter-gatherers may choose to forgo or, alternatively, initiate food production, Keeley (1995) conducted a detailed analysis of ethnographic case studies involving people living in many different environments and with diverse backgrounds, concluding that intensification of food-getting activities is highly unlikely to be directed toward plants if exploitable aquatic fauna are available in adequate supplies. In other cases, however, horticultural and perhaps arboricultural practices were transferred to the Caribbean Islands along with propagules—either seeds, stem cuttings, or rootstocks—ensuring continued production of what must have been key or preferred cultivated plants. Each of the island groups offered wild resources that were tapped by the colonists.

SOUTHERN CARIBBEAN REGION, THE BAHAMAS, AND THE TURKS AND CAICOS

Some similarities exist between the Bahamas and the small offshore Venezuelan islands. Both groups of islands are adjacent to larger, more ecologically diverse landmasses: the South American mainland in the case of the Venezuelan islands and the Greater Antilles in the case of the Bahamas. Both were settled late in the prehistory of the West Indies, and in both cases conch, sea turtles, reef fishes, and salt were important resources making these small, dry islands attractive. It is likely that these islands and their resources were known for some time before they were actually settled. People originating from different segments of the mainland coast settled the Venezuelan islands. Similarly, people from different islands of the Greater Antilles settled the Bahamas archipelago. Possibly the similarities between the two groups of islands end here.

The material culture of course differs between the two groups of islands, the one allied with the complex societies of central Venezuela and the other with those of the Greater Antilles. However, raw materials common to the two groups provided the opportunity for convergent use. For example, the conch that flourish in the shallow-water sea grass beds of both areas could be seen as a rich food resource and the raw material for tools and ornaments (Antczak 1999b; Carlson 1995). According to a modern survey, the estimated catches of conchs around the Venezuelan islands and around the Turks and Caicos are in the same order of magnitude, 120 to 300 individual conchs per person per day (Antczak 1999b:168). The sites in both areas have an exceptionally abundant shell-bead and tool inventory. The Governor's Beach site (GT-2) on Grand Turk was, in fact, primarily a bead manufacturing site (Carlson 1995). In both areas, the climatic conditions and access to salt would have permitted drying the conch meat. This may have been a resource returned to the homelands or retained for later consumption, as Sullivan (1981) suggested.

More remains of mammals were identified from the sites on the Venezuelan offshore islands than in the Bahamas. Two factors may account for this. The richer mainland fauna adjacent to the Venezuelan islands would have been a source of more terrestrial species and the excavations on the Venezuelan Islands were larger, increasing the chance of recovering rare remains. Introductions into the Bahamas include presumed manioc and its cultivation techniques, as well as pottery from Hispaniola and Cuba.

The Bahamas and Turks and Caicos are composed of more islands than those off the coast of Venezuela, and some are larger. Theoretically, this would permit greater independence from the homelands and more localized cultural developments in the Bahamas, at least where freshwater sources were reliable. Such a possibility was cut short by the European expansion. Ironically, people from the Bahamas were enslaved by the Spanish colonists to dive for pearls off Cubagua Island near the coast of Venezuela.

Lesser and Greater Antilles

The Lesser and Greater Antilles differ in scale. The Lesser Antilles is the southerly chain of small islands, many with fertile soils and sufficient rain for horticulture, surrounded by coral reefs and lagoons. In contrast, the Greater Antilles (to the north and west) are composed of large islands with varied habitats, larger rivers and estuaries, and evolved rodent faunas. Exploitation of biotic resources on both groups of islands exhibits flexibility. Sites located on different sides of the islands adjacent to different niches show variation that relates to exploitation of the habitats closest to the sites. In both groups of islands, people living at sites located farther inland relied more on terrestrial resources than did people living on the coast. The larger sizes of the islands in the Greater Antilles permitted location of sites farther from the coast, and a more diverse terrestrial fauna and flora provided a resource base for the inland habitations. A good example of this is the progressively greater relative abundance of terrestrial animals in the series of three Ostionoid sites on Jamaica: Rodney House, White Marl, and Bellevue (Table 7.9). Terrestrial resources make up 29%, 62%, and 89% of the vertebrate fauna in these sites, which are located approximately 1, 5, and 10 km inland, respectively. Similarly, Hope Estate, St. Martin, is 2 km inland and has abundant land animals, 43% in the early and 53% in the later Saladoid vertebrate assemblages (Table 6.3).

The flexibility in exploitation can be seen on islands where we have studied animal remains from different coastal locations around the island. The post-Saladoid sites on Barbados are located on the eastern (Hillcrest), western (Heywoods), and southern coasts (Silver Sands and Chancery Lane) (Table 6.3). At the two neighboring southern-coast sites people made use of virtually the same distribution of species based on exploited habitats, whereas at the other two sites people relied relatively less on reef fishes and more on pelagic fishes.

Although these variations exist, certain key resources predominate; the evidence of their use is repeated from one site to the next and on separate islands. Among these are buttonwood, lignum-vitae, and strong bark woods from the subtropical dry and coastal forests; mastic-bully and a few other native tree fruits and herbs such as trianthema; land crabs in early Ceramic-age deposits, West Indian topsnails, and parrotfishes. The other general characteristic of the exploitation of wild resources is the great diversity of both plants and animals that were used. A strategy based on a broad subsistence base should have helped ensure a stable economy, as a form of risk management or avoidance (Hayden 1981; Kelly 1985).

HUMAN-RESOURCE DYNAMICS

Sustainability versus Overexploitation

Life on small islands differs from life on the mainland as a result of evolution in relative isolation and in a small area (Grant and Grant 2002a, 2002b; MacArthur and Wilson 1967). In general, animals isolated on islands have evolved with few defenses against large predators and consequently are easy prey for humans. Animals without defenses allowing them to flee, fly, or hide can be quickly overexploited, leading to extirpation or extinction. Dogs that accompanied people into the Caribbean were a further threat to the native fauna, making people more efficient hunters and probably hunting in their own right.

Similarly, slow-growing trees that dominate dry tropical and subtropical forests may not be readily replaced following intensive human extraction pressure. Quickly established in their place will be "pioneer" and secondary successional species. Such seral species typically have an abundance of readily dispersed seeds to initiate new populations that take advantage of cleared areas. Particularly in circumscribed island environments, primary and secondary succession may follow alternate pathways, depending on the scale and nature of disturbance (Barnes et al. 1998; Harris 1984). The regeneration efficiency of primary forest, its dominant trees, and forest succession in general may be impeded by the ongoing disruption of human activities, especially with progressive distance from replacement seed sources as clearing and extraction encompass broader areas (Frelich and Puettmann 1999; Haila 1999; Harris 1984). This, combined with soil disturbance, may explain the increase in secondary forest species observed among the later archaeobotanical assemblages from St. Martin and Nevis. The decline in species like lignum-vitae and the increase in second-growth woods among the charcoal remains suggest that land was increasingly cleared for extraction of wood products and cultivation over the ca. 400–600 span of occupation at Hope Estate (Hoogland 1999:139–140) and during some 1,200 years of human settlement on Nevis (Wilson 1993:26–27) (Chapter 6), and that these human activities increasingly interfered with natural forest regeneration. Climate change may have been an additional variable working in concert with the negative pressures exerted by human groups on the native dry forests. A possible consequence of more land under cultivation is that it provided more favorable habitat for the endemic rice rats that become more abundant in some later deposits at Lesser Antilles sites (Table 6.3).

Emphasis on mangrove woods for fuel represented a different human-forest resource dynamic. Mangrove trees, with their waterborne propagules and stem-sprouting ability (Barnes et al. 1998), potentially have a greater resiliency and survival capacity vis-à-vis sustained human cutting and forest thinning. Emphasis on mangrove species as the primary woods for use as fuelwood may be one reason for the taxonomic consistency within the charcoal assemblage from the En Bas Saline site, Haiti, much as in south Florida archaeological sites (Newsom 1993a, 1993b, 1998a, 1998b; Scarry and Newsom 1992). A question emerges as to why people living in the Lesser Antilles seem to have made little or no use of the same mangrove taxa, particularly once the local terrestrial forests were undergoing change and given the positive characteristics of mangroves mentioned above. Perhaps this reflects cultural preferences; possibly wood harvests from mangroves in their aquatic habitats were in some way viewed with disfavor. The archaeological evidence suggests that Nevis and possibly much of the northern Lesser Antilles was abandoned or relatively de-populated later in prehistory, after an initial (Saladoid–Ostionoid transition) period of rapid population growth (Wilson 1993).

Population Reservoirs

Much as the dominant forest trees, many animal populations on tropical is-lands and their marine shelves do not have large reservoirs of adult individuals to maintain population levels. Most reef fishes and land crabs have pelagic lar-vae that are wonderfully designed for dispersal but thereby may pass an island as they drift in a unidirectional ocean current (Wolcott 1988). During the Saladoid period, land crabs were intensively harvested. Saladoid strata in many archaeological sites are dense crab shell deposits. The abundance of land crabs in the early deposits can be seen in the Hichmans site on Nevis and Hope Estate on St. Martin, where crabs make up 39% and 21% of the invertebrate remains, respectively (Table 6.9). In a comparison of the early and late deposits from Tutu, the relative abundance of land crabs declines from 45% to 27% (Wing et al. 2001:154). The quickest way to collect a lot of crabs is to capture them during their spawning migration (deFrance 1990). This would have a multiplier effect on the crab population by removing eggs for the next genera-tion even before they are deposited into the sea. The sizes of the crabs declined through time, and these creatures were a rare commodity in the later, post-Saladoid deposits (Tables 6.7 and 7.6a).

   Land snails are abundant in many dense crab-shell middens (Tables 6.9, 7.5, and 7.9). Most of these land snails are very small and are incidental to the fau-nal assemblages. They are attracted to the moist humus of the midden refuse. It is possible that slow accumulation of crab shells that make up such a large proportion of the animals' weight allowed more time for snails to be incorpo-rated. Therefore the abundance of small land snails may be more a guide to midden formation than to human subsistence.

Island Shelf

The size of the island shelf, the permanence of rivers, and the volume of fresh-water runoff limit inshore marine resources. Fresh water is vital for direct hu-man use, for plants and animals sharing the island ecosystem, and for estuarine organisms. Estuarine development is dependent on the size and conformation of river mouths. Island shelves are also proportional to the size of fringing and patch reefs they can support. Coral reefs are among the most productive and diverse habitats in the world (Connell 1978). The coral-reef animals were, in fact, most intensively exploited by people living along the shore of the islands throughout the West Indies (Wing 2001b).

Decrease in Fish Sizes

Through time several changes in the remains of reef fishes have taken place (Wing and Wing 2001). A significant decline in the sizes of reef fishes is apparent in the later deposits of sites occupied for lengthy periods. Size based on the width of the vertebral centra correlates well with body weight (Table 4.2). The decline in size is accompanied by a shift in species composition from a predominance of predatory fishes high in the trophic level, such as grouper and snapper, to a relatively greater abundance of omnivores and herbivores low in the trophic level, such as parrotfishes and surgeonfishes (Table 6.8). There is not only a decline in average size but also a decline in the range in sizes, as indicated by a lower standard deviation. The average estimated size of unidentified fishes (of which reef fishes were probably a major component) decreased from 1,099 g in the earlier deposit to 204 g in the later deposit on neighboring sites on Nevis (Table 6.7) and from 204 g in the early deposit to 84 g in the later deposit at the Tutu site on St. Thomas (Table 7.6a). Both the decline in size and the decrease in relative abundance of predatory species are indications of overfishing. Reef fishes such as grouper, snapper, grunt, parrotfish, and surgeonfish, which on average weigh only between 120 to 128 g, have not reached their full growth potential. Continuation of the same fishing techniques throughout the occupation of the site, catches made up of small juvenile individuals, is "growth overfishing." This is different from the faunal assemblage from Sulphur Ghaut site (JO-2) on Nevis, where small juvenile grunts appeared to be targeted; they make up approximately 35% of the remains. In this case, fishing in the nursery grounds is the more likely explanation (Kozuch and Wing 2004).

Biomass Change

At the same time we see evidence for overfishing of the coral reef fauna, we also see an increase in offshore pelagic fishes such as tuna, large jacks, flyingfishes, and in some sites herrings. This shift is seen in comparisons of the relative estimated biomass of reef and pelagic fishes (Tables 6.10 and 7.6b). Fishing in offshore waters would have required the use of watercraft and acceptance of the increased danger of that enterprise. Yet it appeared to have been the choice in favor of fishing the reefs farther along the coast. This change in the fishing economy came at a time when the human population had grown (Wilson 1989, 1993), as described above. Possibly, people living in other settlements controlled more distant reefs, precluding continuation of focus on fishing among the reefs. This change to offshore fishing also suggests that the fishermen were confident with their watercraft and had efficient equipment, probably including hooks, lines, and nets.

Economic Change and Cultural Development

Clearly we can document differences in the plant and animal assemblages from West Indian sites. However, in evaluating differences between assemblages, care must be taken to consider environmental circumstances, the resources available to the occupants living in different locations, and the level of technology. Assemblage changes in one location may indicate economic change brought about by human-induced environmental change or an economic choice. For various reasons, environmental and social, some communities will have greater ability or desire to mobilize more resources and intensify food production than others. Widespread changes that are similar from site to site suggest regional economic change resulting from environmental degradation or innovation of production intensification. Archaic-age and early Saladoid–period faunal assemblages appear in general to be more similar to one another than do the assemblages in later periods. In part this may be the result of animal populations that had not been exploited to levels below sustainability during initial occupation.

Such changes may have had considerable bearing on the dynamics and trajectory in social complexity and organization from Archaic people to the later groups of the region, including those described as chiefdoms. Among the classic characteristics of chiefdom society are control of the access to resources such as food and raw or rare materials and mobilization of production. Both the animal and plant assemblages demonstrate some unique differences between earlier and later occupations. For example, only with the later Ceramic-age Ostionoid occupations is there evidence for maize; evidently during that period it became part of an apparently diversified base of plant taxa grown and exploited, at least in the Greater Antilles and Virgin Islands. Associated also with this period in some areas is evidence of technological innovations such as agricultural terraces and irrigation systems to expand agricultural production. This, and the presence of separate races of maize and likely also root-crop cultivars (therefore knowledge of plant life cycles and control over planting and harvests), as well as the presence of additional exotics and special-purpose plants such as tobacco, implies increasing social complexity and perhaps also the presence of managerial elites.

Much remains to be clarified concerning diet choice and economic decision making in general in the Caribbean during all periods of human settlement. Similarly, regional settlement patterns and Ceramic-age site hierarchies on individual islands and within the different subregions of larger islands are little understood. We know less about the relations and interactions between contemporaneous communities on islands and in the region, even though this would serve to illuminate some of the internal and external sociopolitical dynamics and provide a clearer basis for understanding some of the underpinnings of evolving social complexity. For example, it may be that the relationship between sites such as Tibes and nearby El Bronce in southwestern Puerto Rico was analogous to that of Mississippian centers in eastern North America and their affiliated smaller farmsteads or hamlets dispersed in the surrounding countryside (Anderson 1999; Mehrer 1995). We might then anticipate that the material cultures as well as the biotic assemblages, that is, subsistence aspects, of Tibes and El Bronce should exhibit some elements in common, but they should differ by degrees according to the nature of the two settlements (i.e., Tibes as an early center of sociopolitical authority, on the one hand, and El Bronce as a smaller, generally contemporaneous but somewhat autonomous settlement that [presumably] interacted with the center, on the other). To this end, Newsom (1999b) conducted a comparative analysis of the faunal assemblages from Tibes and El Bronce in an effort to explore this relationship or minimally to compare the two sites from a socioeconomic perspective. This analysis focused on how the two sets of faunal remains from the sites partition among the different faunal classes as a possible reflection of differences in exploitation practices or access to resources—in other words, whether the same or different resources were exploited or available between the sites, and whether these were used at about the same levels and intensities or some were emphasized over others in view of the social distinctions between the sites. The results of this analysis demonstrated some definitive similarities—for example, marine fish proved prominent at both sites, comprising 56% and 54% of the vertebrate MNI from El Bronce and Tibes, respectively—and the proportional similarity (Towner 1992) between the two faunal assemblages is 71%. But important differences were noted in terms of the types and relative abundance of organisms, combining both vertebrate and invertebrate data. For example, using the Shannon Index (H') to compare both species richness and evenness,* Tibes was found to have a considerably more diverse and even fauna, relative to El Bronce. The lower diversity (H' = 0.270) and evenness (J' = 0.319) for El Bronce indicate a more narrow, focused subsistence base, largely the result of emphasis on marine molluscs and fish. In contrast, higher diversity (H' = 0.564) and evenness (J' = 0.668) values for Tibes indicate a

*Evenness (Pileu's Index [J']) is incorporated into the Shannon Index; basically this is a measure of equitability and can clarify how species abundances are distributed among individual taxa, thus serving as a reflection of the degree of exploitation or emphasis on different groups of fauna (Ludwig and Reynolds 1988).

broader, more diverse resource base. The pattern of plant resources from the two sites parallels that of the faunal remains, with Tibes exhibiting much greater diversity and equitability (Tables 7.7 and 7.8). These differences are undoubtedly partly explained by Tibes being a larger community, but the differences appear to be more in kind, that is, quality, than a matter of simple abundance or quantities. At El Bronce, for example, reptiles (primarily sea turtles) and mammals, especially hutía, contributed 3% and 2%, respectively, of the MNI for the total faunal sample, whereas at Tibes terrestrial vertebrates seem to make up a greater proportion of the faunal classes: mammals (hutía and guinea pig, both exotics) totaled 9% of the MNI, birds 5%, and reptiles 2%. Moreover, only at Tibes was guinea pig identified, as well as evening primrose, the cojóbana-type wood, and other items. In general, the zooarchaeological and archaeobotanical data appear to suggest greater scope and breadth of diet and resource-procurement patterns associated with Tibes, as a chiefly center, relative to the nearby settlement of El Bronce, a smaller community or farmstead. To what extent the differences in biotic materials reflect different aspects of the culture and various activities associated with the functioning of the two sites is yet to be determined. Hypothetically at least, the greater diversity and richness that seem to characterize Tibes are related to differences in consumption or redistribution of food and other items inherent to the operation of a chiefly center.

INTRODUCED PLANTS AND ANIMALS: RESOURCE MANAGEMENT

Introductions and Crop Diversity

"The rule that migrating people bring their plants and animals with them" has few exceptions (Crosby 1986:81). Our studies indicate that some of the earliest introductions of plants, such as yellow sapote, avocado, and sapodilla, may have originated from Central America during the Archaic age. Thus it would seem that either from the outset or as part of later cultural innovations that took place in the islands, Archaic hunter-gatherers in the West Indies had entered into the "middle ground" (Smith 2001) of low-level food production, exerting some measure of control over plant food resources. However, the majority of introductions of fully domestic plants and animals appear to have come primarily from northeastern South America and later, during the Ceramic-age migrations of sedentary root-crop horticulturists. Among the introductions are domestic dogs and guinea pigs, the staple plant manioc, trees like achiote and Panama tree, and perhaps also papaya, sweet potato, pepper, peanut, and tobacco, among others (as described in Chapter 7). The maize grown in the Caribbean also has the potential to have originated from races developed or long cultivated in lowland South America (Oliver 2001) rather than from Meso-american maize, though this remains to be verified. The historic records mention at least seven types of root crops that were cultivated by the Taino Indians at the time of European contact. Manioc and sweet potato were singled out as the most important plant staples in the islands; the former was the primary crop. The premier position of manioc, as Peterson (1997:128) has pointed out, was also reflected in the fact that one of the two supreme Taino deities was Jocahu or Yucahu, the "lord of cassava and the sea" (among the Spanish-speaking people of the Caribbean, manioc is still known as yuca, a name possibly recalling the Taino epithet). Sugary sweet potatoes called batata were distinguished from less sweet cultivars that were known as age (or axe, aje) (Sauer 1966:54). Aside from manioc and sweet potatoes, other root crops mentioned in the historic chronicles include yautía (*Xanthosoma* sp.), ararú or arrowroot (*Maranta arundinacea*), ilerén (*Calathea* sp.), yampee (*Dioscorea trifida*), and an edible-rooted form of *Canna* sp. (Fernández de Oviedo 1959). All of these, with the possible exception of yampee (which may actually represent an early introduction from Africa), and depending on the particular species, are native to northern South America (Liogier and Martorell 2000:250, 259, 262). Crops were grown together in *conucos*, the series of small, circular earthen mounds that provided growing platforms (as described in Chapter 7). Although there is much to be discovered and clarified concerning Taino and earlier crops, field preparation, and garden systems, for now we can specify with greater certainty some of the actual crops and infer some aspects of their growth and requirements. From the Greater Antilles sites manioc and possibly also sweet potato have been identified, as from En Bas Saline, Haiti, as well as maize and some of the other taxa mentioned above (Chapter 7). Tentative indications for the archaeological presence of some of the other root crops come from plant microremains from Puerto Rico and the Bahamas (Chapters 7 and 8).

As mentioned before, the evidence for manioc cultivation comes more from the remains of the griddle sherds and other artifacts used to cook the prepared tubers than from the plant parts themselves, with the exception of those from En Bas Saline. The South American lowland traditions for cultivation and preparation of manioc tubers are complex because of the poisonous constituents in the tuber that must be removed to make it edible. It is likely that both "bitter manioc" cultivars, so called because they contain a higher percentage of hydrocyanic acid in the tubers than occurs in the "sweet manioc" cultivars, were cultivated in the Caribbean (as described in Chapter 3). Bitter manioc is most widely cultivated in the lowland tropics, possibly because the poisonous ingredients repel pests and the starchy tuber can be stored for a longer time (in the ground or as dry "bread") than the sweet manioc; these cultivars also demonstrate higher yields, evidently by virtue of their ability to repel insect attack by means of the chemical defense system (Wilson and Dufour 2002). Preparation and cooking detoxifies the poisonous cyanogenetic glucosides in extracted manioc juices. Meat, fish, and other ingredients cooked with the juices produced a traditional specialty called a pepper pot. It is likely that small fishes whose remains are found in generally good condition were added to the pepper pot and then the bony residue was discarded on the midden. Both dogs and manioc were widespread and an integral part of the West Indian economy in the past as today.

This does not appear to have been the situation with regard to prehistoric maize. There is no evidence to suggest that it was ever used as intensively in the islands as in mainland areas. Basically we infer that given the volume of research and number of paleoethnobotanical studies that have now been conducted or are under way in the Caribbean, it seems reasonable to expect that maize should be turning up more frequently if it had ever achieved the level of importance as occurred prehistorically in other areas of the Americas. Rather, maize remains are scantily present and have been recovered only from two sites in the entire region (Newsom and Pearsall 2003). A few pollen records hint at a slightly wider occurrence (as described in Chapter 7) though these are still relatively late, there exist problems with dating, and the individual quantities (grain counts) are still very low (Newsom 1993a). Thus comes the question of whether maize was ever grown as a staple in the West Indies. Certainly the evidence suggests it was not grown and stored as quantities of dried grain, that is, as a storable surplus. This is consistent with what is indicated in the ethnohistoric documents: that maize was a secondary crop or was somehow regarded differently than as a pivotal staple. The predominant forms in which maize seems to have been consumed in the West Indies are the green state, that is, immature, including roasted kernels or raw maize: "when the ears are tender they are eaten almost like milk" (Fernández de Oviedo 1959:14–15; and see Ortega and Guerrero 1981; Sauer 1966; Sturtevant 1961). This description conforms to low-intensity use, more as a vegetable, supplement, or "curiosity" (Pearsall 1994) than as a staple carbohydrate source (dried kernels, ground meal, and flour). This form of use—harvesting the grain before it is fully ripened and hard—would leave few traces in the archaeological record, so our current understanding of the timing and areas where maize may have been adopted is potentially very biased. However, it is probable that maize was first transported to the West Indies at a relatively late date. It does not appear to have become a staple in parts of northern lowland South America until well after the first Saladoid migrants entered the Caribbean Islands (Merwe et al. 1981; Oliver 2001; Pearsall 1994; Roosevelt 1980; Sanoja and Vargas 1983; Zucchi et al. 1984). After its introduction the insular environment may have been less conducive to growing maize than that in source regions, leading to a period of adjustment and experimentation. Moreover, Keegan (personal communication 1993) has suggested, and we are inclined to agree, that maize would have represented an expensive source of protein and therefore would never have been emphasized in the Caribbean as long as alternative protein sources (e.g., marine resources) were available at a lower economic cost. This hypothesis is supported by Keeley's (1995) ethnographic research mentioned earlier, emphasizing the key role of aquatic protein sources when available. It is also possible that maize was simply overshadowed in the Caribbean by the primary system of root cropping that seems to have been fully a part of the Ceramic-age subsistence from the beginning (Davis 1988b; Rouse 1986, 1992). This would parallel Pearsall's (1994) explanation for the delayed spread of maize into northeastern South America. Finally, perhaps telling is the very restricted nature of the presence of maize at En Bas Saline (Newsom 1998a; Newsom and Deagan 1994): its strong association with the centrally positioned elite area of the site provides a basis for hypothesizing that restricted elite access to maize may have operated in the prehistoric Caribbean. Perhaps this also extended to evening primrose and a few other plants. Restricted access to maize by privileged social segments has been suggested as a factor in the early stages of the introduction of maize into other regions, for example, southeastern North America (Smith 1990).

Home Garden Structure, Diversity, and Multifunctionality

Another important sphere where domesticated or otherwise useful plants for foods, medicines, utilitarian, and special purposes are maintained is the intimate setting of dooryard or home gardens. According to Las Casas (quoted in Sauer 1966:57), "they planted small trees of manzanillas for purgative use adjacent to their houses, as something they esteemed greatly." Such plants recovered from Caribbean sites (we infer) include trees, shrubs, vines, and herbs; among them avocado, yellow sapote, sapodilla (níspero [*Manilkara* sp.]), achiote, papaya, peppers, passion fruit, evening primrose, tobacco, and possibly also gourds and/or squash, cotton, cojóbana, and others. As indicated above, maize is associated exclusively with later prehistoric contexts and may have had some ritual significance or association with elites, perhaps similar to the guinea pig, at least at En Bas Saline as indicated above. We can speculate that perhaps maize or particular cultivars or races of maize in the Caribbean, like tobacco (Chapter 1), were imbued with some special significance (Ford 1994), and these cultivars were always or at times grown in the close setting of home gardens. Home gardens are perfect venues for experimentation with plants. Some of the other plants, such as cotton, may be the products of local West Indian domestication, where the idea of controlled breeding of plants was applied to West Indian endemic species. Currently, however, insufficient data exist to explore this possibility. Seeds or more seeds, such as from cotton and papaya, are required for sufficient specimen populations from which to collect the range of morphometric data needed to evaluate the possible presence of incipient or fully domesticated plants, and to discern any possibility of in situ domestication. There is no evidence to demonstrate that particular plants were domesticated locally, that is, in the Caribbean Islands, though the evidently wider range and later disappearance of plants such as evening primrose may reflect an inability to survive without human intervention. The human population decline following European contact may have disrupted the maintenance of plants and animals that were in a quasi-domestic status such as (perhaps) the evening primrose.

Introduced Domestic Animals

Animals that were fully domesticated and introduced into the West Indies, probably from northern South America, include dogs and guinea pigs. Of these, dogs, which have accompanied people throughout the world, are most abundant and widespread in the West Indies. In the West Indies dogs appear in Ceramic-age sites. Ethnographic accounts describe successful hunting with dogs (Sauer 1966:58–59, 100). Dogs are typically recovered from burials and often associated with human burials, as was seen at the Sorcé site on Vieques Island and the Silver Sands Site on Barbados. Few remains are associated with midden refuse. This would indicate that before the European expansion, most dogs were not consumed. Spanish accounts of natives eating dogs may have been given during periods of starvation (Sauer 1966:58).

The conformation of dogs from the West Indies is similar. They are small and probably represent a founder population with inbred characteristics. A founder effect has been demonstrated in a human population of Puerto Rico, adding credence to the same effect in their dog companions (Toro-Labrador et al. 1999). Ethnographic accounts describe successful hunting with dogs (Sauer 1966:58–59, 100). In many (30%) of the dogs from the Sorcé site on Vieques Island, and in single specimens from other sites, the crown of the lower fourth premolar had been broken out at some time during the life of the animal, producing a slot in the lower tooth row (Wing 1991b). Mutilation of that single tooth was a regular practice for some reason. One speculation is that it may have allowed a place to anchor a muzzle-like restraint. Zeder (personal communication, 1983) identified dogs with the same tooth mutilation from San Lorenzo, Ecuador, and also suggested that this may have accommodated some binding that acted as a restraint. This may have been a means of controlling the dogs and discouraging their independent hunting of endemic and introduced rodents.

The emerging picture of the distribution of guinea pigs has too many gaps to chart the course of the introduction of this animal. It originated from South America, but whether it was transported up the Lesser Antillean island chain to the Greater Antilles or directly across the Caribbean Sea to Hispaniola and Puerto Rico, and then south along the Lesser Antilles as far as Antigua, is not certain. Guinea pigs are absent from the southern Lesser Antilles, leaving no trail of a northward journey. They appear in many late prehistoric deposits, including sites on Curaçao, Antigua, St. Johns, Vieques, Puerto Rico, and the Dominican Republic. Their remains are rare, though all are from midden contexts. Thus far they have not been found as burials or in clearly ceremonial features except perhaps at the Cinnamon Bay site on St. John. They are reported from a special-purpose site, Tibes, possibly suggesting that these animals were reserved for occasional activities or for elite individuals. Fernández de Oviedo (1959) made the observation that guinea pigs were being eaten in Santo Domingo in the Dominican Republic. No archaeological remains have been studied to support this account or to gauge the relative importance (if any) of guinea pigs in the diet at the time of contact between Native Americans and Europeans.

Guinea pigs were domesticated in the Andes at least 7,000 years ago, where they were used in many special ways. They were and still are a feast food, a sacrificial animal, and an animal used in divination and curing (Morales 1995). In the West Indies they were known as cori, probably a loan word from cuy, the name they are called in the Andes (Cecil Brown, personal communication 1995). It is likely that guinea pigs were introduced into the West Indies accompanied by such cultural traditions as their name and at least some of the traditional Andean uses. These specialized uses may explain the widely dispersed records of guinea pigs and their rarity in midden contexts.

Introduction of Other Animals

In addition to domesticated animals, a number of managed animals were imported. Chief among these is the agouti (*Dasyprocta leporina*) and hutía (*Isolobodon portoricensis*). Agoutis are associated with people throughout tropical America. Although agouti are not common at any site, they are relatively more common in the sites closest to the South American mainland and decrease in relative abundance at sites in the northern Lesser Antilles. They are absent from the Virgin Islands and the Greater Antilles. They became naturalized on most of the islands south of St. Kitts. However, in the face of land clearing and introduced European animals, agouti may have become extirpated from most of the Lesser Antilles (Westermann 1953). A similar decline in relative abundance is seen in the hutía from its center of abundance in Puerto Rico out to the smaller Virgin Islands to the east. Both the agouti and the hutía were maintained in captivity and introduced from island to island by people. MacArthur and Wilson (1967) envisioned the decline in animal abundance distant from the source as a natural distribution rather than as animals associated with and cared for by people. However, the observed decline suggests difficulty people had in maintaining these animals increasingly far from their source.

Management of Animals in Captivity

The decline in these captive animals, agouti and hutía, may exemplify principles of island biogeography and also reveals some constraints of animal management. Care of these animals required providing food and opportunities for breeding as well as restraints of some sort that would keep them accessible and protected them from dogs. Restraints such as cages or collars and leads probably would have been made of wood or plant fibers. Large rodents such as agouti and hutía could easily chew such devices. The other alternative would have been to tame these animals so that they would not wander far, in which case dogs would have been restrained or controlled to prevent hunting.

No Increased Production of Domestic Animals

Increased production of domestic and captive animals would have augmented the post-Saladoid meat supply in the Lesser Antilles. However, agoutis are not abundantly represented at any site studied thus far. An agouti was excavated from a burial on St. Kitts, suggesting this animal was given some special treatment (Goodwin 1976). The hutía of the Greater Antilles and Virgin Islands were successfully managed to contribute substantially to the diets of people living inland on Puerto Rico, at least. For example, at the El Bronce site inland from the southern coast of Puerto Rico, hutía constitute 17% of the vertebrate fauna (Reitz 1985).

In Jamaica the native cony (*Geocapromys brownii*) was successfully exploited at increasing levels of intensity with distance from the coast. Conies make up 82% of the vertebrate fauna at the Bellevue site, which is 10 km inland. Conies may have been wild, abundant, and reliably caught, or they may have been kept in captivity and readily accessible (Wilkins 2001). The closely related *Geocapromys ingrahami* of the Bahamas is not abundant in archaeological contexts. Species of *Geocapromys* and other rodent taxa are beginning to be reported from archaeological sites in Cuba (e.g., Córdova Medina et al. 1997), but we have limited information concerning their relative abundances and overall distributions.

Other large rodents were used and moved from island to island. The Cuban capromyid rodent, *Capromys pilorides*, was also kept in captivity and was introduced into Hispaniola. This species is a very common constituent in Cuban sites. Other endemic rodents are identified from Cuban sites (Córdova and

Arredondo 1988; Morgan and Woods 1986; Pino [in press]). This begs the question of why some cultivated plants and captive animals seem not to have been fully domesticated. It was already mentioned that the seed remains of native plants exhibit none of the signs of true domesticates. To reiterate, however, possibly at least some of these organisms were in incipient stages of domestication and so lacked the anatomical and morphological signatures commonly associated with domestication in plants and animals. Again, supplies of aquatic resources may have been a factor in some areas; in Cuba freshwater fish reportedly were kept in pens in large numbers (Sauer 1966:58).

Maintaining Captive Animals

Another consideration is that these captive animals may not have been easy to maintain. The only suspicion we have of this is that they were not more intensively used when some fisheries began to decline, and they diminish in relative abundance farther from their sources. Because some of these animals are now extinct, it is not possible to determine where the maintenance problems lay. For example, successful domestication requires controlling the animal's movements, providing sufficient food of adequate quality, and ensuring conditions necessary for unconstrained breeding and rearing of young. The biology of most of these animals, with the exception of the agouti and cony, is not well enough known to understand what behavioral or physiological requirements could not be met (Smythe 1978; Wilkins 2001).

The animals kept in captivity in the West Indies never reached full domestication and, in fact, became extinct like the hutía, endangered, like the cony in the Bahamas and Jamaica, and extirpated on most islands, like the agouti during historic times. With disruption of the human population, these animals were no longer maintained even at minimal levels. Increases in human populations from Europe and Africa, plantation agriculture, and introduction of firearms all had a part in endangering cony populations. These animals persist only in the most remote areas or under strict conservation controls. Introduction of chickens, pigs, and other Old World domesticates that can be easily and cheaply reared has taken some of the pressure off native hunted animals. On the other hand, introduction of predators such as the mongoose has contributed to the demise of native fauna.

During the Ceramic age the number of plants that were probably cultivated increased. Cultivated and tended plants included fruit trees and garden crops, as we indicated earlier. In the Greater Antilles agriculture intensified in some regions with construction of terraces for planting crops and evidently also irrigation systems in some parts of Hispaniola. Such major projects require a managed workforce and imply a greater commitment to agricultural production in general. This almost certainly corresponds with the declines in animal protein sources in some areas, coupled with competition for land in conjunction with increasing human populations. If our assumptions about maize are correct, as outlined above, this intensification was focused on heightened root-crop production rather than on grains and seed crops.

MATERIALS PROMOTING A RICH LIFE

Fiber Industries

Plant fibers were used throughout the Caribbean for construction of cloth, netting, and baskets. We know this from several lines of evidence, even though the actual fibers are not generally preserved in archaeological contexts. Several accounts by Spaniards describe the very fine weaving of hammocks made and used by the Taíno. In fact, the word *hammock* is derived from the Taíno word *hamaca* (Lovén 1935; Rouse 1992). Evidence for mats and baskets is seen in the impressions of woven matting on pottery. Particularly rich and diverse examples of mat and basketry impressions are seen in pottery of the Bahamas, much of which may derive from palm leaves or their retted fibers (Hutcheson 2001). Baskets (bags and boxes) are the primary tool for gathering plants or shellfish. An expandable basketry tube known as a *cibucán* or *tipití* (Olazagasti 1997; Oliver 2001) is a traditional way of squeezing the poisonous juices from bitter manioc, the carbohydrate staple of lowland South America and the Caribbean. Evidence for cordage and netting comes from early accounts of fishing and indirectly from the fishes that must have been caught with nets, traps, or hooks and lines.

Plants and Plant Products Essential to Fishing Industries

The faunal assemblages demonstrate that a diverse array of animals was caught. The characteristics of these animals suggest the types of equipment that may have been used. Some cordage probably would have been part of snares or traps used to catch rodents, birds, and lizards. Cordage would of course be an integral part of hook-and-line fishing. Very few examples of hooks have been recognized from archaeological contexts. However, presumably they were used to catch carnivorous fishes such as groupers, snappers, and tuna. Because hook-and-line fishing was likely practiced, hooks were probably made of some plant material (perhaps the robust thorns from certain trees) and the line of plant fiber cordage. Neither preserves well in archaeological contexts, aside from deep caves and waterlogged deposits with exceptional organic preservation. Estimates of maximum fish size based on vertebral measurements are 18.5 kg for the largest fish measured, a snapper, and an average of 4 kg for the little tunny that became common during the post-Saladoid (Wing 2001a, 2001b). Cordage strength and hook size determine the sizes of fishes caught (Salls 1989). Similarly, the mesh gauge of netting and the size and conformation of nets determine the sizes and kinds of fishes caught. Many of the faunal assemblages recovered using fine-gauge screens include herring and silversides. Both are small schooling fishes that swim near the surface of the water and can most easily be caught with fine-gauge nets. A traditional net form still in use today in the lowland circum-Caribbean is a hand net with a rigid, circular rim (Roth 1924:plate 48B). It is also likely that nets in the form of seines were used; however, cast nets were probably not in use during pre-Columbian times (Rostlund 1952:82). Reef fishes are typically caught in traps. These were traditionally made of wood and cane (more likely split palm petioles) in the shape of an S with a conical entrance at both ends. Although basketry fish traps have developed around the world, it is likely that this form evolved in the Americas. Today fish traps are made with chicken wire stretched over a wooden frame.

An unusual method of catching fishes described in documents is with suckerfish or remora (Echeneidae) on a tether, which is pulled in when the remora attaches to a sea turtle or larger fish (Lovén 1935:425). This noteworthy technique apparently has been used in other parts of the world. We have not encountered any remora remains at any site and thus cannot confirm that they were used for this or any other purpose.

Documents mention the use of certain plants, generally termed barbasco, as being effective as fish poisons (Sauer 1966:58). The leguminous trees (*Lonchicarpus* and *Piscidia* [Record and Hess 1943:288, 308]) are known to have properties that stun fish: the bark or certain other parts are pulverized and then dispersed in quiet waters. Based on the fishes in the faunal assemblages, it is not possible to identify those that might have been caught in this manner.

RITUAL OR SPECIAL-PURPOSE USE OF PLANTS, ANIMALS, OR THEIR PARTS

High- or Differential-Status Indicators

During the post-Saladoid periods, when populations had grown and significant social change was under way, we see for the most part no clear evidence for unequal distribution of resources within or between sites that might correspond with some of the social complexity inferred by archaeologists (Curet 1996; Keegan 2000), aside from Newsom's study (1999b) comparing sites in southern Puerto Rico. The only other possible indication of differential access to particular rare commodities or those that may have been imbued with some special social significance is seen in the distribution of guinea pigs and possibly also maize, evening primrose, and cojóbana, as described above and in Chapter 7. Both maize and evening primrose were primarily associated with the high-status area of the site at En Bas Saline, Haiti, specifically the center of the site where the cacique's residence was situated (Newsom 1998a; Newsom and Deagan 1994). This would seem to denote a status apart from more mundane food items and a strong association with power and status. Perhaps similarly at Tibes, another paramount center, both evening primrose and the cojóbana-type wood—two potentially narcotic plants—are associated with an area of the site that may have been reserved for elites or special functions (Newsom and Curet 2003); however, more data are needed to clarify this spatial association and characterization of the site deposits. In addition to En Bas Saline and Tibes, evening primrose was recovered from NCS-4, another civic-ceremonial center, and a few additional Ostionoid sites (Table 7.7). Although admittedly highly speculative, this distribution may be explained if this plant is indeed the herb gioia (see Chapter 1) of ethnohistoric mention (Rouse 1992:14) and was used at these sites as part of rituals and other special purposes.

Fully domesticated guinea pigs were introduced from South America. Again, they occur only in later deposits (e.g., at NCS-4 and Tibes on Puerto Rico) and have been identified from sites in Curaçao, Antigua, St. Thomas, Vieques Island, and Hispaniola. Curaçao is closest to the South American source. The people living on the islands off the coast of South America were engaged in the trade of animals and animal parts, including guinea pigs (Antczak 1999b; Wing 2004). Guinea pigs are most common in Greater Antillean sites and are reported on Hispaniola. Vieques Island, close to Puerto Rico, may have benefited from this proximity. Cinnamon Bay on St. John and both NCS-4 and Tibes on Puerto Rico are believed to have been civic-ceremonial centers. The presence of guinea pigs at these sites denotes some special regard for this animal. Guinea pigs are absent from the Tutu Archaeological Village on neighboring St. Thomas (for example) and from various other sites in the Virgin Islands and Puerto Rico. The presence of guinea pigs at two sites on Antigua but not elsewhere in the Lesser Antilles suggests some special trade relationship between the people of Antigua and those living on the Greater Antilles or St. Johns. There might have been access to a special resource on Antigua, such as flint for stone tools.

West Indian dogs from prehistoric contexts have many traits in common. The dogs are small, and many exhibit congenital loss of the first lower premolar and the last lower molar. They were treated in the same way throughout the islands. A high percentage of them had the fourth lower premolar broken out during life. Most dogs were buried and sometimes associated with a human burial, as we have indicated. Their teeth, usually the canines and sometimes the first lower molar, were modified by a hole pierced in the root so that the tooth could be strung. Such teeth are described from human burials where they may have been a ritual offering.

Shell Beads and Wooden Objects

Shell beads were perhaps another special commodity for which access was controlled and limited. The special qualities or significance attached to particular types of beads may have been due to unique colors, characteristics, or species rarity. The Governor's Beach site (GT-2) on Grand Turk was evidently devoted to the manufacture of beads (Carlson 1995). The craftsmen working at that site were probably Taino from the Greater Antilles, possibly Hispaniola, rather than Lucayans from the Bahamas based on the presence at the site of Greater Antillean pottery. These artisans produced shell beads between A.D. 1100 and 1200. Beads made of queen conch and red jewelbox shell were probably strung and used as ornaments with social and religious significance. Shell and semiprecious stone beads and ornaments would have represented rare and valuable objects, embodying an investment of time, and consequently imbued with social power. Red (jewelbox shells) and white shell (queen conch) beads formed the decorative patterns on woven cotton belts, features of the cacique paraphernalia symbolizing power (Olazagasti 1997). According to documents, two beaded belts were given to Columbus during his first contact with Lucayans as symbols of alliance, power, and leadership (Alegría 1995, 1997b; Carlson 1995:102 [Dunn and Kelley 1989:263]). One beaded belt still in existence comes from an archaeological context, but the others are from unknown proveniences and exhibit a combination of Taino, African, and European characteristics (Alegría 1995; Rouse 1992:159–160). The belts, made of cotton, would have been preserved archaeologically only under extraordinary circumstances, again such as in dry caves or wet sites. If, as the documents describe, the beaded belts were associated with individuals who had controlling power, these artifacts would be uncommon. The Governor's Beach site "has provided a rare insight into craft specialization activities during the period of rising complexity of the Taino chiefdoms" (Carlson 1995:97).

Artisans at the Governor's Beach site followed a tradition of shell-bead making begun during the Saladoid period. A particularly rich and diverse bead and pendant collection was excavated from the Sorcé site on Vieques Island (Chanlatte Baik 1983). Shell beads at Sorcé were made of helmets, tritons, and conchs. Similarly, at the Hope Estate site on St. Martin, shell beads are made of conch and jewelbox shells and the shells of other molluscs (Weydert 1994). The shells most often used in bead production (such as conchs, helmets, and jewelboxes) are found in the coastal waters near most sites. Yet the abundance of worked shell varies among sites. Shell beads seem to overlap with semiprecious stone beads in some similar shapes and probably in many functions. They differ in the availability of the raw material. Beads were for personal adornment, probably signified social status, and represented wealth (Lovén 1935).

The history of the trade of semiprecious stone, the raw material for stone beads, and the reconstruction of the techniques for making beads and ornaments are central to understanding this aspect of material culture. The natural rarity of these materials, the distant trade networks needed to obtain them, and their value-added transformation into beads or amulets with social significance place these objects in a category of special significance (Cody 1991; Watters and Scaglion 1994). Although these beads and amulets have been found at many sites throughout the Caribbean, the centers of bead production are identified in Grenada, Montserrat, and Vieques (Watters and Scaglion 1994).

Wooden figurines or "idols" and stools (duhos) decorated with figures of deities (zemis) were a sign of chiefly rank or other high status, such as accorded the shaman or behique (Olazagasti 1997). The chiefs or chieftains, the caciques (Keegan et al. 1998), as well as the behiques were individuals believed to have the power to mediate between the everyday and spirit worlds, and they performed ceremonies important to the ongoing belief systems and ritual cycles of Taino society. Wooden idols and other figurines had a central role in the ritual reenactments of Taino cosmology and the functioning of cemíism (Oliver 1997a, 1997c). Special magical and spiritual properties were attributed to the particular woods used to carve the idols, such as lignum-vitae or guayácan (Ortiz 1947:115–118). The presence of these and other objects seemingly testifies to the presence of the stratified society of chiefdoms (Rouse 1992:123). Wood and decorative materials including shell and gold, as well as perhaps maize and other plants, are evidence of this social complexity and the role that biotic resources can play in social interaction spheres.

ARCHAEOLOGICAL RECORD AND TECHNIQUES

Recovery Strategies

Biological resources are deeply integrated into human existence. The majority of the plant and animal remains excavated from refuse middens and habitation deposits are the inedible residues of food items or of food preparation and cooking (e.g., charcoal fragments from spent fuelwood). Essential for reconstruction of the past diet and the full range of utilized plants and animals is a recovery strategy that provides for recovery of an adequate sample sieved through fine-gauge screen. The most efficient procedure is to use nested geological sieves separating large bone and shell with a 6 mm sieve, and a 4 mm sieve and finer sieves for plant materials and smaller faunal remains (as discussed in Chapter 4). Although small faunal organisms recovered in this way may seem insignificant, they can cumulatively provide substantial amounts of protein and calcium to the diet. Furthermore, the recovery of a full array of organisms provides information about the habitats that were exploited and the methods that might have been used to catch the represented animals. It is also possible that small organisms and seeds may be caught or gathered on a daily basis, while a distant fishing expedition may be undertaken only occasionally. Fine-gauge sieving (down to 0.4 mm) is the only way to effectively recover very small items such as tobacco seeds and shark dermal denticles, among others, and so retrieve the full complement of paleoethnobiological materials. When recovery is optimal, estimates can be made of the amount of food these remains might have provided or of the relative significance of different biotic resources. Allometric formulas based on animal weights or seed sizes and measurements of modern specimens can be applied to the archaeological remains. Carefully reasoned application of such allometric formulas can be used, for example, to estimate meat or soft-tissue weights, as well as fruit volumes represented by the archaeological remains.

Some types of plant and animal foods will not be registered in the archaeological refuse and are difficult or impossible to account for. These include animals with heavy skeletons or shells that might be butchered on the shore and only the meat brought back to the home site, such as marine mammals: manatee, monk seals, and cetaceans. We seldom find skeletal parts of these animals. The conch is another animal with a heavy shell that might be discarded and only the soft body taken back to the site. Like edible greens and plant tubers, which are generally consumed in their entirety and, even when not, are composed primarily of soft, unlignified cells, making them highly perishable, a whole array of animals and animal products have no hard parts likely to be preserved. Among these are sea turtle eggs. Sea turtles lay many eggs at a predictable time of year on Caribbean beaches; their eggs are relished by people and other animals. Some birds such as shearwaters and boobies come to islands to nest at regular intervals. Their eggs and young might also have provided a tasty treat and left no evidence. It is possible to detect the presence of laying female birds by medullary bone (stores of calcium used for eggshell production). However, neither medullary bone nor the bones of juvenile birds have been reported for the Caribbean. Insects and honey (or similar sugary exudates from plants) are important nutrients favored by many people. Insects are a regular source of food and nutrition in many regions, including tropical America (Marconi et al. 2002). Insect remains are recovered, identified, and analyzed by zooarchaeologists with entomological training who work with the same care used to recover small seeds and plant parts. Research on insects from archaeological deposits has unfortunately not been done in the Caribbean. Similarly, analysis of trace organic residues such as blood proteins and fats found on stone tools or ceramic vessels, which might verify the use of otherwise obscure items, has yet to be undertaken in the Caribbean.

Isotope Analysis May Account for Missing Remains

It is conceivable that some of these missing dietary constituents might be detected in isotopic or trace mineral analysis of human bone. Stokes (1998) studied the stable isotopes of carbon (δ^{13} C) and nitrogen (δ^{15} N) from a series of human skeletons throughout the West Indies. Stable isotopic analysis of bone apatite carbonate and collagen provides information on different aspects of the past diet. The organic component reflects protein sources in the diet and the inorganic component the whole diet (Ambrose and Norr 1993). In her study of the isotopic signatures of 102 human skeletons, Stokes (1998) concluded that the contributions of marine and terrestrial foods to the diet did not change significantly between the Saladoid and the post-Saladoid periods. She also found that people who lived on larger, more diverse, and less isolated islands had a greater proportion of terrestrial foods in their diets. Conversely, people who lived on smaller, more remote, low-limestone islands with poor soils and depauperate land faunas relied more heavily on foods from the sea.

Stable isotope analysis provides signatures that can be used to evaluate the entire diet (both plant and animal portions and protein alone). Stable isotope and faunal data are in agreement at sites where both analyses are available. For example, in the Bahamas Stokes (1998:195) found that "diets were based heavily on marine protein and C_3 cultigens such as manioc." At Hope Estate Stokes (1998:222) found isotope values indicating diets based more on terrestrial animals than the diets of people on other small islands of the Lesser Antilles. She also found that the signature for the sites on Saba indicated a diet close to that at Hope Estate with respect to its terrestrial and marine components. This may be the effect of land crabs, which provide a more terrestrial characteristic to the diet. Stokes (1998:204) also found that the δ^{15} N values are higher for the sites on Saba than for other islands. A high value for δ^{15} N indicated consumption of animals high in the food web. On Saba those may have been sharks found at those sites and generally not elsewhere in the West Indies.

Stable isotopic values also may provide insight into the plant foods that were consumed by prehistoric people, and the staple crops that were cultivated during the Caribbean Ceramic age. The material culture remains in the form of artifacts mentioned in previous chapters, the plant remains, and isotopic signatures all point to manioc as a staple crop, with maize adopted very late in prehistory and then only at some sites and in some low-intensity uses. This is further verification of the lowland South American heritage of the West Indian people, but it exemplifies the unique nature of Caribbean subsistence.

EUROPEAN CONQUEST

The human biogeography of the Caribbean at the time of historic contact was the result of centuries of complex cultural, historical, and ecological processes. This unique cultural evolution and human-landscape dynamic came to an abrupt end beginning in A.D. 1492, truncated by the European conquest. The human population of the West Indies was decimated by the European expansion (Crosby 1986; Rouse 1992), and the rich cultural heritage was rapidly swept away by historical events. Many encounters between island people and colonizing Europeans ended in the tragic and drastic loss of island populations, in part through outright aggression and enslavement but also the more insidious spread of disease through populations without immunities. Ironically, many of the most devastating diseases came about through close contact between people and their domestic animals (e.g., smallpox).

These human and faunal changes experienced in the West Indies with the arrival of Columbus and subsequent voyages have been called the European takeover (Crosby 1986). Just before the arrival of Europeans, the cultures in the West Indies had developed stratified social organization, widespread trade and social networks, intensive agriculture, and they had effected major landscape changes. There is some evidence that overexploitation of resources accompanied population growth during the Ceramic age. These developments were met by expanded technologies, including offshore fishing, intensification of agriculture in some areas and islands, and additions of new cultivated crops and fruit trees. It is impossible to guess whether captive animals and cultivated native plants might have become fully domesticated if Europeans had arrived later. Unfortunately, many plants, such as manioc, and fish and shellfish from the surrounding seas are viewed disparagingly as low-class foods in portions of the West Indies today. Thus prejudices extending to cuisine and other cultural conditions persist 500 years after the first encounter between two peoples in the West Indies.

Appendix A

Table A.1. Animal resources used by Ceramic-age people living in the Netherlands Antilles

Taxa			Islands/Sites				
			Aruba Tanki Flip	Curaçao Santa Barbara		Bonaire Wanápa	
Family	Scientific Name	Common Name		MNI	%	MNI	%
Terrestrial							
Cebidae	*Cebus* sp.	capuchin monkey	X	0		1	2.4
Felidae	*Felis pardalis*	ocelot		0		1	2.4
Cervidae	*Mazama* sp.	brocket deer		1	0.5		
Cervidae	*Odocoileus* sp.	white-tailed deer	X	0			
Muridae	*Calomys bummelincki*	vesper mouse		2	1.1		
Rodentia		rodent	X	2	1.1	4	9.5
Caviidae	*Cavia porcellus*	guinea pig		1	0.5		
Agoutidae	*Agouti paca*	paca		1	0.5		
Accipitridae	*Buteo* cf. *lineatus*	red-shouldered hawk		1	0.5		
Columbidae	cf. *Columba* sp.	pigeon		0		1	2.4
Columbidae	cf. *Columbina* sp.	ground dove		0		1	2.4
		pigeon or dove		2	1.1	3	7.1
Tytonidae	*Tyto alba*	barn owl		0		1	2.0
Salientia		frogs and toads	X	0			
Gekkonidae	*Gekko gekko*	gecko	X	0			
Teidae	*Ameiva* sp.	ameiva	X	0			
Iguanidae	*Iguana iguana*	iguana		11	6.0	3	7.1
Lacertilia		small lizard		0		1	2.4
Subtotal				21	11.5	16	38.1

Freshwater or Shore

Family		Common name					
Ardeidae	*Ardea herodius*	great blue heron		1	0.5	0	
Anatidae		indeterminate duck		1	0.5	0	
Falconidae	*Polyborus plancus*	caracara		1	0.5	0	
Charadriidae		plover		1	0.5	0	
Scolopacidae	*Numenius phaeoptus*	whimbrel		2	1.1	0	
Laridae	*Sterna fuscata*	sooty tern		12	6.6	0	
Laridae	*Sterna hirundo*	common tern		1	0.5	0	
Laridae		indeterminate tern or gull		3	1.6	0	
Testudines		freshwater turtle	X	2	1.1	0	
Subtotal				24	13.2	0	

Shallow Inshore Waters

Family		Common name					
Phocidae	*Monachus tropicalis*	W.I. monk seal		1	0.5	0	
Delphinidae	cf. *Stenella* sp.	spotted dolphin		1	0.5	0	
Cheloniidae		sea turtle	X	3	1.6	1	2.4
Lamniformes		sharks	X	0		2	4.8
Carcharhinidae		requiem shark	X	5	2.7	0	
Rajiformes		rays	X	4	2.2	1	2.4
Myliobatidae	*Aetobatis narinari*	spotted eagle ray	X	0		1	2.4
Elopidae	*Elops saurus*	ladyfish	X	1	0.5	1	2.4
Elopidae	*Megalops atlanticus*	tarpon	X	0		0	
Albulidae	*Albula vulpes*	bonefish	X	2	1.1	1	2.4
Malacanthidae	*Malacanthus plumieri*	sand tilefish	X	1	0.5	0	
Carangidae	*Caranx hippos*	crevalle jack		1	0.5	1	2.4
Carangidae	*Caranx latus*	horse-eye jack		3	1.6	1	2.4
Carangidae	*Caranx ruber*	bar jack		1	0.5	0	

Continued on the next page

Table A.1. Continued

	Taxa		Islands/Sites				
			Aruba Tanki Flip	Curaçao Santa Barbara		Bonaire Wanápa	
Family	Scientific Name	Common Name		MNI	%	MNI	%
Carangidae	*Caranx* sp.	jack	X	2	1.1	0	
		jacks	X	4	2.2	0	
Gerreidae	*Diapterus* sp.	mojarra		1	0.5	0	
Sparidae		porgy	X	1	0.5	0	
Sciaenidae		drum	X	0		0	
Kyphosidae		sea chub	X	0		0	
Ephippidae	*Chaetodipterus faber*	Atlantic spadefish	X	0		0	
Mugilidae	*Mugil* sp.	mullet	X	1	0.5	1	2.4
Sphyraenidae		barracuda	X	4	2.2	1	2.4
Ostrachiidae		boxfishes		1	0.5	0	
Subtotal				37	20.3	10	23.8
Coral Reefs							
Holocentridae	*Holocentrus* sp.	squirrelfish	X	0		1	2.4
Serranidae	*Epinephelus* sp.	grouper	X	8	4.4	0	
Serranidae	*Mycteroperca* sp.	grouper	X	5	2.7	0	
Serranidae		grouper	X	8	4.4	0	

Family	Genus/species	Common name		Count	%	Count	%
Lutjanidae	*Lutjanus* sp.	snapper		7	3.8	4	9.5
Lutjanidae		snapper		13	7.1	0	
Haemulidae	*Anisotremus* sp.	grunt		2	1.1	0	
Haemulidae	*Haemulon* sp.	grunt		21	11.5	4	9.5
Haemulidae		grunt	X	4	2.2	0	
Pomacanthidae		angelfish		2	1.1	0	
Labridae	*Bodianus* sp.	hogfish		1	0.5	0	
Labridae		wrasse	X	0		0	
Scaridae	*Scarus* sp.	parrotfish	X	7	3.8	1	2.4
Scaridae	*Sparisoma* sp.	parrotfish	X	8	4.4	2	4.8
Scaridae	*Sparisoma viride*	stoplight parrotfish	X	8	4.4		
Acanthuridae	*Acanthurus* sp.	surgeonfish	X	0		1	2.4
Balistidae	*Balistes* sp.	triggerfish		1	0.5	0	
Balistidae		black durgon		2	1.1	0	
Balistidae	*Melichthys niger*	triggerfishes	X	1	0.5	0	
Subtotal				98	53.8	13	31.0
Pelagic							
Clupeidae		herring	X	0		1	2.4
Belonidae		needlefish	X	1	0.5	2	4.8
Scombridae	*Euthynnus* sp.	little tunny	X	1	0.5	0	
Scombridae		mackerals	X	0		0	
Subtotal				2	1.1	3	7.1
Total vertebrate				182		42	

Continued on the next page

Table A.1. *Continued*

Family	Taxa Scientific Name	Common Name	Aruba Tanki Flip	Curaçao Santa Barbara MNI	%	Bonaire Wanápa MNI	%
Terrestrial Crabs							
Coenobitidae	*Coenobita clypeatus*	land hermit crab		8	15.4	4	44.4
Gecarcinidae	*Cardisoma guanhumi*	land crab		11	21.2	0	
Gecarcinidae		land crab		30	57.7	4	44.4
Shallow Water Crabs							
Portunidae	*Callinectes* sp.	swimming crabs		3	5.8	1	11.1
Total crab				52		9	
Total				234		51	

Note: Abundance is measured by minimum number of individuals (MNI) and expressed as a percentage. Species presence indicated by X in Tanki Flip (Grouard 1997). Families are arranged according to the habitats in which they are usually found.

Table A.2. Survey of molluscs from Tanki Flip, Aruba

	Taxa		Abundance
Family/Order	Scientific Name	Common Name	Tanki Flip
Terrestrial			
Bulimulidae	*Orthalicus maracaibensis*	tree snail	32
Rocky and Sandy Intertidal			
Polyplacophora		chiton	42
Mytilidae	*Brachiodontes citrinus*	mussel	41
Fissurellidae	*Fissurella* sp.	limpet	5
Turbibidae	*Lithopoma caelatum*	carved starsnail	1
Trochidae	*Cittarium pica*	W.I. topsnail	58
Neritidae	*Nerita* spp.	nerites	57
Littorinidae	*Nodolittorina tuberculata*	periwinkle	4
Littorinidae	*Tectarius muricatus*	false pricklywinkle	10
Muricidae	*Chicoreus brevifrons*	murex	33
Muricidae	*Chicoreus pomum*	apple murex	1
Muricidae	*Plicopurpura patula*	widemouth rocksnail	2
Shallow Inshore Waters (rocky, sandy, or attached to roots)			
Archidae	*Arca zebra*	turkey wing	1
Isognomonidae	*Isognomon radiata*	purse oyster	206
Pectinidae	*Lyropecten nodosus*	scallop	1
Lucinidae	*Codakia orbicularis*	tiger lucine	91
Cardiidae	*Trachycardium* sp.	pricklycockle	4
Tellinidae	*Tellina radiata*	sunrise tellin	1
Veneridae		venus	3
Strombidae	*Strombus gigas*	queen conch	1122
Calyptraeidae	*Crucibulum auricola*	W.I. cup-and-saucer	13
Vermatidae	*Petaloconchus irregularis*	wormsnail	4
Cypraeidae	*Macrocypraea zebra*	measled cowrie	1
Cassidae		helmet	2
Tonnidae	*Tonna maculosa*	tun	1
Turbinelidae	*Vasum muricatum*	Caribbean vase	3
Melongenidae	*Melongena melongena*	conch	1
Columbellidae	*Columbella mericatoria*	W.I. dovesnail	3
	Nitidella nitida	glossy dovesnail	1
Olividae	*Oliva reticularis*	olive	10
Bullidae	*Bulla* sp.	bubble	2

Source: Reinink 1997

Note: Abundance is measured by the frequency with which each species was encountered in the Tanki Flip site.

Appendix B

Table B.1. Vertebrate remains identified from the Pearls site, Grenada (GREN P3, 5N/17W level 10-30)

Taxa		Site	
		Pearls	
Scientific Name	Common Name	MNI	%
Terrestrial			
Didelphis sp.	opossum	2	4.9
Dasyprocta sp.	agouti	4	9.8
Oryzomyini	rice rats	2	4.9
Iguana sp.	iguana	1	2.4
Subtotal		9	22.0
Freshwater or Shore			
Puffinus lhermanieri	Audubon's shearwater	1	2.4
Sterna sp.	tern	1	2.4
Subtotal		2	4.9
Shallow Inshore Waters			
Cheloniidae	sea turtles	1	2.4
Lamniformes	shark	1	2.4
Carcharhinus sp.	requiem shark	1	2.4
Elops saurus	ladyfish	1	2.4
Centropomus sp.	snook	1	2.4
Caranx hippos	crevalle jack	3	7.3
Caranx latus	horse-eye jack	1	2.4
Gobiomorus dormator	bigmouth sleeper	1	2.4
Subtotal		10	24.4
Coral Reefs			
Muraenidae	moray eels	1	2.4
Holocentrus sp.	squirrelfish	1	2.4
Epinephelus sp.	grouper	2	4.9
Lutjanus sp.	snapper	2	4.9
Haemulon sp.	grunt	1	2.4
Bodianus sp.	hogfish	1	2.4
Labridae	wrasses	1	2.4
Scarus sp.	parrotfish	1	2.4
Sparisoma sp.	parrotfish	2	4.9
Acanthurus sp.	surgeonfish	1	2.4
Subtotal		13	31.7

Continued on the next page

Table B.1. *Continued*

Taxa		Site	
		Pearls	
Scientific Name	Common Name	MNI	%
Pelagic			
Exocoetidae	flyingfishes	1	2.4
Belonidae	needlefishes	2	4.9
Auxis sp.	mackerel	2	4.9
Scombridae	tuna	2	4.9
Subtotal		7	17.1
Total		41	

Note: Abundance is based on minimum number of individuals (MNI) and expressed as a percentage. Families are arranged according to the habitats in which they are usually found.

Table B.2. Vertebrate remains identified from Saladoid deposits in Barbados

Taxa		Sites					
Scientific Name	Common Name	Hillcrest		Chancery		Little Welches	
		MNI	%	MNI	%	MNI	%
Terrestrial							
Oryzomyini	rice rats	0		0		1	4.8
Canis familiaris	domestic dog	1	3.8	0		0	
Indeterminate snake	snake	0		0		1	4.8
Subtotal		1	3.8	0		2	9.5
Shallow Inshore Waters							
Cheloniidae	sea turtle	0		0		1	4.8
Carcharhinidae	requiem sharks	1	3.8	0		0	
Albula vulpes	bonefish	0		1	6.7	0	
Caranx sp.	jack	2	7.7	2	13.3	0	
Selar crumenophthalmus	bigeye scad	5	19.2	0		3	14.3
Carangidae	jacks	0		0		2	9.5
Subtotal		8	30.8	3	20.0	6	28.6
Coral Reefs							
Serranidae	groupers	0		0		1	4.8
Haemulon sp.	grunt	0		1	6.7	0	
Bodianus sp.	hogfish	0		0		1	4.8
Halichoeres sp.	wrasse	1	3.8	1	6.7	1	4.8
Scarus sp.	parrotfish	0		2	13.3	1	4.8
Sparisoma sp.	parrotfish	9	34.6	3	20.0	5	23.8
Acanthurus sp.	surgeonfish	1	3.8	2	13.3	1	4.8
Balistidae	triggerfishes	1	3.8	1	6.7	0	
Subtotal		12	46.2	10	66.7	10	47.6
Pelagic							
Clupeidae	herrings	1	3.8	0		0	
Exocoetidae	flyingfishes	1	3.8	0		0	
Belonidae	needlefishes	0		1	6.7	0	
cf. *Seriola* sp.	amberjack	1	3.8	0		0	
Scombridae	tuna	2	7.7	1	6.7	3	14.3
Subtotal		5	19.2	2	13.3	3	14.3
Total		26		15		21	

Note: Abundance is based on minimum number of individuals (MNI) and expressed as a percentage. Families are arranged according to the habitats in which they are usually found.

Table B.3. Vertebrate remains identified from post-Saladoid deposits in Barbados

| Taxa | | | Sites | | | | | | |
| | | Hillcrest | | Silver Sands | | Chancery Lane | | Heywoods | |
Scientific Name	Common Name	MNI	%	MNI	%	MNI	%	MNI	%
Terrestrial									
Oryzomyini	rice rats	2	10	22	4.8	2	3.0	0	
Indeterminate rodent	rodent	0		0		0		1	2
Canis familiaris	domestic dog	1	5	15	3.3	2	3.0	1	2
Columbidae	pigeon	0		1	0.2	0		0	
Mimus sp.	mockingbird	0		1	0.2	0		0	
Indeterminate lizard	lizard	0		0		0		1	2
Indeterminate snake	snake	1	5	1	0.2	2	3.0	0	
Subtotal		4	20	40	8.8	6	9.0	3	6
Freshwater or Shore									
Puffinus lherminieri	Audubon's shearwater	0		1	0.2	0		0	
Dendrocygna sp.	tree duck	0		2	0.4	0		0	
Aythya sp.	duck	0		1	0.2	0		0	
Porphyrula martinica	purple gallinule	0		2	0.4	0		0	
Laridae	gull	0		1	0.2	0		0	
Indeterminate bird	bird	1	5	0		1	1.5	0	
Anuran	frog or toad	0		1	0.2	0		0	
Subtotal		1	5	8	1.8	1	1.5	0	

Shallow Inshore Waters

Chelonia mydas	green turtle	0		1	0.2	0		0	
Cheloniidae	sea turtle	1	5	9	2.0	2	3.0	4	8
Ginglymostoma cirratum	nurse shark	0		1	0.2	0		0	
Carcharhinus limbatus	blacktip shark	0		1	0.2	0		0	
Galeocerdo cuvieri	tiger shark	0		1	0.2	0		0	
Carcharhinidae	requiem sharks	0		2	0.4	0		0	
Indeterminate shark	shark	0		0		1	1.5	2	4
Rajiformes	rays	0		2	0.4	0		0	
Centropomus sp.	snook	0		0		1	1.5	0	
Caranx crysos	blue runner	0		3	0.7	0		0	
Caranx hippos	crevalle jack	0		1	0.2	0		0	
Caranx latus	horse-eye jack	1	5	14	3.1	1	1.5	0	
Caranx lugubris	black jack	0		3	0.7	0		0	
cf. *Trachinotus* sp.	pompano	0		2	0.4	0		0	
Carangidae	jacks	1	5	0		0		2	4
Sphyraena sp.	barracuda	0		1	0.2	0		0	
Lactophrys sp.	boxfish	0		2	0.4	0		0	
Subtotal		3	15	43	9.5	5	7.5	8	16

Coral Reefs

Muraenidae	moray eels	0		2	0.4	0		0	
Holocentrus sp.	squirrelfish	0		4	0.9	0		0	
Scorpaena sp.	scorpionfish	0		2	0.4	0		0	
Epinephelus sp.	grouper	0		11	2.4	3	4.5	0	
Caranx ruber	bar jack	0		8	1.8	1	1.5	0	
Lutjanidae	snappers	1	5	5	1.1	1	1.5	1	2
Anisotremus sp.	margate	0		1	0.2	0		0	
Haemulon sp.	grunt	1	5	14	3.1	1	1.5	1	2

Continued on the next page

Table B.3. *Continued*

| Taxa | | Sites | | | | | | | |
Scientific Name	Common Name	Hillcrest MNI	%	Silver Sands MNI	%	Chancery Lane MNI	%	Heywoods MNI	%
Bodianus sp.	hogfish	0		5	1.1	1	1.5	0	
Halichoeres sp.	wrasse	0		5	1.1	2	3.0	0	
Lachnolaimus sp.	hogfish	0		1	0.2	0		0	
Labridae	wrasse	0		3	0.7	0		0	
Scarus sp.	parrotfish	0		11	2.4	6	9.0	2	4
Sparisoma sp.	parrotfish	4	20	104	22.9	20	29.9	3	6
Acanthurus sp.	surgeonfish	1	5	120	26.4	7	10.4	1	2
Balistidae	triggerfishes	1	5	25	5.5	4	6.0	1	2
Diodon sp.	porcupinefish	0		6	1.3	0		0	
Subtotal		8	40	327	72.0	46	68.7	9	18
Pelagic									
Clupeidae	herring	0		0		1	1.5	1	2
Exocoetidae	flyingfishes	4	20	8	1.8	4	6.0	18	36
Belonidae	needlefishes	0		6	1.3	0		2	4
Seriola sp.	amberjack	0		1	0.2	0		0	
Auxis sp.	mackerel	0		4	0.9	0		0	
Euthynnus alletteratus	little tunny	0		3	0.7	0		0	
Scombridae	tuna	0		14	3.1	4	6.0	9	18
Subtotal		4	20	36	7.9	9	13.4	30	60
Total		20		454		67		50	

Note: Abundance is based on minimum number of individuals (MNI) and expressed as a percentage. Families are arranged according to the habitats in which they are usually found.

Table B.4. Vertebrate remains identified from the Trants site, Montserrat

Taxa		Site Trants	
Scientific Name	Common Name	MNI	%
Terrestrial			
Oryzomyini A	small rice rat	2	2.1
Oryzomyini B	large rice rat	3	3.1
Indeterminate rodent	rodent	8	8.2
Canis familiaris	domestic dog	2	2.1
Columbidae	pigeons	7	7.2
Passeriformes	song birds	8	8.2
Iguana sp.	iguana	5	5.2
Teiidae	whiptails	3	3.1
Ameiva sp.	ameiva	2	2.1
Indeterminate snake	snake	4	4.1
Subtotal		44	45.4
Freshwater or Shore			
Anatidae	ducks	1	1.0
Subtotal		1	1.0
Shallow Inshore Waters			
Cheloniidae	sea turtles	2	2.1
Carcharhinidae	requiem shark	1	1.0
Caranx sp.	jack	2	2.1
Selene sp.	lookdown	1	1.0
Trachinotus goodei	palometa	2	2.1
Carangidae	jacks	2	2.1
Sparidae	porgies	1	1.0
Sciaenidae	drums	1	1.0
Gobiidae	gobies	1	1.0
Subtotal		13	13.4
Coral Reefs			
Epinephelus sp.	grouper	9	9.3
Mycteroperca sp.	grouper	16	16.5
Lutjanus sp.	snapper	1	1.0
Ocyurus chrysurus	yellowtail snapper	1	1.0
Anisotremus sp.	margate	2	2.1
Haemulon sp.	grunt	1	1.0
Halichoeres sp.	wrasse	3	3.1
Labridae	wrasses	1	1.0
Scaridae	parrotfishes	1	1.0

Continued on the next page

Table B.4. *Continued*

Taxa		Site Trants	
Scientific Name	Common Name	MNI	%
Balistidae	triggerfishes	3	3.1
Subtotal		38	39.2
Pelagic			
Scombridae	tuna	1	1.0
Subtotal		1	1.0
Total		97	

Source: Reitz 1994: 306–307, 1/8-inch sample

Note: Abundance is based on minimum number of individuals (MNI) and expressed as a percentage. Families are arranged according to the habitats in which they are usually found.

Table B.5. Faunal remains identified from the Saladoid site, Hichmans (GE-5 55,15 level 20–40 and 50–60) on Nevis

Taxa		Site Hichmans	
Scientific Name	Common Name	MNI	%
Vertebrates			
Terrestrial			
Oryzomyini	rice rats	19	29.7
Dasyprocta leporina	agouti	2	3.1
Anous sp.	noddy	1	1.6
Zenaida sp.	dove	1	1.6
Columbidae	pigeons and doves	5	7.8
Iguana delicatessima	iguana	4	6.3
Subtotal		32	50.0
Freshwater or Shore			
Rallidae	rails	1	1.6
Subtotal		1	1.6

Continued on the next page

Table B.5. *Continued*

| Taxa | | Site Hichmans | |
| | | MNI | % |
Scientific Name	Common Name		
Shallow Inshore Waters			
cf. *Monachus tropicalis*	W.I. monk seal	1	1.6
Cheloniidae	sea turtle	2	3.1
Caranx sp.	jack	1	1.6
Subtotal		4	6.3
Coral Reefs			
Holocentrus sp.	squirrelfish	1	1.6
Epinephelus sp.	grouper	3	4.7
Serranidae	groupers	5	7.8
Lutjanidae	snappers	1	1.6
Haemulon sp.	grunt	3	4.7
Halichoeres sp.	wrasse	2	3.1
Sparisoma sp.	parrotfish	2	3.1
Acanthurus sp.	surgeonfish	1	1.6
Balistidae	triggerfishes	2	3.1
Diodon sp.	porcupinefish	1	1.6
Subtotal		21	32.8
Pelagic			
Clupeidae	herrings	1	1.6
Belonidae	needlefishes	2	3.1
Scombridae	tuna	3	4.7
Subtotal		6	9.4
Total vertebrates		64	
Invertebrates			
Terrestrial–Crabs			
Coenobita clypeatus	land hermit crab	2	0.7
Gecarcinidae	land crab	110	37.8
Subtotal		112	38.5
Terrestrial–Snails			
Bulimulidae	tree snails	93	32.0
Subtotal		93	32.0
Rocky Intertidal			
Fissurelidae	keyhole limpet	2	0.7
Trochidae	topsnails	21	7.2
Neritidae	nerites	34	11.7
Cerithiidae	ceriths	1	0.3

Continued on the next page

Table B.5. *Continued*

Taxa		Site Hichmans	
Scientific Name	Common Name	MNI	%
Littorinidae	periwinkle	1	0.3
Muricidae	murex	3	1.0
Chitonidae	chitons	12	4.1
Subtotal		74	25.4
Shallow Inshore Waters (rocky, sandy, or attached to roots)			
Chamidae	jewelboxes	2	0.7
Turbibidae	turbans	4	1.4
Cassidae	helmets	3	1.0
Ranellidae	triton	1	0.3
Subtotal		10	3.4
Reef—Crabs and Molluscs			
Mithrax sp.	clinging crab	2	0.7
Subtotal		2	0.7
Total invertebrates		291	
Total fauna		355	

Note: Abundance is based on minimum number of individuals (MNI) and expressed as a percentage. Families are arranged according to the habitats in which they are usually found.

Table B.6. Faunal remains identified from post-Saladoid sites on Nevis

Taxa		Sites			
		Sulphur Ghaut		Indian Castle	
Scientific Name	Common Name	MNI	%	MNI	%
Vertebrates					
Terrestrial					
Brachphyllum sp.	bat	0		1	0.8
Oryzomyini	rice rats	9	5.2	8	6.4
Dasyprocta leporina	agouti	2	1.2	1	0.8
Indeterminate bird	bird	1	0.6	3	2.4
Indeterminate snake	snake	1	0.6	2	1.6
Anolis sp.	anole	0		2	1.6

Continued on the next page

Table B.6. *Continued*

Taxa		Sites			
		Sulphur Ghaut		Indian Castle	
Scientific Name	Common Name	MNI	%	MNI	%
Iguana delicatissima	iguana	2	1.2	1	0.8
Ameiva erythrocephala	ameiva	0		1	0.8
Indeterminate lacertilia	lizard	1	0.6	1	0.8
Indeterminate turtle	turtle	0		1	0.8
Subtotal		16	9.3	21	16.8
Shallow Inshore Waters					
Carcharhinus cf. *limbatus*	blacktip shark	0		1	0.8
Caranx sp.	jack	0		3	2.4
Selar crumenophthalmus	bigeye scad	11	6.4	3	2.4
Carangidae	jacks	2	1.2	0	
Eucinostomus sp.	mojarra	11	6.4	0	
Gerres cinereus	yellowfin mojarra	1	0.6	0	
Gerreidae	mojarras	0		1	0.8
Bairdiella sp.	croaker	1	0.6	0	
Mullidae	goatfishes	0		1	0.8
Sphyraena sp.	barracuda	2	1.2	1	0.8
Ostrachiidae	boxfishes	2	1.2	0	
Subtotal		30	17.4	10	8.0
Coral Reefs					
Holocentridae	squirrelfishes	4	2.3	4	3.2
Serranidae	groupers	20	11.6	18	14.4
Lutjanidae	snappers	6	3.5	4	3.2
Haemulon sp.	grunt	0		3	2.4
Haemulidae	grunts	62	36.0	3	2.4
Microspathodon chrysurus	yellowtail damselfish	0		1	0.8
Bodianus sp.	hogfish	0		1	0.8
Halichoeres sp.	wrasse	2	1.2	5	4.0
Labridae	wrasses	0		1	0.8
Scarus sp.	parrotfish	0		2	1.6
Sparisoma sp.	parrotfish	5	2.9	10	8.0
Acanthurus sp.	surgeonfish	6	3.5	28	22.4
Balistidae	triggerfishes	3	1.7	4	3.2
Diodontidae	porcupinefishes	1	0.6	0	
Subtotal		109	63.4	84	67.2
Pelagic					
Clupeidae	herrings	4	2.3	3	2.4
Hemiramphus cf. *brasiliensis*	halfbeak	2	1.2	0	

Continued on the next page

Table B.6. *Continued*

Taxa		Sites			
		Sulphur Ghaut		Indian Castle	
Scientific Name	Common Name	MNI	%	MNI	%
Exocoetidae	flyingfishes	4	2.3	1	0.8
Belonidae	needlefishes	3	1.7	3	2.4
Scombridae	tuna	4	2.3	3	2.4
Subtotal		17	9.9	10	8.0
Total vertebrates		172		125	
Invertebrates					
Terrestrial—Crabs					
Coenobita clypeatus	land hermit crab	150	4.0	9	2.1
Gecarcinidae	land crabs	33	0.9	22	5.2
Subtotal		183	4.8	31	7.3
Terrestrial—Snails					
Subulinidae	awlsnails	1	0.0	0	
Bulimulidae	treesnails	129	3.4	89	21.1
Subtotal		130	3.4	89	21.1
Rocky and Sandy Intertidal					
Balanus sp.	barnacle	37	1.0	0	
Paguridae	hermit crabs	1	0.0	0	
Mytilidae	mussels	3	0.1	0	
Donax denticulata	donax	2971	78.5	61	14.5
Lottiidae	limpets	4	0.1	0	
Fissurellidae	keyhole limpets	1	0.0	0	
Trochidae	topsnails	33	0.9	49	11.6
Neritidae	nerites	118	3.1	93	22.0
Cerithiidae	ceriths	2	0.1	0	
Littorinidae	periwinkles	7	0.2	14	3.3
Hipponicidae	hoofsnails	2	0.1	0	
Muricidae	murex	67	1.8	7	1.7
Fasciolariidae	latirus	4	0.1	1	0.2
Columbellidae	dovesnails	10	0.3	0	
Chitonidae	chitons	18	0.5	29	6.9
Mopaliidae	chitons	0		2	0.5
Subtotal		3278	86.6	256	60.7
Shallow Inshore Waters (rocky, sandy, or attached to roots)					
Echinoidea	sea urchin	21	0.6	4	0.9
Majidae	spider crabs	0		1	0.2
Xanthidae	mud crabs	2	0.1	4	0.9

Continued on the next page

Table B.6. *Continued*

Taxa		Sites			
		Sulphur Ghaut		Indian Castle	
Scientific Name	Common Name	MNI	%	MNI	%
Portunidae	swimming crabs	1	0.0	1	0.2
Arcidae	arks	53	1.4	0	
Noetiidae	arks	1	0.0	0	
Glycymerididae	bittersweets	1	0.0	0	
Pteriidae	pearl oysters	1	0.0	0	
Plicatulidae	kittenpaws	1	0.0	0	
Pectinidae	scallops	1	0.0	0	
Ostreidae	oysters	8	0.2	0	
Gryphaeidae	oysters	1	0.0	0	
Lucinidae	lucines	3	0.1	5	1.2
Chamidae	jewelboxes	9	0.2	0	
Cardiidae	cockles	2	0.1	0	
Tellinidae	tellins	1	0.0	0	
Veneridae	venuses	2	0.1	0	
Turbinidae	turbans	45	1.2	18	4.3
Planaxidae	planaxis	17	0.4	5	1.2
Strombidae	conchs	4	0.1	4	0.9
Calyptraeidae	slippersnails	9	0.2	0	
Naticidae	moonsnails	1	0.0	1	0.2
Cassidae	helmets	2	0.1	0	
Tonnidae	tuns	3	0.1	0	
Ranellidae	tritons	0		1	0.2
Nassariidae	nassas	2	0.1	0	
Olividae	olives	4	0.1	0	
Conidae	cones	1	0.0	0	
Subtotal		196	5.2	44	10.4
Coral reefs					
Palinuridae	spiny lobsters	0		2	0.5
Subtotal		0		2	0.5
Total invertebrates		3787		422	
Total fauna		3959		547	

Note: Sulphur Ghaut (JO-2 9N level 20–40) is located on the southwestern coast and Indian Castle (GE-1 95-2 level 20–40) on the southeastern coast. Abundance is based on minimum number of individuals (MNI) and expressed as a percentage. Families are arranged according to the habitats in which they are usually found.

Table B.7. Vertebrate remains identified from Golden Rock, St. Eustatius

Taxa		Site Golden Rock	
Scientific Name	Common Name	MNI	%
Terrestrial			
Chiroptera	bats	1	0.2
Oryzomyini	rice rats	66	12.6
Dasyprocta leporina	agouti	2	0.4
Columbidae	pigeons	5	1.0
Passeriformes	perching birds	9	1.7
Indeterminate bird	bird	1	0.2
Iguana sp.	iguana	2	0.4
Anolis sp.	anole	7	1.3
Ameiva sp.	racerunner	4	0.8
Gekkonidae	gecko	1	0.2
Indeterminate snake	snake	3	0.6
Subtotal		101	19.2
Freshwater or Shore			
Phaethontidae	tropic bird	1	0.2
Ardeidae	herons	1	0.2
Subtotal		2	0.4
Shallow Inshore Waters			
Cheloniidae	sea turtle	3	0.6
Chondrichthyes	sharks and rays	2	0.4
Caranx sp.	jack	34	6.5
Sparidae	porgies	2	0.4
Sciaenidae	drums	1	0.2
Mullidae	goatfishes	1	0.2
Kyphosidae	sea chubs	2	0.4
Subtotal		45	8.6
Coral Reefs			
Holocentridae	squirrelfishes	11	2.1
Serranidae	grouper	65	12.4
Lutjanidae	snapper	15	2.9
Haemulidae	grunt	20	3.8
Labridae	wrasses	17	3.2
Scaridae	parrotfishes	19	3.6
Acanthuridae	surgeonfishes	6	1.1
Balistidae	triggerfishes	8	1.5
Diodontidae	porcupinefishes	1	0.2
Subtotal		162	30.9

Continued on the next page

Table B.7. *Continued*

Taxa		Site Golden Rock	
Scientific Name	Common Name	MNI	%
Pelagic			
Exocoetidae	flyingfishes	10	1.9
Belonidae	needlefishes	4	0.8
Trachurus or *Decapterus*	scad	187	35.6
Scombridae	tuna	14	2.7
Subtotal		215	41.0
Total		525	

Source: van der Klift 1992

Note: Abundance is based on minimum number of individuals (MNI) and expressed as a percentage. Families are arranged according to the habitats in which they are usually found.

Table B.8. Faunal remains identified from early and late Saladoid deposits at Hope Estate, St. Martin

Taxa		Site Hope Estate			
		Unit 16 zone 18		Unit 10 zone 3	
Scientific Name	Common Name	MNI	%	MNI	%
Vertebrates					
Terrestrial					
Oryzomyini	rice rats	2	2.9	25	28.1
Canis familiaris	domestic dog	0		1	1.1
Columbidae	pigeons	18	25.7	10	11.2
Margarops sp.	thrasher	0		0	
Mimidae	mockingbirds	6	8.6	3	3.4
Passeriformes	perching birds	1	1.4	2	2.2
Ameiva sp.	racerunner	1	1.4	5	5.6
Iguana delicatissima	iguana	1	1.4	0	
Iguanidae	iguanas	0		0	
Alsophis rijersmai	racer	1	1.4	1	1.1
Subtotal		30	42.9	47	52.8
Freshwater or Shore					
Phoenicopterus ruber	flamingo	1	1.4	1	1.1
cf. *Larus philadelphia*	gull	2	2.9	0	
Subtotal		3	4.3	1	1.1

Continued on the next page

Table B.8. *Continued*

Taxa		Site Hope Estate			
		Unit 16 zone 18		Unit 10 zone 3	
Scientific Name	Common Name	MNI	%	MNI	%
Shallow Inshore Waters					
Cheloniidae	sea turtle	1	1.4	1	1.1
Carcharhinus sp.	requiem shark	0		1	1.1
Caranx crysos	blue runner	6	8.6	8	9.0
Caranx sp.	jack	1	1.4	1	1.1
Selar crumenophthalmus	bigeye scad	0		2	2.2
Trachinotus sp.	pompano	0		1	1.1
Carangidae	jacks	0		0	
Calamus sp.	porgy	0		1	1.1
Sparidae	porgies	1	1.4	0	
Mugil sp.	mullet	0		1	1.1
Polydactylus spp.	threadfin	2	2.9	0	
Subtotal		11	15.7	16	18.0
Coral Reefs					
Epinephelus sp.	grouper	1	1.4	0	
Serranidae	groupers	3	4.3	3	3.4
Lutjanus spp.	snapper	3	4.3	4	4.5
Anisotremus sp.	margate	1	1.4	0	
Haemulon spp.	grunt	2	2.9	3	3.4
Haemulidae	grunts	2	2.9	1	1.1
Halichoeres spp.	wrasse	2	2.9	3	3.4
Labridae	wrasses	1	1.4	0	
Scarus sp.	parrotfish	1	1.4	2	2.2
Sparisoma spp.	parrotfish	4	5.7	4	4.5
Balistidae	triggerfishes	2	2.9	1	1.1
Diodon sp.	porcupinefish	1	1.4	0	
Subtotal		23	32.9	21	23.6
Pelagic					
Belonidae	needlefishes	3	4.3	3	3.4
Scombridae	tuna	0		1	1.1
Subtotal		3	4.3	4	4.5
Total vertebrates		70		89	

Continued on the next page

Table B.8. *Continued*

| Taxa | | Site Hope Estate | | | |
| | | Unit 16 zone 18 | | Unit 10 zone 3 | |
Scientific Name	Common Name	MNI	%	MNI	%
Invertebrates					
Terrestrial–Crabs					
Coenobita clypeatus	land hermit crab	47	6.6	15	1
Gecarcinidae	land crabs	102	14.3	31	3
Subtotal		149	20.8	46	4
Terrestrial–Snails					
Subulinidae	awlsnails	109	15.2	0	
Bulimulidae	treesnails	210	29.4	836	78
Xanthonychidae	seagrape snails	44	6.2	94	9
Stylommatophora	terrestrial snails	0		60	6
Subtotal		363	50.8	990	93
Rocky Intertidal					
Mytilidae	mussels	5	0.7	0	
Lottiidae	limpets	2	0.3	3	0
Turbinidae	starsnail	0		1	0
Trochidae	topsnails	2	0.3	2	0
Neritidae	nerites	12	1.7	2	0
Cerithiidae	ceriths	18	2.5	1	0
Modulidae	buttonsnail	0		1	0
Littorinidae	periwinkles	23	3.2	5	0
Muricidae	murex	1	0.1	0	
Columbellidae	dovesnails	2	0.3	0	
Chitonidae	chitons	2	0.3	2	0
Subtotal		67	9.4	17	2
Shallow Inshore Waters					
Echinoidea	sea urchins	1	0.1	1	0
Arcidae	arks	1	0.1	2	0
Pteriidae	pearl oysters	3	0.4	0	
Spondylidae	thorny oysters	1	0.1	1	0
Lucinidae	lucines	3	0.4	1	0
Chamidae	jewelboxes	106	14.8	5	0

Continued on the next page

Table B.8. *Continued*

Taxa		Site Hope Estate			
		Unit 16 zone 18		Unit 10 zone 3	
Scientific Name	Common Name	MNI	%	MNI	%
Veneridae	venuses	1	0.1	0	
Turbinidae	turbins	1	0.1	0	
Vermetidae	wormsnails	3	0.4	0	
Ovulidae	flamingo tongues	5	0.7	0	
Ranellidae	tritons	2	0.3	0	
Buccinidae	whelks	1	0.1	0	
Nassariidae	nassas	1	0.1	0	
Fasciolariidae	latirus	3	0.4	0	
Olividae	olive	0		3	0
Conidae	cones	4	0.6	0	
Subtotal		136	19.0	13	1
Total invertebrates		715		1066	
Total fauna		785		1155	

Note: The early deposit is Unit 16 zone 18 and the late deposit is Unit 10 zone 3. Abundance is based on minimum number of individuals (MNI) and expressed as a percentage. Families are arranged according to the habitats in which they are usually found.

Appendix C

Table C.1. Vertebrate remains identified from sites on Vieques and the Virgin

Taxa			Islands/Sites	
			Vieques	
			Luján	
Family	Scientific Name	Common Name	MNI	%
Terrestrial				
Nesophontidae	*Nesophontes edithae*	insectivore	3	1.5
Caviidae	*Cavia porcellus*	guinea pig	2	1.0
Capromyidae	*Isolobodon portoricensis*	hutia	18	9.0
Canidae	*Canis familiaris*	dog	1	0.5
Columbidae		pigeons	2	1.0
Strigidae	*Otis nudipes*	screech owl	0	
Iguanidae	*Iguana/Cyclura*	iguana	3	1.5
Sauria		lizard	1	0.5
Serpentes		snake	1	0.5
Subtotal			31	15.6
Freshwater or Shore				
Procellaridae	*Puffinus* sp.	shearwater	1	0.5
Ardeidae	*Egretta alba*	great egret	1	0.5
Pandionidae	*Pandion haliaetus*	osprey	1	0.5
Rallidae	*Porphyrula/Fulica*	rails	4	2.0
Testudines		turtles	1	0.5
Subtotal			8	4.0
Shallow Inshore Waters				
Trichechidae	*Trichechus manatus*	manatee	1	0.5
Cheloniidae		sea turtles	4	2.0
Carcharhinidae		requiem sharks	2	1.0
Rajiformes		rays	3	1.5
Elopidae	*Elops/Megalops*	ladyfish/tarpon	6	3.0
Albulidae	*Albula vulpes*	bonefish	1	0.5
Centropomidae	*Centropomus* sp.	snook	2	1.0
Atherinidae		silversides	0	
Malacanthidae	*Malacanthus plumieri*	sand tilefish	1	0.5
Carangidae	*Caranx* spp.	jacks	3	1.5
Gerreidae		mojarra	1	0.5
Haemulidae		grunts	0	
Sparidae		porgy	5	2.5
Sciaenidae	*Bairdiella* sp.	croaker	0	
Mullidae	*Mulloidichthyes martinicus*	yellow goatfish	0	

Islands

Islands/Sites											
St. Thomas				St. John				Tortola		Jost van Dyke	
Tutu Early		Tutu Late		Trunk Bay		Cinnamon Bay		Paraquita		Cape Wright	
MNI	%	MNI	%	MNI	%	MNI	%	MNI	%	MNI	%
0		0		0		0		0		0	
0		0		0		0		0		0	
3	2.5	5	3.3	2	1.1	3	2.0	3	10.0	5	5.1
0		0		0		0		0		0	
1	0.8	2	1.3	0		0		1	3.3	0	
0		0		0		1	0.7	0		0	
1	0.8	4	2.6	0		1	0.7	0		0	
1	0.8	4	2.6	2	1.1	0		1	3.3	0	
1	0.8	1	0.7	2	1.1	2	1.4	0		0	
7	5.8	16	10.6	6	3.4	7	4.8	5	16.7	5	5.1
0		0		2	1.1	0		0		1	1.0
0		0		0		0		0		0	
0		0		0		0		0		0	
0		1	0.7	2	1.1	0		0		0	
1	0.8	1	0.7	2	1.1	2	1.4	1	3.3	0	
1	0.8	2	1.3	6	3.4	2	1.4	1	3.3	1	1.0
0		0		0		0		1	3.3	0	
2	1.7	2	1.3	1	0.6	0		0		3	3.0
0		0		0		0		0		1	1.0
0		4	2.6	1	0.6	1	0.7	0		0	
0		2	1.3	0		1	0.7	0		0	
0		0		0		0		1	3.3	0	
0		0		0		0		0		0	
0		1	0.7	0		0		0		0	
0		0		0		0		0		0	
19	15.7	8	5.3	12	6.7	8	5.4	1	3.3	9	9.1
1	0.8	1	0.7	0		0		0		0	
0		22	14.6	0		0		0		0	
3	2.5	9	6.0	3	1.7	4	2.7	1	3.3	5	5.1
0		0		1	0.6	0		0		0	
0		1	0.7	1	0.6	0		0		0	

Continued on the next page

Table C.1. *Continued*

Taxa			Islands/Sites	
			Vieques	
			Luján	
Family	Scientific Name	Common Name	MNI	%
Kyphosidae	*Kyphosus* sp.	sea chub	0	
Mugilidae	*Mugil* sp.	mullet	3	1.5
Sphyraenidae	*Sphyraena* sp.	barracuda	4	2.0
Clinidae		clinids	0	
Eleotridae	*Dormitator maculatus*	fat sleeper	0	
Eleotridae	*Gobiomorus dormitor*	bigmouth sleeper	0	
Ostrachiidae	*Lactophrys* sp.	boxfish	2	1.0
Subtotal			38	19.1
Coral Reefs				
Muraenidae		moray	2	1.0
Holocentridae	*Holocentrus* sp.	squirrelfish	0	
Serranidae	*Epinephelus* sp.	grouper	13	6.5
Serranidae	*Diplectrum/Mycteroperca*	groupers	3	1.5
Lutjanidae	*Lutjanus/Ocyurus*	snapper	9	4.5
Haemulidae	*Anisotremus/Haemulon*	grunt	12	6.0
Pomacanthidae	*Holocanthus/Pomacanthus*	angelfish	3	1.5
Pomacentridae	*Abudefduf/Microspathodon*	damselfish	0	
Labridae	*Bodianus/Halichoeres*	wrasse	3	1.5
Labridae	*Lachnolaimus maximus*	hogfish	18	9.0
Scaridae	*Scarus* sp.	parrotfish	5	2.5
Scaridae	*Sparisoma* sp.	parrotfish	24	12.1
Acanthuridae	*Acanthurus* sp.	surgeonfish	5	2.5
Balistidae	*Balistes* sp.	triggerfish	13	6.5
Diodontidae	*Diodon* sp.	porcupinefish	6	3.0
Subtotal			116	58.3
Pelagic				
Clupeidae		herring	0	
Exocoetidae		flyingfishes	0	
Belonidae		needlefishes	5	2.5
Scombridae	*Euthynnus* sp.	tuna	1	0.5
Subtotal			6	3.0
Total			199	

Note: Abundance is based on minimum numbers of individuals (MNI) and expressed as 1380 B.P. and from a later deposit (N2036 E1842, level B) with a date of 560 B.P. Luján to the habitats in which they are usually found.

	Islands/Sites											

	Islands/Sites											
	St. Thomas				St. John				Tortola		Jost van Dyke	
	Tutu Early		Tutu Late		Trunk Bay		Cinnamon Bay		Paraquita		Cape Wright	
	MNI	%	MNI	%	MNI	%	MNI	%	MNI	%	MNI	%
	1	0.8	0		0		0		0		0	
	0		3	2.0	0		0		0		1	1.0
	1	0.8	2	1.3	0		3	2.0	1	3.3	1	1.0
	0		0		1	0.6	0		0		0	
	2	1.7	0		0		0		0		0	
	0		4	2.6	0		0		0		0	
	0		3	2.0	2	1.1	2	1.4	0		1	1.0
	29	24.0	62	41.1	22	12.4	19	12.9	4	13.3	21	21.2
	0		2	1.3	2	1.1	1	0.7	1	3.3	1	1.0
	0		2	1.3	17	9.6	3	2.0	1	3.3	4	4.0
	9	7.4	5	3.3	10	5.6	10	6.8	1	3.3	2	2.0
	2	1.7	1	0.7	8	4.5	0		0		5	5.1
	18	14.9	14	9.3	21	11.8	22	15.0	1	3.3	7	7.1
	14	11.6	0		13	7.3	20	13.6	1	3.3	3	3.0
	0		0		0		0		0		0	
	0		1	0.7	2	1.1	0		0		0	
	8	6.6	3	2.0	7	3.9	3	2.0	2	6.7	5	5.1
	0		0		0		0		0		0	
	0		3	2.0	6	3.4	2	1.4	2	6.7	4	4.0
	12	9.9	17	11.3	42	23.6	42	28.6	7	23.3	13	13.1
	1	0.8	3	2.0	1	0.6	1	0.7	2	6.7	5	5.1
	3	2.5	2	1.3	3	1.7	2	1.4	0		2	2.0
	3	2.5	4	2.6	2	1.1	2	1.4	1	3.3	4	4.0
	70	57.9	57	37.7	134	75.3	108	73.5	19	63.3	55	55.6
	2	1.7	5	3.3	2	1.1	2	1.4	1	3.3	2	2.0
	8	6.6	2	1.3	4	2.2	0		0		0	
	4	3.3	6	4.0	2	1.1	4	2.7	0		8	8.1
	0		1	0.7	2	1.1	5	3.4	0		7	7.1
	14	11.6	14	9.3	10	5.6	11	7.5	1	3.3	17	17.2
	121		151		178		147		30		99	

a percentage. The data from Tutu come from an early deposit (N2044 E1837, level I) with a date of
data come from Midden A and B. Other samples are totals for the site. Families are arranged according

Table C.2. Invertebrate remains identified from sites on Vieques and the Virgin Islands

Taxa			Islands/Sites									
			Vieques		St. Thomas				St. John			
			Lujan		Tutu Early		Tutu Late		Trunk Bay		Cinnamon Bay	
Family	Scientific Name	Common Name	MNI	%	MNI	%	MNI	%	MNI	%	MNI	%
Terrestrial Crustaceans												
Coenobitidae	*Coenobita clypeatus*	land hermit crab	2	0.0	3	0.6	12	5.4	10	2.6	6	2.2
Paguridae		hermit crab	0		0		7	3.2	0		0	
Gecarcinidae		land crab	24	0.3	85	18.3	32	14.5	6	1.6	5	1.9
Subtotal			26	0.4	88	18.9	51	23.1	16	4.2	11	4.1
Terrestrial Molluscs												
Annulariidae	*Chondropoma* sp.	horn	0		0		1	0.5	0		0	
Pyramidellidae	*Cingulina* sp.	pyram	0		0		0		0		0	
Subulinidae	*Opeas* sp.	awlsnail	0		237	51.0	8	3.6	0		0	
Spiraxidae		wolfsnail	0		3	0.6	0		0		0	
Bulimulidae	*Bulimulus guadaloupensis*	bulimulus	21	0.3	69	14.8	8	3.6	0		0	
Sagdidae		mudcloak	0		27	5.8	7	3.2	0		0	
Camaenidae	*Caracolus/Polydontes*	land snails	449	6.1	2	0.4	12	5.4	0		0	
Subtotal			470	6.4	338	72.7	36	16.3	0*		0*	
Rocky Intertidal												
Fissurellidae		limpet	12	0.2	1	0.2	1	0.5	17	4.5	0*	
Lottiidae	*Lottia* sp.	limpet	18	0.2	0		9	4.1	62	16.4	0*	
Turbinidae	*Lithopoma* spp.	starsnails	177	2.4	0		0		0		0	
Turbinidae	*Astrea/Turbo*	starsnails	50	0.7	1	0.2	1	0.5	7	1.8	2	0.7

Family	Taxon	Common name	n	%	n	%	n	%	n	%	n	%
Trochidae	*Cittarium pica*	W.I. topsnail	1297	17.8	14	3.0	56	25.3	168	44.3	112	41.9
Neritidae		nerites	166	2.3	10	2.2	7	3.2	9	2.4	58	21.7
Cerithidae	*Cerithium* spp.	cerith	10	0.1	0		3	1.4	2	0.5	1	0.4
Littorinidae		periwinkles	90	1.2	2	0.4	3	1.4	12	3.2	4	1.5
Hipponicidae	*Hipponix* sp.	hoofsnail	0		0		0		2	0.5	0	
Calyptraeidae		slippershells	0		0		0		0		3	1.1
Muricidae		murex/rocksnails	50	0.7	1	0.2	0		3	0.8	5	1.9
Chitonidae	*Acanthopleura* sp.	chiton	92	1.3	5	1.1	15	6.8	0		9	3.4
Subtotal			1962	26.9	34	7.3	95	43.0	282	74.4	194	72.7

Shallow Inshore Waters (rocky, sandy, or attached to roots)

Family	Taxon	Common name	n	%	n	%	n	%	n	%	n	%
Majidae		spider crab	0		0		1	0.5	1	0.3	1	0.4
Portunidae		swimming crab	4	0.1	0		1	0.5	0		0	
Mytilidae	*Brachiodontes* sp.	mussel	49	0.7	0		2	0.9	2	0.5	3	1.1
Archidae	*Anadara notabilis*	eared ark	10	0.1	0		1	0.5	5	1.3	2	0.7
Archidae	*Arca zebra*	turkey wing	0		0		0		0		14	5.2
Glycymeridae	*Glycymeris pectinata*	bittersweet	0		0		0		0		1	0.4
Pteriidae	*Pinctada radiata*	pearl oyster	0		0		0		0		5	1.9
Isognomonidae	*Isognomon alatus*	tree-oyster	1837	25.2	0		0		1	0.3	0	
Limidae	*Lima* sp.	fileclam	0		0		0		1	0.3	0	
Pectinidae	*Lyropecten nodosus*	scallop	0		0		0		0		1	0.4
Ostreidae	*Crassostrea rhizophora*	Caribbean oyster	1478	20.2	0		0		0		0	
Lucinidae	*Anodontia alba*	buttercup lucine	76	1.0	0		0		0		0	
Lucinidae	*Codakia orbicularis*	tiger lucine	376	5.1	0		16	7.2	4	1.1	9	3.4
Lucinidae	*Lucina pectinata*	thick lucine	578	7.9	1	0.2	0		0		0	
Lucinidae		lucine	0		0		1	0.5	3	0.8	0	
Chamidae	*Chama* sp.	jewelbox	2	0	0		1	0.5	0		4	1.5
Cardiidae		cockle	2	0	0		0		3	0.8	0	
Tellinidae	*Tellina* sp.	tellin	3	0	1	0.2	1	0.5	0		0	
Donacidae	*Donax denticulatum*	coquina	326	4.5	0		0		48	12.7	5	1.9
Psammobiidae	*Asaphis* sp.	asaphis	0		2	0.4	0		0		4	1.5
Veneridae		venus	61	0.8	0		10	4.5	1	0.3	2	0.7

Continued on the next page

Table C.2. Continued

Taxa			Islands/Sites									
Family	Scient'fic Name	Common Name	Vieques		St. Thomas				St. John		St. John	
			Lujan		Tutu Early		Tutu Late		Trunk Bay		Cinnamon Bay	
			MNI	%	MNI	%	MNI	%	MNI	%	MNI	%
Dentaliidae	*Dentalium* sp.	tusksnail	0		0		1	0.5	0		1	0.4
Planaxidae	*Supplanaxis* sp.	planaxis	0		0		0		5	1.3	0	
Modulidae	*Modulus* sp.	buttonsnail	0		0		3	1.4	1	0.3	0	
Strombidae	*Strombus* spp.	conch	8	0.1	0		0		1	0.3	2	0.7
Naticidae	*Polinices* sp.	moonsnail	4	0.1	0		0		0		2	0.7
Cassidae	*Cassis/Phalium*	cowrie	2	0	0		0		0		0	
Tonnidae	*Tonna* sp.	tun	1	0	0		0		0		0	
Ranellidae	*Cymatium* sp.	triton	9	0.1	1	0.2	0		1	0.3	1	0.4
Buccinidae		phos	3	0	0		0		1	0.3	0	
Fasciolariidae		tulip	12	0.2	0		0		0		1	0.4
Columbellidae		dovesnail	0		0		0		0		2	0.7
Olividae	*Oliva* sp.	olive	0		0		0		2	0.5	0	
Turbinellidae	*Vasum* sp.	vase	1	0	0		0		1	0.3	0	
Marginellidae		marginella	1	0	0		0		0		0	
Conidae	*Conus* sp.	cone	0		0		1	0.5	0		2	0.7
Subtotal			4843	66.3	5	1.1	39	17.6	81	21.4	62	23.2
Total			7301		465		221		379		267	

* indicates unquantified remains

Note: Abundance is based on minimum number of individuals (MNI) and expressed as a percentage. The data from Tutu come from an early deposit (N2044 E1837, level I) with a date of 1380 B.P. and from a later deposit (N2036 E1842, level B) with a date of 560 B.P. Families are arranged according to the habitats in which they are usually found.

Table C.3. Vertebrate remains identified from sites in the Greater Antilles

Taxa			Islands/Sites							
			Puerto Rico				Hispaniola		Jamaica	
			El Bronce		Maisabel		En Bas Saline		White Marl	
Family/Order	Scientific Name	Common Name	MNI	%	MNI	%	MNI	%	MNI	%
Terrestrial										
Capromyidae	Geocapromys browni	cony	0		0		0		357	50.1
Capromyidae	Plagiodontia sp.	hutia	0		1	0.5	1	0.5	0	
Capromyidae	Isolobodon portoricensis	hutia	20	17.4	2	1.1	9	4.5	0	
Capromyidae		hutia	0		1	0.5	0		0	
Echimyidae	Brotomys voratus	spiny rat	0		0		3	1.5	0	
Cricetidae	Oryzomys antillarum	rice rat	0		0		0		14	2.0
Canidae	Canis familiaris	domestic dog	1	0.9	0		0		5	0.7
Columbidae		pigeons	0		7	3.7	0		0	
Passeriformes		perching birds	0		7	3.7	0		0	
Bird		bird	0		0		3	1.5	27	3.8
Iguanidae		iguanas	0		7	3.7	4	2	38	5.3
Anguidae		anguid lizards	0		1	0.5	5	2.5	0	
Teiidae	Ameiva spp.	racerunner	3	2.6	1	0.5	1	0.5	0	
Sauria		lizards	1	0.9	1	0.5	0		0	
Colubridae	Alsophis portoricensis	ground snake	11	9.6	2	1.1	3	1.5	0	
Serpentes		snakes	0		3	1.6	1	0.5	0	
Subtotal			36	31.3	33	17.5	30	15	441	61.9

Continued on the next page

Table C.3. *Continued*

Taxa			Islands/Sites								
			Puerto Rico				Hispaniola		Jamaica		
			El Bronce		Maisabel		En Bas Saline		White Marl		
Family/Order	Scientific Name	Common Name	MNI	%	MNI	%	MNI	%	MNI	%	
Freshwater or Shore											
Anatidae		ducks	0		1	0.5	0		0		
Rallidae		rails	1	0.9	0		1	0.5	0		
Emydidae	*Trachemys decussata*	pond turtle	11	9.6	2	1.1	3	1.5	0		
Anura		frog or toad	2	1.7	2	1.1	2	1	0		
Subtotal			14	12.2	5	2.6	6	3	0		
Shallow Inshore Waters											
Trichechidae	*Trichechus manatus*	manatee	0		0		0		1	0.1	
Crocodylidae	*Crocodylus acutus*	crocodile	0		0		0		5	0.7	
Cheloniidae		sea turtles	1	0.9	0		1	0.5	20	2.8	
Carcharhinidae	*Rhizoprionodon* sp.	sharpnose shark	0		0		1	0.5	0		
Carcharhinidae		requiem shark	1	0.9	0		0		0		
Chondrichthys		sharks	0		0		0		33	4.6	
Rajiformes		skate or ray	1	0.9	0		0		1	0.1	
Elopidae	*Elops saurus*	ladyfish	2	1.7	0		0		7	1.0	
Elopidae	*Megalops atlanticus*	tarpon	0		0		0		1	0.1	
Albulidae	*Albula vulpes*	bonefish	0		0		4	2	0		
Anguilliformes		eels	0		1	0.5	1	0.5	0		

Family	Genus/species	Common name								
Centropomidae	*Centropomus* sp.	snook	0		6	3.2	3	1.5	40	5.6
Carangidae		jacks	2	1.7	11	5.8	12	6	18	2.5
Gerreidae	*Diapterus* spp.	mojarra	1	0.9	3	1.6	2	1	0	
Gerreidae		mojarra	1	0.9	3	1.6	1	0.5	4	0.6
Sparidae		porgies	1	0.9	1	0.5	4	2	20	2.8
Sciaenidae	*Larimus fasciatus*	banded drum	3	2.6	0		0		0	
Sciaenidae	*Micropogonias furnieri*	croaker	3	2.6	0		0		0	
Sciaenidae		drums	0		4	2.1	1	0.5	0	
Mugilidae	*Mugil* sp.	mullet	4	3.5	6	3.2	4	2	22	3.1
Sphyraenidae	*Sphyraena* sp.	barracuda	1	0.9	1	0.5	5	2.5	12	1.7
Eleotridae	*Gobiomorus dormitor*	bigmouth sleeper	8	7.0	6	3.2	2	1	16	2.2
Eleotridae		sleepers	15	13.0	0		0		0	
Gobiidae	*Gobionellus* sp.	goby	0		1	0.5	1	0.5	0	
Ostrachiidae	*Lactophrys* sp.	boxfish	0		1	0.5	3	1.5	0	
Tetraodontidae	*Sphoeroides* sp.	pufferfish	0		0		2	1	0	
Subtotal			44	38.3	44	23.3	47	23.5	200	28.1
Coral Reefs										
Holocentridae	*Holocentrus* sp.	squirrelfish	0		2	1.1	5	2.5	0	
Scorpaenidae	*Scorpaena* spp.	scorpionfish	1	0.9	0		0		0	
Serranidae	*Epinephelus* sp.	grouper	0		8	4.2	16	8	11	1.5
Lutjanidae	*Lutjanus* sp.	snapper	4	3.5	9	4.8	12	6	27	3.8
Lutjanidae	*Ocyurus crysurus*	yellowtail	0		0		1	0.5	0	
Haemulidae	*Conodon nobilis*	barred grunt	1	0.9	0		0		0	
Haemulidae	*Haemulon* sp.	grunt	1	0.9	8	4.2	18	9	7	1.0
Haemulidae		grunts	2	1.7	4	2.1	0		0	
Pomacanthidae		angelfishes	0		1	0.5	1	0.5	0	
Pomacentridae	*Abudefduf* sp.	damselfish	0		1	0.5	0		0	
Labridae		wrasses	1	0.9	11	5.8	8	4	1	0.1

Continued on the next page

Table C.3. *Continued*

	Taxa			Islands/Sites						
			Puerto Rico				Hispaniola		Jamaica	
			El Bronce		Maisabel		En Bas Saline		White Marl	
Family/Order	Scientific Name	Common Name	MNI	%	MNI	%	MNI	%	MNI	%
Scaridae	*Sparisoma* sp.	parrotfish	4	3.5	6	3.2	34	17	7	1.0
Scaridae		parrotfishes	2	1.7	1	0.5	3	1.5	0	
Acanthuridae	*Acanthurus* sp.	surgeonfish	0		3	1.6	3	1.5	1	0.1
Balistidae		triggerfishes	1	0.9	7	3.7	4	2	8	1.1
Tetraodontidae	*Diodon* sp.	porcupinefish	3	2.6	3	1.6	3	1.5	6	0.8
Subtotal			20	17.4	64	33.9	108	54	68	9.5
Pelagic										
Clupeidae		herrings	0		27	14.3	0		0	
Exocoetidae		flyingfishes	0		3	1.6	8	4	0	
Belonidae		needlefishes	0		9	4.8	1	0.5	3	0.4
Scombridae	*Scomberomorus* sp.	mackeral	0		1	0.5	0		0	
Scombridae	*Thunnus* sp.	tuna	0		1	0.5	0		1	0.1
Scombridae		tunas	1	0.9	2	1.1	0		0	
Subtotal			1	0.9	43	22.8	9	4.5	4	0.6
Total			115		189		200		713	

Source: El Bronce (Reitz 1985); Maisabel (deFrance 1990); White Marl (Wing 1972)

Note: En Bas Saline data are from feature 15, FS *6750, 6751, 6752*. Abundance is based on minimum number of individuals (MNI) and expressed as a percentage. Families are arranged according to the habitats in which they are usually found.

Table C.4. Invertebrate remains identified from sites in the Greater Antilles

Taxa			Islands/Sites			
			Puerto Rico		Hispaniola	
			Maisabel		En Bas Saline	
Family/Order	Scientific Name	Common Name	MNI	%	MNI	%
Terrestrial Crustaceans						
Gecarcinidae		land crab	7	0.4	2	0.0
Subtotal			7	0.4	2	0.0
Terrestrial Molluscs						
Stylommatophora		land snails	1586	89.3	1	0.0
Subtotal			1586	89.3	1	0.0
Rocky Intertidal						
Fissurellidae	*Fissurella* sp.	limpet	23	1.3	0	
Lottiidae	*Lottia* sp.	limpet	3	0.2	0	
Trochidae	*Cittarium pica*	W.I. topsnail	7	0.4	0	
Trochidae		margarites	1	0.1	1	0.0
Turbinidae	*Astrea/Turbo*	starsnail	4	0.2	4	0.0
Neritidae	*Nerita/Neritina*	nerites	66	3.7	32	0.3
Cerithidae		ceriths	6	0.3	34	0.3
Littorinidae		periwinkles	36	2.0	2	0.0
Calyptraeidae	*Crepidula* sp.	slippersnail	1	0.1	0	
Muricidae	*Chicoreus pomum*	apple murex	0		4	0.0
Muricidae	*Stramonita rustica*	rocksnail	1	0.1	1	0.0
Fasciolaridae	*Fasciolaria lilium*	tulip	0		1	0.0
Columbellidae	*Columbella/Mitrella*	dovesnail	1	0.1	3	0.0
Chitonidae		chitons	15	0.8	0	
Subtotal			164	9.2	82	0.7
Shallow Inshore (rocky, sandy, or attached to roots)						
Portunidae		swimming crabs	0		5	0.0
Brachyura		crabs	0		2	0.0
Mytilidae	*Brachiodontes* sp.	mussel	0		45	0.4
Arcidae	*Anadara* spp.	arks	0		24	0.2
Arcidae		arks	1	0.1	0	
Pteriidae	*Pteria colymbus*	wing-oyster	0		3	0.0
Isognomonidae	*Isognomon alatus*	flat tree-oyster	0		52	0.5
Pinnidae		penshell	0		1	0.0
Pectinidae	*Argopecten gibbus*	calico scallop	0		1	0.0
Pectinidae		scallops	1	0.1	0	
Ostreidae	*Crassostrea virginica*	oyster	0		133	1.2
Ostreidae	*Ostrea equestris*	crested oyster	0		31	0.3

Continued on the next page

Table C.4. *Continued*

Taxa			Islands/Sites			
			Puerto Rico		Hispaniola	
			Maisabel		En Bas Saline	
Family/Order	Scientific Name	Common Name	MNI	%	MNI	%
Lucinidae	*Anodontia alba*	buttercup lucine	0		6	0.1
Lucinidae	*Codakia orbicularis*	tiger lucine	1	0.1	137	1.2
Lucinidae	*Lucina pectinata*	thick lucine	0		57	0.5
Chamidae	*Chama* sp.	jewelbox	2	0.1	0	
Cardiidae	*Trachycardium* sp.	pricklycockle	0		3	0.0
Mactridae	*Mulinia* sp.	surfclam	0		13	0.1
Tellinidae	*Tellina fausta*	favored tellin	0		5	0.0
Donacidae	*Donax* sp.	coquina	2	0.1	203	1.8
Donacidae	*Iphygenia brasiliana*	giant coquina	0		6	0.1
Solecurtidae	*Tagelus plebeius*	stout tagelus	0		4	0.0
Dreissenidae	*Mytilopsis* sp.	false mussel	0		44	0.4
Veneridae	*Anomalicardia brasiliana*	pointed venus	0		54	0.5
Veneridae	*Chione cancellata*	cross-barred venus	0		166	1.5
Veneridae	*Periglypta/Pitar*	venus/pitar	1	0.1	1	0.0
Veneridae	*Prototheca granulata*	beaded venus	0		84	0.8
Veneridae		venus/pitar	0		2	0.0
Planaxidae	*Supplanaxis nucleus*	planaxis	0		1	0.0
Modulidae	*Modulus modulus*	buttonsnail	0		22	0.2
Rissoidae	*Zebina browniana*	smooth risso	1	0.1	0	
Strombidae	*Strombus* sp.	conch	3	0.2	36	0.3
Natacidae	*Polinices* sp.	moonsnail	2	0.1	0	
Renallidae	*Charonia tritonis*	trumpet triton	0		1	0.0
Buccinidae	*Engoniphos* sp.	whelk	1	0.1	0	
Nassariidae	*Nassarius vibex*	nassa	1	0.1	1	0.0
Olividae	*Olive* sp.	olive	1	0.1	0	
Conidae	*Conus* sp.	cone	0		1	0.0
Bullidae	*Bulla striata*	striate bubble	0		4	0.0
Haminoeidae	*Haminoea* sp.	glassy-bubble	0		1	0.0
Elobiidae	*Melampus* sp.	melampus	2	0.1	9883	88.9
Subtotal			19	1.1	11032	99.2
Total			1776		11117	

Source: Maisabel (deFrance 1990)

Note: Abundance is based on minimum number of individuals (MNI) and expressed as a percentage. Families are arranged according to the habitats in which they are usually found.

Appendix D

Table D.1. Vertebrate remains identified from the Coralie site (GT-3), Grand Turk.

Taxa			Site Coralie	
Family/Order	Scientific Name	Common Name	MNI	%
Terrestrial				
Pandionidae	*Pandion haliaetus*	osprey	1	0.1
Columbidae	*Columba leucocephala*	white-crowned pigeon	2	0.2
Columbidae	*Zenaida aurita*	zenaida dove	1	0.1
Columbidae	*Geotrygon chrysia*	Key West quail dove	2	0.2
Psittacidae	*Amazona leucocephala*	Cuban parrot	2	0.2
Psittacidae	*Amazona* sp.	parrot	1	0.1
Tyrannidae	*Tyrannus dominicensis*	gray kingbird	1	0.1
Corvidae	*Corvus nasicus*	Cuban crow	6	0.6
Testudinidae	*Geochelone* sp.	tortoise	18	1.9
Iguanidae	*Cyclura carinata*	rock iguana	386	40.3
Iguanidae	*Cyclura* sp.	iguana	1	0.1
Iguanidae	*Leiocephalus psammadromus*	curlytail lizard	12	1.3
Boidae	*Epicrates chrysogaster*	boa	2	0.2
Subtotal			435	45.4
Freshwater or Shore				
Sulidae	*Sula dactylatra*	blue-faced booby	7	0.7
Sulidae	*Sula sula*	red-footed booby	7	0.7
Ardeidae	*Ardea herodias*	great blue heron	2	0.2
Ardeidae	*Egretta rufescens*	reddish egret	1	0.1
Ardeidae	*Nyctannasa violacea*	yellow-crowned night heron	1	0.1
Threskiornithidae	*Eudocimus ruber*	scarlet ibis	1	0.1
Phoenicopteridae	*Phoenicopterus ruber*	flamingo	2	0.2
Anatidae	*Dendrocygna arborea*	W.I. tree duck	4	0.4
Haematropodidae	*Haematropus palliatus*	American oystercatcher	1	0.1
Scolopacidae	*Limnodromus griseus*	American dowitcher	1	0.1
Burhinidae	*Burhinus bistriatus*	double-striped thick-knee	2	0.2
Laridae	*Larus atricilla*	laughing gull	2	0.2
Subtotal			31	3.2
Shallow Inshore Waters				
Cheloniidae	*Chelonia mydas*	green sea turtle	50	5.2
Cheloniidae	*Caretta caretta*	hawksbill turtle	1	0.1
Carcharhinidae	*Carcharhinus* sp.	requiem shark	4	0.4
Dasyatidae	*Dasyatus americanus*	southern stingray	7	0.7
Albulidae	*Albula vulpes*	bonefish	27	2.8
Carangidae	*Caranx hippos*	crevalle jack	1	0.1
Carangidae	*Trachinotus* cf. *falcatus*	permit	2	0.2
Sparidae	*Calamus* sp.	porgy	5	0.5
Kyphosidae	*Kyphosus sectatrix*	sea chub	4	0.4

Continued on the next page

Table D.1. *Continued.*

Taxa			Site Coralie	
Family/Order	Scientific Name	Common Name	MNI	%
Sphyraenidae	*Sphyraena barracuda*	barracuda	6	0.6
Scombridae	cf. *Scomberomorus* sp.	mackerel	1	0.1
Bothidae	*Bothus lunatus*	peacock flounder	2	0.2
Ostraciidae	*Lacophyrs* sp.	boxfish	12	1.3
Tetraodontidae	*Sphoeroides* cf. *testudineus*	checked puffer	2	0.2
Subtotal			124	12.9
Coral Reefs				
Holocentridae	*Holocentrus ascensionis*	squirrelfish	5	0.5
Serranidae	*Epinephelus striatus*	Nassau grouper	4	0.4
Serranidae	*Epinephelus* sp.	grouper	32	3.3
Serranidae	*Mycteroperca* sp.	grouper	1	0.1
Carangidae	*Caranx crysos*	blue runner	3	0.3
Carangidae	*Caranx ruber*	bar jack	9	0.9
Carangidae	*Caranx* sp.	jack	4	0.4
Lutjanidae	*Lutjanus* spp.	snappers	59	6.2
Haemulidae	*Haemulon* spp.	grunts	167	17.4
Labridae	*Bodianus rufus*	Spanish hogfish	4	0.4
Labridae	*Halichoeres radiatus*	puddingwife	25	2.6
Scaridae	*Scarus* sp.	parrotfish	25	2.6
Scaridae	*Sparisoma* sp.	parrotfish	12	1.3
Acanthuridae	*Acanthurus* sp.	surgeonfish	2	0.2
Balistidae	*Balistes vetula*	queen triggerfish	7	0.7
Diodontidae	*Diodon* cf. *hystrix*	porcupinefish	9	0.9
Subtotal			368	38.4
Total			958	

Source: Carlson 1999

Table D.2. Vertebrate remains identified from sites in Middle Caicos

Taxa			Sites					
			MC-6		MC-12		MC-32	
Family/Order	Scientific Name	Common Name	MNI	%	MNI	%	MNI	%
Terrestrial								
Capromyidae	*Geocapromys ingrahami*	Bahaman hutia	1	0.7	0		0	
Canidae	*Canis familiaris*	dog	0		1	0.8	0	
Columbidae		pigeons	0		0		1	1.0
Indeterminate bird		bird	0		0		2	2.1
Iguanidae	*Anolis* sp.	anole	1	0.7	0		0	
Iguanidae	*Cyclura* sp.	rock iguana	11	7.9	2	1.6	1	1.0
Iguanidae		iguana	0		1	0.8	2	2.1
Boidae	*Tropidophis* sp.	boa	0		0		1	1.0
Subtotal			13	9.4	4	3.1	7	7.2
Freshwater or Shore								
Podicipedidae		grebes	1	0.7	0		0	
Ardeidae		herons	1	0.7	0		1	1.0
Pandionidae		ospreys	1	0.7	0		0	
Rallidae		rails	1	0.7	0		0	
Laridae		gulls	0		1	0.8	0	
Testudinidae	*Trachemys* sp.	pond turtle	0		0		1	1.0
Subtotal			4	2.9	1	0.8	2	2.1

Shallow Inshore Waters

Family	Genus/species	Common name						
Cheloniidae	*Caretta caretta*	loggerhead	0		0		1	1.0
Cheloniidae		sea turtles	4	2.9	1	0.8	0	
Ginglymostomidae	*Ginglymostoma cirratum*	nurse shark	1	0.7	0		0	
Carcharhinidae	*Carcharhinus* sp.	requiem shark	1	0.7	0		0	
Dasyatidae	*Dasyatis* sp.	stingray	0		1	0.8	0	
Elopidae	*Elops saurus*	ladyfish	0		0		3	3.1
Albulidae	*Albula vulpes*	bonefish	37	26.6	10	7.9	3	3.1
Centropomidae	*Centropomus* sp.	snook	1	0.7	0		1	1.0
Carangidae	*Selene vomer*	lookdown	1	0.7	0		0	
Carangidae		jacks	0		2	1.6	0	
Gerreidae	*Eucinostomus* sp.	mojarra	10	7.2	0		0	
Gerreidae		mojarra	4	2.9	0		9	9.3
Sparidae	*Calamus* sp.	porgy	2	1.4	0		6	6.2
Sparidae/Sciaenidae		porgy/drum	1	0.7	0		2	2.1
Sphyraenidae	*Sphyraena* sp.	barracuda	3	2.2	1	0.8	1	1.0
Ostraciidae	*Lactophrys* sp.	boxfish	1	0.7	1	0.8	2	2.1
Tetraodontidae	*Sphoeroides* sp.	pufferfish	1	0.7	0		2	2.1
Subtotal			67	48.2	16	12.6	30	30.9

Coral Reefs

Family	Genus/species	Common name						
Muraenidae	*Gymnothorax* sp.	moray eel	1	0.7	0		0	
Serranidae	*Epinephelus striatus*	Nassau grouper	0		0		6	6.2
Serranidae	*Epinephelus* sp.	grouper	5	3.6	5	3.9	0	
Serranidae		grouper	0		1	0.8	0	
Carangidae	*Caranx* spp.	jacks	3	2.2	0		5	5.2
Lutjanidae	*Lutjanus* sp.	snapper	12	8.6	3	2.4	9	9.3

Continued on the next page

Table D.2. *Continued*

Taxa			Sites					
			MC-6		MC-12		MC-32	
Family/Order	Scientific Name	Common Name	MNI	%	MNI	%	MNI	%
Haemulidae	*Haemulon* sp.	grunt	10	7.2	7	5.5	10	10.3
Labridae	*Halichoeres* sp.	wrasse	1	0.7	5	3.9	2	2.1
Labridae	*Lachnolaimus maximus*	hogfish	0		1	0.8	0	
Labridae		wrasses	0		0		2	2.1
Scaridae	*Scarus* sp.	parrotfish	9	6.5	10	7.9	4	4.1
Scaridae	*Sparisoma* sp.	parrotfish	7	5.0	60	47.2	10	10.3
Acanthuridae	*Acanthurus* sp.	surgeonfish	2	1.4	4	3.1	5	5.2
Balistidae	*Balistes* sp.	triggerfish	1	0.7	4	3.1	0	
Balistidae		triggerfish	0		0		3	3.1
Diodontidae	*Diodon* sp.	porcupinefish	1	0.7	6	4.7	2	2.1
Subtotal			52	37.4	106	83.5	58	59.8
Pelagic								
Belonidae		needlefishes	3	2.2	0		0	
Subtotal			3	2.2	0			
Total			139		127		97	

Source: MC-6 and MC-12 (Wing and Scudder 1983) and MC-32 (Carlson 1994).

Table D.3. Invertebrate remains identified from the Coralie site (GT-3), Grand Turk

Family/Order	Scientific Name	Common Name	MNI	%
Terrestrial Crustaceans				
Coenobitidae	*Coenobita clypeatus*	land hermit crab	9	0.7
Gecarcinidae		land crab	85	6.6
Subtotal			94	7.3
Rocky Intertidal (also above high tide on vegetation)				
Fissurellidae		limpet	6	0.5
Fissurellidae	*Diodora cayenensis*	keyhole limpet	2	0.2
Turbinidae	*Astralium phoebium*	longspine starsnail	2	0.2
Turbinidae	*Lithopoma tectum*	W.I. starsnail	1	0.1
Trochidae	*Cittarium pica*	W.I. topsnail	79	6.1
Neritidae	*Nerita* spp.	nerites	159	12.3
Littorinidae	*Cenchritis muricatus*	beaded periwinkle	19	1.5
Littorinidae	*Littorina angulifera*	mangrove periwinkle	1	0.1
Littorinidae	*Nodolittorina dilatata*	pricklywinkle	1	0.1
Cerithidae	*Cerithium* sp.	cerith	1	0.1
Hipponicidae	*Hipponix antiquatus*	hoofsnail	1	0.1
Ranellidae	*Cymatium muricinum*	knobbed triton	3	0.2
Muricidae	*Chicoreus pomum*	apple murex	15	1.2
Muricidae	*Plicopurpura patula*	rocksnail	1	0.1
Chitonidae	*Acanthopleura granulata*	chiton	14	1.1
Subtotal			305	23.7
Shallow Inshore (rocky, sandy, among coral, or attached to roots)				
Palinuridae	*Panularis argus*	spiny lobster	33	2.6
Portunidae	*Callinectes sapidus*	blue crab	2	0.2
Mytilidae	*Brachiodontes* sp.	mussel	31	2.4
Archidae	*Anadara notabilis*	eared ark	1	0.1
Archidae	*Arca zebra*	turkey wing	3	0.2
Archidae	*Barbatia* sp.	ark	2	0.2
Pteriidae	*Pinctada imbricata*	pearl oyster	3	0.2
Limidae	*Lima scabra*	rough fileclam	3	0.2
Spondylidae	*Spondylus americanus*	thorny oyster	2	0.2
Lucinidae	*Anodontia alba*	buttercup lucine	4	0.3
Lucinidae	*Codakia orbicularis*	tiger lucine	49	3.8
Lucinidae	*Divalinga quadrisculcata*	cross-hatched lucine	10	0.8
Lucinidae	*Lucina pensylvanica*	Pennsylvania lucine	2	0.2
Ungulinidae	*Diplodonta* sp.	diplodon	1	0.1
Cardiidae	*Americardia media*	cockle	1	0.1
Cardiidae	*Laevicardium laevigatum*	eggcockle	5	0.4
Tellinidae	*Tellina fausta*	favored tellin	2	0.2

Continued on the next page

Table D.3. *Continued*

Taxa			Site Coralie	
Family/Order	Scientific Name	Common Name	MNI	%
Tellinidae	*Tellina listeri*	speckled tellin	43	3.3
Tellinidae	*Tellina radiata*	sunrise tellin	61	4.7
Psammobiidae	*Asaphis deflorata*	gaudy sanguin	25	1.9
Veneridae	*Chione cancellata*	cross-barred venus	81	6.3
Veneridae	*Periglypta listeri*	princess venus	2	0.2
Strombidae	*Strombus gigas*	conch	395	30.6
Cypraeidae	*Macrocypraea zebra*	measled cowrie	6	0.5
Naticidae	*Naticarius canrena*	colorful moonsnail	3	0.2
Naticidae	*Polinices lacteus*	milk moonsnail	1	0.1
Naticidae	*Tectonatica pusilla*	miniature moonsnail	2	0.2
Cassidae	*Cypraecassis tecticulus*	cowrie-helmet	1	0.1
Tonnidae	*Tonna pennata*	partridge tun	2	0.2
Ranellidae	*Charonia variegata*	trumpet triton	2	0.2
Bursidae	*Bursa* sp.	frogsnail	1	0.1
Columbellidae	*Columbella mercatoria*	dovesnail	2	0.2
Columbellidae		dovesnail	1	0.1
Fasciolaridae	*Fasciolaria tulipa*	tulip	7	0.5
Olividae	*Oliva* sp.	olive	4	0.3
Olividae	*Olivella* sp.	dwarf olive	11	0.9
Terebridae	*Terebra dislocata*	auger	1	0.1
Bullidae	*Bulla striata*	bubble	32	2.5
Echinidae	*Tripneustes ventricosus*	sea egg	1	0.1
Subtotal			838	65.0
Reef				
Chamidae	*Chama macrophylla*	leafy jewelbox	4	0.3
Chamidae	*Chama sarda*	cherry jewelbox	48	3.7
Subtotal			52	
Total			1289	

Source: Carlson 1999

Table D.4. Vertebrate remains identified from sites on Crooked Island and Samana Cay

			Islands/Sites					
	Taxa		Crooked Island		Samana Cay			
			CK-14		SM-2		SM-7	
Family/Order	Scientific Name	Common Name	MNI	%	MNI	%	MNI	%
Terrestrial and Shore								
Capromyidae	*Geocapromys ingrahami*	hutia	6	3.2	0		0	
Sulidae	*Sula leucogaster*	brown booby	1	0.5	0		0	
Laridae	*Sterna* sp.	tern	0		0		1	0.5
Iguanidae	*Anolis scriptus*	anole	0		2	1.0	2	1.1
Subtotal			7	3.8	2	1.0	3	1.6
Shallow Inshore Waters								
Crocodylidae	*Crocodylus* sp.	crocodile	1	0.5	0		0	
Carcharhiniformes		sharks	0		1	0.5	0	
Carangidae	*Selar crumenophthalmus*	big-eye scad	0		6	3.1	3	1.6
Carangidae		jacks	1	0.5	2	1.0	0	
Sparidae	*Calamus pennatula*	pluma	1	0.5	0		0	
Sparidae	*Calamus* spp.	porgy	14	7.6	0		0	
Sparidae	*Archosargus* sp.	porgy	1	0.5	0		0	
Sphyraenidae	*Sphyraena barracuda*	barracuda	1	0.5	0		0	
Ostrachiidae	*Lactophrys* sp.	boxfish	2	1.1	1	0.5	0	
Subtotal			21	11.4	10	5.1	3	1.6

Continued on the next page

Table D.4. Continued

Family/Order	Scientific Name	Common Name	Crooked Island CK-14 MNI	CK-14 %	Samana Cay SM-2 MNI	SM-2 %	SM-7 MNI	SM-7 %
Coral Reefs								
Holocentridae		squirrelfish	0		1	0.5	6	3.2
Serranidae	*Epinephelus fulvus*	coney	2	1.1	0		0	
Serranidae	*Epinephelus* spp.	grouper	25	13.5	0		0	
Serranidae		groupers	0		2	1.0	0	
Priacanthidae		bigeyes	0		0		1	0.5
Carangidae	*Caranx* cf. *ruber*	bar jack	0		8	4.1	3	1.6
Carangidae	*Caranx* sp.	jack	3	1.6	0		0	
Lutjanidae	*Lutjanus* sp.	snapper	7	3.8	0		0	
Haemulidae	*Haemulon steindachneri*	Latin grunt	1	0.5	0		0	
Haemulidae	*Haemulon* spp.	grunt	17	9.2	0		0	
Labridae	*Halichoeres* spp.	wrasse	6	3.2	0		0	
Labridae		wrasses	1	0.5	1	0.5	0	
Scaridae	*Scarus guacamaia*	rainbow parrotfish	2	1.1	0		0	
Scaridae	*Scarus* sp.	parrotfish	24	13.0	8	4.1	2	1.1
Scaridae	*Sparisoma viride*	stoplight parrotfish	25	13.5	0		0	
Scaridae	*Sparisoma* spp.	parrotfish	14	7.6	12	6.1	5	2.7

Family	Taxon	Common name	n	%	n	%	n	%
Acanthuridae	*Acanthurus coeruleus*	blue tang	2	1.1	0		0	
Acanthuridae	*Acanthurus* spp.	surgeonfish	17	9.2	5	2.6	1	0.5
Balistidae	*Balistes* sp.	triggerfish	3	1.6	0		0	
Balistidae	*Melichthys niger*	black durgon	1	0.5	0		0	
Balistidae		triggerfishes	2	1.1	1	0.5	1	0.5
Diodontidae	*Diodon* sp.	porcupinefish	3	1.6	1	0.5	2	1.1
Subtotal			155	83.8	39	19.9	21	11.3
Pelagic and Sargassum								
Exocoetidae		flyingfishes	0		19	9.7	8	4.3
Belonidae		needlefishes	1	0.5	0		0	
Carangidae	*Alectis ciliaris*	African pompano	1	0.5	0		0	
Mullidae	cf. *Mullus auratus*	red goatfish	0		121	61.7	129	69.4
Scombridae		tuna	0		5	2.6	22	11.8
Subtotal			2	1.1	145	74.0	159	85.5
Total			185		196		186	

Source: CK-14 on Crooked Island (deFrance 1991) and SM-2 and SM-7 on Samana Cay (Kozuch data)

Table D.5. Vertebrate remains identified from four sites on San Salvador

Taxa			Sites							
			Palmetto Grove		Minnis Ward		Long Bay		Three Dog	
Family/Order	Scientific Name	Common Name	MNI	%	MNI	%	MNI	%	MNI	%
Terrestrial and Freshwater										
Capromyidae	Geocapromys ingrahami	hutia	3	0.3	0		1	0.7	0	
Indeterminate bird		bird	1	0.1	0		1	0.7	0	
Iguanidae	Anolis sp.	anole	0		0		1	0.7	0	
Iguanidae	Cyclura rileyi	rock iguana	5	0.5	0		0		0	
Emydidae	Trachemys sp.	pond turtle	0		0		0		1	1.8
Subtotal			9	0.9	0		3	2.1	1	1.8
Shallow Inshore Waters										
Cheloniidae		sea turtle	0		3	7.9	1	0.7	1	1.8
Lamniformes		sharks	0		0		1	0.7	0	
Carcharhinidae		requiem shark	1	0.1	0		0		0	
Sphyrnidae	Sphyrna sp.	hammerhead shark	1	0.1	0		0		0	
Rajiformes		rays	0		1	2.6	0		0	
Albulidae	Albula vulpes	bonefish	0		0		1	0.7	0	
Malacanthidae	Malacanthus plumieri	sand tilefish	0		0		6	4.2	0	
Carangidae	Caranx sp.	jacks	0		0		1	0.7	1	1.8
Carangidae		jacks	1	0.1	0		0		0	
Gerreidae	Eucinostomus sp.	mojarra	0		0		1	0.7	0	
Sparidae	Calamus sp.	porgy	1	0.1	0		0		0	
Sphyraenidae	Sphyraena sp.	barracuda	4	0.4	0		1	0.7	1	1.8

Family	Species	Common name	#	%	#	%	#	%	#	%
Bothidae	*Botbus* cf. *lunattus*	peacock flounder	0		0		1	0.7	0	
Ostrachiidae		boxfish	0		0		1	0.7	0	
Subtotal			8	0.8	4	10.5	14	9.8	3	5.3
Coral Reefs										
Holocentridae	*Holocentrus* sp.	squirrelfish	0		0		1	0.7	0	
Serranidae	*Epinephelus fulva*	coney	8	0.8	0		0		0	
Serranidae	*Epinephelus guttatus*	red hind	1	0.1	0		0		0	
Serranidae	*Epinephelus striatus*	Nassau grouper	41	4.1	0		0		0	
Serranidae	*Epinephelus* sp.	grouper	38	3.8	6	15.8	13	9.1	3	5.3
Serranidae	*Mycteroperca* sp.	grouper	17	1.7	0		2	1.4	0	
Serranidae		grouper	10	1.0	0		8	5.6	1	1.8
Carangidae	*Caranx ruber*	bar jack	9	0.9	0		0		0	
Lutjanidae	*Lutjanus* sp.	snapper	8	0.8	0		2	1.4	1	1.8
Haemulidae	*Haemulon* sp.	grunt	6	0.6	0		2	1.4	0	
Labridae	*Halichoeres* sp.	wrasse	0		1	2.6	10	7.0	5	8.8
Labridae	*Lachnolaimus maximus*	hogfish	33	3.3	0		0		0	
Labridae		wrasses	52	5.2	0		0		0	
Scaridae	*Scarus* spp.	parrotfish	64	6.5	3	7.9	12	8.4	2	3.5
Scaridae	*Sparisoma* spp.	parrotfish	610	61.6	16	42.1	52	36.4	38	66.7
Acanthuridae	*Acanthurus* sp.	surgeonfish	27	2.7	2	5.3	20	14.0	2	3.5
Balistidae		triggerfishes	47	4.7	3	7.9	2	1.4	1	1.8
Diodontidae		porcupinefishes	3	0.3	1	2.6	1	0.7	0	
Subtotal			974	98.3	32	84.2	125	87.4	53	93.0
Offshore and Pelagic										
Atherinidae		anchovies	0		0		1	0.7	0	
Scombridae		tuna	0		2	5.3	0		0	
Subtotal			0		2	5.3	1	0.7	0	
Total			991		38		143		57	

Source: Palmetto Grove (Wing 1969), Minnis Ward (Winter and Wing 1995), Long Bay, and Three Dog (Berman 1994).

Table D.6. Invertebrate remains identified from the Three Dog site, San Salvador

Taxa			Site Three Dog	
Family/Order	Scientific Name	Common Name	MNI	%
Terrestrial Crustaceans				
Coenobitidae	*Coenobita clypeatus*	land hermit crab	1	0.9
Gecarcinidae		land crab	11	9.8
Subtotal			12	10.7
Terrestrial Molluscs				
Stylommatophora	3 species			
Subtotal	not quantified			
Rocky Intertidal (also above high tide on vegetation)				
Acmaeidae	*Notoacmaea antillarum*	Antillean limpet	1	0.9
Turbinidae	*Lithopoma caelatum*	carved starsnail	1	0.9
Neritidae		nerites	6	5.4
Cerithidae	*Cerithium* spp.	cerith	4	3.6
Subtotal			12	10.7
Shallow Inshore (rocky, sandy, among coral, or attached to roots)				
Archidae	*Arca* cf. *imbricata*	mossy ark	1	0.9
Archidae	*Barbatia* sp.	ark	6	5.4
Glycymeridae	*Glycymeris* sp.	bittersweet	19	17.0
Lucinidae	*Codakia* cf. *orbicularis*	tiger lucine	1	0.9
Lucinidae	*Divalinga quadrisulcata*	cross-hatched lucine	4	3.6
Lucinidae	*Lucina pectinata*	thick lucine	4	3.6
Chamidae	*Chama sarda*	cherry jewelbox	2	1.8
Chamidae		jewelbox	1	0.9
Cardiidae	*Americardium guppyi*	strawberry-cockle	17	15.2
Cardiidae	*Laevicardium laevigatus*	eggcockle	1	0.9
Tellinidae	*Strigilla* cf. *mirabilis*	strigilla	1	0.9
Tellinidae	*Tellina radiata*	sunrise tellin	10	8.9
Veneridae	*Chione cancellata*	cross-barred venus	5	4.5
Veneridae	*Pitar* sp.	pitar	1	0.9
Modulidae	*Modulus modulus*	buttonsnail	2	1.8
Strombidae	*Strombus gigas*	conch	1	0.9
Cypraeidae		cowrie	1	0.9
Naticidae	*Naticarius canrena*	colorful moonsnail	4	3.6
Columbellidae	*Columbella mercatoria*	W.I. dovesnail	4	3.6
Mitridae	*Mitra nodulosa*	beaded miter	1	0.9
Conidae	*Conus* sp.	cone	1	0.9
Bullidae	*Bulla striata*	bubble	1	0.9
Subtotal			88	78.6
Total			112	

Source: Berman 1994

References Cited

Acevedo-Rodríguez, P.
  1996   *Flora of St. John: U.S. Virgin Islands.* New York Botanical Garden, Bronx.
Adams, C. D.
  1972   *Flowering Plants of Jamaica.* University of the West Indies, Mona, Jamaica.
Alegría, R. E.
  1981   El uso de la terminología etno-histórica para designar las culturas aborígines de las Antillas. Cuadernos Prehispánicas. Seminario de Historia de América, University of Valladolid.
  1983   *Ball Courts and Ceremonial Plazas in the West Indies.* Yale University Publications in Anthropology No. 79. Yale University Press, New Haven.
  1995   Apuntes sobre la vestimenta y los adornos de los caciques Taínos de las Antilles y de la parafernalia asociada a sus funciones mágico-religiosas. In *Proceedings of the XV International Congress for Caribbean Archaeology*, edited by R. E. Alegría and M. Rodríguez, pp. 295–309. Centro de Estudios Avanzados de Puerto Rico Y Caribe, San Juan, Puerto Rico.
  1997a   An Introduction to Taino Culture and History. In *Taino Precolumbian Art and Culture from the Caribbean*, edited by F. Bercht, E. Brodsky, J. A. Farmer, and D. Taylor, pp. 18–33. Monacelli Press and El Museo del Barrio, New York.
  1997b   The Study of Aboriginal Peoples: Multiple Ways of Knowing. *The Indigenous People of the Caribbean*, edited by S. M. Wilson, pp. 11–19. University Press of Florida, Gainesville.
Allaire, L.
  1997a   The Lesser Antilles before Columbus. In *The Indigenous People of the Caribbean*, edited by S. M. Wilson, pp. 20–28. University Press of Florida, Gainesville.
  1997b   The Caribs of the Lesser Antilles. In *The Indigenous People of the Caribbean*, edited by S. M. Wilson, pp. 177–185. University Press of Florida, Gainesville.

Ambrose, S. H., and L. Norr
  1993   Experimental Evidence for the Relationship of the Carbon Isotope Ratios of
         Whole Diet and Dietary Protein to Those of Bone Collagen and Carbonate.
         In *Prehistoric Human Bone: Archaeology at the Molecular Level*, edited by J. B.
         Lambert and G. Grupe, pp. 1–37. Springer Verlag, New York.
Amorosi, T., P. Buckland, A. Dugmore, J. H. Ingimundarson, and T. H. McGovern
  1997   Raiding the Landscape: Human Impact in the Scandinavian North Atlantic.
         Human Ecology 25(3):491–518.
Anderson, D. G.
  1999   Examining Chiefdoms in the Southeast: An Application of Multiscalar Analy-
         sis. In *Great Towns and Regional Polities in the Prehistoric American Southwest and
         Southeast*, edited by J. E. Neitzel, pp. 215–241. University of New Mexico
         Press, Albuquerque.
Antczak, A. T.
  1991   La pesca marina prehispanica en el archipelago de Los Roques, Venezuela. In
         *Proceedings of the fourteenth Congress of the International Association for Caribbean
         Archaeology*, edited by A. Cummins and P. King, pp. 504–518. Barbados Mu-
         seum and Historical Society.
  1995   Mammal Bone remains from the Late Prehistoric Amerindian Sites on Los
         Roques Archipelago, Venezuela: An Interpretation. In *Proceedings of the XVIth
         International Congress for Caribbean Archaeology*, pp. 83–99. Conseil Régional
         de la Guadeloupe, Basse Terre.
  1999a Reading beyond the Taxonomic List: The Non-ceramic Evidence and the
         (Re)construction of the Social Past. Paper presented at the XVIII Congress
         for Caribbean Archaeology, Grenada.
  1999b Late Prehistoric Economy and Society of the Islands off the Coast of Vene-
         zuela: A Contextual Interpretation of the Non-Ceramic Evidence. Ph.D. dis-
         sertation, Institute of Archaeology, University College, London.
Antczak, A. T., and M. M. Antczak
  1991   Análisis del sistema de los asentamientos prehistóricos en el archipiélago de
         Los Roques. *Montalban* No. 23, pp. 335–386. Universidad Católico Andrés
         Bello, Caracas.
Antczak, M. M., and A. T. Antczak
  1992   Avances en la arqueologia de las islas Venezolanas. In *Avances en Arqueologia
         Venezolana*, edited by J. Fernández and R. Gassón, pp. 53–92. Editorial Acta
         Cientifica, Caracas.
Ayensu, E. S
  1981   *Medicinal Plants of the West Indies*. Reference Publications, Algonac, Michigan.
Bailey, L. H., and E. Z. Bailey
  1976   *Hortus Third: A Concise Dictionary of Plants Cultivated in the United States and
         Canada*. (Revised and expanded by the staff of the L. H. Bailey Hortorium,
         Cornell University). Simon and Schuster Macmillan, New York.
Baker, R. J., and H. H. Genoways
  1978   Zoogeography of Antillean bats. In *Zoogeography in the Caribbean*, edited by

F. G. Gill, pp. 35–97. Academy of Natural Sciences of Philadelphia, Special Publication No. 13.

Barnes, B. V., D. R. Zak, S. R Denton, and S. H. Spurr
1998   *Forest Ecology.* 4th ed. John Wiley and Sons, New York.

Beard, J. S.
1944   Climax Vegetation in Tropical America. *Ecology* 25:127–58.
1949   *The Natural Vegetation of the Windward and Leeward Islands.* Oxford Forestry Memoirs 21:1–192.
1955   Classification of Tropical American Vegetation Types. *Ecology* 36:89–100.

Beckerman, S.
1994   Hunting and Fishing in Amazonia: Hold the Answers, What Are the Questions? In *Amazonian Indians, From Prehistory to the Present: Anthropological Perspectives,* edited by A. Roosevelt, 177–200. University of Arizona Press, Tucson.

Behrensmeyer, A. K., J. D. Damuth, W. A. DiMichele, R. Potts, H. Sues, and S. L. Wing
1992   *Terrestrial Ecosystems through Time: Evolutionary Paleoecology of Terrestrial Plants and Animals.* University of Chicago Press, Chicago.

Berlocher, S. H.
1998   Origins: A Brief History of Research on Speciation. In *Endless Forms: Species and Speciation,* edited by D. J. Howard and S. H. Berlocher, pp. 3–15. Oxford University Press, New York.

Berman, M. J.
1994   Preliminary Report on a Vertebrate Assemblage Excavated from the Three Dog Site, San Salvador, Bahamas. In *Proceedings of the Fifth Natural History of the Bahamas Conference,* edited by L. B. Kass, pp. 5–13. Bahamas Field Station, San Salvador, Bahamas.

Berman, M. J., and P. L. Gnivecki
1995   Colonization of the Bahama archipelago: A Reappraisal. Colonization of Islands, edited by J. F. Cherry. *World Archaeology* 26(3):421–441.

Berman, M. J., and D. M. Pearsall
2000   Plants, People, and Culture in the Prehistoric Central Bahamas: A View from the Three Dog site, an Early Lucayan Settlement on San Salvador Island, Bahamas. *Latin American Antiquity* 11(3): 219–239.

Bond, J.
1985   *Birds and the West Indies.* Houghton Mifflin, Boston.

Bretting, P. K., M. M. Goodman, and C. W. Stuber
1987   Karyological and Isozyme Variation in West Indian and Allied American Mainland Races of Maize. *American Journal of Botany* 74(11):1601–1613.

Broeders, F. M. A.
1967   *Handleiding tot het Gebruik van Inheemse en Ingevoerde Planten op Aruba, Bonaire en Curaçao.* Boekhandel "St.-Augustinus," Curaçao.

Brown, W. L.
1953   Maize of the West Indies. *Tropical Agriculture* 30:141–170.
1960   *Races of Maize in the West Indies.* National Academy of Sciences, National Re-

search Council Publication No. 792, Government Printing Office, Washington, D.C.

Brown, W. L., and M. M. Goodman
1977   Races of Corn. In *Corn and Corn Improvement*, edited by G. F. Sprague, pp. 49–88. American Society of Agronomy, Madison, Wisconsin.

Bullen, R. P.
1964   *The Archaeology of Grenada, West Indies*. Contributions of the Florida State Museum, Social Sciences No. 11.

Bullock, S. H., H. A. Mooney, and E. Medina (editors)
1995   *Seasonally Dry Tropical Forests*. Cambridge University Press, Cambridge.

Burgess, G. H., and R. Franz
1989   Zoogeography of the Antillean Freshwater Fish Fauna. In *Biogeography of the West Indies: Past, present, and future*, edited by C. A. Woods, pp. 263–304. Sandhill Crane Press, Gainesville, Florida.

Burney, D. A.
1997   Tropical Islands as Paleoecological Laboratories: Gauging the Consequences of Human Arrival. *Human Ecology* 25(3):437–457.

Burney, D. A., and L. P. Burney
1994   Holocene Charcoal Stratigraphy from Laguna Tortuguero, Puerto Rico, and the Timing of Human Arrival on the Island. *Journal of Archaeological Science* 21:273–281.

Carlson, L. A.
1994   Analysis of the vertebrate fauna from MC-32 on the north coast of Middle Caicos, Turks and Caicos Islands, B.W.I. Manuscript on file at the Florida Museum of Natural History, Gainesville.
1995   Strings of Command: Manufacture and Utilization of Shell Beads among the Taino. In *Proceedings of the XV International Congress for Caribbean Archaeology*, edited by R. E. Alegía and M. Rodríguez, pp. 97–109. Centro de Estudios Avanzados de Puerto Rico y el Caribe, Puerto Rico.
1999   *Aftermath of a Feast: Human Colonization of the Southern Bahamian Archipelago and Its Effects on the Indigenous Fauna*. Ph.D. dissertation, Department of Anthropology, University of Florida. University Microfilms, Ann Arbor, Michigan.

Carr, M. E., B. S. Phillips, and M. O. Bagby
1985   Xerophytic Species Evaluated for Renewable Energy Resources. *Economic Botany* 39(4):505–513.

Chanlatte Baik, L. A.
1983   *Catalogo arqueologia de Vieques*. Centro de Investigaciones Arqueológicas. Universidad de Puerto Rico, Rio Piedras.

Cherry, J. F.
1984   The Initial Colonization of the West Mediterranean Islands in the Light of Island Biogeography and Palaeogeography. In *The Deya Conference of Prehistory. Early Settlement of the West Mediterranean Islands and the Peripheral Areas*, edited by W. H. Waldren, R. Chapman, J. Lewthwaite, and R.-C. Kennard, pp. 35–67. BAR International Series 229. British Archaeological Reports, Oxford.

Cody, A.
1991   Distribution of Exotic Stone Artifacts through the Lesser Antilles: Their Implications for Prehistoric Interactions and Exchange. In *Proceedings of the Fourteenth Congress of the International Association for Caribbean Archaeology*, edited by A. Cummins and P. King, pp. 204–226. Barbados Museum and Historical Society.

Connell, J. H.
1978   Diversity in Tropical Rain Forests and Coral Reefs. *Science* 199:1302–1310.

Córdova, A. P., and O. Arredondo
1988   Análisis de restos dietarios del sitio archeológico El Mango, Rio Cauto, Granma. *Anuario de Arqueologia:*112–132. Editorial Academia, La Habana.

Córdova Medina, A., R. Crespo Díaz, and O. Jiménez Vázquez
1997   Importancia Arqueologica y zoological del sitio Solapa del Silex. *El Caribe Arqueológico:*78–83.

Correll, D. S., and H. B. Correll
1982   *Flora of the Bahama Archipelago (Including the Turks and Caicos Islands)* (reprinted 1996). A. R. G. Gantner Verlag K.-G, Vaduz.

Costanza, R., J. Cumberland, H. Daly, R. Goodland, and R. Norgaard
1997   *An Introduction to Ecological Economics.* St. Lucie Press, Boca Raton, Florida.

Cowan, C. W.
1997   Evolutionary Changes Associated with the Domestication of *Cucurbita pepo:* Evidence from Eastern Kentucky. In *People, Plants, and Landscapes: Studies in Paleoethnobotany*, edited by K. J. Gremillion, pp. 63–85. University of Alabama Press, Tuscaloosa.

Crosby, A. W.
1986   *Ecological Imperialism: The Biological Expansion of Europe, 900–1900.* University of Cambridge Press, Cambridge.

Curet, L. A.
1996   Ideology, Chiefly Power, and Material Culture: An Example from the Greater Antilles. *Latin American Antiquity* 7:114–131.
1998   New Formulae for Estimating Prehistoric Populations for Lowland South America and the Caribbean. *Antiquity* 72:359–375.

Curet, L. A., L. A. Newsom, and S. deFrance
1998   *Report on the 1996–1997 Research at the Civic-Ceremonial Center of Tibes, Ponce, Puerto Rico.* Report to Latin American Archaeology Program of the Heinz Family Foundation, Pittsburgh.

Curet, L. A., L. A. Newsom, and D. Welch
2003   Space and Time in the Civic-ceremonial Center of Tibes, Ponce, Puerto Rico. *Proceedings of the XIX International Congress for Caribbean Archaeology*, edited by L. Alofs and R. Dijkhoff, pp. 142–155. Oranjestad, Aruba.

Curet, L. A., and J. R. Oliver
1998   Mortuary Practices, Social Development, and Ideology in Pre-Columbian Puerto Rico. *Latin American Antiquity* 9(3):217–239.

Curtis, J. H., M. Brenner, and D. A. Hodell
  2001   Climate Change in the Circum-Caribbean (Late Pleistocene to present) and Implications for Regional Biogeography. In *Biogeography of the West Indies: Patterns and Perspectives*, edited by C. A. Woods and F. E. Sergile, pp. 35–54. CRC Press, Boca Raton, Florida.
Dacal Moure, R., and M. Rivero de la Calle
  1996   *Art and Archaeology of Pre-Columbian Cuba*. University of Pittsburgh Press, Pennsylvania.
Daubenmire, R.
  1978   *Plant Geography*. Academic Press, New York.
Davis, D. D.
  1988a Calibration of the Ceramic Period Chronology for Antigua, West Indies. *Southeastern Archaeology* 7:52–60.
  1988b Coastal Biogeography and Human Subsistence: Examples from the West Indies. *Archaeology of Eastern North America* 16:177–185.
  1993   Archaic Blade Production on Antigua, West Indies. *American Antiquity* 58: 688–697.
Deagan, K. D.
  1987   Initial Encounters: Arawak responses to European Contact at the En Bas Saline Site, Haiti. In *Proceedings of the First San Salvador Conference*, edited by D. T. Gerace, pp. 341–359. CCFL Bahamian Field Station, Fort Lauderdale, Florida.
De Boer, B. A.
  1996   *Our Plants and Trees: Curaçao, Bonaire, Aruba*. Stichting Dierenbescherming, Curaçao.
Decker, D. S., and L. A. Newsom
  1988   Numerical Analysis of Archaeological *Cucurbita pepo* Seeds from Hontoon Island, Florida. *Journal of Ethnobiology* 8(1):35–44.
deFrance, S. D.
  1990   Zooarchaeological Investigations of an Early Ceramic Age Frontier Community in the Caribbean, Maisabel Site, Puerto Rico. *Antropológica* 73–74, pp. 3–180. Fundación la Salle, Instituto Caribe de Antropológica y Sociología, Caracas.
  1991   Zooarchaeological research on Lucayan Taino subsistence: Crooked Island, Bahamas. Manuscript on file at the Florida Museum of Natural History, Gainesville.
  1997   *Faunal Material Recovered from the 1996 Test Excavations at the Tibes Ceremonial Site, Puerto Rico*. Submitted to L. Antonio Curet and Lee Newsom, Tibes Archaeological Project, Field Museum of Natural History, Chicago, and Pennsylvania State University, University Park.
Delgado Ceballos, L., S. Angelbello Izquierdo, and S. Silva García
  2000   Primer reporte de semillas quemadas de maní en el residuario Birama. *El Caribe Arqueológico* 4:40–44.

Diamond, J. M.
  1975   Assembly of Species Communities. In *Ecology and Evolution of Communities*,
          edited by M. L. Cody and J. M. Diamond, pp. 342–444. Harvard University
          Press, Cambridge.
  1995   Easter's End. *Discover* 16(8):63–69.
  1997   Paradises Lost. *Discover* 18(11):69–79.
Dobkin de Rios, M.
  1984   *Hallucinogens: Cross-Cultural Perspectives.* University of New Mexico Press, Al-
          buquerque.
Domning, D. P., Emery, R. J., Portell, R. W., Donovan, S. K., and K. S. Schindler
  1997   Oldest West Indian Land Mammal: Rhinocerotoid Ungulate from the Eocene
          of Jamaica. *Journal of Vertebrate Paleontology* 17:541–638.
Drewett, P. L.
  1991   *Prehistoric Barbados.* Archetype Publication for the Institute of Archaeology,
          University College London and Barbados Museum and Historical Society.
Drewett, P. L., M. H. Harris, L. A. Newsom, and E. S. Wing.
  1993   Excavations at Heywoods, Barbados, and the Economic Basis of the Suazoid
          Period in the Lesser Antilles. *Proceedings of the Prehistoric Society* 59:113–137.
Drewett, P. L., B. Bates, M. Bennell, L. Drewett, S. Fitzpatrick, M. Hill Harris,
G. Hunt, L. Newsom, I. Quitmyer, G. Rogers, S. Scudder, and E. Wing.
  2000   *Prehistoric Settlements in the Caribbean: Fieldwork in Barbados, Tortola, and the
          Cayman Islands,* edited by P. L. Drewett. Archetype Publications, London.
Drewett, P. L., G. Rogers, L. A. Newsom
  2000   Economy and Subsistence II: Shellfish and Plant Remains. In *Prehistoric settle-
          ments in the Caribbean: Fieldwork in Barbados, Tortola and the Cayman Islands,*
          edited by P. L. Drewett, pp. 155–165. Archetype Publications, London.
Dufour, D. L.
  1994   Diet and Nutritional Status of Amazonian Peoples. In *Amazonian Indians,
          From Prehistory to the Present: Anthropological Perspectives,* edited by A. Roose-
          velt, pp. 151–175. University of Arizona Press, Tucson.
Dunn, O. and J. E. Kelley Jr.
  1989   *The Diario of Christopher Columbus's First Voyage to America 1492–1493. Ab-
          stracted by Fray Bartolomé de las Casas.* University of Oklahoma Press, Norman.
Eisenberg, J. F.
  1989   *Mammals of the Neotropics: The Northern Neotropics.* Vol. 1. University of Chi-
          cago Press.
Ewel, J. J.
  1986   Designing Agricultural Ecosystems for the Humid Tropics. *Annual Review of
          Ecological Systematics* 17:245–271.
Ewel, J., C. Berish, B. Brown, N. Price, and J. Raich
  1981   Slash and Burn Impacts on a Costa Rican Wet Forest Site. *Ecology* 62(3):
          816–829.
Ewel, J. J., and J. L. Whitmore
  1973   *The Ecological Life Zones of Puerto Rico and the U.S. Virgin Islands.* Forest Service

Research Paper ITF-18. U.S.D.A. Forest Service, Institute of Tropical Forestry, Río Piedras, Puerto Rico.

Fandrich, J. E.

1990   *Subsistence at Pearls, Grenada, W.I. (200 A.D.).* In Progress Report on the Archaeological Excavations at the Site of Pearls, Grenada, August 1989, edited by W. F. Keegan and A. Cody. Miscellaneous Project Report No. 44. Florida Museum of Natural History.

Fernández Mendez, E. (compiler)

1995   Memoria de D. Alexandro O'Reylly Sobre la Isla de Puerto Rico, Año 1765. (A. Tapia, 1945, Biblioteca Historica de Puerto Rico. Instituto de Literatura, San Juan). Pp. 237–269 in *Cronicas de Puerto Rico: Desde la Conquista Hasta Nuestros Dias (1493–1599).* Universidad de Puerto Rico, Río Piedras.

Fernández de Oviedo, Gonzalo

1959   [1526]. *Natural History of the West Indies* (Translated by Sterling A. Stoudemire). University of North Carolina Studies in the Romance Languages and Literature No. 32. University of North Carolina Press, Chapel Hill.

Fischer, W. (editor)

1978   FAO Species Identification Sheets for Fishery Purposes, Western Central Atlantic (fishing area 31). FAO United Nations, Rome.

Fitzhugh, B., and T. L. Hunt

1997   Introduction: Islands as Laboratories: Archaeological Research in Comparative Perspective. *Human Ecology* 25(3):379–383.

Flemming, C., and R. D. E. MacPhee

1999   Redetermination of Holotype of *Isolobodon portoricensis* (Rodentia, Capromyidae), with Notes on Recent Mammalian Extinctions in Puerto Rico. *American Museum Noviates* 3278:1–11.

Ford, R. I.

1994   Corn Is Our Mother. In *Corn and Culture in the Prehistoric New World*, edited by C. Johannessen and C. A. Hastorf, pp. 513–525. Westview Press, Boulder, Colorado.

Fortuna, L.

1978   Analysis polinico de Sanate Abajo. *Boletin del Museo del Hombre Dominicano* 10:125–130.

Frelich, L. E., and K. J. Puettmann

1999   Restoration Ecology. In *Maintaining Biodiversity in Forest Ecosystems*, edited by M. J. Hunter Jr., pp. 499–524. Cambridge University Press, Cambridge.

García Arévalo, M. A., and J. Tavares

1978   Presentation (Arqueología de Sanate). *Boletin del Museo del Hombre Dominicano* 10:31–44.

Gaston, K. J., and S. L. Chown

1999   Geographic Range Size and Speciation. In *Evolution of Biological Diversity*, edited by A. E. Magurran and R. M. May, pp. 236–259. Oxford University Press, New York.

Gentry, A. H.
  1995   Diversity and Floristic Composition of Neotropical Dry Forests. In *Seasonally Dry Tropical Forests*, edited by S. H. Bullock, H. A. Mooney, and E. Medina. Cambridge University Press, Cambridge.

Gilmore, M. P., W. H. Eshbaugh, and A. M. Greenberg
  2002   The Use, Construction, and Importance of Canoes among the Maijuna of the Peruvian Amazon. *Economic Botany* 56(1):10–26.

Goodwin, R. C.
  1976   Archaeological Investigations on St. Kitts, West Indies: A Progress Report. In *Public Works*, pp. 32–58. Government of St. Kitts, Nevis, and Anguilla.

  1980   Demographic Change and the Crab-shell Dichotomy. *Proceedings of the International Congress for the Study of the Pre-Columbian Cultures of the Lesser Antilles* 8:45–68. Tempe, Arizona.

Grant, P. R., and B. R. Grant
  2002a   Adaptive Radiation of Darwin's Finches. *American Scientist* 90:130–139.

  2002b   Unpredictable Evolution in a 30-Year Study of Darwin's Finches. *Science* 296:707–711.

Greig, J.
  1989   *Archaeobotany*. Handbooks for Archaeologists No. 4. European Science Foundation, Strasbourg.

Grouard, S.
  1997   Tanki Flip Faunal Remains. In *The Archaeology of Aruba: The Tanki Flip Site*, edited by A. H. Vesteeg and S. Rostain, pp. 257–264. Archaeological Museum Aruba No. 8 and Foundation for Scientific Research in Caribbean Region No. 141, Aruba and Amsterdam.

Gumbs, F.
  1981   Agriculture in the Wider Caribbean. *Ambio* 10(6):335–339.

Gunn, C. R., and J. V. Dennis
  1976   *World Guide to Tropical Drift Seeds and Fruits*. Quadrangle/New York Times, New York.

Haila, Y.
  1999   Islands and Fragments. In *Maintaining Biodiversity in Forest Ecosystems*, edited by M. L. Hunter Jr., pp. 234–264. Cambridge University Press, Cambridge.

Harris, L. D.
  1984   *The Fragmented Forest: Island Biogeography Theory and the Preservation of Biotic Diversity*. University of Chicago Press, Chicago.

Hastorf, C. A.
  1999   Cultural Implications of Crop Introductions in Andean Prehistory. In *The Prehistory of Food, Appetites for Change*, edited by C. Gosden and J. Hather, pp. 35–58. One World Archaeology, Routledge, London.

Hather, J. G.
  1994   Introduction. In *Tropical Archaeobotany: Applications and New Developments*, edited by J. G. Hather, pp. 1–8. Routledge, London.

Haviser, J. B.

1985   *The St. Michielsberg Site: Preliminary Archaeological Observations of an Archaic Settlement on Curaçao*. Reports of the Institute of Archaeology and Anthropology of the Netherlands Antilles 2, Curaçao.

1987   *Amerindian Cultural Geography on Curaçao*. Natuurwetenschappelijke Studiekring voor Suriname en de Nederlandse Antillen No. 120. Utrecht, The Netherlands.

1989   A Comparison of Amerindian Insular Adaptive Strategies on Curaçao. In *Early Ceramic Population Lifeways and Adaptive Strategies in the Caribbean*, edited by P. E. Siegel, pp. 3–28. BAR International Series 506. British Archaeological Reports, Oxford.

1991a   *The First Bonaireans*. Reports of the Archaeological-Anthropological Institute of the Netherlands Antilles No. 10.

1991b   Prehistoric Cultural Development on Bonaire, Netherlands Antilles. In *Proceedings of the Fourteenth Congress of the International Association for Caribbean Archaeology*, edited by A. Cummins and P. King, pp. 237–261. Barbados Museum and Historical Society, Barbados.

1991c   Development of a Prehistoric Interaction Sphere in the Northern Lesser Antilles. *New West Indian Guide* 65:129–151.

1997   Settlement Strategies in the Early Ceramic Age. In *The Indigenous People of the Caribbean*, edited by S. M. Wilson, pp. 57–69. University of Florida Press, Gainesville.

Hayden, B.

1981   Subsistence and Ecological Adaptations of Modern Hunter-Gatherers. In *Omnivorous Primates: Hunting and Gathering in Human Evolution*, edited by G. Teleki and R. Harding, pp. 344–422. Columbia University Press, New York.

Hedges, S. B.

2001   Biogeography of the West Indies: An Overview. In *Biogeography of the West Indies: Patterns and Perspectives*, edited by C. A. Woods and F. E. Sergile, pp. 15–33. CRC Press, Boca Raton, Florida.

Hernández Cano, J., and R. Navarrete Pujol

1999   Semillas carbonizadas del residuario protoarcaico La Batea, Santiago de Cuba. Presunciones Etnobotánicas. *El Caribe Arqueológico* 3:70–73.

Higuera-Gundy, A.

1989   Recent Vegetation Changes in Southern Haiti. In *Biogeography of the West Indies: Past, Present, and Future*, edited by C. A. Woods, pp. 191–200. Sandhill Crane Press, Gainesville, Florida.

1991   Antillean Vegetational History and Paleoclimate Reconstructed from the Paleolimnological Record of Lake Miragoane, Haiti. Ph.D. dissertation, Department of Botany, University of Florida, Gainesville.

Higuera-Gundy, A., M. Brenner, D. A. Hodell, J. H. Curtis, B. W. Leyden, and M. W. Binford

1999   A 10,300 ¹⁴C Record of Climate and Vegetation Change from Haiti. *Quaternary Research* 52:159–170.

Hodell, D. A., M. Brenner, J. H. Curtis, and T. Guilderson
  2001   Solar Forcing of Drought Frequency in the Maya Lowlands. *Science* 292:1367–1370.

Holdridge, L. R.
  1947   Determination of World Plant Formations from Simple Climatic Data. *Science* 105:367–368.
  1967   *Life Zone Ecology.* Tropical Science Center, San Jose, Costa Rica.

Holdridge, L. R., W. C. Grenke, W. H. Hatheway, T. Liang, and J. A. Tosi Jr.
  1971   *Forest Environments in Tropical Life Zones: A Pilot Study.* Pergamon Press, Oxford.

Hoogland, M. L. P.
  1999   In Search of the Native Population of Pre-Columbian Saba (400–1450 A.D.). Ph.D. dissertation, Rijksuniversiteit Leiden, The Netherlands.

Hooijer, D. A.
  1960   *Mammalian Remains from Indian Sites on Aruba.* Studies on the Fauna of Curaçao and other Caribbean Islands No. 49, pp. 154–157.
  1963   Mammalian Remains from an Indian site on Curaçao. *Studies on the Fauna of Curaçao and other Caribbean Islands* No. 64, pp. 119–122.

Honychurch, P. N.
  1986   *Caribbean Wild Plants and Their Uses.* Macmillan, London.

Howard, R. A.
  1973   The Vegetation of the Antilles. In *Vegetation and vegetational history of northern Latin America*, edited by A. Graham, pp. 1–23. Elsevier Scientific, New York.
  1979   Flora of the West Indies. In *Tropical Botany*, edited by K. Larsen and L. B. Holm-Nielsen, pp. 239–250. Academic Press, New York.
  1988   *Flora of the Lesser Antilles: Leeward and Windward Islands, Dicotyledoneae.* Vol. 4, Pt. 1. Arnold Arboretum, Harvard University, Jamaica Plain, Massachusetts.
  1989   *Flora of the Lesser Antilles: Leeward and Windward Islands, Dicotyledoneae.* Vol. 6, Pt. 3. Arnold Arboretum, Harvard University, Jamaica Plain, Massachusetts.

Husson, A. M.
  1960   *De Zoogdieren van de Nederlandse Antillen.* Natuurwetenschappelijke Werkgroep Nederlandse Antillen, Curaçao.

Hutcheson, C. D.
  2001   Reweaving the Strands: Continued Exploration into the Basketry Technology of Prehistoric Bahamians. In *Proceedings of the XVIIIth International Congress for Caribbean Archaeology*, edited by G. Richard, pp. 185–198. Conseil Régional de la Guadeloupe, Basse Terre.

Irwin, G.
  1992   *The Prehistoric Exploration of the Pacific.* University of Cambridge Press.

Iturralde-Vinent, M. A., and R. D. E MacPhee
  1999   *Paleogeography of the Caribbean Region: Implications for Cenozoic Biogeography.* Bulletin of the American Museum of Natural History 238:1–95.

Jackson, J. B.C.
  1997   Reefs since Columbus. *Coral Reefs* 16, Supplement:23–32.

Jackson, J. B.C., A. F. Budd, and J. M. Pandolfi

1996 The Shifting Balance of Natural Communities? In *Evolutionary Paleobiology*, edited by D. Jablonski, D. H. Edwin, and J. H. Lipps, pp. 89–127. University of Chicago Press, Chicago.

Jardines Macías, J., and J. Calvera Roses

1999 Estructuras de viviendas aborígenes en Los Buchillones. *El Caribe Arqueologico* 3:44–52.

Johannessen, S.

1988 Plant Remains and Culture Change: Are Paleoethnobotanical Data Better Than We Think? In *Current Paleoethnobotany: Analytical Methods and Cultural Interpretations of Archaeological Plant Remains*, edited by C. A. Hastorf and V. S. Popper, pp. 119–144. University of Chicago Press, Chicago.

Johnson, K. F.

1976 A Preliminary Faunal Analysis of Cinnamon Hill, Jamaica. *Archaeology-Jamaica Newsletter*:9–18.

Jones, A. R.

1985 Dietary Change and Human Population at Indian Creek, Antigua. *American Antiquity* 50(3):518–536.

Judd, W. S.

2001 Phylogeny and Biogeography of Lyonia sect. Lyonia (Ericaceae). In *Biogeography of the West Indies: Patterns and Perspectives*. 2nd ed. Edited by C. A. Woods and F. E. Sergile, pp. 63–75. CRC Press, Boca Raton, Florida.

Judge, J.

1986 Where Columbus Found the New World. *National Geographic* 170(5): 566–599.

Kaye, Q.

2001 The Paraphernalia Associated with Intoxicant Use by Prehistoric Caribbean Islanders, with Particular Reference to Spouted Ceramic Bowls. In *Proceedings of the XVIIIth International Congress for Caribbean Archaeology*, edited by G. Richard, pp. 199–213. Conseil Régional de la Guadeloupe, Basse Terre.

Keegan, W. F.

1992 *The People Who Discovered Columbus: The Prehistory of the Bahamas*. University Press of Florida, Gainesville.

1994 West Indian Archaeology. 1. Overview and Foragers. *Journal of Archaeological Research* 2(3):255–284.

1997a "No man [or woman] is an island": Elements of Taino Social Organization. In *The Indigenous People of the Caribbean*, edited by S. M. Wilson, pp. 111–117. University Press of Florida, Gainesville.

1997b *Bahamian Archaeology: Life in the Bahamas and Turks and Caicos before Columbus*. Media Publishing, Nassau.

2000 West Indian Archaeology. 3. Ceramic Age. *Journal of Archaeological Research* 8(2):135–167.

Keegan, W. F., and A. Cody

1990 *Progress Report on the Archaeological Excavations at the Site of Pearls, Grenada,*

August 1989. Miscellaneous Project Report No. 44. Florida Museum of Natural History, Gainesville.

Keegan, W. F., and M. J. DeNiro
1988 Stable Carbon- and Nitrogen-Isotope Ratios of Bone Collagen Used to Study Coral-Reef and Terrestrial Components of Prehistoric Bahamian Diet. *American Antiquity* 53(2):320–336.

Keegan, W. F., and J. M. Diamond
1987 Colonization of Islands by Humans: A Biogeographical Perspective. In *Advances in Archaeological Method and Theory,* vol. 10, edited by M. Schiffer, pp. 49–92. Academic Press, New York.

Keegan, W. F., M. Maclachlan, B. Byrne
1998 Social Foundations of the Taíno Caciques. In *Chiefdoms and Chieftancy in the Americas,* pp. 217–244. University Press of Florida, Gainesville.

Keeley, L. H.
1995 Protoaricultural Practices among Hunter-Gatherers: A Cross-Cultural Survey. In *Last Hunters, First Farmers,* edited by T. D. Price and A. B. Gebauer, pp. 243–272. School of American Research Press, Santa Fe, New Mexico.

Kelly, R. L.
1995 *The Foraging Spectrum: Diversity in Hunter-Gatherer Lifeways.* Smithsonian Institution Press, Washington, D.C.

King, F. B.
1994 Variability in Cob and Kernel Characteristics of North American Maize Cultivars. In *Corn and Culture in the Prehistoric New World,* edited by S. Johannessen and C. A. Hastorf, pp. 35–54. Westview Press, Boulder, Colorado.

Kirch, P. V.
1980 The Archaeological Study of Adaptation: Theoretical and Methodological Issues. In *Advances in Archaeological Method and Theory,* vol. 3, edited by M. B. Shiffer, pp. 101–157. Academic Press, New York.
1984 *The Evolution of Polynesian Chiefdoms.* Cambridge University Press, Cambridge.
1986 *Island Societies: Archaeological Approaches to Evolution and Transformation.* Cambridge University Press, Cambridge.

Klift, H. M. van der.
1992 Faunal Remains of Golden Rock. In *The Archaeology of St. Eustatius: The Golden Rock Site,* edited by A. H. Versteeg and K. Schinkel, pp. 74–83. St. Eustatius Historical Foundation No. 2 and Foundation for Scientific Research in the Caribbean No. 131, Amsterdam.

Klinken, G. J. van.
1991 *Dating and Dietary Reconstruction by Isotopic Analysis of Amino Acids in Fossil Bone Collagen—with Special Reference to the Caribbean.* Publications of the Foundation for Scientific Research in the Caribbean Region No. 128, Amsterdam.

Koopman, K. F.
1989 Review and Analysis of the Bats of the West Indies. In *Biogeography of the West*

Indies: Past, Present, and Future, edited by C. A. Woods, pp. 635–644. Sandhill Crane Press, Gainesville, Florida.

Kozuch, L., and E. S. Wing
  2004 Animal Remains from Archaeological Sites on Nevis. In *The Prehistory of Nevis*, edited by S. M. Wilson. Yale University Press, New Haven (in press).

Krieger, H. W.
  1930 *The Aborigines of the Ancient Island of Hispaniola.* Annual Report of the Board of Regents of the Smithsonian Institution for 1929, pp. 473–506, Government Printing Office, Washington, D.C.

Kruge, M. A., B. A. Stankiewicz, J. C. Crelling, A. Montanari, and D. F. Bensley
  1994 Fossil Charcoal in Cretaceous-Tertiary Boundary Strata: Evidence for Catastrophic Firestorm and Megawave. *Geochimica et Cosmochimica Acta* 58(4): 1393–1397.

Larsen, C. S.
  1997 *Bioarchaeology: Interpreting Behavior from the Human Skeleton.* Cambridge University Press, Cambridge.

Larsen, C. S., R. L. Kelly, C. B. Ruff, M. J. Schoeninger, and D. L. Hutchinson
  1996 Biobehavioral Adaptations in the Western Great Basin. In *Case Studies in Environmental Archaeology*, edited by E. J. Reitz, L. A. Newsom, and S. J. Scudder, pp. 149–174. Plenum Press, New York.

Las Casas, Fray Bartolomé de.
  1971 [1527–1565] *History of the Indies.* Translated and edited by Andree Collard. Harper and Row, New York.

Levin, D. A.
  2000 *The Origin, Expansion, and Demise of Plant Species.* Oxford University Press, New York.

Levin, S.
  1983 Food Production and Population Size in the Lesser Antilles. *Human Ecology* 11(3):321–338.

Levy, T. E., and A. F. C. Holl
  2002 Migrations, Ethnogenesis, and Settlement Dynamics: Israelites in Iron Age Canaan and Shuwa-Arabs in the Chad Basin. *Journal of Anthropological Archaeology* 21:83–118.

Liogier, H. A.
  1989 *La Flora de la Española V.* Universidad Central del Este, Volumen LXIX, Serie Científica 26. Santo Domingo, República Dominicana.

Liogier, H. A., and L. F. Martorell
  1982 *Flora of Puerto Rico and Adjacent Islands; A Systematic Synopsis.* Editorial de la Universidad de Puerto Rico, Rio Piedras, Puerto Rico.
  2000 *Flora of Puerto Rico and Adjacent Islands: A Systematic Synopsis.* 2nd ed. Editorial de la Universidad de Puerto Rico, Rio Piedras, Puerto Rico.

Lippold, L. K.
  1991 Animal Resources Utilized by Saladoid People at Pearls, Grenada, West Indies. In *Proceedings of the Thirteenth International Congress for Caribbean Archae-*

ology, edited by E. N. Ayubi and J. B. Haviser, pp. 264–268. Report of the Archaeological-Anthropological Institute of the Netherlands Antilles No. 9 Curaçao.

Little, E. L., Jr.
  1983 *Common Fuelwood Crops: A Handbook for Their Identification.* Communi-Tech Associates, Morgantown, West Virginia.

Little, E. L., Jr., and F. H. Wadsworth
  1964 *Common Trees of Puerto Rico and the Virgin Islands, Second Volume.* U.S.D.A. Forest Service, Agriculture Handbook No. 449. U.S. Government Printing Office, Washington, D.C.

Lovén, S.
  1935 *Origins of the Taino Culture, West Indies.* Elanders Bokfrycheri Äkfieborlag, Göteborg.

Ludwig, J. A., and J. F. Reynolds
  1988 *Statistical Ecology: A Primer on Methods and Computing.* John Wiley and Sons, New York.

Lugo, A. E., R. Schmidt, and S. Brown
  1981 Tropical forests of the Caribbean. *Ambio* 10(6):318–324.

Lundberg, E. R.
  1989 *Preceramic Procurement Patterns at Krum Bay, Virgin Islands.* Ph.D. dissertation, University of Illinois, Urbana. University Microfilms, Ann Arbor, Michigan.
  1991 Interrelationships between Preceramic Complexes of Puerto Rico and the Virgin Islands. In *Proceedings of the Thirteenth International Congress for Caribbean Archaeology*, edited by E. N. Ayubi and J. B. Haviser, pp. 73–85. Archaeological-Anthropological Institute of the Netherlands Antilles No. 9.

MacArthur, R. H., and E. O. Wilson
  1967 *The Theory of Island Biogeography.* Monographs in Population Biology No. 1. Princeton University Press, Princeton.

MacFadden, B. J.
  1980 Rafting Mammals or Drifting Islands? Biogeography of the Greater Antillean Insectivores *Nesophontes* and *Solenodon. Journal of Biogeography* 7:11–22.

Marconi, S., P. Manzi, L. Pizzoferrato, E. Buscardo, H. Cerda, D. Lopez Hernandez, and M. G. Paoletti
  2002 Nutritional Evaluation of Terrestrial Invertebrates as Traditional Food in Amazonia. *Biotropica* 34(2):273–280.

Martin, F. W., C. W. Campbell, and R. M. Ruberte
  1987 *Perennial Edible Fruits of the Tropics: An Inventory.* U.S. Department of Agriculture, Agriculture Handbook No. 642. U.S. Government Printing Office, Washington, D.C.

May, R. M., and M. P. H. Stumpf
  2000 Species-Area Relations in Tropical Forests. *Science* 290(5499):2084–2086.

Meehan, B.
  1982 *Shell Bed to Shell Midden.* Australian Institute of Aboriginal Studies. Canberra.

Mehrer, M. W.
  1995   *Cahokia's Countryside: Household Archaeology, Settlement Patterns, and Social Power.* Northern Illinois University Press, DeKalb.
Merwe, N. J. van der, A. C. Roosevelt, and J. C. Vogel
  1981   Isotopic Evidence for Prehistoric Subsistence Change at Parmana, Venezuela. *Nature* 292:536–538.
Miller, N. F.
  1988   Ratios in Paleoethnobotanical Analysis. In *Current Paleoethnobotany: Analytical Methods and Cultural Interpretations of Archaeological Plant Remains,* edited by C. A. Hastorf and V. S. Popper, pp. 72–85. University of Chicago Press, Chicago.
Moerman, D. E.
  1986   *Medicinal Plants of Native America.* Research Reports in Ethnobotany, Contribution 2. University of Michigan Museum of Anthropology Technical Reports No. 19. Ann Arbor.
Morales, E.
  1995   *The Guinea Pig: Healing, Food, and Ritual in the Andes.* University of Arizona Press, Tucson.
Morgan, G. S.
  1989   Fossil Chiroptera and Rodentia from the Bahamas, and the Historical Biogeography of the Bahamian Mammalian Fauna. In *Biogeography of the West Indies,* edited by C. A. Woods, pp. 685–740. Sandhill Crane Press, Gainesville, Florida.
Morgan, G. S., and C. A. Woods
  1986   Extinction and the Zoogeography of West Indian land mammals. *Biological Journal of the Linnean Society* 28:167–203.
Morton, J. F.
  1990   *Wild Plants for Survival in South Florida.* Fairchild Tropical Garden, Miami, Florida.
Murphy, P. G., and A. E. Lugo
  1995   Dry Forests of Central America and the Caribbean. In *Seasonally Dry Tropical Forests,* edited by S. H. Bullock, H. A. Mooney, and E. Medina, pp. 9–34. Cambridge University Press, Cambridge.
Nadal, J., F. Morban Laucer, A. Perguero
  1991   Current Research: Greater Antilles (Manoguayabo site, Dominican Republic). *American Antiquity* 56(1):145.
Narganes, Y. M.
  1982   Vertebrate Faunal Remains from Sorcé, Vieques, Puerto Rico. Masters thesis, Department of Anthropology, University of Georgia, Athens.
  1991   Los restos faunísticos del Sitio de Puerto Ferro, Vieques, Puerto Rico. *Proceedings of the Fourteenth Congress of the International Association for Caribbean Archaeology,* edited by A. Cummins and P. King, pp. 94–114. Barbados Museum and Historical Society, Barbados.

1997a   *Analysis de los restos faunisticos de Maruca: primero parte, vertebrados and inverte-brados.* Submitted to Arql. Miguel Rodrígiez. Toa Baja, Puerto Rico.

1997b   *Analysis de los restos faunisticos de Maruca, Ponce: segunda parte, moluscos.* Submitted to Arql. Miguel Rodrígiez. Toa Baja, Puerto Rico.

National Academy of Sciences

1980   *Firewood Crops: Shrub and Tree Species for Energy Production.* National Academy of Sciences, Washington, D.C.

1983   *Firewood Crops: Shrub and Tree Species for Energy Production.* Vol. 2. National Academy Press, Washington, D.C.

1991   *Microlivestock: Little-Known Small Animals with a Promising Economic Future.* National Academy Press, Washington, D.C.

Nelson, J. S.

1984   *Fishes of the World.* John Wiley and Sons, New York.

Newsom, L. A.

1987   Analysis of Botanical Remains from Hontoon Island (8Vo202), Florida: 1980–1985 Excavations. *Florida Anthropologist* 40(1):47–84.

1988   Archaeobotanical Analysis of Three Features from a Prehistoric Habitation Site. In *Puerto Rico: El Fresal, Cuyón, Aibonito. Pp. C1–13 in Mitigación Arqueológica Franja del Yacimiento Area B, Barrio Cuyón, Aibonito, Puerto Rico.* (M. J. Melendez). U.S. Department of Agriculture Programa de Finca Familiares Titulo VI.

1991   Paleoethnobotanical Analysis of Midden Remains from the Wanápa Site (B-016), Bonaire, West Indies. Pp. 242–262 in *The first Bonairians* (J. B. Haviser Jr.). Institute of Archaeology and Anthropology, Netherlands Antilles, Curaçao.

1992   Wood Exploitation at Golden Rock (GR-1). In *The archaeology of St. Eustatius: The Golden Rock site*, edited by A. H. Versteeg and K. Schinkel, pp. 213–227. St. Eustatius Historical Foundation No. 2 and the Foundation for Scientific Research in the Caribbean Region No. 131. Amsterdam.

1993a   *Native West Indian Plant Use.* Ph.D. dissertation, Department of Anthropology, University of Florida. University Microfilms, Ann Arbor, Michigan.

1993b   Plants and People: Cultural, Biological, and Ecological Responses to Wood Exploitation. In *Foraging and Farming in the Eastern Woodlands*, edited by C. M. Scarry, pp. 115–137. University Press of Florida, Gainesville.

1995a   *Archaeobotanical Analysis of Feature Deposits from Barrazas site, Carolina, Puerto Rico.* Submitted to M. Meléndez and the Municipality of Carolina.

1995b   *Archaeobotanical Analysis of Aklis site, St. Croix, U.S. Virgin Islands.* Submitted to Panamerican Consultants, New York, and the National Park Service, Southeastern Regional Office, Atlanta.

1997   Carbonized Wood Remains from Tanki Flip. In *The Archaeology of Aruba: The Tanki Flip Site*, edited by A. H. Versteeg and S. Rostain, pp. 347–352. Archaeological Museum Aruba No. 8 and Foundation for Scientific Research in the Caribbean Region No. 141. Aruba and Amsterdam.

1998a   Mangroves and Root Crops: Archaeobotanical Record from En Bas Saline, Haiti. In *Proceedings of the XVIth International Congress for Caribbean Archaeology*, edited by G. Richard, pp. 52–66. Conséil Regional de la Guadeloupe, Basse Terre.

1998b   Archaeobotanical Research at the Shell Ridge Midden, Palmer Site (8So2), Sarasota County, Florida. *Florida Anthropologist* 51(4):207–222.

1999a   *Archaeobotanical Analysis of Plant Remains Site Luján I, Vieques Island, Commonwealth of Puerto Rico.* Report to V. Rivera Calderón and the Municipality of Vieques.

1999b   Cambios en la estrategias de subsistencia en el area de Ponce, del Archaico al Taino. Paper presented in the symposium: "Arqueología Prehistorica de Ponce y sus Hallazgos más Importantes," 17 February, Ponce, Puerto Rico.

2001   *Archaeobotanical Analysis of Plant Remains from the Trunk Bay site, St. John, U.S. Virgin Islands.* Submitted to Ken Wild and the U.S. National Park Service, St. John.

2002   Concerning North America (invited editorial). *Antiquity* 76(292):287–310.

2004   Tubers, Fruits, and Fuel: Paleoethnobotanical Investigation of the Dynamics between Culture and the Forested Environment on Nevis, Lesser Antilles. In *The prehistory of Nevis*, edited by S. M. Wilson. Yale University Press, New Haven (in press).

Newsom, L. A., and L. A. Curet

2000   *Report on the 1998–1999 Field Seasons of the Proyecto Arqueologico del Centro Ceremonial de Tibes (Puerto Rico).* Report to Committee for Research and Exploration, National Geographic Society, Washington, D.C.

2003   Biodiversity and Natural Capital: Toward Understanding the Ecological Economics of the Tibes Archaeological Site. In *Proceedings of the XIX International Congress for Caribbean Archaeology*, edited by L. Alofs and R. Dijkhoff, pp. 156–167. Oranjestad, Aruba.

Newsom, L. A., and K. A. Deagan

1994   *Zea mays* in the West Indies: The Archaeological and Early Historic Record. In *Corn and culture in the prehistoric New World*, edited by S. Johannessen and C. A. Hastorf, pp. 203–217. Westview Press, Boulder, Colorado.

Newsom, L. A. and J. Molengraaff

1999   Paleoethnobotanical analysis. In *Archaeological investigations on St. Martin (Lesser Antilles): The Sites of Norman Estates, Anse des Pères, and Hope Estate, with a Contribution to the "La Hueca Problem,"* edited by C. L. Hofman and M. L. P. Hoogland, pp. 229–247. Archaeological Studies Leiden University, Faculty of Archaeology, Leiden, The Netherlands.

Newsom, L. A., and D. M. Pearsall

2003   Temporal and Spatial Trends Indicated by a Survey of Archaeobotanical Data from the Caribbean islands. In *People and Plants in Ancient North America I: East*, edited by P. Minnis, pp. 347–412. Smithsonian Institution Press, Washington D.C.

Nieuwolt, S.
  1977   *Tropical Climatology.* John Wiley and Sons, London.
Nieves-Rivera, A. M., J. Muñoz-Vasquez, and C. Betancourt-López
  1995   Hallucinogens used by the Taino Indians in the West Indies. *Atenea: Facultad de Artes y Ciencias:*15(1–2):125–139 (Universidad de Puerto Rico, Mayagüez).
Norman, M. J. T., C. J. Pearson, and P. G. E. Searle
  1995   *The Ecology of Tropical Food Crops.* 2nd ed. Cambridge University Press, Cambridge.
Odum, E. P.
  1971   *Fundamentals of Ecology.* 3rd. ed. Saunders, Philadelphia.
Olazagasti, I.
  1997   The Material Culture of the Taino Indians. In *The Indigenous People of the Caribbean*, edited by S. M. Wilson, pp. 131–139. University Press of Florida, Gainesville.
Oliver, J. R.
  1997a The Taino Cosmos. In *The Indigenous People of the Caribbean*, edited by S. M. Wilson, pp. 140–153. University Press of Florida, Gainesville.
  1997b Dabajouroid Archaeology: Settlements and House Structures: an Overview from Mainland Western Venezuela. In *The Archaeology of Aruba: The Tanki Flip Site*, edited by A. H. Versteeg and S. Rostain, pp. 363–428. Archaeological Museum Aruba No. 8 and Foundation for Scientific Research in the Caribbean Region No. 141. Aruba and Amsterdam.
  1997c *El Centro Ceremonial de Caguana, Puerto Rico: Simbolismo Iconografico, Cosmovision, y el poderio Caciquil Taino de Boriquen.* Fundación Anthropológica Arqueológica e Histórica de Puerto Rico, San Juan.
  1999   The "La Hueca Problem" in Puerto Rico and the Caribbean: Old Problems, New Perspectives, Possible Solutions. In *Archaeological Investigations on St. Martin (Lesser Antilles): The Sites of Normal Estate, Anse des Pères, and Hope Estate, with a Contribution to the "La Hueca Problem,"* edited by C. L. Hofman and M. L. P. Hoogland, pp. 253–297. Archaeological Studies Leiden University, Faculty of Archaeology, Leiden University, The Netherlands.
  2001   The Archaeology of Forest Foraging and Agricultural Production in Amazonia. In *Unknown Amazon*, edited by C. McEwan, C. Barreto, and E. Neves, pp. 50–85. British Museum Press, London.
Oliver, J., J. A. Rivera Fontán, and L. A. Newsom
  1999   Arqueología del Barrio Caguana: resultados preliminares de las temporadas 1996–1997. In *Trabajos de investigación arqueológica en Puerto Rico*, edited by J. A. Rivera Fontán, pp. 7–26. Publicación ocasional de la División de Arqueologia, Instituto de Cultura Puertorriqueña, Puerto Rico.
Olson, S. L., and G. K. Pregill
  1982   Introduction to the Paleontology of Bahamian Vertebrates. In *Fossil Vertebrates from the Bahamas*, edited by S. L. Olson, pp. 1–7. Smithsonian Contributions to Paleobiology No. 48.

Ortega, E., and J. Guerrero
  1981   *Cuatro Nuevos Sitios Paleoarchaicos en las Isla de Santo Domingo.* Ediciones Museo del Hombre Dominicano, Santo Domingo.

Ortiz, F.
  1947   *Cuban Counterpoint: Tobacco and Sugar.* Translated from the Spanish by H. de Onís. Introduction by B. Malinowski. Alfred A. Knopf, New York.

Ortíz Agilú, J. J., Rivera Meléndez, J., Principe Jácome, A., Mélendez Maiz, M. and M. Lavergne Colberg
  1991   Intensive Agriculture in Pre-Columbian West Indies: The Case for Terraces. In *Proceedings of the Fourteenth Congress of the International Association for Caribbean Archaeology,* edited by A. Cummins and P. King, pp. 278–285. Barbados Museum and Historical Society, Barbados.

Ottenwalder, J. A.
  2001   Systematics and Biogeography of the West Indian Genus Solenodon. In *Biogeography of the West Indies: Patterns and Perspectives.* 2nd ed. Edited by C. A. Woods and F. E. Sergile, pp. 253–329. CRC Press, Boca Raton, Florida.

Patton, M.
  1996   *Islands in Time: Island Sociogeography and Mediterranean Prehistory.* Routledge, London.

Pauly, D.
  1995   Anecdotes and the Shifting Baseline Syndrome of Fisheries. *Trends in Ecological Evolution* 10:430.

Pearsall, D. M.
  1985   Analysis of Soil Phytoliths and Botanical Macroremains from El Bronce Archaeological Site, Ponce, Puerto Rico. Appendix in *Archaeological data recovery at El Bronce, Puerto Rico, Final Report Phase 2.* United States Army Corps of Engineers, Jacksonville District.
  1989   Plant Utilization at the Krum Bay Site, St. Thomas U.S.V.I. Appendix C in *Preceramic procurement patterns at Krum Bay, Virgin Islands* (E. R. Lundberg). Ph.D. dissertation, University of Illinois, Urbana. University Microfilms, Ann Arbor.
  1994   Issues in the Analysis and Interpretation of Archaeological Maize in South America. In *Corn and Culture in the Prehistoric New World,* edited by S. Johannessen and C. A. Hastorf, pp. 245–272. Westview Press, Boulder, Colorado.
  2000   *Paleoethnobotany: A Handbook of Procedures.* Academic Press, New York.
  2002   Analysis of Charred Botanical Remains from the Tutu Site, U.S. Virgin Islands. In *The Tutu Archaeological Village Site: A Multidisciplinary Case Study in Human Adaptation,* edited by E. Righter. Routledge, London.

Petersen, J. B.
  1997   Taino, Island Carib, and Prehistoric Amerindian Economies in the West Indies: Tropical Forest Adaptations to Island Environments. In *The Indigenous People of the Caribbean,* edited by S. M. Wilson, pp. 118–130. University Press of Florida, Gainesville.

Pianka, E. R.
  2000   *Evolutionary Ecology*, 6th ed. Addison Wesley, San Francisco.
Pickersgill, B.
  1984   Migrations of Chili Peppers, *Capsicum* spp., in the Americas. In *Pre-Columbian Plant Migrations*, edited by D. Stone, pp. 106–123. Papers of the Peabody Museum of Archaeology and Ethnology Vol. 76. Harvard University Press, Cambridge.
Pino, M.
  2004   Associations of Terrestrial Mammals of Cuba with Evidence of Aboriginal Cultures. In *The Mammals of the West Indies*, edited by C. A. Woods, R. Borroto, and F. Sergile. University Press of Florida, Gainesville (in press).
Piperno, D. R.
  2002   Phytolith and Pollen Analysis at the Tutu Site, St. Thomas, U.S. Virgin Islands. In *The Tutu Archaeological Village Site: A Multidisciplinary Case Study in Human Adaptation*, edited by E. Righter. Routledge, London.
Poinar, G. Jr., and R. Poinar
  1999   *The Amber Forest: A Reconstruction of a Vanished World.* Princeton University Press, Princeton.
Popper, V. S.
  1988   Selecting Quantitative Measurements in Paleoethnobotany. In *Current Paleoethnobotany: Analytical Methods and Cultural Interpretations of Archaeological Plant Remains*, edited by C. A. Hastorf and V. S. Popper, pp. 53–71. University of Chicago Press, Chicago.
Prance, G. T.
  1984   The Pejibaye, *Guilielma gasipaes* (HBK) Bailey, and the Papaya, *Carica papaya* L. In *Pre-Columbian Plant Migration*, edited by D. Stone, pp. 85–104. Papers of the Peabody Museum of Archaeology and Ethnology Vol. 76, Harvard University Press, Cambridge.
Pregill, G. K., and S. L. Olson
  1981   Zoogeography of West Indian Vertebrates in Relation to Pleistocene Climatic Cycles. *Annual Review of Ecology and Systematics* 12:75–98.
Pregill, G. K., D. W. Steadman, and D. R. Watters
  1994   Late Quaternary Vertebrate Faunas of the Lesser Antilles: Historical Components of Caribbean Biogeography. *Bulletin of Carnegie Museum of Natural History* No. 30. Pittsburgh.
Prugh, T., R. Costanza, J. H. Cumberland, H. E. Daly, R. Goodland, and R. B. Norgaard
  1999   *Natural Capital and Human Economic Survival.* 2nd ed. Lewis, Boca Raton, Florida.
Quammen, D.
  1996   *The Song of the Dodo: Island Biogeography in an Age of Extinctions.* Scribner, New York.
Quitmyer, I. R.
  2003   The Zooarchaeology of Cinnamon Bay (12Vam 2–3), St. John, U.S. Virgin

Islands: The Pre-Columbian Overexploitation of Animal Resources. *Bulletin of the Florida Museum of Natural History*, Gainesville (in press).

Quitmyer, I. R., and L. Kozuch
1996   *Phase II Zooarchaeology at Finca Valencia (NCS-1) and Site NCS-4, Northwest Puerto Rico.* Submitted to LAW Caribe and on file at the Florida Museum of Natural History, Gainesville.

Quitmyer, I. R., and R. K. Brown
2001   *The Zooarchaeology of the Site NCS-4: A Native American Farmstead on the Rio Indio, Northwest Puerto Rico.* Submitted to C. Solis at LAW Caribe, Puerto Rico.

Quitmyer, I. R., and E. S. Wing
2001   *The Luján I site: A Record of Native American Animal Use on Vieques Island, Puerto Rico.* Submitted to Virginia Rivera and on file in Environmental Archaeology, Florida Museum of Natural History, Gainesville.

Rainbird, P.
1994   Prehistory in the Northwest Tropical Pacific: The Caroline, Mariana, and Marshall Islands. *Journal of World Prehistory* 8(3):293–349.

Rainey, F. G.
1940   Porto Rican Archaeology. *Scientific survey of Porto Rico and the Virgin Islands.* Vol. 18, Pt. 1. New York Academy of Sciences.

Record, S. J., and R. W. Hess
1943   *Timbers of the New World.* Yale University Press, New Haven.
1942–   Keys to American Woods. In *Tropical Woods* 72:19–29 (1942), 73:23–42 (1943),
1948   75:8–26 (1943), 76:32–47 (1944), 85:1–19 (1946), 94:29–52 (1948).

Redmond, C. L.
1999   *Human Impact on Ancient Environments.* University of Arizona Press, Tucson.

Rehm, S., and G. Espig
1991   *The Cultivated Plants of the Tropics and Subtropics: Cultivation, Economic Value, and Utilization.* IAT Institute of Agronomy in the Tropics, University of Göttingen. Verlag Josef Margraf, Weikersheim, West Germany.

Reice, S. R.
2001   *The Silver Lining: The Benefits of Natural Disasters.* Princeton University Press, Princeton.

Reinink, A.
1997   Tanki Flip shell. In *The Archaeology of Aruba: The Tanki Flip Site*, edited by A. H. Versteeg and S. Rostain, pp. 127–157. Archaeological Museum Aruba No. 8 and Foundation for Scientific Research in the Caribbean Region No. 141. Aruba and Amsterdam.

Reis, K. R., and D. W. Steadman
1997   Archaeology of Trants, Montserrat, Pt. 5. Prehistoric Avifauna. *Annals of Carnegie Museum* 68(4):275–287.

Reitz, E. J.
1985   Vertebrate Fauna from El Bronce Archaeological Site, Puerto Rico. Appendix C in *Archaeological Data Recovery at El Bronce, Puerto Rico, Final Report*

Phase 2, edited by L. S. Robinson, E. R. Lundberg, and J. B. Walker. Report to the United States Army Corps of Engineers, Jacksonville, District.

1989   Vertebrate Fauna from Krum Bay, Virgin Islands. Appendix B In *Preceramic Procurement Patterns at Krum Bay, Virgin Islands*, by E. R. Lundberg. Ph.D. dissertation, University of Illinois, Urbana. University Microfilms, Ann Arbor.

1994   Archaeology of Trants, Montserrat. Pt. 2. Vertebrate Fauna. *Annals of Carnegie Museum* 63(4):297–317.

Reitz, E. J., and B. G. McEwan

1995   Animals, Environment, and the Spanish Diet at Puerto Real. In *Puerto Real: The Archaeology of a Sixteenth-Century Spanish Town in Hispaniola*, edited by K. Deagan, pp. 287–334. University Press of Florida, Gainesville.

Reitz, E. J., and E. S. Wing

1999   *Zooarchaeology.* Cambridge University Press, Cambridge.

Ricklefs, R. E., and G. W. Cox

1972   Taxon Cycles in the West Indian Avifauna. *American Naturalist* 106:195–219.

Ricklefs, R. E., and D. Schluter (editors)

1993   *Species Diversity in Ecological Communities: Historical and Geographic Perspectives.* University of Chicago Press, Chicago.

Rímoli, R. O.

1977   Nuevas citas para mamiferos precolombinos en la Hispañiola. *Cuadernos del Cendia* 259(5):3–15.

Rindos, D.

1984   *The Origins of Agriculture: An Evolutionary Perspective.* Academic Press, Orlando, Florida.

Roberts, C. M.

1997   Connectivity and Management of Caribbean Coral Reefs. *Science* 278:1454–1457.

Rodríguez López, M.

1997a   Maruca, Ponce. *Ocho Trabajos de Investigación Arqueológica en Puerto Rico: Secundo Encuentro de Investigadores*, 17–30. Publicación Ocasional de la División de Arqueología, Instituto de Cultura Puertorriqueña, San Juan, Puerto Rico.

1997b   Religious Beliefs of the Saladoid People. Pp. 80–87 in *The Indigenous People of the Caribbean*, edited by S. M. Wilson. University Press of Florida, Gainesville.

Roe, P. G.

1989   A Grammatical Analysis of Cedrosan Saladoid Vessel Form Categories and Surface Decoration: Aesthetic and Technological Styles in Early Antillean Ceramics. In *Early Ceramic Population Lifeways and Adaptive Strategies in the Caribbean*, edited by P. E. Siegel, pp. 267–382. BAR International Series 506. British Archaeological Reports, Oxford.

Roosevelt, A. C.

1980   *Parmana: Prehistoric Maize and Manioc Subsistence along the Amazon and Orinoco.* Academic Press, New York.

Rostlund, E.
    1952   *Freshwater Fish and Fishing in Native North America.* University of California
            Publications in Geography Vol. 9. University of California Press, Berkeley.

Roth, W. E.
    1924   *An Introductory Study of the Arts, Crafts, and Customs of the Guiana Indians.* 38th
            Annual Report of U.S. Bureau of American Ethnology. Washington, D.C.

Rouse, I.
    1986   *Migrations in Prehistory: Inferring Population Movements from Cultural Remains.*
            Yale University Press, New Haven.

    1989   Peopling and Repeopling of the West Indies. In *Biogeography of the West Indies:
            Past, Present, and Future,* edited by C. A. Woods, pp. 119–135. Sandhill Crane
            Press, Gainesville, Florida.

    1992   *The Tainos: Rise and Decline of the People who Greeted Columbus.* Yale University
            Press, New Haven.

Rouse, I., and R. E. Alegría
    1990   *Excavations at María de la Cruz Cave and Hacienda Grande Village Site, Loiza,
            Puerto Rico.* Yale University Publications in Anthropology No. 80, New Haven.

Russ, G. R.
    1991   Coral Reef Fisheries: Effects and Yields. In *The Ecology of Fishes on Coral Reefs,*
            edited by P. F. Sale, pp. 601–635. Academic Press, San Diego.

Salls, R. A.
    1989   To Catch a Fish: Some Limitations on Prehistoric Fishing in Southern Cali-
            fornia with Special Reference to Native Plant Fiber Fishing Line. *Journal of
            Ethnobiology* 9(2):173–199.

Sandford, M. K.
    2002   Human Remains from the Tutu Site. In *The Tutu Archaeological Village Site: A
            Multidisciplinary Case Study in Human Adaptation,* edited by E. Righter. Rout-
            ledge, London.

Sanoja, M., and I. Vargas
    1983   New Light on the Prehistory of Eastern Venezuela. *Advances in World Archae-
            ology* 2:205–244.

Sauer, C. O.
    1966   *The Early Spanish Main.* University of California Press, Berkeley.

Sauget, J. S., and E. E. Liogier
    1957   *Flora de Cuba.* Pt. 3. Contribuciones Ocasionales del Museo de Historia Natu-
            ral. Del Colegio de la Salle, Numero 13. Havana, Cuba.

Scarry, C. M., and L. A. Newsom
    1992   Archaeobotanical Research in the Calusa Heartland. In *Culture and Environ-
            ment in the Domain of the Calusa,* edited by W. H. Marquardt, pp. 375–401.
            Institute of Archaeology and Paleoenvironmental Studies Monograph No. 1,
            University of Florida, Gainesville.

Schinkel, K.
    1992   The Golden Rock Features. In *The Archaeology of St. Eustatius: The Golden
            Rock Site,* edited by A. H. Versteeg and K. Schinkel, pp. 143–212. St. Eusta-

tius Historical Foundation No. 2 and the Foundation for Scientific Research in the Caribbean Region No. 131. Amsterdam, The Netherlands.

Schwimmer, E.
1980 The Anthropology of Religious Practices. In *People and Culture: A Survey of Cultural Anthropology*, edited by I. Rossi, pp. 511–537. J. F. Bergin, New York.

Scudder, S.
1991 Early Arawak Subsistence Strategies on the South Coast of Jamaica. In *Proceedings of the Thirteenth International Congress for Caribbean Archaeology*, edited by E. N. Ayubi and J. B. Haviser, pp. 297–315. Reports of the Archaeological-Anthropological Institute of the Netherlands Antilles No. 9.

Sears, W. H. and S. O. Sullivan
1978 Bahamas Prehistory. *American Antiquity* 43(1):3–25.

Serrand, N.
1997 Tanki Flip Shell: Artifacts with a Relatively High Level of Modification. In *The Archaeology of Aruba: The Tanki Flip Site*, edited by A. H. Versteeg and S. Rostain, pp. 189–217. Archaeological Museum Aruba No. 8 and Foundation for Scientific Research in the Caribbean Region No. 141. Aruba and Amsterdam.

Shafer, C. L.
1990 *Nature Reserves: Island Theory and Conservation Practice*. Smithsonian Institution Press, Washington, D.C.

Siegel, P. E. (editor)
1989 *Early Ceramic Population Lifeways and Adaptive Strategies in the Caribbean*. BAR International Series 506. British Archaeological Reports, Oxford.
1991 Saladoid Survival Strategies: Evidence from Site Locations. In *Proceedings of the Fourteenth International Congress for Caribbean Archaeology*, edited by A. Cummins and P. King, pp. 315–337. Barbados Museum and Historical Society, St. Ann's Garrison, Barbados.

Simpson, G. G.
1956 Zoogeography of West Indian Land Mammals. *American Museum Noviates* 1759:1–28.

Smith, B. D.
1995 Seed Plant Domestication in Eastern North America. In *Last Hunters, First Farmers*, edited by T. D. Price and A. B. Gebauer, pp. 193–213. School of American Research, Advanced Seminar Series, Santa Fe, New Mexico.
2001 Low-level Food Production. *Journal of Archaeological Research* 9(1):1–43.

Smith, B. D. (editor)
1990 *The Mississippian Emergence*. Smithsonian Institution Press, Washington, D.C.

Smythe, N.
1978 The Natural History of the Central American Agouti (*Dasyprocta punctata*). *Smithsonian Contribution in Zoology* 257:1–52.

Steadman, D. W.
1995 Prehistoric Extinctions of Pacific Island Birds: Biodiversity Meets Zooarchaeology. *Science* 267:1123–31.

1999   Prehistoric Human Impact on Island Faunas: A Comparison of Oceania and the West Indies. Paper presented at the XVIIIth Congress for Caribbean Archaeology, Grenada, West Indies. July. 11–17.

Steadman, D. W., D. R. Watters, E. J. Reitz, and G. K. Pregill
1984   Vertebrates from Archaeological Sites on Montserrat, West Indies. *Annals of Carnegie Museum* 53:1–29.

Stoffers, A. L.
1956   *Studies on the Flora of Curaçao and other Caribbean Islands.* Vol. 1: *The Vegetation of the Netherlands Antilles.* Uitgaven "Natuurwetenschappelijke Studiekring voor Suriname en de Nederlandse Antillen," Utrecht. Martinus Nijhoff, The Hague, Netherlands.

Stokes, A. V.
1998   *A Biogeographic Survey of Prehistoric Human Diet in the West Indies Using Stable Isotopes.* Ph.D. dissertation, Department of Anthropology, University of Florida. University Microfilms, Ann Arbor, Michigan.

Sturtevant, W. C.
1961   Taino Agriculture. In *The Evolution of Horticultural Systems in Native South America: Causes and Consequences*, edited by J. Wilbert, pp. 68–73. Anthropologica Supplement 2.

Sullivan, Shaun D.
1981   *Prehistoric Patterns of Exploitation and Colonization in the Turks and Caicos Islands.* Ph.D. dissertation, University of Illinois, Urbana. University Microfilms, Ann Arbor.

Taverne, Y. and A. H. Verteeg
1992   Golden Rock Shells. In *The Archaeology of St. Eustatius: The Golden Rock Site*, edited by A. H. Versteeg and K. Schinkel, pp. 84–92. St. Eustatius Historical Foundation No. 2 and Foundation for Scientific Research in the Caribbean No. 131, Amsterdam.

Teixeira, S. R., J. B. Dixon, G. N. White, and L. A. Newsom
2002   Charcoal in Soils: A Preliminary Review. In *Soil Mineralogy with Environmental Applications*, edited by J. B. Dixon, pp. 819–830. SSSA Book Series No. 7. Soil Science Society of America, Madison, Wisconsin.

Terrell, J. E.
1997   The Postponed Agenda: Archaeology and Human Biogeography in the Twenty-First Century. *Human Ecology* 25(3):419–436.

Tomblin, J.
1981   Earthquakes, Volcanoes and Hurricanes: A Review of Natural Hazards and Vulnerability in the West Indies. *Ambio* 10(6):340–345.

Toro-Labrador, A. Sanchez-Crespo, V. Ho-Fung, M. Estevez-Montero, Lobaina-Manzavet, D. A. Padovani-Claudio, H. Sanchez-Cruz, P. Ortiz-Bermudez, J. C. Martinez-Cruzado
1999   Mitochondrial DNA Evidence for a Founder Effect in the Colonization of Puerto Rico by Its Indigenous People. Paper presented at the XVIIIth Congress for Caribbean Archaeology, Grenada, West Indies.

Towner, H.
  1992   *Ecostat: an Ecological Analysis Program.* Trinity Software, Campton, New Hampshire.
Vandermeer, J., I. G. de la Cerda, D. Boucher, I. Perfecto, J. Ruiz
  2000   Hurricane Disturbance and Tropical Tree Species Diversity. *Science* 290: 788–791.
Veloz Maggiolo, M.
  1993   *La Isla de Santo Domingo antes de Colon.* Banco Central de la República Dominicana, Santo Domingo.
  1996   La chola, un alimento con su historia. *Barril sin Fondo (Antropologia para curiosos).* S. A. de Colores, Santo Domingo, Republica Dominica.
  1997   The Daily Life of the Taíno People. In *Taíno: Pre-Columbian Art and Culture from the Caribbean*, pp. 34–45. Monacelli Press and El Museo del Barrio, New York.
Veloz Maggiolo, M., and B. Vega
  1982   The Antillean Preceramic: A New Approximation. *Journal of New World Archaeology* 5:33–44.
Versteeg, A. H.
  1991   *The Indians of Aruba.* Archaeological Museum Aruba No. 4.
Versteeg, A. H. and K. Schinkel
  1992   *The Archaeology of St. Eustatius: The Golden Rock Site.* St. Eustatius Historical Foundation No. 2 and Foundation for Scientific Research in the Caribbean Region No. 131. Amsterdam.
Versteeg, A. H., J. Tacoma, and P. van de Velde
  1990   *Archaeological Investigations on Aruba: The Malmok Cemetery.* Archaeological Museum Aruba No. 2 and Foundation for Scientific Research in the Caribbean Region No. 126.
Wagner, G. E.
  1988   Comparability among Recovery Techniques. In *Current Paleoethnobotany: Analytical Methods and Cultural Interpretations of Archaeological Plant Remains*, edited by C. A. Hastorf and V. S. Popper, pp. 17–35. University of Chicago Press, Chicago.
Wartluft, J. L., and S. White
  1984   *Comparing Simple Charcoal Production Technologies for the Caribbean: Montserrat Fuelwood/Charcoal/Cookstove Project.* Volunteers in Technical Assistance, Arlington, Virginia.
Watson, P. J.
  1997   The Shaping of Modern Paleoethnobotany. In *People, Plants, and Landscapes: Studies in Paleoethnobotany*, edited by K. J. Gremillion, pp. 13–22. University of Alabama Press, Tuscaloosa.
Watters, D. R.
  1997   Maritime Trade in the Prehistoric Eastern Caribbean. In *The Indigenous People of the Caribbean*, edited by S. M. Wilson, pp. 88–99. University of Florida Press, Gainesville.

Watters, D. R., and R. Scaglion
  1994   Beads and Pendants from Trants, Montserrat: Implications for the Prehis-
          toric Lapidary Industry of the Caribbean. *Annals of Carnegie Museum* 63(3):
          215–237.

Watts, D.
  1987   *The West Indies: Patterns of Development, Culture and Environmental Change
          since 1492.* Cambridge University Press, Cambridge.

Westermann, J. H.
  1953   *Nature Preservation in the Caribbean.* Scientific Research in Surinam and the
          Netherlands Antilles, Utrecht No. 9.

Weydert, N.
  1994   The Hope Estate Shells, Technological and Food Resources by Arawaks In-
          dians. Association Archeologique, Hope Estate Edition No. 3, pp. 9–11.
          St. Martin.

Whidden, H. P., and R. J. Asher
  2001   The Origin of the Greater Antillean Insectivorans. In *Biogeography of the West
          Indies: Patterns and Perspectives.* 2nd ed. Edited by C. A. Woods and F. E. Ser-
          gile, pp. 237–252. CRC Press, Boca Raton, Florida.

Whittaker, R. J.
  1998   *Island Biogeography: Ecology, Evolution, and Conservation.* Oxford University
          Press, Oxford.

Wild, K.
  2001   Investigations of a "Caney" at Cinnamon Bay, St. John, and Social Ideology in
          the Virgin Islands as Reflected in Pre-Columbian Ceramics. In *Proceedings of
          the XVIIIth International Congress for Caribbean Archaeology,* edited by G. Rich-
          ard, pp. 304–310. Conseil Régional de la Guadeloupe, Basse Terre.

Wilkins, L.
  2001   Status and Distribution of the Jamaican hutía (*Geocapromys brownii*) and a Re-
          introduction of a Captive Bred Population. Masters thesis, Center for Latin
          American Studies, University of Florida, Gainesville.

Williams, E. E.
  1989   Old Problems and New Opportunities in West Indian Biogeography. In *Bio-
          geography of the West Indies: Past, Present, and Future,* edited by C. A. Woods,
          pp. 1–46. Sandhill Crane Press, Gainesville, Florida.

Williams, R. O. and R. O. Williams Jr.
  1961   *The Useful and Ornamental Plants of Trinidad and Tobago.* Guardian Commer-
          cial Printery, Port-of-Spain.

Williamson, I. and M. D. Sabath
  1982   Island Population, Land Area, and Climate: A Case Study of the Marshall Is-
          lands. *Human Ecology* 10(1):71–84.
  1984   Small Population Instability and Island Settlement Patterns. *Human Ecology*
          12(1):21–34.

Wilson, S. M.
  1989   The Prehistoric Settlement Pattern of Nevis, West Indies. *Journal of Field Ar-
          chaeology* 16:427–450.

1990a Taino Elite Integration and Social Complexity on Hispaniola. In *Proceedings of the Eleventh International Congress for Caribbean Archaeology*, edited by A. G. Pantel Tekakis, I. Vargas Arenas, and M. Sanjoa Obediente, pp. 517–521. La Fundación Arqueológica, Antropológica e História de Puerto Rico, San Juan.

1990b *Hispaniola: Caribbean Chiefdoms in the Age of Columbus.* University of Alabama Press, Tuscaloosa.

1993 Structure and History: Combining Archaeology and Ethnohistory in the Contact Period Caribbean. In *Ethnohistory and Archaeology: Approaches to Post-contact Change in the Americas*, edited by J. D. Rogers and S. M. Wilson, pp. 19–30. Plenum Press, New York.

1997a Introduction. In *The Indigenous People of the Caribbean*, edited by S. M. Wilson, pp. 1–8. University Press of Florida, Gainesville.

Wilson, S. M. (editor)

1997b *The Indigenous People of the Caribbean.* University Press of Florida, Gainesville.

2001 The Prehistory and Early History of the Caribbean. In *Biogeography of the West Indies: Patterns and Perspectives*. 2nd ed. Edited by C. A. Woods and F. E. Sergile, pp. 519–527. CRC Press, Boca Raton, Florida.

Wilson, S. M., H. B. Iceland, and T. R. Hester

1998 Preceramic connections between Yucatan and the Caribbean. *Latin American Antiquity* 9(4):342–352.

Wilson, W. M., and D. L. Dufour

2002 Why "Bitter" Cassava? Productivity of "Bitter" and "Sweet" Cassava in a Tukanoan Indian Settlement in the Northwest Amazon. *Economic Botany* 56(1):49–57.

Wing, E. S.

1969 Vertebrate Remains Excavated from San Salvador Island, Bahamas. *Caribbean Journal of Science* 9(1–2):25–29.

1972 Identification and Interpretation of Faunal Remains. In *The White Marl Site in Jamaica*, edited by J. Silverberg, pp. 18–35. Mimeograph Report, Department of Anthropology, University of Wisconsin, Milwaukee.

1977 The Bellevue Site (K-13). *Archaeology-Jamaica Newsletter*:2–13.

1989 Human Exploitation of Animal Resources in the Caribbean. In *Biogeography of the West Indies*, edited by C. A. Woods, pp. 137–152. Sandhill Crane Press, Gainesville, Florida.

1991a Economy and Subsistence I-Faunal Remains. In *Prehistoric Barbados*, edited by P. L. Drewett, pp. 134–152. Archetype Publications, London.

1991b Dog Remains from the Sorcé Site on Vieques Island, Puerto Rico. In *Beamers, Bobwhites, and Blue-Points*, edited by J. R. Purdue, W. E. Klippel, and Bonnie W. Styles, 379–386. Illinois State Museum Scientific Papers Vol. 23 and University of Tennessee, Department of Anthropology Report of Investigations No. 52.

1993 The Realm between Wild and Domestic. In *Skeletons in her Cupboard*, edited by A. Clason, S. Payne, H.-P. Uerpmann, pp. 243–250. Oxbow Monograph 34. Oxford.

1995 Rice Rats and Saladoid People as seen at Hope Estate. In *Proceedings of the*

XV International Congress for Caribbean Archaeology, edited by R. E. Alegría and M. Rodríguez, pp. 219–231. Centro de Estudios Avanzados de Puerto Rico y Caribe, Fundación Puertorriqueña de las Humanidades y la Universidad del Turabo, San Juan, Puerto Rico.

1996   Vertebrate Remains Excavated from the Sites of Spring Bay and Kelbey's Ridge, Saba, Netherlands West Indies. Pp. 261–279 in *In Search of the Native Population of Pre-Columbian Saba (400–1450 A.D.) Part Two* (M. L. P. Hoogland). Ph.D. dissertation, Rijksuniversiteit Leiden, The Netherlands.

1997   The Animal Remains. In *The Spring Head Petroglyph Cave: A Sample Excavation*, edited by P. L. Drewett, pp. 55–57. Journal of the Barbados Museum and Historical Society, vol. 43.

1999   Animal Remains from the Indian Creek Site, Antigua. In *Excavations at the Indian Creek site, Antigua, West Indies*, edited by I. Rouse and B. Faber Morse, pp. 51–66. Yale University Publications in Anthropology No. 82. New Haven.

2000   Economy and Subsistence I—Animal Remains from Sites on Barbados and Tortola. In *Prehistoric settlements in the Caribbean: Fieldwork in Barbados, Tortola and the Cayman Islands*, edited by P. L. Drewett, pp. 147–153. Archetype Publications, London.

2001a   The Sustainability of Resources Used by Native Americans on Four Caribbean Islands. *International Journal of Osteoarchaeology* 11:112–126.

2001b   Native American Use of Animals in the Caribbean. In *Biogeography of the West Indies: Patterns and Perspectives*. 2nd ed. Edited by C. A. Woods and F. Sergile, pp. 418–518. CRC Press, Boca Raton, Florida.

2004   Zooarchaeology of West Indian Land Mammals. In *Mammals of the West Indies*, edited by C. A. Woods, R. Borrota, and F. Sergile. University Press of Florida, Gainesville (in press).

Wing, E. S., S. D. deFrance, and L. Kozuch

2002   Faunal Remains from the Tutu Archaeological Village Site, St. Thomas. In *The Tutu Archaeological Village Site: A Multidisciplinary Case Study in Human Adaptation*, edited by E. Righter. Routledge, London.

Wing, E. S., C. E. Ray, and C. A. Hoffman Jr.

1968   Vertebrate Remains from Indian sites on Antigua, West Indies. *Caribbean Journal of Science* 8(3–4):123–129.

Wing, E. S. and E. J. Reitz

1982   Prehistoric Fishing Communities of the Caribbean. *Journal of New World Archaeology* 5(2):13–32.

Wing, E. S., and S. J. Scudder

1980   Use of Animals by the Prehistoric Inhabitants of St. Kitts, West Indies. *Proceedings of the Eighth International Congress for the Study of Pre-Columbian Cultures of the Lesser Antilles*. Arizona State University, Anthropological Research Papers No. 22: 237–245.

1983   Animal Exploitation by People Living on a Tropical Marine Edge. In *Animals and Archaeology*, edited by C. Grigson and J. Clutton-Brock, pp. 197–210. BAR International Series 183. British Archaeological Reports, Oxford.

Wing, S. R., and E. S. Wing
  2001   Prehistoric Fisheries in the Caribbean. *Coral Reefs* 20:1–8.

Winter, J. H., and D. M. Pearsall
  1991   A Wooden Mortar of the Lucayans. In *Proceedings of the Fourteenth Congress of the International Association for Caribbean Archaeology*, edited by A. Cummins and P. King, pp. 586–590. Barbados Museum and Historical Association.

Winter, J. H., and E. S. Wing
  1995   A refuse midden at the Minnis Ward site San Salvador, Bahamas. In *Proceedings of the XV International Congress for Caribbean Archaeology*, edited by R. E. Alegria and M. Rodriquez, pp. 423–433. Centro de Estudios Avancados de Puerto Rico y el Caribe, Puerto Rico.

Winter, J. H., E. Wing, L. Newsom, A. Fierro, and D. McDonald
  1999   A Lucayan Funeral Offering in Major's Cave, San Salvador, Bahamas. In *Seventeenth International Congress for Caribbean Archaeology*, edited by J. Winter, p. 21. Nassau, Bahamas.

Winterhalder, B., and C. Goland
  1997   An Evolutionary Ecology Perspective on Diet Choice, Risk, and Plant Domestication. In *People, Plants, and Landscapes: Studies in Paleoethnobotany*, edited by K. J. Gremillion, pp. 123–160. University of Alabama Press, Tuscaloosa.

Wolcott, T. G.
  1988   Ecology. In *The Biology of Land Crabs*, edited by W. W. Burggren and B. R. McMahon, pp. 55–96. University of Cambridge Press.

Woods, C. A.
  1989   The Biogeography of West Indian Rodents. In *Biogeography of the West Indies: Past, Present, and Future*, edited by C. A. Woods, pp. 741–797. Sandhill Crane Press, Gainesville.

  2001   Introduction and Historical Overview of Patterns of West Indian Biogeography. In *Biogeography of the West Indies: Patterns and Perspectives.* 2nd ed. Edited by C. A. Woods and F. E. Sergile, pp. 1–14. CRC Press, Boca Raton, Florida.

Woods, C. A., R. Borroto Paez, and C. W. Kilpatrick
  2001   Insular Patterns and Radiations of West Indian Rodents. In *Biogeography of the West Indies: Patterns and Perspectives.* 2nd ed. Edited by C. A. Woods and F. E. Sergile, pp. 335–353. CRC Press, Boca Raton, Florida.

Zucchi, A., K. Tarble, and E. Vaz
  1984   The Ceramic Sequence and New TL and C-14 Dates for the Aguerito Site of the Middle Orinoco, Venezuela. *Journal of Field Archaeology* 11:155–180.

Index

MacArthur, Robert, 17, 26, 205–6
macaw (*Ara autochthones*), 6
maceration, 47
macrobotanical research, 35
madder (Rubiaceae) family, 6
maga wood (*Thespesia grandiflora,* syn.
  Montezuma grandiflora), 162
Maggiolo, Marcio Veloz, 29
magicoreligious ceremonies, 34
mahogany (*Swietenia mahogani*), 23, 186
Maijuna, 55
Maisabel, Puerto Rico: changes in reef
  and inshore fish components, 165–66;
  fauna, 165; maga wood (*Thespesia grandiflora,* syn. *Montezuma grandiflora*), 162;
  marine resources, 118; molluscs, 166;
  postholes and house floors, 5; sweet potato or native *Ipomoea* sp. (pollen), 154
maize (*Zea mays*): "Chandelle" (popcorn),
  155, 157; En Bas Saline, 155, 157, 201,
  203; floury-endosperm kernels, 157;
  Greater Antilles, 154, 155, 198; high-
  status use, 203, 210; introduction, 200–
  201; later Ceramic-age Ostionoid occupations, 198; low-intensity uses, 214;
  race "Early Caribbean," 155; as a secondary crop, 202–3; Tutu, 129, 155; Virgin Islands, 155, 198
Major's Cave, San Salvador, 182, 183, 186
Malmok, Aruba, 61
malnutrition, 53
malocas, 32
mammals: at El Bronce, 200; marine, 24,
  71; on southern Caribbean Islands, 60;
  Venezuelan islands, 193
managed animals, 205, 206
managerial elites, 198
manatee (*Trichechus manatus*), 52, 213
manchineel, 67
mangroves (*Avicennia germinans, Conocarpus
  erectus, Laguncularia racemosa, Rhizophora mangle*), 21, 63, 141; En Bas
  Saline, 160–61; exploited for wood,
  23, 167–68, 195; Greater Antilles, 117,
  121; Lesser Antilles, 78; use by marine
  animals as nursery areas, 17. *See also*
  black mangrove; red mangrove
manioc (*Manihot esculenta*): in the Bahamas,

183; detoxification, 3–4; En Bas Saline,
  155, 156; Greater Antilles, 154, 201; introduction of, 108, 200; Lesser Antilles,
  79; as most important plant staple, 29,
  191, 201–2, 214; poisonous compounds,
  3, 201; time to harvest, 28
Manoguayabo, Dominican Republic, 154
manzanillas, 203
Marantaceae, Greater Antilles, 154–55
Margarita Island, 12, 58, 60, 73
margay (*Felis weidii*), 72
María de la Cruz rockshelter, Puerto Rico,
  120, 121
Marie Galante, 77
marine ecosystems, 2, 21
marine resources: as alternative protein
  sources, 192; human impacts, 1; mammals, 24, 71; southern Caribbean Islands, 58, 62, 67–72; and technological
  innovations, 29
maritime knowledge, 27
Marshall Islands, 28
marsupials, 15
Martinique, 77
Maruca, Puerto Rico, 31, 120; vertebrate
  remains identified from Archaic age
  sites, 124–25
marunguey or guáyiga (*Zamia* sp.;
  Cycadaceae), 118
mastic-bully (*Sideroxylon* sp.), 91, 143; Barbados, 94; Ceramic-age deposits in Virgin Islands and Vieques, 129; Greater
  Antilles, 169; Grenada, 87; Hope Estate, 103; key resource, 194; Krum Bay,
  120; Lesser Antilles, 108; Nevis and
  Antiqua, 84; wood, 94
material culture, 8, 61–62
maví (*Colubrina* sp.), 143
mayten (*Maytenus* sp.), 104
MC-6, Middle Caicos, 180
MC-12, Middle Caicos, 180
MC-32, Middle Caicos, 180
measurements, 49
medicinal properties: of plants, 3, 4, 67,
  86, 108, 156–57
Mediterranean Islands, 27
medullary bone, 213
mesophytic forests, 13, 22

Mexican poppy (*Argemone mexicana*), 86
microbotanical remains, 8, 57
microliths, 30
microphyllous woodlands, 22, 23
microremains: indicators of landscape modification and change, 57
mid-Cenozoic period, 11
midden deposits, 42, 71, 196
Middle Caicos, 180, 181, 187; three archaeological sites, 180–81; vertebrate remains identified from sites in, 260–62
migration(s), 191
mind-altering substances: derived from plants, 4, 5, 34
minimum number of individuals (MNI), 49
Miragoane, Lake, 18–19
Mississippian centers, 199
mist forest, 116
moist forest, 21
molluscs: Archaic age sites in Greater Antilles and Virgin Islands, 121, 126–27, 128; as diet staple, 3, 25, 29; Hichmans' Shell Heap, Nevis, 80; Maisabel and En Bas Saline, 166; preparing specimens, 47; Tanki Flip, Aruba, 223; used for food, 31
mongoose, 207
monkey. *See* capuchin monkey (*Cebus* sp.)
monk seal (*Monachus tropicalis*), 24, 54, 61, 72, 213
monotypic species, 17
montane forests, 21, 116
Montserrat, 77, 94–98; Trant's site, 94–95, 231–32; Windward Bluff site, 95
More's Island, 183
mortuary patterns, 119
mountain ridges: vegetation formations, 19
mullet (Mugilidae), 117, 135, 165

naborías, 33
narcotic snuff, 4, 143
Narganes, Yvonne, 35, 136
nassau grouper (*Epinephelus striatus*), 69
Native Americans: in the Caribbean Islands, 1; depopulation of subsequent to European contact, 28; introduction of manioc, 3. *See also* human colonization, of West Indian Archipelago

navigation guides, 27
NCS-1, Puerto Rico: evening primrose (*Oenothera* sp., Onagraceae), 156; guinea pigs (*Cavia porcellus*), 164; maga wood (*Thespesia grandiflora*, syn. *Montezuma grandiflora*), 162
NCS-4, Puerto Rico, 210
nearshore habitats, 2, 17
needlefishes (Belonidae), 135, 165, 166
negative economic ecology trends, 77
Neotropics, 10, 23
nerites (Neritidae), 87, 141, 166, 181
Nesophontes sp., 16
nested geological sieves, 212
Netherlands Antilles ("ABC" islands), 12, 36, 58; animal resources used by Ceramic-age people living in, 218–22; Archaic-age occupation between 1370 B.C. and A.D. 470, 30; Ceramic-age cultures, 73–74; Ceramic-age plant resources, 64; exotic fauna, 74; fuelwood, 74; marine resources around, 58; pottery styles, 61; rainfall, 13; settlement by Ceramic-age people, 33
net making, 183
netting, 53, 208, 209
Nevis, 77, 98–101, 108; changes in species composition and size, 100–101; comparison of the sizes of selected animals from sites on, 102; depopulation, 196; faunal remains from post-Saladoid sites, 234–37; rice rats, 100; sea grape, 108; secondary forest species, 195; second-growth trees, 109; tree snails, 100. *See also* Hichmans' Shell Heap, Nevis
New Providence, 174
Newsom, Lee, 58, 62, 66, 99, 160, 162, 168, 169, 170, 199, 202, 203
niche expansion, 159
Nieves-Rivera, A. M., 5
níspero or sapodilla (*Manilkara* cf. *M. zapota*), 120, 121
nitainos, 33
nitrogen isotopes, 53
Norr, L., 53
North Creek, 180
northeast trade winds, 13
number identified (NI), 49

size profiles: interpretation of, 49
sleeper (Eleotridae), 165
SM-2, Samana Cay, 181
SM-7, Samana Cay, 181
small-leaved (microphyll) shrubs, 23
smallpox, 215
snails, 3, 7; land, 2, 140, 196; seagrape
(Xanthonychidae), 105; tree, 100, 105;
West Indian topsnail (*Cittarium pica*),
80, 84, 87, 101, 140–41, 181, 194
snapper (Lutjanidae), 68, 95, 105, 128,
138, 197
snares, 208
snook (Centropomidae), 165
snuff, 4, 156
"social memory," 191
social stratification, 33, 198
soil: calcareous, 19; constituents, 2; disturbance, 195; erosion, 2; negative effects
of cropping on, 110; nutrient status, 2;
and plant cultivation, 19; sandy, 19, 22
Solenodon sp., 16
Sombrero, 77
Sorcé site, Vieques Island: dogs, 204; shell
beads, 211
soursop (*Annona* sp.), 94, 108, 143
South America: lowland traditions for
cultivation and preparation of manioc
tubers, 201; settlement-resource interaction with Caribbean Islands, 31, 75, 190
South Equatorial Current, 75
special-purpose use: of plants, animals, or
their parts, 4, 209–12
speciation, 18
species: grouping of, 51
species-area. *See* rarefaction curve
species-area relations, 55
species diversity: influence of geography
on, 17, 55–56
species extirpations, 27, 55, 207
species richness, 55–56
spiny palm (*Acrocomia aculeata*), 87, 94
spiritual belief systems: and biological
resources, 189
Spring Bay site, Saba, 137
spurge family (Euphorbiaceae), 66
squirrelfishes (Holocentridae), 71, 181
St. Barthelemy, 77

St. Croix, 120
St. Eustatius, 5, 77, 101–3
St. John: Beach Access site, 120; Cinnamon Bay, 129, 138, 141, 164, 205, 210;
cultural resources survey, 120; guinea
pigs (*Cavia porcellus*), 205; special trade
relationship with Antigua, 210; Trunk
Bay, 129, 138, 141
St. Kitts, 77, 206
St. Lucia, 21, 77
St. Martin, 77, 103–5, 195
St. Michielsberg, Caraçao, 61
St. Vincent, 77
stable isotope analysis, 8, 12, 214
staple crops, 2; Greater Antilles, 154–59;
manioc, 29, 191, 201–2, 214; molluscs,
3, 25, 29; primary starch, 183; root
crops, 31, 170
starch grains, 8
star grass or coquí (*Hypoxis* sp.), 158
Steadman, David, 35, 45, 55, 95
Sterculiaceae, 143
stinking toe pods, 94, 108
Stokes, Ann, 8, 53, 214
stone tools, 29
stools (*duhos*), 212
stoplight parrotfish (*Sparisoma viride*),
68, 187
stopper (*Eugenia* sp.), 186
storms, 15
strand vegetation, 22, 117
strata, 44
stress, in human populations, 54
strong bark (*Bourreria* sp.), 186; Bahamas,
183; Hope Estate, 104; key resource,
194; Lesser Antilles, 106, 109; southern Caribbean, 63; Sulphur Ghaut,
99; Tibes, 161; Trant's site, 95; Virgin
Islands and Vieques, 135; wood, 98
subsistence: defined, 1; economies, vari-
ance in diversity of species, 45; practices, 121, 192; and resource exploitation, 50–51
subtropical, 10, 20
subtropical rain forest, 21
succulent leaves, 21
suckerfish/remora (Echeneidae), 209
sugarcane production, 23